The Legacy
of Middle School
Leaders

In Their Own Words

The inaugural volume in
The Handbook of Resources in Middle Level Education
Steven B. Mertens and Vincent A. Anfara, Jr., *Series Editors*

The Legacy of Middle School Leaders

In Their Own Words

Tracy W. Smith

Appalachian State University

C. Kenneth McEwin

Appalachian State University

MIDDLE LEVEL EDUCATION RESEARCH
SPECIAL INTEREST GROUP

INFORMATION AGE PUBLISHING, INC.
Charlotte, NC • www.infoagepub.com

Cataloging-in-Publication Data is available from the Library of Congress

ISBN: 978-1-61735-472-4 (paperback)
        978-1-61735-473-1 (hardcover)
        978-1-61735-474-8 (e-book)

Printed in the United States of America

MIDDLE LEVEL EDUCATION RESEARCH
SPECIAL INTEREST GROUP

The Handbook of Resources in Middle Level Education and
The Handbook of Research in Middle Level Education are endorsed
by the Middle Level Education Research Special Interest Group,
an affiliate of the American Educational Research Association.

As stated in the organization's Constitution, the purpose of MLER is
to improve, promote, and disseminate educational research
reflecting early adolescence and middle-level education.

Contents

PART **II**

Prominent Leaders in Middle School Education   91

PART **III**

Voices of the Past and Visions for the Future   343

Introduction to
The Handbook of Resources
in Middle Level Education *Series*

W̶e are pleased to introduce *The Handbook of Resources in Middle Level Education,* a companion series to *The Handbook of Research in Middle Level Education.* Started in 2000 after a sufficient amount of encouragement from George Johnson, President and Publisher of Information Age Publishing, the first volume of *The Handbook of Research in Middle Level Education* was released in 2001 under the editorship of Vincent A. Anfara, Jr. At that time the Middle Level Education Research Special Interest Group (MLER SIG) of the American Educational Research Association (AERA) voted to endorse this series. Since that first volume was released in 2001, seven additional volumes have been published including: *Middle School Curriculum, Instruction, and Assessment* (Anfara & Stacki, 2002); *Leaders for a Movement: Professional Preparation and Development of Middle Level Teachers and Administrators* (Andrews & Anfara, 2003); *Reforming Middle Level Education: Considerations for Policymakers* (Thompson, 2004); *Making a Difference: Action Research in Middle Level Education* (Caskey, 2005); *The Young Adolescent and the Middle School* (Mertens, Anfara, & Caskey, 2007), *An International Look at Educating Young Adolescents* (Mertens, Anfara, & Roney, 2009); and *Voices from the Middle: Narrative Inquiry By, For, and About the Middle Level Community* (Malu, 2010). Additionally, the first-ever *Encyclopedia of Middle Grades Education* (Anfara, Andrews, & Mertens) was released in 2005.

The Legacy of Middle School Leaders, pages ix–xi
Copyright © 2011 by Information Age Publishing
ix

Discussions about the need for this new book series, *The Handbook of Resources in Middle Level Education*, have spanned the past two years. Over the course of that timeframe, numerous conversations at the annual meetings of the National Middle School Association (NMSA), the American Educational Research Association (AERA), and the National Forum to Accelerate Middle-Grades Reform were held in which colleagues noted the need for resources as they prepared to teach new or revised courses or start new programs in middle grades education. It was not uncommon for colleagues and interested parties to voice their desire to examine exemplary syllabi, examples of course assignments and their related rubrics for grading, as well as annotated bibliographies on various topics and a list of seminal works in the field of middle grades education. From these numerous discussions, the need for this second book series became more evident and its distinctiveness became even more apparent. While the intent of the first book series, *The Handbook of Resources in Middle Level Education*, is to focus on research related to middle grades education, this new series provides faculty and colleagues in institutions of higher education with quality resources that will be invaluable in the preparation of future middle grades' teachers and administrators.

The first volume of *The Handbook of Resources in Middle Level Education, The Legacy of Middle Level Leaders: In Their Own Words*, is authored by Tracy Smith and Ken McEwin. We felt that documenting and preserving the legacy and influence of the founders and prominent leaders of the middle school movement was an ideal match with the intended purpose of this new book series. It is fitting that this first volume in the new book series was released at the symposium, "Celebrating the Legacy of the Middle Schools and Envisioning Its Future." This symposium, held May 18–20, 2011 on the campus of Georgia College and State University in Milledgeville, GA, was sponsored by Southeast Regional Professors of Middle Level Education, the National Association of Professor of Middle Level Education (NaPoMLE), and Georgia College and State University.

While the original *Handbook* series was developed to disseminate research focusing on varying topics in middle level education, this companion series was developed, in part, to provide our MLER SIG colleagues with a venue for the publication of resources useful in promoting, supporting, and advocating for the education of young adolescents. It is our hope that future volumes in this book series will include collections of undergraduate and graduate-level course syllabi, course assignments and projects, annotated bibliographies, and other materials and resources found useful in the preparation of middle grades teachers and administrators. We invite our colleagues to offer their suggestions for future volumes and we welcome volunteers to assist in developing these proposed volumes.

We wish to thank our many colleagues and the people who have made the first book series extremely successful. The eight volumes of that series and an encyclopedia contain the research and scholarly work of hundreds of middle grades researchers. A needed publication outlet was created by the series since the field of middle grades was absent any handbooks or encyclopedias which are so common to numerous other fields of inquiry. We hope that *The Handbook of Resources in Middle Level Education* will be as successful and fill a current void in our field.

Steven B. Mertens
Illinois State University

Vincent A. Anfara, Jr.
The University of Tennessee, Knoxville
Series Editors

Acknowledgements

This work would not have been possible without the help and support of many individuals and groups who have been committed to telling the story of the history of the Middle School Movement. First, we would like to thank Dr. Barbara Blackburn for her significant and essential contributions to this work. Without her help developing the research protocols, traveling to interview locations, securing funds, operating video equipment, developing video materials, and coordinating many of the logistics of the interviews, this project would not have been possible. Major changes in her life and career led to her leaving the project in 2009.

We are especially grateful for the cooperation of the prominent middle level leaders who willingly permitted us to record the rather extensive interviews that became The Legacy Project's primary data source. We were fortunate to have John H. Lounsbury, one of the founders of middle school education, as our editor and adviser during the writing of this book. His excellent editorial skills and comprehensive knowledge of middle level education greatly enhanced the quality of the book.

During the course of the project, we obtained a series of small research grants from the respective research team institutions (Appalachian State University and Winthrop University). We thank Michael Jacobson, our department chair, our middle grades colleagues, and other university administrators and colleagues in these institutions for their support of this work. We are grateful to have had such wonderful technical support as well. Numerous technology experts have helped us ensure the security of our

The Legacy of Middle School Leaders, pages xiii–xiv
Copyright © 2011 by Information Age Publishing
All rights of reproduction in any form reserved.

materials on servers and hard drives. We have been fortunate to have a series of Appalachian State University graduate students committed to this effort. Ana Haywood, Erin Hemric, Ricky Rhea, and Ashley Tipton have transcribed, edited, digitized, provided feedback, and grown professionally from their involvement in this work.

Finally, we are hopeful that the next generation of middle level educators and leaders will draw on and be informed and inspired by the Legacy Project materials. The participants profiled in this book, by their examples, have taught us the importance and value of pouring our professional lives into the lives of others.

PREFACE

The Middle School Legacy Project

The Middle Level Education Legacy Project had its beginnings in 2002 when Tracy Smith and Ken McEwin were discussing their fear that much of the history of the middle school movement was being lost over time. McEwin had mentioned William Alexander to some middle level educators in leadership positions, and they did not know who he was or that he is considered the father of the middle school. Without this knowledge, they could not appreciate the rich history of the education tier of which they were a part. McEwin and Smith had also noticed that some middle level professors, especially those new in their positions, lacked a comprehensive understanding of the early years of the middle school movement and sought resources that could provide that knowledge for them and their students. Smith and Barbara Blackburn, who had been doctoral students together and were teaching in middle grades programs at Appalachian State University and Winthrop University respectively, continued this discussion, noting that they had been fortunate to have mentors who had shared much of this history with them. However, they were concerned that those most knowledgeable about the history of the middle school movement had retired

The Legacy of Middle School Leaders, pages xv–xix
Copyright © 2011 by Information Age Publishing
All rights of reproduction in any form reserved.

or would soon do so and were "handing over the reins" of leadership to newcomers to middle level education. During a break at the 2002 National Middle School Association Conference in Portland, Oregon, Smith and Blackburn began to formulate specific plans for a project that would preserve that history. Upon returning, they met with McEwin, and the Middle Level Education Legacy Project emerged. The official description of the project is as follows:

> This study is an investigation of the history of a major educational reform in American education—the Middle School Movement. It will provide insight about current middle level education reform efforts through an investigation and discussion of the context in which these reforms have occurred; an analysis of factors that led to the development, evolution, and progress of middle level education; a summary of key features of these reforms; and a critical analysis of their impact on the future of middle level schooling.
>
> Contemporary middle schools are the result of a major American educational reform movement that has impacted many thousands of the nation's private and public schools. The far-reaching effects of this movement have not been fully documented nor their effects clearly determined. This research project will begin an important process of carefully studying and preserving the history of American middle schools by creating a shared record based on the collective experience and knowledge of the founders and pioneers of this effort. The Middle Level Education Legacy Project will provide a meaningful record of achievement in middle level education. The final products will include written and video documentation and analysis of the following: a) contributions of middle level leaders, b) critical events and incidents, c) origins and roles of organizations, associations, and groups, d) key publications, and e) other contextual factors that have affected the development of middle school education.

Unlike many historical research studies that rely primarily on document review, the major data source was a series of videotaped interviews with pioneer leaders. Transcriptions of these interviews captured and preserved the voices and views of these prominent leaders in middle level education in the hopes that their wisdom and experiences would provide a foundation on which to build a promising future for middle level education.

Because the full study is so broad in scope, we divided data collection and study into three phases. During Phase I, we focused on the interviews that were our main data source. This decision was made primarily because of the urgency to capture on video- and audio-tapes the thoughts and experiences of those pioneer leaders of the movement while they were still healthy and active. Ultimately we conducted, recorded, and transcribed 18 structured interviews during the period 2003–2007. The interview protocol was structured so that the researchers would be able to analyze patterns and draw conclusions across the set of participants. However, the interviewers also used their discretion about asking additional probing or follow-up questions to elicit thorough responses and information from each individual participant. The full interview protocol is included as the Appendix. Those interviewed were given an opportunity to check their transcriptions for accuracy. Readers should realize that these transcriptions are just that: unrehearsed, recorded conversations. They are often not the sort of polished prose that one would expect in published writings, but they are informally expressed and genuine thoughts of these leaders.

Participants were chosen based on their known and substantive contributions to middle level education. Selection criteria included a combination of various factors including authorship of significant and influential publications and presentations, a minimum of 25 years of active involvement in middle level education, substantial service, peer recognition, and a public record of advocacy for young adolescents. The eighteen participants chosen were:

John R. Arnold

Alfred A. Arth

James A. Beane

Sherrel K. Bergmann

Thomas S. Dickinson

Nancy M. Doda

Thomas O. Erb

Thomas E. Gatewood

Paul S. George

J. Howard Johnston

Joan S. Lipsitz

John H. Lounsbury

C. Kenneth McEwin

Chris Stevenson

John H. Swaim

Sue Swaim

Conrad F. Toepfer, Jr.

Gordon F. Vars

Phase II of the Middle Level Education Legacy Project will focus on document review and continued analysis of interview data that will draw together the thoughts of the interviewees on specific topics such as curriculum integration and advisory. Video materials and teaching resources will be developed during this phase. Phase III of the study will focus on a holistic analysis of both primary and secondary source data as well as dissemination plans that would put these materials before educators, policymakers, and anyone interested in the education and welfare of young adolescents.

The Middle Level Education Legacy Project is an historical, exploratory, and qualitative research project. When judged against Creswell (2009), the study answers what he terms the "epistemological question" through a qualitative paradigm. Specifically, a qualitative design calls for the researchers to interact with those in the study, minimizing distance. Face-to-face interviews provided the medium for the researcher-participant interaction needed. Miles and Huberman (1994) detail the recurring features of qualitative inquiry. When compared to their list, several criteria emerge as particularly relevant to this study:

1. The role of the researcher is to gain an overview of the context under study from a holistic viewpoint.
2. The researcher is attempting to gather data on the perceptions that exist with those involved in the study from an "insider" perspective.
3. One of the major tasks is to explain how people in the particular setting come to "understand, account for, take action, and otherwise manage their day-to-day situations" (p. 7).

Qualitative data emphasizes people's lived experiences and are useful for describing people's meanings (Miles & Huberman, 1994), their "perceptions, assumptions, prejudgments, presuppositions" (van Manen, 1977) and for connecting those meanings to their world (Miles & Huberman, 1994). The rich, descriptive nature of the data is critical. Vivid, real-world, context-based descriptions provide a more complex and accurate depiction of the occurrences.

This book, which is essentially a report on Phase I of the Legacy Project, comes now in response to the request of middle level educators with whom we have shared portions of this work at professional conferences. They have requested that these materials be made available prior to the completion of all phases of the study. This book is comprised of four sections. The brief introduction provides a description of the context and origins of the middle school movement. The second section is devoted to the five individuals widely recognized as the founders of the middle school movement. It opens with biographical and publication information on William M. Alexander and Donald H. Eichhorn, both of whom are deceased, along with examples of their works. These are followed by biographical and publication information and interview transcriptions of John H. Lounsbury, Conrad F. Toepfer, Jr., and Gordon F. Vars. The third section includes the biographical and publication information and interview transcriptions of the other early prominent leaders in middle school education selected to be included in the project. The final section of the book includes a synthesis of patterns and findings across the set of participants, statements of the participants' views about the current status of middle school education, and their observations about the future of middle school education.

References

Creswell, J. W. (2009). *Research design: Qualitative, quantitative, and mixed methods approaches.* Thousand Oaks, CA: Sage Publications.

Miles, M. B., & Huberman, A. M. (1994). *Qualitative data analysis: An expanded sourcebook.* Thousand Oaks, CA: Sage Publications.

Van Manen, M. (1977). Linking ways of knowing with ways of being practical. *Curriculum and Inquiry, 6*(3), 205–228.

INTRODUCTION

The Context and Origins of the Middle School Movement

In July 1963, William Alexander, noted curriculum authority and chairperson of the Department of Education at the George Peabody College for Teachers in Nashville, Tennessee, delivered a speech at a conference on the junior high school held at Cornell University. In what proved to be a landmark address, Alexander proposed "a new school in the middle," one with its own status in the K–12 vertical system of American education, rather than a "junior" version of another level of schooling. This speech provided the catalyst and is considered to be the start of the Middle School Movement.

Many middle level leaders participating in this study expressed their belief that Alexander's proposal resonated so positively with American educators because the social and historical context provided a ripe environment for change. Erb explained that "the whole period of the 1960s was a period of social questioning, agitation, and change. It was an opportune time to try new things." America was in the midst of the Vietnam Conflict and the Civil

The Legacy of Middle School Leaders, pages xxi–xxvi
Copyright © 2011 by Information Age Publishing
All rights of reproduction in any form reserved.

and Women's Rights Movements. Other early participants in the transition to middle schools describe the historical context as "more open than it is today" (Arnold) and "a good moment in terms of the possibility of change" (Beane). More specifically, they recall that it was "a time of liberality in education and the freedom that came with the 1960s" (George). Beane suggests that there was emerging from the progressive critics like Kozol a general sense that "there is something wrong with education." Toepfer compared the educational context of the 1960s to the first decade of the twenty-first century:

> In the 1960s, there was a greater sense of hope in our nation. While some of it may have been naïveté, many felt that the terrible things the world had witnessed in World War II and the Korean Conflict might be over. There was confidence and trust, and people seemed to look at things more non-judgmentally. People also looked at educational changes with more open minds. There was a trusting relationship between parents and educators not there anymore. Today, the public often criticizes schools and faults teachers almost immediately for things they do not understand or with which they disagree. When the middle school movement flourished, there was more participatory democracy and tolerance to try new approaches. Educators could more readily try new practices without their being challenged before results could show their value.

Gatewood further illuminates the importance of the timing of Alexander's proposal:

> In the 1960s . . . a lot of questioning was going on—questions about our government, questions about our leadership, questions about war, and questions about education. Being on college campuses at that time and being part of all this change was an energizing and exciting time to live because everything was up for grabs. Literally, every institution was under attack and was being questioned, so middle schools came along and provided a solution, an answer to one of those questions about "what do we do about the junior high?"

Many of the middle school leaders cited here were young professors at the time of Alexander's proposal. The 1960s were characterized by revolutionary ways of thinking and real change in the cultural fabric of American life. Young people in the 1960s were not content to follow in the footsteps of the generation ahead of them; they wanted change. The changes affected education, values, lifestyles, laws, and entertainment. Dickinson described it as "a period where experimentation was something that was going on in the schools" and that Alexander's ideas "found fertile ground" in the social and political climate of the late 1960s.

In addition to the context of schooling and education, Lipsitz notes that at this time in the history of the world, the study of early adolescence was a non-field. Early adolescence was not being studied in the context of education nor was it being studied in disciplines such as medicine, psychology, or sociology: "It was amazing to me that you could have an age group that everybody knew was important and that nobody was willing to pay attention to."

With a missionary fervor, emerging middle school advocates involved themselves in an effort to rescue young adolescents from the "wasteland" that the junior high was characterized as by Silberman (1970). In the beginning, the middle school "philosophy" was driven by an ethical or moral commitment to respect and respond to the developmental needs of young adolescents. This commitment led to the belief that they deserved their own schools and programs, designed in response to their unique needs and characteristics.

The Middle School Movement arose, in part, because, at a time when Americans were open to change—especially social change, middle level educators like Alexander recognized deficits in both junior high schools and the upper grades of elementary schools. He acknowledged that many of the components he proposed for the new middle school had their roots in the rationale used for the junior high school movement but that the implementation and application of those components had been lost as junior high schools "became in time almost duplicate copies of their senior high schools in terms of credit and grading systems, methods of teaching, time schedules, and student activities" (Alexander & George, 1981, p. 11).

However, it would be erroneous to assume that the only reason middle schools became prevalent was dissatisfaction with what the junior high school had become. Rather, the reasons middle schools became prominent are varied and complex. Middle schools grew in popularity in large part as a response to shifting demographics, including the need to find room in public schools for the offspring of the baby boom that were causing overcrowded conditions in elementary schools. In addition, in some cases, establishing or restructuring schools to middle schools became a means to comply with desegregation mandates. School districts could desegregate their middle schools as they transitioned students from their segregated elementary schools. While these practical and political forces increased the prevalence of middle schools, they were not the primary forces that influenced the belief system that shaped the middle school movement.

Because of the varied backgrounds and experiences of its early leaders, the middle school philosophy has roots in several academic perspectives, including developmental psychology, democratic education, and core curriculum all of which were grounded in progressive education. As a true grassroots innovation in American public education, middle school education was not conceived from a single specific philosophy or theory. Rather, middle schools were established, at the district level at least in part, in response to the demographic, political, and moral issues of the early 1960s. Over time, however, the middle school concept evolved. As middle level educators began to meet together at conferences and institutes, they brought to these gatherings their own perspectives, influenced by their backgrounds and experiences. At the same time, they began to build a collective identity around a set of shared beliefs.

As this collective identity developed, educational organizations began to dedicate time and attention to middle level education and to commission statements and reports about the philosophical and practical aspects of establishing developmentally responsive middle schools. In 1975, the ASCD Working Group on the Adolescent Learner published *The Middle School We Need* (Gatewood & Dilg, 1975). In 1980, the National Middle School Association (NMSA) commissioned a writing group to articulate the shared ideals of their organization, and in 1982, the first edition of *This We Believe*, the official position statement of NMSA, was published. In 1985, the Middle Level Council of NASSP published *An Agenda for Excellence at the Middle Level.* In 1989, The Carnegie Corporation of New York issued *Turning Points: Preparing American Youth for the 21st Century*, a landmark report which recognized the need to strengthen the academic core of middle schools and establish caring, supportive environments that value young adolescents. *This We Believe* has been revised and published in 1995, 2003, and 2010. Also in 2000, the Carnegie Corporation issued *Turning Points 2000: Educating Adolescents in the 21st Century*, by Anthony Jackson and Gayle Davis, an in-depth update of its 1989 report.

As evidence of the far-reaching impact of Alexander's speech and his conception of contemporary middle schools, *The New York Times* published the following information about Alexander and his conception of middle schools on the occasion of his death in 1996 (Pace, 1996):

> William M. Alexander, an educator who was a leader in the movement to supplant conventional junior high schools with middle schools that provide young adolescents with a smaller and more intimate educational environment, died on Tuesday at his home in Gainesville, Fla. He was 84. Dr. Alexander, who retired in 1977 after 14 years as professor of education at

the University of Florida, became convinced in the early 1960's that most conventional junior high schools had become rather static, being modeled on programs at senior high schools. He and others began to advocate specific programs and other ideas for middle schools, and in the decades since then, thousands of middle schools have been established around the United States. Middle school pupils variously range in age from 11 to 14 or from 10 to 15. They are generally in the fifth through the eighth grades. The main ingredients of the middle-school concept, according to *The Middle School Journal*, a professional publication, include a comprehensive curriculum plan, team planning and teaching, various instructional plans and health and physical education programs tailored to meet the needs of adolescent students.

The journal said a turning point in Dr. Alexander's career came in 1963, while he was waiting at La Guardia Airport for a plane to Ithaca, N.Y., where he was to address a Cornell University conference on the junior high school. Then and there, he decided to recommend in his address to the conference that, as the journal put it, "the concept of junior high schools be changed to middle schools that were designed to be more responsive to the needs and interests of young adolescents." He presented the proposal, and the middle school movement is often said to have begun at that time.

Now that the middle school movement is almost five decades old, it is most appropriate to examine its origins and development. The Legacy Project was undertaken primarily to deepen the understanding of this movement so that contemporary middle level educators and other stakeholders could benefit from the collective experiences and wisdom of early leaders.

References

Alexander, W. (1963, July). *The junior high school: A changing view.* Paper presented at the Tenth Annual Conference for School Administrators: A National Conference on the Junior High School, Ithaca, NY. Available at EJ590059.

Alexander, W. M., & George, P. S. (1981). *The exemplary middle school.* New York: Holt, Rinehart and Winston.

Carnegie Council on Adolescent Development. (1989). *Turning points: Preparing American youth for the 21st century.* New York: Carnegie Corporation of New York.

Gatewood, T., & Dilg, C. (1975). *The middle school we need.* A report from the ASCD Working Group on the Emerging Adolescent Learner. Washington, DC: Association for Supervision and Curriculum Development. (ERIC Document Reproduction Service No. ED 113 821)

Jackson, A., & Davis, G. (2000). *Turning points 2000: Educating adolescents in the 21st century.* New York: Teachers College Press.

Pace, E. (August 29, 1996). William M. Alexander, 84, dies: Fostered idea of middle schools. *The New York Times*. Retrieved from http://www.nytimes.com/1996/08/29/us/william-m-alexander-84-dies-fostered-idea-of-middle-schools.html?scp=1&sq=william%20m.%20alexander&st=cse

National Association of Secondary School Principals' Council on Middle Level Education. (1985). *An agenda for excellence at the middle level*. A statement by NASSP's Council on Middle Level Education. Reston, VA: National Association of Secondary School Principals.

National Middle School Association. (1982). *This we believe*. Columbus, OH: Author.

National Middle School Association. (1995). *This we believe: Developmentally responsive middle level schools*. Columbus, OH: Author.

National Middle School Association. (2003). *This we believe: Successful schools for young adolescents*. Westerville, OH: Author.

National Middle School Association. (2010). *This we believe: Keys to educating young adolescents*. Westerville, OH: Author.

Silberman, C.E. (1970). *Crisis in the classroom: The remaking of American education*. New York: Random House.

PART **I**

Founders of the Middle School Movement

1

William M. Alexander
(1912–1996)

---

*A characteristic to be sought in the middle school of the future is a flexible
curriculum, permitting and indeed aiding pupils to progress at different
rates and to different depths.*

Because of his pioneering work in the conceptualization and establishment of the middle school, Dr. William (Bill) M. Alexander is widely recognized as the "father of the middle school." He proposed the creation of middle schools in 1963 and conducted the first comprehensive national study of middle schools in 1968. Dr. Alexander's visionary research effort provided the baseline for subsequent studies of the implementation of middle school organization that provided a critical measure of the growth and implementation of programs and practices in middle schools over four decades. Alexander was senior author of one of the first books on middle school education. Although he always modestly pointed out that other early leaders had also conceived the need for developmentally responsive middle schools, there is no doubt he played a pivotal role in middle level education.

The Legacy of Middle School Leaders, pages 3–15
Copyright © 2011 by Information Age Publishing
3

Because he was already established as a world-renowned curriculum expert, his 1963 proposal calling for the creation of developmentally responsive middle schools gave essential credibility to the middle school movement.

Following graduation from Bethel College in McKenzie, Tennessee, Alexander began his career as a teacher in the McKenzie School District in 1934. He received his master's degree in education and history from George Peabody College for Teachers and his Doctor of Philosophy degree from Columbia University. He was Assistant Director of Curriculum for the Cincinnati Public Schools and then a Professor of Education at the University of Tennessee from 1941 to 1943 when he received a United States Naval Reserve commission and served in the Naval Orientation Training Program at Princeton University. After serving in the Navy, he accepted the position of Director of Curriculum with the Battle Creek School District, Battle Creek, Michigan. In 1950, Dr. Alexander became Superintendent of the Winnetka, Illinois Elementary School District. It was in Winnetka that he had the first opportunity to learn about a grades 6–8 school that later became one of his models for the newly conceptualized middle school. After leaving Winnetka, he accepted a position with the School of Education at the University of Miami.

In 1958, Dr. Alexander returned to Peabody College to teach and chair the Education Department. He continued to write prolifically and was president of the Association for Supervision and Curriculum Development. Then In 1963, Alexander became Professor at the University of Florida where he remained until his retirement in 1977. During his tenure there, he chaired the Department of Curriculum and Instruction and the Department of Educational Leadership.

In the 1960s, Alexander became frustrated with the failures of the junior high school to implement programs and practices that reflected what was known about young adolescent development. He was asked to deliver a keynote address at the 1963 Cornell University Conference on The Dynamic Junior High School. This was problematic because he realized that most junior high schools had become static and adopted programs and practices of the senior high school while largely ignoring students' developmental needs. So he prepared a speech proposing a new school called the *middle school*. His address, *The Junior High School: A Changing View* follows in its entirety. This proposal for a new transitional school in the middle received wide recognition and played a major role in guiding the collective vision of what middle level schools could and should be.

After the Cornell conference, Dr. Alexander and his colleagues wrote and spoke widely about the newly conceptualized middle school. *The*

Emergent Middle School, which he co-authored with Emmett Williams, Mary Compton, Vynce Hines, and Dan Prescott, was published in 1968. This classic book included a status report on the middle school movement and provided a comprehensive rationale and program guidelines for the establishment of developmentally responsive middle schools.

The key components of the middle school Alexander proposed were: (1) a comprehensive middle school curriculum plan based on young adolescent development; (2) advisory programs; (3) continuous progress arrangements; (4) team planning and teaching; (5) diverse instructional strategies; (6) exploratory courses and experiences; (7) health and physical education programs; and (8) planning and evaluation systems. An additional theme that ran throughout all his works was the necessity of creating specialized middle level teacher preparation programs. In an interview conducted in 1982 by John Lounsbury, Alexander stated:

> The lack of specific teacher preparation was a major blind spot in teacher education.... We need the strong support of Department of Education faculties who are interested in preparing people for teaching at the middle level, who are knowledgeable in this field, who are not resisting reorganization of their original bailiwicks of elementary and secondary education, and through the force of their leadership are helping to build up the program of middle schools. (p. 5)

Alexander, with the help of Ken McEwin, replicated the 1968 study, *A Survey of Organizational Patterns of Reorganized Middle Schools,* previously cited, 20 years later in 1988. *The Exemplary Middle School,* co-authored with his University of Florida colleague Dr. Paul S. George, was published in 1981 and became the standard text which helped define the middle school for many thousands of university students and middle level practitioners across the nation.

Dr. Alexander received many awards during his career. He was recipient of the John H. Lounsbury Distinguished Service Award from National Middle School Association (NMSA) in 1981. In 1982, he was given special recognition by the National Association of Secondary School Principals for his leadership in middle level education. He also received a significant award for Sustained Contribution in the Field of Curriculum from the American Educational Research Association in 1983. Alexander held many leadership positions in professional associations including president of ASCD and membership on the NMSA's Critical Issues and Publications Committees. He was a member of the team that developed the first *This We Believe* and a Laureate Counselor of Kappa Delta Pi.

Selected Publications

Alexander, W. M. (1963). The junior high school: A changing view. In R. David (Ed.), *Moving forward from the past: Early writings and current reflections of middle school founders* (pp. 3–13). Columbus, OH: National Middle School Association.

Alexander, W. M. (1968). *A survey of organizational patterns of reorganized middle schools.* Washington, DC: United States Department of Education.

Alexander, W. M. (1969). The new school in the middle, *Phi Delta Kappan, 50,* 355–357.

Alexander, W. M. (1978). How fares the middle school movement? *Middle School Journal, 9*(3), 19–21.

Alexander, W. M., & George, P. S. (1981). *The exemplary middle school.* New York: Holt, Rinehart, and Winston.

Alexander, W. M. (1984). The middle school emerges and flourishes. In J. H Lounsbury (Ed.), *Perspectives: Middle school education 1964–1984* (pp. 14–29). Columbus, OH: National Middle School Association.

Alexander, W. M., & McEwin, C. K. (1988). *Preparing to teach at the middle level.* Columbus, OH: National Middle School Association.

Alexander, W. M., & McEwin, C. K. (1989). *Schools in the middle: Status and progress.* Columbus, OH: National Middle School Association.

Alexander, W. M. (1991). Wandering and wondering in education. In D. L. Burleson (Ed.), *Reflections: Personal essays of thirty-three distinguished educators* (pp. 1–14). Bloomington, IN: Phi Delta Kappa.

McEwin, C. K., & Alexander, W. M. (1990). *Middle level programs and practices in elementary schools: Report of a national study.* Columbus, OH: National Middle School Association.

The Junior High School: A Changing View

William M. Alexander

Presented at the Tenth Annual Conference for School Administrators: A National Conference on the Dynamic Junior High School, Cornell University, July, 1963

It is not my task to summarize or seek to interpret what has gone before. Rather, Professor Johnson asked me to look forward with you, attempting to "identify the features of the junior high school that seem to be undergoing change and those which seem to endure." And so, I shall start out with a review of four characteristics of the junior high school which have been somewhat continuously sought and, to varying degrees, attained. Of these characteristics, I would also ask: Should they continue, and why or why not? Then I shall describe three other characteristics which many of us seek in the middle school of the future, and close my presentation with some hypotheses as to a partial, tentative model of this new middle school we need.

Characteristics of the Junior High School Which Continue

From its beginnings, the junior high school has sought to be a *transitional* or *bridge* institution between the elementary and the high school. This characteristic has been vigorously questioned both as to its appropriateness and its actual development.

As to appropriateness, certainly there is need to ease the transition of learners from childhood to adolescence. This type of transition function is more relevant to my second characteristic, however. Also, as long as the program and organization of the elementary schools differed sharply, there was, and is, real need for a bridge between the self-contained classroom of the elementary school with its broad and flexible units of work and the departmentalized program of the high school with its relatively greater emphasis on subjects and specialization. These differences are becoming much less sharp, however, as subjects are once again being pushed downward, as departmentalization of various sorts is again spreading in the elementary grades, as vertical curriculum planning in the major subjects makes more progress. That is, there are the distinct signs, commented on in Professor Broudy's paper and elsewhere, that the differences between the last years of the elementary school and the first ones of the high school—junior, senior, four year, or six year—are not nearly so severe and distinct as a decade ago, or indeed as many feel they should be.

However needed a transition is between the elementary and the high school, there are grave doubts as to the functioning of the junior high school in this regard. It is an interesting commentary on this function of the entire junior high school that after these schools had been widely established, a return from their departmentalized organization á lá the high school was sought in the block-time or core program. The chief justification of this program is to ease the transition from elementary to junior high school—a clear admission that the usually departmentalized program and organization of the junior high school tended to defeat the transitional function. Other evidence abounds that the "junior" high school has typically been a secondary school following the four-year high school model rather than being an in-between school, bridging a gap between elementary and secondary education. As Professor Johnson pointed out in his *Saturday Review* article, the transition that was originally of greatest concern was that of making "the academic initiation at grade nine easier for pupils" rather than the transition from grade six to seven or the one represented by pubescence. The general adoption by junior high schools of the schedule, the activity program, and the organization of the high school attests to the dominance of the idea that the bridge was fundamentally a vestibule added at the front door of the high school.

Thus, there is a major question as to whether the junior high school as it now exists should defend its existence on the transitional basis. Indeed we doubt whether any institution can have real purpose and vitality if its role is subordinated either to the separate institutions it bridges or the one for which it serves a preparatory function. I would vote for elimination of the separateness of current elementary, junior and senior high schools, with the resulting need for bridges, and for instead a 12- to 14-year institution, with three levels in its vertical structure, each of which has a program and organization appropriate to its place in a sequential educational pattern. Thus, there would be a lower, middle, and upper level or a primary, middle, and high school.

The second continuing characteristic of the junior high school is its composite of efforts to have a *program of its own especially adopted to the needs of preadolescent and early adolescent pupils.* All of us would undoubtedly like to see these efforts succeed in leading children successfully through pubescence and from the dependency of childhood to a resourceful, responsible, independence of adolescence. The catch here lies in the great variations between the sexes and among individuals in each as so clearly pointed out in Professor Wattenberg's paper, as to when these changes occur. Apparently, if we would really have one school to bridge the gap from childhood to adolescence for all pupils, even nearly all pupils, it would have to enroll pupils from ages 10 through 16, or grades 5 through 10. Perhaps we should have to settle instead for a school which serves a vestibule function for pubescence and adolescence for many, perhaps most children, rather than for high school.

Despite the criticisms already made here and elsewhere, we should affirm the belief that junior high school, even as a "junior" institution, has provided for some needs of the preadolescent, certainly better than in the narrower program of the eight grade elementary school or of the more regimented one of the high school. In good junior high schools, boys and girls have had more of the freedom of movement they need, more appropriate health and physical education, more chances to participate in planning and managing their own activities, more resources for help on their problems of growing up, and more opportunities to explore new interests and to develop new aspirations. All of these features we would definitely continue in the middle school of the future.

A third continuing characteristic of the junior high school has been *its program of exploratory experiences*. Once a prevocational education function, exploration has been broadened to include a wider variety of possible interests. There seems little disagreement that the youngster of twelve and above needs many and varied opportunities to identify and/or deepen worthwhile interests, and all of us would applaud what junior high schools have done to this end. However, the recent pressures on schools to give greater emphasis to the academic subjects may be curtailing the exploratory feature. Earlier languages, more mathematics and science, more homework, may mean for many pupils less time and energy for the fine arts, for homemaking and industrial arts, and for such special interests as dramatics, journalism, musical performance, scouting, camping, outside jobs, and general reading.

Furthermore, many view the 6-, 9-, 12-, or even 18-weeks elective courses in grades 8 and 9 as inadequate exploration. In some areas these may be the only possibilities, but we wonder if different scheduling and a different relationship of subjects and activities might facilitate many independent experiences and projects developing either from the classroom, the counseling situation, the activity program, or just from the pupil's expressed interests? Could the middle school give more emphasis to independent study and activity as an aid to the transition from childhood to adolescence? Perhaps we need more special interests centers competently supervised and operated on a flexible time basis in which children can get guidance and experience in such varied activities as reading, acting, writing, painting, ceramics, mechanics of the automobile and home, typing, photography, and personal grooming and many others.

The fourth characteristic of the junior high school is one all support – *continued general education*. Probably most of us would heartily agree with our hosts here at Cornell that there is great need to underline the intellectual growth phase of this program. Certainly curriculum planning at the junior high school level has been no more successful than elsewhere, perhaps less so, in defining the scope and sequence of an adequate general education. Possibly the difficulty has lain in part in the feeling that the subjects in "junior" high school must be very different from the elementary school, although repetition has continued. My own view is that the junior high school break has unwittingly hastened the disrespect for intellectual activity too common among adolescents. Has the "junior" high school, with its imitation of the high school activity and social programs, hastened and fixed more firmly the ideals of athletic prowess (boys) and popularity (girls) over academic brilliance as reported in Coleman's study of the *Adolescent Society*?

Continued general education in the junior high school must indeed give a new emphasis to intellectual development. This it must do, I believe, by more skillful teaching and more careful curriculum planning, rather than by more, or even continued, pressures on grades, and preparation for high school and college.

Other Characteristics to be Sought in the Middle School

Several factors point to the need for vigorous attempt in the middle school to focus on the *individualization of instruction*. Although the primary school certainly pays attention to individual differences, its program is most of all one of integration of young children into accepted patterns of communication and social behavior. Habits of conformity are well-enough developed in most 10-to-12 year-olds to indicate a need for opening up opportunities for individual deviations of a wholesome and promising variety.

I was impressed by Dr. Paul Torrance's report recently of studies in youngsters' creative behavior that showed a decided slump for many children beginning about the fourth grade. Is our emphasis on the group and on conformity in the middle grades contributing to the inhibition of creative ideas and activities?

We are all familiar, too, with the characteristic resistance to schools and schooling which begins to be expressed even in the third and fourth grades. Whether real or fancied, the apparent disposition of many children to discount educational purposes and programs reflects inadequate motivation to intellectual achievement. It is at this level, too, that underachievement is first readily identified. The potential drop-out is noted, and the need for individual help and stimulation weighs heavily on the conscientious, sympathetic teacher.

Ability grouping and programs for special groups may be only hiding the needs of the individual in the group. Whether he be the potential artist, or drop-out, the intellectually stimulated or unmotivated, Johnny needs all the attention he can get from a teacher who knows him well and respects his individuality. To help in individualization, the middle school needs to provide adequate diagnostic and guidance services. It also needs to permit teachers to work individually with children and their parents. All of the other known aids to individualization—for example, a variety of learning resources, time and place for independent study, self-evaluation devices, individual projects, opportunities for varied pupil roles in classroom and school organizations—should be abundant in the middle school years.

A related second characteristic to be sought in the middle school of the future is a *flexible curriculum*, permitting and indeed aiding pupils to progress at different rates and to different depths. Although the requirements of continued general education make mandatory some beginning points and goals in the basic curriculum fields, minimum grade standards subject by subject can defeat the aims of intellectual development. Programmed instructional materials in mathematics and language arts may help to pace individual's learning progress. Unit-of-work approaches in social studies and science can provide differentiated tasks for learners. In matters of performance, individuals can be challenged to seek their own level of attainment in playing an instrument, using paints and easels, or hitting a softball.

But even greater flexibility must come through a reconsideration of classroom organization and procedure. The middle grades seem none too early to initiate some pupils into plans of curriculum differentiation which provide certain ones to work on reading improvement in a reading center, while some classmates are reading in the classroom under their teacher's guidance and still others are using the library for more challenging materials. Or a few pupils may be working with a speech teacher, others preparing a dramatic presentation, and others in the language laboratory learning a modern foreign language.

In all studies continued attention would be given to the learning process itself. The teacher demonstrates how sources are used to get answers to real questions, and pupils apply the procedures to questions they investigate. Reference books, textbooks, interviews, current newspapers and magazines, and other sources are fully utilized as methods of inquiry; they replace methods of memorization as the focal points of teaching and learning. Although facts are kept central, fact-finding rather than fact-memorizing and reciting is emphasized in the flexible curriculum of essential learning processes instead of minimum essentials of definitions, dates, and details in general. The curriculum which should be characteristic of the middle school must reflect such an educational belief as was stated by the Winnetka Public Schools as their No. 1 objective in a recent publication of *Beliefs and Objectives*, under the heading of "Give Primary and Unremitting Devotion to Intellectual Growth." The statement in part is as follows:

Intellectual growth means much more than an increasing competence in the academic content of the curriculum. We must endeavor to stimulate in the child a love for learning, an attitude of inquiry, a passion for truth and beauty, a questioning mind. The learning of right answers is not enough...beyond answers alone, we must help children ask right questions, and discover their answers through creative thinking, reasoning, judging, and understanding. We must help children know that learning is its own reward, uncluttered by momentary symbolic rewards for accomplishments or penalties for failures.

Learning can best flourish when teachers, supported by adequate materials, create a climate in which children are genuinely desirous of learning. It will flourish when children become, through the teacher's stimulation, self-motivated, knowing that learning is necessary and important, and why they are engaged upon it. And it behooves us to be sure that it is necessary and important. Conclusions, values, solutions to problems are not taught...they are learned, created, possessed internally by the child, having been excited by the teacher, and having been led by the teacher to the place where the answers might be found.

A final, and somewhat summarizing, characteristic to be sought in the middle school is an *emphasis on values.* In the upper or high school boys and girls are beset by conflicts in value systems. In the early school years, these conflicts were less real or absent. Between the primary and later years is a real opportunity for the school to provide leadership in fixing values which will survive the perils ahead. As boys and girls are challenged in the middle grades to assume responsibility for their own actions, to respect each other and the adults with whom they associate, and to distinguish right from wrong, truth from falsehood, they can grow to a real independence. Every class, every pupil-teacher conversation, every school activity is a setting for the development of values. The responsiveness of the older children and preadolescent makes the middle grades an especially desirable level for a continuing emphasis on this aspect of education.

A Tentative Model for the New Middle School

The "changing view" I have seen and reflected here is by now obvious to you as a view of a middle unit in a vertically planned educational system. This unit or school may compromise what is now called junior high school; however, this unit is really a third quarter, too much like the final quarter. Perhaps it will be the grade 6-8 unit, now growing in popularity. I would personally prefer to see it as near a middle unit as possible, namely, what now constitutes grades 5–8.

Experimentation with a new middle school (best developed in new building programs, although it could be accomplished by modifying present junior high school structures), should serve several purposes, it is suggested:

1. It would give this unit a status of its own, rather than a "Junior" classification.
2. It would facilitate the introduction in grades 5 and 6 of some specialization and team teaching in staffing patterns.
3. It would also facilitate the reorganization of teacher education sorely needed to provide teachers competent for the middle school; since existing patterns of neither elementary nor secondary teacher training would suffice, a new pattern would have to be developed.
4. A clearly defined middle unit should more easily have the other characteristics already described as desirable, than the typical junior high school: (1) a well-articulated 12- to 14-year system of education; (2) preparation for, even transition to, adolescence; (3) continued general education; and (4) abundant opportunities for exploration of interests, individualization of instruction, a flexible curriculum, and emphasis on values.

I hope that the suggestions made here do not amount to the "major surgery" Dr. Johnson mentioned in his *Saturday Review* article as being often prescribed by critics; he stated that these proposals generally had "about as much chance of being pulled off as has the abolition of the income tax." I hope the specifics of this tentative model now proposed may get some further consideration and tried out as applicable, perhaps in a few complete experimental units.

I. *The Program* might have these phases:
A. *Learning skills*: reading, speaking, computation skills continued from the elementary school, with new emphases on use of library tools and self-teaching devices.
B. *Other common learnings*: literature, social studies, languages, mathematics, science, and fine arts, following a sequence of instruction in these areas planned for grades K–12.
C. *Personal development*: health and physical education geared to the 10- 14 year old; individually planned experiences in foreign languages, typing, fine and practical arts, and remedial basic skills; other exploratory experiences through independent study and a program of special interest activities and student-managed enterprises; close relationship with a counselor-teacher through-

out the middle school; and adequate diagnostic tests, parent conferences, and other data sources for counseling.

II. *The organization* of the middle school might include these arrangements:

    A. A team of three to five teachers (one or two especially competent in language arts and social studies, one or two in science and mathematics, and one in the fine arts and/or languages) could be assigned to each group of 75 to 150 pupils, on a team basis. These teachers would be responsible for about two-thirds of the instruction of these pupils, on a team basis according to such plans as are appropriate to curriculum goals, teacher competencies, and school organization.

    B. Each pupil would be a member of a small homeroom group, which would be assigned to one of the team members for counseling and individual scheduling for special programs.

    C. Each pupil would participate daily in a program of health and physical education directed by a specialist in this area.

    D. Such special instructional and/or laboratory centers as the following would be available for several purposes, with each center manned by a teacher competent in individualized instruction: reading; writing; speech; mathematics; library; foreign languages; typing; music; art; industrial arts; home economics; dramatics. Pupils would be scheduled for work in these centers on an individualized basis for both short-term and long-term instruction as needed.

    E. The basic instructional units (75 to 150 pupils) and the homeroom groups (3 to 5 in each unit) would be organized on a heterogeneous basis as to ability. The teaching team might arrange some instruction in basic skills by groups determined for this purpose according to status in the skills concerned.

III. *Personnel arrangements* might include:

    A. A principal whose major duties involve the coordination of basic instructional units and special instructional centers, and leadership in curriculum planning and evaluation activities.

    B. An assistant principal (assuming 500 or more pupils) to manage supporting administrative and auxiliary school services and to supervise record-keeping, clerical, and fiscal operations.

    C. Special staff positions: curriculum research and evaluation, psychological services, health services, etc.

    D. Classification of teachers as either (1) homeroom or (2) special center, there being no differential in status or salary due to this classification.

E. Homeroom teacher would work with pupils about two-thirds of their scheduled time and have one-third available for team planning, individual preparation, and parent conferences. Special center teachers would have an appropriate period available daily for individual preparation and conferences with teaching team members.

F. Employment and assignment of faculty based on:
  1. Five to six years' college training and three or more years' successful teaching experience before permanent license.
  2. For all teachers a major in their teaching field(s) through the master's degree, with adequate professional education of a practice-oriented nature.
  3. Equivalent of a doctorate in the field of specialization for all administrative and special staff positions.
  4. Salary schedule provisions for recognition of superior training and performance.

2

Donald H. Eichhorn
(1934–2001)

> *The middle school must be a strong learning school where every child is expected to achieve and helped to learn and it should be accomplished in a humane, positive, and dynamic environment.*

Donald H. Eichhorn provided a distinctive leadership role in the middle school movement. He was a pioneer in the implementation of developmentally responsive middle schools in Upper St. Clair, Pennsylvania, where he spent the first 26 years of his career. While serving as Assistant Superintendent, he worked with the principals of Fort Couch Middle School and Boyce Middle School to create middle schools that were multi-aged, with young adolescents grouped for instruction based on developmental readiness. These two middle schools served as early models for other school districts that were planning to create new middle schools. Visitors from across the country and around the world came to learn from the exemplary programs and practices at these schools. In 1979, Dr. Eichhorn became superintendent of the Lewisburg Area School District, Lewisburg, Pennsylvania,

The Legacy of Middle School Leaders, pages 17–26
Copyright © 2011 by Information Age Publishing
All rights of reproduction in any form reserved.

where he served until his retirement. His dissertation, *Nongraded Middle School: Supporting Theory and Conceptualized Functional Model*, was the basis for his 1966 book *The Middle School*, the first middle school book written. In the book he used the term *transescence*, which he had coined, to give an identity to this level or stage of development which begins prior to the onset of puberty and extends through the early stages of adolescence. A theme that always ran through his publications, professional presentations, and consultancies was the uniqueness of the age group and the need to base decisions about middle school curriculum, instruction, and schooling on that uniqueness.

Dr. Eichhorn received his undergraduate degree in health education at Slippery Rock University and his master's and doctorate from the University of Pittsburg. Considered to be a consummate scholar–practitioner who put theoretical, pioneering ideas into practice, he was active professionally conducting research, writing, speaking, and working with schools and districts in the United States and abroad. He chaired the influential ASCD's Council on the Emerging Adolescent and served in various capacities in NMSA and National Association of Secondary School Principals (NASSP). As a testament to the lasting importance of his work, the National Middle School Association (NMSA) dedicated its 1991 Annual Conference to him celebrating the 25th anniversary of the publication of *The Middle School*. Eichhorn was the recipient of the highest award given by NMSA, The John H. Lounsbury Distinguished Service Award (1983). He also received the Gruhn-Forrest Long-Melton Award for distinguished service and leadership in middle level education given by NASSP (1999). The Pennsylvania Middle School Association presented Dr. Eichhorn with an Achievement Award and established the Donald H. Eichhorn Award for Excellence in Middle Level Education in his honor. Additionally, the Lewisburg, Pennsylvania School District named an award-winning middle school in his honor, the Donald H. Eichhorn Middle School.

Selected Publications

Eichhorn, D. H. (1968). Middle school reorganization: A new dimension. *Theory Into Practice, 7*(3), 111–113.

Eichhorn, D. H. (1973). The Boyce medical study. In H. Atkins & P. Pumerantz (Eds), *Educational dimensions of the emerging adolescent learner*. Washington, DC: Association for Supervision and Curriculum Development.

Eichhorn, D. H. (1977). Middle school: The beauty of diversity. *Middle School Journal, 8*(1), 3, 18–19.

Eichhorn, D. H. (1980). The school. In M. Johnson (Ed.), *Toward adolescence: The middle school years* (79th yearbook of the National Society for the Study of Education) (pp. 56–73). Chicago, IL: University of Chicago Press.

Eichhorn, D. H. (1983). Focus on the learner leads a clearer middle level picture. *NASSP Bulletin, 67*, 45–48.

Eichhorn, D. H. (1984). The nature of transescents. In J. H. Lounsbury (Ed.), *Perspectives: middle school education 1964–1984* (pp. 30–38). Columbus, OH: National Middle School Association.

Eichhorn, D. H. (1987). *The middle school.* Columbus, OH: National Middle School Association and Reston, VA: National Association of Secondary School Principals. [Reprinted from D. H. Eichhorn (1966). *The middle school.* New York: Center for Applied Research in Education.

Eichhorn, D. H. (1991). *Five visions as a basis for strategic planning for middle schools.* Mechanicsburg, PA: Pennsylvania Middle School Association.

Eichhorn, D. H. (1998). Donald H. Eichhorn reflects: Considering it all. In R. David, (Ed.), *Moving forward from the past: Early writings and current reflections of middle school founders* (pp. 78–95). Columbus, OH: National Middle School Association.

The Middle School:
The Beauty of Diversity

Keynote Address presented at the National Middle School Association Annual Conference, November 19, 1976. This speech was published in the Middle School Journal in February, 1977.

During World War II, there was a refrain in one of the popular morale building songs of the day which went something like this, "We did it before and we can do it again." While the expression emerged in a different world and for a different purpose, somehow its haunting lyric fits a concern in this place in our time.

We have been down the road to middle school education twice in this century. A strange thing happened on the *road* to the junior high school— we ultimately forgot the students. We designed the road bed out of concrete and designed the motels along its route all with the same dining rooms. We made the road a limited access highway with standard speed limits. We built bridges like the one over the River Kwai where the bridge became more important than the purpose of its construction. In short, we bowed to the efficiency of the road and somehow forgot the traveler's desire and need to see the countryside, readily bypassed the need for the traveler to get to the next stop. The trip simply could not tolerate engine trouble or flat tires. An even stranger thing might happen on the road to the middle school—we might forget the students again. Certainly, we have improved the road by adding rotaries, cloverleafs, and rest stops. But somehow, the traveler finds it all too easy to miss the richness of the journey because she must return to the *basic* highway as quickly as possible.

I am sure you must be wondering if this talk is taking you on a detour away from the conference. I hope not as I feel at this crossroads in the middle school movement, a detour might be in the best interests of the journey. At least, it should give us pause to restudy the map and assure ourselves that the message on the sign which reads "Temporary Inconvenience, Permanent Improvement" is accurate.

All of us are familiar with the past history of schools for youngsters in the middle. There is a lesson, I believe, in these past programs. The lesson is simply that effective schools are schools designed around the characteristics and needs of transescents. By concentrating on pedagogy, learning strategies, and administrative things, we find ourselves rushing madly from one extreme of the philosophic pendulum to the other—from traditional to progressive back to traditional and on and on. If we are to "Arch the Gap," I suggest we focus on students. The only rationale which makes sense is the uniqueness of the students in the middle school.

There is no question we possess enough organizational weapons in our arsenal to ensure success. But we cannot run effective schools designed only for organizational strategies. I have said on many occasions if I had a choice between four outstanding self-contained teachers and four mediocre team members I certainly would choose the former. If I had a choice between a faculty housed in an 1890 building who focuses on the characteristics and needs of students or a group of teachers concerned mostly with team arrangements in a 1976 open space school, I surely would again choose the former. I am not suggesting that team teaching, open space, etc. are less desirable than self-contained, closed spaced instruction. I am merely suggesting that organization, in the final analysis, is secondary in importance to an attitude, knowledge, and understanding of students among teachers and principals.

Impressions of Middle School Students

To me, the most fascinating aspect of transescents is their diversity. To set up a curriculum based upon the premise that seventh grade is for seventh graders neglects one basic element and that is how does one describe a seventh grader? A seventh grader may be six feet, two inches with a deep voice or four feet, four inches hoping to grow. She might be observed awkwardly navigating the stairs or she might score a perfect 10.0 in Olympic parallel bar competition. He may be unable to read the comic page or he might be solving problems in tenth grade geometry. Wearing mouth braces, she might be playing with her jump rope or she might be aspiring in a sophisticated way to Miss Teenage America. He might be curious, enthusiastic, and interested or he might be turned off. He might be an alcoholic or he might be a little leaguer.

It is these vast differences which make these youngsters so challenging. We persist, however, in stereotyping seventh graders as seventh graders. We standardize test scores and declare any student not average or better as a failure. We manipulate diversity so it fits what adults say all seventh graders should be. Albert Einstein once said, "It is in fact nothing short of a miracle that the modern methods of instruction have not yet entirely strangled the holy curiosity of inquiry for this delicate plant, aside from stimulation, stands mainly in the need of freedom; without this it goes to wrack and ruin without fail."

It seems to me the acceptance of the stereotype and the rejections of diversity lead to a very sterile middle school experience. Certainly, middle school students have always been this way and surely will remain in the future. Frances Bacon writing in *Essays: of Young and Age* seemed to express it quite well: "Young men are fitter to invent than to judge: fitter for execution than for counsel, and fitter for new projects than for settled business." While Bacon has not been a part of the middle school movement, this perceptiveness of youth might guide us.

I am certain that I need not review for this audience the scientific growth characteristics of youngsters in transition from childhood to adolescence. All respectable middle school rationales contain these stark facts. Rather, I thought I might remind you of those traits which make middle schoolers such delightful human beings as well as rich building blocks for effective programs. One such trait is their creative sense of humor. I recall one such incident which makes the point. When we started our middle school, some of the residents became unduly alarmed. As a result, we had a number of meetings with large groups of parents in an attempt to allay their fears. One day on the way to the large group instruction room to meet with a group of parents, I met Sally in the hall. She said, "Mr. Eichhorn, do you know I brought my two white mice to school?" I said "No, but I am happy you did." She said, "I am too but somehow they got loose in the large group instruction room. Do you think the mothers will mind?"

As Students See the Middle School

What is middle school? Well, one youngster says, "A middle school is a school where you are too old to be in elementary school and too young to be in high school. In other words, it's no fun." Another remarked, "The middle school has some boring teachers and rotten grilled cheese sandwiches. You always get homework and you sit in uncomfortable desks. But, it's an okay school." Another student said, "A place to go after they go to elementary school and come out a lot more mixed up and confused." Signed, "The Shadow." One student gave almost a textbook definition. She said, "It's the school for grades that aren't children, but still aren't adults." The last definition reminded me of the story Emmett Williams of the University of Florida tells. Emmett said he was meeting with a group of sixth graders and he asked them if they knew what the term transescent meant. One obviously mature student said, "Sure it's the stage between childhood and adultery."

Of course, they have their serious side also. Their power of observation is great. One city of Pittsburgh youngster said, "The kids at this school work together better than in any school I have ever been to. They act like they have been working together for years. I think it probably has something to do with the happy, bright, and free atmosphere." Occasionally, one is too observant. For example, regarding teachers, one said, "My teachers are very nice. But my math teacher isn't fair sometimes. And my reading teacher likes to leave the room, well very often. It seems like she don't want to teach class." Regarding the curriculum, one youngster remarked, "The science, reading, social studies, language arts, math, and spelling are all okay—if you like them." Some cannot make up their minds about curriculum, like this boy who said, "Another thing I hate about school is that we have a lot of subjects we don't need like music. Even though I like them, I'd rather be outside playing football." Loyalty is an ever present concern. "I love this school. To me it's a home away from home," remarked one Pittsburgh youth. Another said, "When I come to school every day I walk boldly because I know I am going to the best school in the nation."

We believe flexible arrangements are helpful but one student obviously disagrees. She wrote, "My schedule has been changed. I'm very unhappy. In my new class, I have no friends." We also believe schools should be efficient but one student remarked, "I really like reading, and this means a lot to me. I hope the library will be open to all students all the time."

Some of critics have said that we have middle schools because we need new buildings. In this regard, one Upper St. Clair youth says, "They have middle schools so that elementary schools aren't too crowded." His friend agreed. He said, "They put us here because they don't want us hanging around little kids."

Let me share one final gem with you which proves that our belief that some youngsters are in formal operations is accurate. This student says, "A middle school is a place where kids who are still linked to the elementary school and those who look up to the high school go to learn what's ahead. It is a place where gym uniforms are *out* and bubble gum is *in*. Where sixth graders can feel as mighty as eighth graders and vice versa. To go to a middle school means some teachers think you act too young and some think you act too old. A middle school is a really nice place."

I have attempted to present you a mental picture of youngsters, a rather special group of youngsters in a rather special time in their educational lives. It seems to me that this message is highly consistent with what I have observed as the foundation of this Association. The task is now to translate the electricity one feels whenever middle school educators get together into middle school programs when we are apart.

The Challenges Ahead

What are the challenges which face us? One certainly can only suggest a few areas which appear to be the most vital.

The Challenge to Keep Our Movement Dynamic

By resisting institutional rigidity, the middle school has remained a dynamic concept. We have been criticized for a lack of uniformity. Middle schools in Atlanta are different from middle schools in Indiana, critics claim. So be it. I firmly believe when middle schools find *the* model—*the* right program for all schools, then we will need to start a third movement this Century. The strength of middle schools lies in their ability to create programs for students wherever they may be. The history of all institutions whether these are churches, governments, or schools, tells us whenever rigidity and the inability to adjust occur, that institution ceases to be an effective force.

The Challenge to Develop Schools Which Excite and Inspire

If returning to basics means that middle schools should become places of mental drudgery, then I am opposed. Middle schoolers are curious, enthusiastic, and mercurial human beings. To condemn them to a school which deprives them of their very nature is to create a school which is doomed to failure. In Shakespeare's play, *As You Like It*, he describes one phase of life in this way, "And then the whining school boy, with his satchel and shining morning face, creeping like snail unwilling to go to school." We don't need middle schools where youngsters with shining faces are unwilling to go.

The Challenge to Create Instructional Programs Which Expect Students to Learn and Curriculum Which Challenges Their Intellect

Middle school students in this time of relative innocence in their lives desire nothing more than to learn. One Pittsburg youngster said it best. He said "We are learning a lot, but some of the children are not learning enough. I know I'm slow and I need more help. I would like to be like other children—smart."

Perhaps our greatest challenge is to develop a curriculum which expects, requires, and insists on all students learning. Mauritz Johnston, an outstanding junior high school leader, once said, "It is an affront to adolescents to assume that they cannot or will not respond to a program with a serious intellectual emphasis." Provided with a suitable background and placed in a setting in which intellectual activity is not deprecated, most of them are quite capable of dealing formally with abstract notions that serve to explain the world around them and invest their experiences with meaning."

The middle school must be a strong learning school where every child is expected to achieve and helped to learn, and it should be accomplished in a humane, positive, and dynamic environment. A middle school should be considered a learning laboratory where curiosity is the cornerstone; where students are able to pursue learning in their style not our style, where creativity and divergent thinking are admired at least as much as convergent thinking, where students respect and admire learning rather than only the grades they receive, and where students can learn that youngsters of different races, religions, sex, and ethnic backgrounds can begin to understand and appreciate their differences.

The Challenge to Broaden our Base of Knowledge Regarding the Physical Characteristics of Middle School Students

Over the years, we have relied heavily on the psycho-educational field for our knowledge of students and the type of program we should provide. I would like to suggest, in addition to these basic fields, we create an alliance of knowledge with the medical profession. The one factor which totally permeates the lives of students at this age is their physical growth and the ramifications socially and emotionally of this growth. Havighurst, writing in his famous *Developmental Tasks and Education,* said it so well. He said, "The period from twelve to eighteen is primarily one of physical and social maturing.... The principal lessons are emotional and social, not intellectual." One youngster at Fort Couch said it more succinctly, "It's a point in your life where you do most of your growing up."

It seems to me, as we look ahead to the 1980s, such an alliance with the medical profession would provide educators with immense knowledge. Medical researchers are investigating and discovering vast new knowledge regarding pubescence and early adolescence. Such areas as the impact of hormonal changes, stress, nutrition, growth patterns and vascular changes are only the tip of the iceberg. The concept which medical researchers refer to as developmental or biological age, in my judgment, has the potential to revolutionize middle school education.

By accepting the medical concept of developmental age, which is so much more consistent than the graded concept, we would by necessity, restructure the middle level in terms of curriculum, learning strategies, and in other basic ways. Medical men such as J. M. Tanner of the University of London and Allan Drash, Professor of Pediatrics, University of Pittsburg Medical School, have strongly endorsed this concept. Drash, writing in this year's volume of *Transescence* had this to say, "Will curricular changes based on developmental information significantly affect the future course of the student in academic, physical, or emotional terms? ... It seems highly likely that beneficial effects will accrue." I suggest this Association take the lead in building such an alliance with the medical profession. I firmly believe such an alliance would create for middle school educators unlimited opportunities for serving middle school students.

The Challenge to Focus on the Transescent as the Foundation of Program

Throughout my remarks, I have attempted to place the student into perspective. Earlier in my comments I suggested that at times we have taken the wrong road. Let me suggest that now as we consider our journey further, that we consider students as the "engine not the caboose" of the train. If we have courage and the vision to start with the characteristics of students and develop programs in line with those characteristics we will indeed be taking the right road. If we believe the student, not the organization, is the real uniqueness of middle schools, let's test that belief by judging our classrooms and our schools by how effectively they mesh with what students are like in those classrooms and schools.

A poem by Phyliss McGinley titled "Portrait of Girl with Comic Book" sums it up nicely.

Portrait of Girl with Comic Book

Thirteen's no age at all. Thirteen is nothing.
It is not wit, or powder on the face,
Or Wednesday matinees, or misses' clothing,
Or intellect, or grace.
Twelve has its tribal customs. But thirteen
Is neither boys in battered cars nor dolls,
Nor Sara Crewe, or movie magazine,
Or pennants on the walls.

Thirteen keeps diaries and tropical fish
(A month, at most); scorns jump ropes in the spring;
Could not, would fortune grant it, name its wish;
Wants nothing, everything;
Has secrets from itself, friends it despises;
Admits none to the terrors that it feels;
Owns half a hundred masks but no disguises;
And walks upon it heels.

Thirteen's anomalous—not that, not this;
Nor folded bud, or wave that laps a shore,
Or moth proverbial from the chrysalis.
Is the one age defeats the metaphor.
It is not a town, like childhood, strongly walled
But easily surrounded; Is not city.
Nor, quitted once, can it be quite recalled—
Not even with pity.

This is the essence of middle schools. With your commitment and with your care, emphasizing the Beauty of Diversity, middle schools can ultimately achieve their great destiny.

3

John H. Lounsbury

> *We need to study our history and recognize it and learn from it. And one of the things that bothers me now is change is so rampant about everything, that we forget to look at the history and think that everything new is good and everything old is bad. We need to become students of our history.*

Throughout his long and distinguished career, John H. Lounsbury has been a constant, committed advocate for young adolescents as well as for those who teach them and serve them in other ways. His leadership in middle level education spans a period of more than 60 years and includes exemplary teaching, mentoring, leadership, writing, editing, research, and professional service. He has significantly influenced the nature of contemporary middle level education. Because of his special contributions, values, and integrity, he has been referred to as the "conscience of the middle school."

After serving in the United States Army in the Pacific Theatre during World War II, Lounsbury graduated with a BA degree in social studies in 1947 from John B. Stetson University, DeLand, Florida. He began his teach-

The Legacy of Middle School Leaders, pages 27–51
Copyright © 2011 by Information Age Publishing
27

ing career as a junior and senior high school teacher in Wilmington, North Carolina, in 1948. He received his master's degree in secondary education in 1948 and his doctorate in curriculum and instruction in 1954 from George Peabody College for Teachers. After completing his doctorate, Dr. Lounsbury became Chair of the Department of Education at Berry College, Mt. Berry, Georgia and then from 1956–1960 he was Associate Professor of Education at the University of Florida. In 1960, Dr. Lounsbury became Professor of Education and Director of Graduate Studies at Georgia College and State University, Milledgeville, Georgia, and was later named Dean of the School of Education He retired in 1983, in order to devote full time to middle level education.

Dr. Lounsbury edited the *Middle School Journal* from 1976 to 1990, taking the fledgling National Middle School Association's *Middle School Journal* and molding it into the highly respected professional journal that it is today. Lounsbury also served as Chair of NMSA's Publications Committee from 1985 until 2002 when he was named Editor, Professional Publications, a position he continues to hold. During his tenure he has edited and produced some 200 monographs and books.

Lounsbury is also author or co-author of more than 150 articles, two college textbooks, five research reports, and numerous other books and chapters. Among his most significant publications is the book he co-authored with William Van Til and his colleague and fellow founder of the middle school, Gordon Vars. This book, *Modern Education for the Junior High School Years* was published in 1961 with a second edition in 1967. This classic textbook, although focused on the junior high school, informed the conception of the contemporary middle school movement. An additional book that has been an important resource for middle school curriculum is *A Curriculum for the Middle School Years,* which he co-authored with Gordon Vars. Lounsbury has played a prominent role in every edition of *This We Believe,* NMSA's seminal position paper.

Dr. Lounsbury has been a major speaker for more than 100 middle level professional institutes, conventions, and conferences in 49 states, Canada, and Europe. He has served on the Board of Directors for the Association for Supervision and Curriculum Development (ASCD) and was a member of two ASCD Commissions. He was a member of National Association of Secondary School Principals' Middle Level Council, a founder of the Professors of Middle Level Education which became an affiliate organization of NMSA and Co-Director of the Georgia Lighthouse Schools-to-Watch Program.

Dr. Lounsbury is recipient of many awards. In 1978, the National Middle School Association created its highest level award—an Award for

Distinguished Service to Middle Level Education. Dr. Lounsbury was the first recipient of this award, and it was named the John H. Lounsbury Distinguished Service Award. This award is given only when an individual has demonstrated a level of service, integrity, and leadership in middle level education that warrants special recognition. Since that time, many of the persons interviewed for the Middle Level Education Legacy Project have received that reward. Dr. Lounsbury also received awards from many other professional associations including NASSP's William Gruhn-Forrest Long Award for Leadership in Middle Level Education in 1992 and the Distinguished Service Award from the Georgia Middle School Association in 1995. In 1997, Georgia State College and State University named the school of education The John H. Lounsbury School of Education. In 2006, he was recipient of the National Forum to Accelerate Middle Grades Reform Joan Lipsitz Lifetime Achievement Award and was cited in the Congressional Record for his contributions to the field of middle level education. But, as has been noted, John Lounsbury's "greatness comes not from the time he has devoted to his own career, but the time he has given to others. His achievements are recorded not only on his vita, but in the achievements of his colleagues. He measures what he has acquired by what he has given away" (Johnston, 1992, p. 50).

Selected Publications

Lounsbury, J. H. (1960). How the junior high school came to be. *Educational Leadership, 18*, 145–147.

Van Til, W., Vars, G. F., & Lounsbury, J. H. (1960, 1967). *Modern education for the junior high School years.* Indianapolis, IN: The Bobbs-Merrill Company.

Lounsbury, J. H., & Mariani, J. V. (1964). *The junior high school we saw: One day in the eighth grade.* Alexandria, VA: Association for Supervision and Curriculum Development.

Lounsbury, J. H. (1977). Assuring the continued success of middle school. In P. George (Ed.), *The middle school: A look ahead* (pp. 148–153). Columbus, OH: National Middle School Association.

Lounsbury, J. H., & Vars, G. F. (1978). *A curriculum for the middle school years.* New York, NY: Harper and Row.

Lounsbury, J. H. (Ed.). (1984). *Perspectives on middle level education: 1964–1984.* Columbus, OH: National Middle School Association.

Lounsbury, J. H., & Johnston, J. H. (1988). *Life in three sixth grades.* Reston, VA: National Association of Secondary School Principals.

Lounsbury, J. H., & Clark, D. C. (1990). *Inside grade eight: From apathy to excitement.* Reston, VA: National Association of Secondary School Principals.

Lounsbury, J. H. (1991). *As I see it.* Columbus, OH: National Middle School Association.

Johnston, J. H. (1992). John H. Lounsbury: Conscience of the Middle School movement. *Middle School Journal, 24*(2), 45–50.

Lounsbury, J. H. (1998). John Lounsbury reflects: What is past is prologue. In R. David (Ed.), *Moving forward from the past: Early writings and current reflections of middle school founders* (pp. 120–126). Columbus, OH: National Middle School Association and Pittsburgh, PA: Pennsylvania Middle School Association.

George, P. S., & Lounsbury, J. H. (2000). *Making Big Schools Feel Small: Multi-age grouping looping and schools-within-a-school.* Westerville, OH: National Middle School Association.

Lounsbury, J. H. (2009). Deferred but not deterred: A middle school manifesto. *Middle School Journal, 40*(5), 31–36.

Lounsbury, J. H. (in press). Middle level education: A chronological history and personal perspective. In G. Davis (Ed.), *Research to guide practice in middle grades education.* Westerville, OH: National Middle School Association.

John H. Lounsbury[*]

My involvement with the middle school movement came about in a somewhat roundabout way. I started teaching in 1948 as a secondary social studies teacher in Wilmington, North Carolina, was made a department chair and then I was appointed a supervisor. I had a master's degree, which at that time was not common, and so without seeking the position I became a supervisor. One of my first assignments was to convert two elementary schools to junior high schools. I didn't know anything about junior high schools as such, but when I went back to George Peabody College in Nashville, Tennessee for summer graduate work, that became the focus of my study and culminated in 1954 in my dissertation, *The Role and Function of the Junior High School.*

Who or what were your main influences?

I had two professors at George Peabody College who were particularly influential. Louis Armstrong was committed to democracy and helped me understand democracy in education when I studied with him at the master's level. Then at the doctorate level, William Van Til was my major professor, and it was Dr. Van Til who got me into writing and editing as I worked with him as a graduate assistant. He gave me opportunities to assume leadership

---

[*] John Lounsbury was interviewed for the Legacy Project in January 2004.

and to look over his shoulder as he wrote and edited. He was a very skilled writer and editor, and I learned more working as his graduate assistant than I did in any of the classes that I took, which is not an uncommon experience.

I need to go back however, and say that when I got out of the service, I went to John B. Stetson University without really knowing what I wanted to do. I had been a biology major, had two years of college, but somehow realized that wasn't really the field I wanted. At Stetson I was enrolled in a course in history of education, of all things, taught by Dr. Boyce Fowler Ezell. Somehow that course got to me, and I decided then that I wanted to be a teacher. I ended up doing my student teaching in DeLand Junior High School in biology. Interestingly enough, the only participation or observation experience I had as part of my preparation was when I walked into that school to do student teaching. Inconceivable now where we provide field experiences, participation experiences, beginning in the sophomore year, but that was the only experience that I had in the school as a part of my preparation. But it was a good university. Dr. Randolph Carter became my mentor and influenced me significantly.

So, going back to Peabody I got into the middle level arena and in trying to bring about what I referred to as the renaissance of the junior high school, I quickly came to realize that this new idea that was being proposed was in fact the new junior high school and it was much easier to create a new institution than to change one that is well established. And the junior high school, unfortunately, had become very much what its name said it was, a junior high school.

What kinds of middle school literature did you read?

In the beginning, there was no middle school literature. I read junior high school literature, but when I was a doctoral student at Peabody, I had the opportunity not only to read Leonard Koos' book, but also to actually communicate with Dr. Koos and had one letter from Dr. Briggs. And when I went to the University of Florida in 1956, Koos came to Gainesville during the winters and I actually had several personal conversations with him. Thomas Briggs and Leonard Koos were considered to be the fathers of the junior high school. So I read Briggs and Koos, and if you go back and look at the book that Briggs wrote (1920) and read the last paragraph in that book you will find a perfect description of the middle school. The terms just changed, but the message is the same.

I read all these various books and articles having to do with the creation of the junior high school in the 1900s, including Charles W. Elliot's speech before the department of superintendents in 1888 when he first suggested that school programs should be shortened and enriched. It was college prep that was the motivation for the early junior high school, but soon after the college prep people began to promote this idea of extending secondary education downward, other people, public educators, got into it and so the movement changed rather dramatically and by the time of the first real significant junior high schools between 1910 and 1920 really that the impact of that idea was greatly diminished. There were other factors that entered into the junior high school movement that made it a success. One was the economic factor. Some of you who are younger may not realize that back then students were flunked regularly, constantly, you would go into a fifth grade classroom and almost half the class might well be repeating that grade or had already repeated an earlier grade. That was common, and they began to look at the expense of having children repeat grades and where they were repeating the grades most was often in the seventh and eighth grade. So, that was a factor.

Another factor that really came into play and was most important was the individual differences movement. E. L. Thorndike measured people as well as counted words and Cattell and other psychologists began to really make a serious study of how children indeed differed one from another. And where were they most different? At the middle level or junior high school level, and so that had a great deal to do with the growth of the junior high school idea. Still another thing was G. Stanley Hall and his cultural epics theory. He was president of a college, but he was also the first psychologist to write books about the age of adolescence. He wrote a two-volume book, I think it was 1907 and 1909, and that was the first study of adolescence, and he came up with the phrase *storm and stress* to characterize what the young person goes through at this stage of life. He called it a psychological second birth. This promoted the notion that we needed then a distinctive institution for this developmental age group, a different institution. So we needed a junior high school that would in fact recognize these rare and difficult-to-get-along-with adolescents who were going through this great turmoil in their lives, and although that idea has been tempered there is some validity to it. Joan Lipsitz's work helped to temper some of that early notion of tremendous storm and stress but also reinforced the distinctiveness of early adolescence and how it has been underserved.

Are there any other particular theorists or theories that have influenced your educational thought?
I think the student-centered, democratic philosophy I developed under Drs. Armstrong and Van Til really took hold of me. I didn't have an educational philosophy until I was in graduate school, really. It just wasn't

something I thought about. I didn't have strong feelings about education one way or the other. I was not a great student in high school myself. Whole interesting story about that, if we have time we might talk about it, but I developed one during my graduate work. Dr. Van Til who seemed to see in me something I didn't see in myself encouraged me to get a doctorate, something I never would have thought about back then. At that time of course, it was rare, now the master's degree is the expected degree for almost any teacher and the doctorate has become much, much more common. But I also have to give credit to the G.I. Bill as well as to my wife, who worked and supported me. Between the government, my wife, and my part-time jobs, I was able to continue my graduate work and completed my doctorate in 1954 when I was still relatively young.

We have time if you want to share the story.

In high school, education just didn't touch me. I was active in student government, I was active in athletics, and was sociable, had a lot of friends, but schooling just didn't really connect with me at all. As a matter of fact, I was unable to run for Senior Class President, even though I had been Junior Class President because I flunked two subjects and had to go to summer school. I flunked French II and Algebra. And as a result of that I have always avoided math and I've had trouble with it, but my record in high school was very mediocre. Now I mentioned earlier, that I did my student teaching in biology, because when I went off to college that was the only subject that made any sense to me. The only "A" I made in high school was in biology. You could see it, it had a name, it was specific, it really communicated with me. So I started out as a biology major. But I did have some good teachers who meant well, but somehow the formal curriculum just didn't connect.

What was your primary motivation for becoming involved in the middle school movement?

I don't know how to answer that. In a way I just fell into it. It was the educational idea that matched my values and I identified with it and invested my doctoral work in that area. Young adolescents appealed to me and from 1954 on that's been my professional and personal interest really even though actually most of my career has been spent in teacher education itself. But all of my professional activities have been in the middle level.

What is your primary motivation for your continuing involvement in the middle school movement?

Because I really care about it, I believe in it. I'm passionate about it. I genuinely love these kids, this age level, it's just a pleasure to be around them.

And I hate to see them get the short end of it, as they often do, in schools that really don't recognize what wonderful learners they are. How energetic and creative and how ready to go they are, if you just give them a chance. I found in teaching high school seniors, they were so blasé, "Yeah been there, done that." You know, but middle school kids are so captivating.

How would you describe the early years of the middle school movement—and we are defining that as the 1960s and 1970s?

Having failed to bring about the renaissance of the junior high school as Gordon Vars and I tried to do through writings and speeches, we were aware of and associates of William Gruhn and Harl Douglass, who wrote the classic book on the modern junior high school. When the middle school idea came along, we were at first resistant because the middle school advocates, I called them the young Turks, maligned the junior high. Everything about the junior high was wrong, and they came up with this great new idea setting in motion the dichotomy: junior high versus middle school. And we didn't like that; we felt that was an unfair comparison, because the ideas, as I indicated earlier, they are really the same, there isn't a dime's worth of difference between the advocacy of Leonard Koos and Thomas Briggs and the advocacy of William Alexander and all of the rest of us in the middle school movement. We wanted the same thing, to create a school that was designed for this distinctive age group, an age group that had not previously been identified or understood.

One of the interesting things is that our language contains no word for this level. You're either an infant, a child, an adolescent, or adult. When the most critical stage of all is that period between childhood and adolescent and we didn't have a term for it. We said early adolescents, late childhood, emerging adolescents. We created the term *tweeners*. Don Eichhorn created the word transescence to give an identity to this special age group and yet now that the child development specialists have worked on it, it's really pretty obvious that it is in fact the most critical developmental period of all—the greatest period of change. Infants grow as much physically, but infants don't grow socially and intellectually as young adolescents. So no other age level has greater change accompanying it than does the period between the years ten to fifteen. Fascinating age and a reason middle school is so special. It is while they are in the seventh and the eighth grade that they decide who they are, what they believe, what their standards are, what their values are, what they might aspire to be. You don't change people much in high school, you really don't. You add to them, you refine them, but in terms of basic personality and basic values, you don't do much. It always bothers me that high school is seen as the great capstone, the great educational end product. You have to have a new building for it and the building that wasn't good enough for the high schools is good enough then for the junior high school and middle school, when in fact, in terms of having an effect on one's life, no other age level can equal the impact of what happens in the middle level.

How has the middle school concept changed since the early years of the middle school movement?

I don't think it has changed. I think the concept, the ideas have always been there and they've been expressed sometimes with different words. We talk about interdisciplinary planning; we used to talk about student-teacher planning. Some of the terminology has changed but the ideas are the same. And I guess I want to go back and bring up this historical concept. Van Til and Armstrong were progressive educators, no question about it. They were identified with William Heard Kilpatrick, John Dewey, George Counts, all those others who were giants as progressive educators in the 1920s and 1930s and into the 1940s, and as I studied progressive education as a graduate student at Peabody, I became a progressive educator. And it seems to me that the middle school is the rebirth of progressive education. Progressive education was supposed to have been dead and buried and you remember that book by Laurence Cremin that talked about the death of progressive education. Well, it never died. The concept never died. Because progressive education like middle level education is based exclusively on what do we know about kids and what do we know about learning and what is the nature of our society. Those foundations are the same. Progressive education, middle level education, same thing—basing educational experiences on what we know about learning and society and the nature of kids. They're the enduring triangle, the enduring foundations and they're always present.

Now you say, well, aren't all schools based on those practices? The fact of the matter is, and this is a rather radical statement, there is not a single general practice in the way we conduct public education that matches what we know about learning and kids. The whole concept of periods, time frame, there's no research to show that 47 to 50 minutes is the right time for conducting learning activities, or there is no research to show that the best size for a learning class is 25 to 30. None whatsoever. There is no research to show that the best way to present the world to young people is by studying separate subjects, no basis. So all of the basic organizational practices of public education are there only because we've always done it that way. They are not based on psychology, pedagogy, sociology, or anything else. It's hard to realize that. People aren't willing to face that. That's why I keep saying that we've got to quit trying to make schools better as they are and make them instead different. We keep trying to make them better as they are; add a subject here, bring in this, change that, but still keep the basic idea of subjects, classes, and periods even though they are not the proven way to organize education for young adolescents.

Middle school has done more than anything to bring about the value of student/teacher relationships, long term, to bring about interdisciplinary, integrated curriculum, and so on. And all of the things that we advocate, I am convinced are based on what we know about learning and kids. That's why I am so, almost haughty about my comment that the middle school movement has to succeed and will succeed because it has God and Uncle Sam on its side. It's based on human growth and development—the way the good Lord made us—and it's based on the concepts of democracy, our way of life. So it's got to work, but we struggle and struggle to overcome that centuries-old conflict between education as putting in and education as pulling out, to use one overly stated generalization.

How have middle schools changed since the early years of the middle school movement?

Not much. I think probably my greatest disappointment in the development of the middle school movement has been the failure of teams to take advantage of common planning time and to take advantage of the opportunity to improve curriculum. I think in part we made a great stride forward, and teaming has become well established, and well it should, but because we organized our teams by subject area we still tended to teach by subject area and if you go into most middle schools today, with teams, they are still largely departmentalized in their instruction. With limited exception, an occasional interdisciplinary unit, and an occasional correlation, but by and large most middle schools still teach subjects. So I think that's been a big disappointment that we haven't taken advantage of the concept of teaming with common planning time to really alter curriculum and instruction. We've done a great job of dealing with kids and their needs. We've done a good job of taking care of a lot of things in common planning time; meeting with parents, avoiding getting tests on the same day and those sorts of things, but we really haven't taken advantage of what teaming really is designed to do.

The other thing that's been a major problem, I guess, has been the inability of schools to really implement in practice the concept of advisory. The advisor/advisee program which was a good attempt to do it never has been able to take hold, and of course as an old core curriculum advocate, I'm looking for that day when we don't have to deal with the affect in a separate period or separate program, for in an integrative curriculum, the concepts that concern youth are taken care of within the regular curriculum.

As we move beyond interdisciplinary planning to integrative education to thematic units, we really then can focus our instruction on the concerns of young adolescents as well as acquiring the knowledge and concepts from the various disciplines. But it is a slow, slow process, because you see we have institutionalized passive learning. We have built it into our schools. It is into certification, it is into textbooks, it is into school facilities, everything about it is based on the assumption of passive learning. It's very difficult, hard for a teacher to break that and right now we are worse off because of the tremendous prescription and the concern about tests and testing. We are really handicapping teachers' efforts to do better practices.

What were some of the motivations that fueled the growth of the middle school movement?

I may be a little naïve in this, but I think ultimately the terrible state of our society will become obvious to enough people that they will see that we've got to do something about improving society through our schools, and at what grade level are you best able to make a difference? At the middle grades level. And when you look at teenage pregnancies and violence and alcohol and crime and all the rest of it, all of these things are the result of the decisions of individuals, their chosen behaviors. And the thing that worries me now as much as anything is that we have forgotten that education is a matter of changing behavior. We're so focused on test scores and the acquisition of information that we've forgotten what education really is all about. John Ruskin, famous Englishman said, "Education does not mean teaching people to know what they do not know, it means teaching them to behave as they do not behave." And then he went on to say more about turning their literature to lust and so on, but we've forgotten that. What we are really trying to do is improve the behavior of individuals. Governor Maddox was not a popular governor in Georgia, he was kind of a character. He rode his bicycle backwards and he was known as an ardent segregationist and people laughed at him because he did a lot of crazy things and one of the things he said one day when we were so concerned about the terrible prison situation in Georgia. He said, "What we need to get is a better class of prisoners." And people laughed at that, but you know, there's a point there. How are we going to have better schools? By creating better students, better people. We ought to be in the business of improving the behavior of our students, not just improving their ability to take tests and to remember and regurgitate, and I'm afraid we've forgotten that. We're really spending all of our time and efforts on the thing that has the least enduring importance and forgetting the things that have the most enduring importance.

What were some of the motivations that fueled the early growth of the middle school movement?

The middle school movement provided a home base for people who had been concerned about education, for progressive educators who wanted to be progressive, for those that really tried to do a better job, and so folks immediately flocked to the movement because it provided a gathering place for people who were progressive but didn't have anybody to associate with or to organize with until the middle school movement. The National Middle School Association, especially, gave a place for those of us to gather and when you went to one of the early national conferences you sensed, even still do, a religious fervor among National Middle School Association people who really care about kids and are committed. And it's interesting to know how exhibitors comment on how much they prefer to exhibit at the middle school conference than any of the others because the people there want to know about the information, want to get information, find out about newer practices, they stop to learn. If you go to other conferences, it's a whole different tone, the focus of the sessions at NMSA are kid-centered. So, I think, it became the gathering place for progressives who perhaps didn't know they were progressive educators, but people who realized that what they were doing in their schools wasn't really all that it should be and could be.

How were decisions about the directions taken by the middle school movement made?

I don't know that it has taken different directions. I think NMSA inevitably had to spend an inordinate amount of its time and effort getting organized and growing and deciding and formalizing their procedures to go by, but I wouldn't say that I saw any great change in the direction. It was finding the direction, clarifying it, organizing ways for the association to pursue those directions, but I don't see that we have had any big changes in the direction and why should there be? We're on the right track, we know that.

Would you talk about the things that you did discuss, like how decisions were made about how to organize?

Board of directors in their meetings hashed it out. And it was tough in the early years. We had no money and there were some differences of philosophy and the very, very beginning between the administrators because the first group, you know, was an administrators group. And Gordon Vars, Connie Toepfer, and Hal Gaddis and one or two others stood up for making that first Midwest Middle School Association open to all and that was one of the big decisions made and one of the key decisions made. And so the National Middle School Association started from the beginning with open membership and that's been its strength, but also its weakness. It is a strength because whether you're a classroom teacher, a superintendent, or college professor, NMSA welcomes you. It's a weakness because we don't automatically have to be a member. If you're a school counselor, you are expected to join the school counselors' association. If you're a school principal, you join the school principals' group. If you're a middle school teacher, you might join a subject area organization or if you're elementary, you would join ACEI. So NMSA hasn't had an automatic membership by job. Its membership is exclusively focused on the commitment to kids, which is wonderful. It's the only association which is that directed and so whether you're a college president and we've even had some of those, or a classroom teacher, you're no better or no worse. And I think it's a great pride of the Association that we've had classroom teachers as presidents. You don't find that in other associations. There is a rather healthy atmosphere at NMSA where title doesn't carry privilege.

How were other individuals and groups outside middle level education involved in the early years of the middle school movement?

Well, that was a hard thing to do and still a hard thing to do, to get cooperation. We've always sort of dreamed of having an alliance of the middle level educators that would bring in other people and we've struggled with it. We had a great deal of difficulty establishing relationships with NASSP because they were seen as competing and there's still some of that existing. We had somewhat better relationships with NAESP than we have with NASSP. But inevitably there is a problem because principals might join our association instead of joining the principals' groups. Many, of course, join both. I think college people have had the least difficulty there because there's been no real conflict, so we had strong college people in middle school associations.

What was the educational context at the time the middle school movement began?

Of course there was Sputnik. And you had "back to the basics" which reoccurs every few years. It's one of those things that pops up again, but probably Sputnik and the aftermath of that was a major factor; getting to the moon; beating the Russians to the moon; emphasizing science and math, and the inevitable conflict that the middle school advocacy had with established views of traditional schooling, promoting separate subjects. Now the work of, what was his name, the cycles, I can't remember the name of the psychologist. Well, there have been several concepts that have come along the way. Learning theories and so on, but I think basically the middle school movement is progressive education in contemporary dress. Always trying to organize education in ways that match what we know of our kids and learning.

What have been some of the most significant events, incidents, or moments in the middle school movement?

Certainly the creation of the National Middle School Association was a key moment, unequalled. The second big moment was the publication of *This We Believe* in 1982. After a long and arduous developmental period it finally was released and it provided a clear written document that was very important in moving the middle school along because there was a lot of looseness about what we were after. People didn't know, people thought of it as organizational. That was a big moment, no question about it. Then, of course, the second edition of *This We Believe* and now most recently, the third edition. Those have indeed been big moments. The Atlanta conference was the 30th conference. I think any national conference has been a high moment, and the general sessions have been so moving and so emotional. And the roles that student groups play. The student introducers of the keynote speakers. Those have been really significant. I remember the one in Atlanta some years ago, the kid was so moving, so great, and the orchestra at this last year's conference! I mean high class superiors, middle school kids . . . they are so able if you just give them a chance.

Do you have any personal stories to tell about any events?

Well, of course, I can't help but mention when the Lounsbury Award was first given and I was completely surprised, had no notion of it at all. That was a personally moving experience, I was really just floored. During the presidency of Jim Fox, the Lounsbury Award was established. I, of course, did not know that it was being established. I had gotten maybe a year before or maybe two years before, the President's Award because of my work with the *Middle School Journal* and I guess we ought to say something about it at some point too, but I was sitting there after Zacharie Clements, a fascinating speaker had captured us and then Jim Fox got up and began to talk and he said one or two things that had to be me and all of a sudden I realized that and got called up there. It has become something I've had to live up to, in a way, to have my name identified with it, and what a wonderful group of people have been recipients since then. William Alexander was the next one. Ken McEwin was an early one. Gordon Vars, Connie, Paul, you know all the big names, Joan Lipsitz, Sherrel Bergmann, you know, it's been a great thing, and personally humbling, and personally awkward, too, using my name. It's a little uncomfortable to have people use it that way, but so be it.

Earlier I said I should say more about the *Middle School Journal,* and its development. It had started as the *Midwest Middle School Journal* and it was printed, really lithographed, in Glen Maynard's garage. It was, you know, pretty crude, had just two or three articles and Tom Gatewood who had created it from scratch, had pioneered it, at the Atlanta conference, which was the second conference, came up to me and asked me if I would be editor. Now, I don't really know why he asked me to do that, but he did and he knew something of me, I guess. And I agreed and at that time it was purely a little extra thing you did on your own. But in the first year I did the *Middle School Journal,* we made some improvements. Instead of lithographing it in a basement, we went to a printer who used hot lead, linotype. So that year we printed the *Middle School Journal* in that way, literally the old fashioned long rolled out galleys. The printer was there in Indianapolis and I had visited. I mailed the typed articles to him and he mailed the galleys back. After that we began to get better and began to do a much higher quality job with a printer in nearby Macon, Georgia. But it was still cut and paste. It was a growing experience and I had to grow in my own knowledge because I was not prepared in any way officially to be an editor or designer or even a writer. That all came later; I learned by doing.

We were talking about significant events or moments that you might like to talk a little bit about?

This is purely personal and I don't want to sound egotistical in mentioning it, but certainly one of the high moments of my life was when Jeannette Phillips and Neila Conners planned and put on this celebration for me without my knowing anything about it in Long Beach at the national conference. They had invited people, they had written them, people came in tuxes, not everybody came in tuxes, but dressed up. They gathered together in a hotel ballroom. I had no idea of this. George Melton was the guy who was supposed to get me there and had me meet him somewhere to go somewhere and I really didn't know it. When I walked in that ballroom, it was a beautiful setting, tables, nice china and everything, napkins folded up, you know, it was a beautiful dinner meeting and a great big raised head table with my name hanging over it. It was just really overwhelming. They had formal programs, printed programs, it was really done up right. A special evening celebrating me. People spoke, Nancy Doda spoke, Mary Mitchell, my associate who does the *Middle School Journal* publications with me. Everybody, you know, Howard and Connie and all the others there spoke.

It was really a very, very moving experience. I have never been as overcome, even more overcome than when I got the first Lounsbury Award, I think.

One more significant moment in my professional life that should be mentioned. I actually retired from Georgia College in 1983, even though I was just sixty at the time, in order to devote full time to middle school education. I was already editor of the *Middle School Journal* and that had grown and expanded and that was really where my interest was and I got tired of the politics of higher education. Committee meetings were killing me so I retired really earlier than I would have otherwise because I was already involved in it, but the college let me have an office there in the building and it became the publications office of the National Middle School Association. Some years later, a group of faculty members came into my office there one day and said we want to name the School of Education after you. This was their idea and they petitioned the Board of Regents, and so after the usual process of getting approval, they literally did name the School of Education at Georgia College and State University The John H. Lounsbury School of Education, and we had a big ceremony and Sue Swaim came down as a representative of the Middle School Association for that; John Swaim came with her and a number of other people spoke. That was, of course, moving because my wife and daughter and her kids and her husband were all able to be there, too. So that was a highlight, and again it came from a group of faculty members some of whom were still active and some that had retired.

One particularly significant aspect of my life unrelated to middle school deserves mention—my marriage of 57 years to the young lady I met in the fall of 1941when I went to Tusculum College right out of high school. We didn't get married until after I got out of the service, but that's been a major strength in my life—to have that stable and good marriage and the opportunity to devote energies to middle school and other things as well and not have to be torn up with, you know, relationship problems. And the birth of my daughter, the miracle baby if there ever was one, who then had three children of her own, also miracle babies. Those are continuing moments of significance to me—family and so on.

Who or what have been some of the greatest detractors or opponents, meaning negative influences, on middle level education?

The stand patters; the non-progressive educators; the subject matter lovers; the hesitant administrators who are administrators but not instructional leaders; the bureaucracies that establish procedures that make it difficult to make changes; all of these things. The tendency to support "we've always done it that way." And the fear of teachers who will opt for the security of the past even though they know it's not really what it could be, and the many difficulties that teachers are under, ones that really give them a lot of support for not doing anything better, which is unfortunate. I guess those are the things that occur to me.

Closely linked to that, what do you think have been some of the most significant obstacles to the success of the middle level movement?

I guess I would say the number one obstacle in my mind to the implementation of the middle school has been and continues to be lack of understanding on the part of the general public, as well as most of the professionals, about the nature and needs of young adolescents. They still are a misunderstood and little understood and underappreciated group of young people and because they do not understand them, they do not see why we want to do things for them that are not like schools used to be for them. I think that's still the big problem. We've made progress in the last twenty years in that realm, but many parents still are frightened by them. They don't understand them. If parents really understood the nature and needs of young adolescents, they would be at the school house door or the school board's door asking for more time for exploratories even at the expense of so-called academic time, but they do not understand that this is the age when young people need to experience new things, are ready for it, and yet we deny them and say we've got to give more of the same and it shortchanges their lives because they don't get to experience things that they might find of interest and value. If you look at the exploratory program, it is that component of the program that most matches the nature of these kids, certainly nothing about the reading, writing, and arithmetic is particularly developmentally appropriate.

What are some of the mistakes that have been made during the middle school movement that we might be able to learn from today?

The inevitable willingness to compromise. Sometimes it's a necessary thing, but I'm afraid sometimes we have been too ready to "punt on third down" to use that expression. Jonathan Kozol of course said, "Pick battles big enough to matter, but small enough to win." And sometimes middle schools have had to accept the inability to win the battle of interscholastic athletics or having things like the Miss Spring Time contest that Paul George and Nancy Doda used to talk about, you know, things that were like the high school recognizing individuals and separating individuals, sometimes you have to do that. I mean, interscholastic athletics is one example, ability grouping has probably been the one where we've had the most difficulty where sometimes we've had to go along with it because if we tried to cut out ability grouping we could lose the whole middle school and right now that's come back in. I don't know whether you've read about the new book, *The War Against Excellence*, in which I am labeled a radical socialist activist, which is a joke. Anybody that knows me knows better, but that's a whole other story.

What are some of the most important factors that are influencing middle school education today?

Well, the continued recognition that education has to be improved. It has brought attention to education often with the wrong thrust and has pursued a wrong agenda, but nevertheless, it has kept education on the public agenda and even this current conflict with the Commissioner in Minnesota will in the long run advance us because it will give us an opportunity to restate, and I think when people read the new *This We Believe*, our position paper, they will realize that her comments, her views are narrow and inappropriate and misleading and misrepresenting, and that the middle school movement is not in a war against excellence at all. But it is an ongoing battle.

Let's just clarify, you mentioned about the Commissioner.

Just released in the last month, I think, a book by Cheri Pierson Yecke. She was in the United States' Office of Education, and she's just been appointed Commissioner of Education for the State of Minnesota, She has written a book which was her doctoral dissertation entitled *The War Against Excellence: The Rising Tide of Mediocrity in America's Middle Schools*, and she has taken the very narrow position of many parents of gifted children who want gifted children to be treated specially and be challenged at the expense of others. And she has a real passion about it; she's very committed about it. Her own daughter was the original example, but then she misrepresents things. She belittles the work of Johnson and Johnson, who are professors at the University of Minnesota and who are the major names and leading researchers dealing with the whole area of cooperative learning, which she's against because it would reduce tracking. She strongly believes that gifted children need to be challenged, need to be treated separately, and she accuses the middle school movement, despite our beliefs, our real beliefs, of wanting to keep all, make kids all alike, the homogenization of the student body. That isn't what we wanted at all. We have advocated individualism and that's why we talk about the distinctive differences of middle level kids that they are numbered by that and that's why I say democracy is on our side. To each his own. To each to pursue his own interests and so on. So she is way off base, terribly off base. She attacks Paul George ruthlessly. She mentions Ken McEwin and Jim Beane and Sue Swaim and Howard Johnston. A lot of her sources are older ones, she goes back and digs up brain growth periodization and claims it's still widely held when it is not widely held at all. She really clouds her book in a lot of purported scholarship by great numbers of citations, but in fact it's poorly done in terms of scholarship.

Who has benefited the most from the middle school movement?

The kids, of course—who have had a better chance, who've been given a chance to be individuals a little bit more, to do a little more exploring, to have relationships with teachers that involve interaction and dialog rather than just listening and doing right. Certainly the kids have. Then I think another group that has really profited from the middle school movement has been women teachers and women administrators. Other things being equal, which they never are, I would have to say that women make the best middle school principals and I say that, not because men do not also make good middle school principals, but men carry a certain baggage in our culture to an administrative role. They are expected to be bosses; women do not carry that in the same way and so they are more able to be child centered. Of course the tradition of elementary education and all of that, but I have witnessed with great delight the advancement of women in middle level education as team leaders, as administrators, as supervisors. I think women have really profited from middle level education.

Who has benefited the least from the middle school movement?

Well, the people who want to keep the status quo.

Were there regional differences in the way middle school education was developed or defined, for example New England versus the South?

Like junior high school before, middle schools have been found in small places and large places, in urban and rural, and in every state. To a minor degree you would see some special advancement of middle schools early on in the South and in the Midwest, but I don't think that is of any enduring significance. California was perhaps a little slower to come to it. Then in New England you're somewhat handicapped because schools were small to begin with and there wasn't the opportunity to organize middle schools administratively. While on the other hand, where have middle school practices been best developed? Often in Vermont and Maine because of their smallness. And again, smallness has become a recognized significant factor in correlation with quality and that's why we've tried to develop looping, and multi-age teaming, and schools within a school. Things that create a sense of smallness and a continuity of relationship—I think the middle school has done a great deal in that regard, and often that can be done in smaller schools where you don't have to have a separate advisory program to deal with affective concerns of young adolescents and where you can easily have kids two years in a row because you don't have different teachers for different subjects.

So there are a lot of advantages, and one other thing that needs to be pointed out is—unfortunately the public initially came to assume that the middle school movement was about organizing sixth, seventh, and eighth or five through eight schools. It really was not about that. It's really about program. And an eleven year old is an eleven year old whether he's in elementary school or a 12 grade school or 7–12 high school, or wherever he is. So the emphasis always needs to be and should be on providing the right program for young adolescents wherever they are housed. At the same time I would have to say that where possible it is best to have a sixth, seventh, and eighth because you have at least that three year span that involves the vast majority of people who are going through the period of transition. It misses a few fifth grade girls who already had their first period. It misses a few ninth grade boys who haven't quite matured, but by and large it covers that group. But in doing that, we have to help the public to recognize and the profession too that the significant mission of the middle school is to serve diversity, not to serve commonality.

We don't group them together in a middle school because they are alike; we group them together in the middle school because they are different. How do you define a seventh grader? Is it a boy or girl? Early maturer or late maturer? After all, I can take you to a classroom and show you two girls, one of which still plays with Barbie dolls and in that same classroom there's a girl who plays with her own living doll, her own daughter and they are both in the seventh grade. Nowhere in the human life cycle are humans so diverse and so irregular in their rate of development. It isn't that they all go through it at the same time; they go through it not only at a different time, but at a different rate of growth. You've got men, women and children in the same classroom. So the middle school seeks to serve diversity, but how are schools organized and what is the assumption—commonality. If they're seventh graders they need seventh grade English. If they're eighth graders they need eighth grade biology. We make these assumptions about likeness that simply do not hold water. Back in the early 1960s late 1950s there was a big movement for the non-graded primary where kids stay in the primary unit instead of having to be promoted or not promoted at the end of first grade.

My own daughter went to a school at Peabody Lab School where she had the same teacher first and second grade in there together, no problem. If that was theoretically justifiable then, the middle level is even more justifiable because of the degree of diversity. So what we ultimately ought to have is a non-graded intermediate unit, where some kids might spend two years, other kids might spend four years, most will spend three years, but the flexibility within it. That's why multi-age grouping has worked so well in the middle level.

Who do you consider to be among the most influential leaders of the middle school movement and why?

We've already named them. Again I hate to say it because it sounds egotistical, but the Lounsbury Award winners are obviously leaders, but there are others who belong in that category. Leadership in the middle level has been diverse. That's one good thing about it. Some of us may be identified as leaders, have a national recognition level through writings and publications and through speeches, but we've got real leaders in classrooms, teachers, they're the real ones in the long run.

Anybody in particular that you haven't already talked about that you want to mention?

Sue Swaim of course has done a magnificent job to bring stability to our organization that went through a series of turnovers in staff for a variety of reasons as we grew. And she has given stability of leadership. She's also given a national voice to the National Middle School Association. Certainly her work has been so significant, but there are a lot of other things going on. John Norton in Middle Web has helped to communicate. There's so much available now through the internet that has spread the word.

Have there been major debates among middle school leaders focusing on any particular issues or beliefs?

Yes. Debates about heterogeneous grouping. The big one of course, the big debate has been the one that Jim Beane and Paul George have had a couple of conference sessions on—the degree to which curriculum could be and should be integrated as opposed to interdisciplinary. And actually they are not philosophically as far apart as it sometimes looks like they are, but it is clear that given a level of understanding of most teachers getting good interdisciplinary curriculum is about as far as you're able to go now. You've got to keep promoting integration and I think it is going to come and it will come and we have so many successful examples, Mark Springer being probably the best example. Now what, fifteen years he's being doing that successfully in a public school? But it is still beyond the ability of most people to comprehend because teachers have not experienced it themselves. They cannot visualize it and it is a big jump to leave your subject matter and go out on your own and yet when you're able and willing to do it—it does work for kids, for teachers, and for academic achievements. But that's been a big issue and the issue of advisory continues to be big. Ability grouping, integrated curriculum, advisory, those are the big ones.

What have been the roles of women and minorities in the middle school movement?

I think because it is a pioneering movement and because it is seeking change and is committed to change, it has given more attention to and done more for the role of women and minorities. There's been a very strong, conscientious effort on the part of the National Middle School Association Board of Trustees to involve representatives of diverse cultures and minorities and so on. As an Association there was a very clear, overt commitment to that.

What are some examples of ways the middle school movement has affected American education?

We've remade the face of American education, no question about it. Middle school is now seen and heard everywhere. I never will forget how excited I was when I first saw the term middle school used in *USA Today*. And now you can't go through communities where there are schools, you're going to run into middle schools, you don't see junior high schools hardly at all and you don't see much reference to them in the general press. We now have books about middle schools. It's a big change and that's all happened in the last twenty years. We've really remade the face of American Education and 5–3–4 organizational pattern is the accepted way. It's interesting that the original advocacy of 4–4–4 didn't really take hold. Alexander himself was really a strong advocate of five through eight as much as six through eight and actually if you've got a five/six combination, makes a great multiage right there. There's nothing wrong with that, but that does work against a lot of expectations and assumptions.

What educational groups, organizations, and institutions have influenced the middle school movement?

National Middle School Association. National Association of Secondary School Principals has a commitment, did have a commitment to junior high before and has done a lot with middle schools. State associations, affiliates, that's the thing about the National Middle School Association, we have affiliates all over the world and in every state and so that's important. There have been some other groups, like the James Comer Institute at Yale that have studied this age level and promoted things, not directly middle school per se, but other things going on in education which play into it. And the middle school has been the area where you've been able to do the most experimentation with instructional practices, such as cooperative learning because it has been open, it's been the center for experimentation, which the junior high was in the very beginning, incidentally.

Any others?

I think the one thing I didn't mention that I might have mentioned when you said "important influences of the middle school movement" and I mentioned "kids." I think the middle school movement and middle school education has helped kids to maintain a sense of reality and balance that they need. Given the media, the movies, the music, it is awfully hard for kids to make up their mind about what's right and what's wrong as they go through this developmental stage. I think middle school teachers have helped kids dialogue and get a handle on what reality is so that they are not overly influenced by the images they see, hear, and experience. It's awfully difficult to be a middle school kid. It was easy for me to grow up. I didn't always do right, but I knew what was right, now how does a kid know what is right? You know, the models, the examples, it's not easy and I think that is why middle school education is so critical because it—almost far more than any other group, organization, agency—can affect the future. Government can't do it, family can't even do it anymore, church can't do it anymore, I regret that, but the middle school is the one place where we really have a chance to make a difference and that's why I want us to make sure we're focusing on behavior as well as achievement in the narrowest sense. It's critical, and it's a scary time right now.

**Have particular legislative actions significantly influenced the
middle school movement at the state or national level?**

There have been a lot of narrow ones, but in the state of Georgia where we were able, over a great period of years, to get grants for schools that were committed to go to middle schools and that helped to make a big differ-ence. Unfortunately, many schools got the money but didn't really use it in the full way, but there have been major supports in the state of Georgia. We now have a new legislature, new governor, new state superintendent, and you lose about as much as you gain. You take two steps forward and then you struggle not to take two back and just take one back.

What are some ways the middle school movement has influenced middle level curriculum and instruction?

Oh, a great deal because it has been a place where we've done things differently, where we've been less traditional, where we've involved kids more and I think the concept of getting kids involved, I still say the best way, the cheapest way, the easiest way, and the most doable way to improve American education is to involve the kids actively in deciding what to study and how to study it. It's all right at the elementary level for teachers to make all the decisions for the curriculum to be all planned, but when they get to the middle level, Mother Nature provides a golden opportunity to take learning to a new level, to leave rote learning and memorization and to actually get kids involved as they mentally mature, and we don't take advantage of this. We continue to perpetuate passive learning, yet this is the time when they can grow intellectually and mature.

As middle level educators, how do you think we should respond to the current emphasis on student achievement as measured by standardized tests?

With alarm, with distress, and with advocacy of alternatives. We want to improve test scores. Don't ever let anybody think we don't, but what is the best way to improve test scores? The best way to improve test scores is to improve learning and learners. And when you improve learning and learners, tests scores go up, but to focus directly and narrowly on test scores may conceivably give a short term gain under pressure, but it won't last. The only real way is to improve the learning in the classroom, and when they do that, test scores will follow.

Are there lessons we still need to learn from the history of the middle school movement?

Yes, history has repeated itself and we go around in cycles. We need to study our history and recognize it and learn from it. And one of the things that bothers me now is change is so rampant about everything, that we forget to look at the history and think that everything new is good and everything old is bad. We need to become students of our history. I am an old social studies teacher, you can tell that.

How would you characterize the current status of the middle school movement?

Well, I still say it's the green and growing edge of education reform. Middle level education is where action is, where most good things are happening, but it's still struggling, it still hasn't claimed dominance at all, but it is moving, it is working.

Are there particular efforts that need to be made to help ensure the future success of the middle school movement?

Keep on doing what we're doing, spread the message, stand up, talk to parents, talk to citizens, listen to kids, do what we know in our heart and in our professional mind is right and we know it's right, be active professionally, take advantage of the opportunities that present themselves, to speak up for kids and for middle level education, wherever and whenever. And fortunately we are creating or are building a new group of pre-service teachers in many institutions including some in Georgia where the graduates are just excellent, just excellent, who are committed middle school educators. They're going to make the difference.

When you stop and think about it, it's amazing that the middle school movement was able to go as far as it did and as far as it has on teachers who were trained as high school teachers. I mean, we really did a tremendous job with conferences, with staff development, with yeomen efforts to get the middle school idea out when there really was no pre-service training for the early middle school people, and we've got to get administrators who share that philosophy; that's a real handicap right now. We're doing better preparing teachers to be middle school teachers than we are principals. Principals are still pretty much administrators and often they don't have that philosophy, and middle school education is a philosophy, it's a way of life, it's a set of beliefs; it's not a managerial thing, it's not administrative, it's gut-level.

4

Conrad F. Toepfer, Jr.

> *Young people largely finalize their values on issues about gender, race, and religion, during their middle level school years. Thus, middle level programs must continue helping students understand the problems caused by gender, religious, and racial prejudice.*

The contributions that Conrad F. Toepfer, Jr. has made to middle level education are manifold and profound. He is a distinguished scholar, visionary educator, and long-time proponent of middle level programs, practices, and schools that recognize and respect the rights and educational welfare of young adolescents. He is a staunch advocate of social justice, children's rights, and all aspects of authentic middle level curriculum reform. Since the inception of the middle school idea, Toepfer has been a powerful voice for human rights and the need to help young adolescents develop enduring positive attitudes about themselves and others. Human rights, equity, and democracy are themes that prevail throughout Dr. Toepfer's life and career. He believes that one of the most important central challenges to middle level education is educating moral citizens who can responsibly participate in a democratic society.

The Legacy of Middle School Leaders, pages 53–69
Copyright © 2011 by Information Age Publishing
53

Dr. Toepfer was creator and editor of *Transescence: The Journal on Emerging Adolescent Education* which began publication in 1973. He also edited *Dissemination Services on the Middle Grades* beginning in 1970. These two publications, sponsored by Educational Leadership Institute, focused on young adolescents and middle level education and were very important to the development and success of the middle school movement. He is author and coauthor of many professional publications focusing on young adolescent development, middle level schooling, and middle level curriculum. He was one of the authors of the National Middle School Association's (NMSA) first edition of *This We Believe*, its 1982 position statement.

Before his retirement, Dr. Toepfer made numerous keynote addresses and presentations at professional conferences across the nation. These speeches and presentations challenged audiences to collaborate in establishing developmentally responsive middle schools that recognized, honored, and valued the unique characteristics, interests, and needs of young adolescents. He also served as consultant to hundreds of schools in New York and across the nation as he helped them make the transition to middle schools. Additionally, he worked with middle schools in other countries such as Belgium, Germany, and Switzerland and assisted in the establishment of the European League for Middle Level Education.

Dr. Toepfer received his undergraduate degree in 1955 and his master's degree in 1956 from the State University of New York–Buffalo. His major in both degrees was English, and he planned to teach English literature at the senior high school level. Fortunately for middle level education, he became a core teacher at Cleveland Junior/Senior High School in Cheektowaga, New York, where he taught until 1960. He later became Curriculum Coordinator at Newfane Central School, Newfane, New York. Dr. Toepfer received his doctorate in curriculum planning from the State University of New York–Buffalo in 1962. He then accepted a faculty position in the Department of Curriculum Development and Instructional Media at State University of New York–Buffalo. Toepfer was Associate Professor of Education at the University of Georgia, Athens, Georgia, from 1979–1981. Then he returned to the State University of New York, Buffalo and served as Professor in the Department of Curriculum Development and Instructional Media until his retirement in 2000. He mentored numerous doctoral students, and many of these people (e.g., James Beane) have followed in his footsteps to become national middle level leaders.

The notable work of Dr. Toepfer has been recognized on many occasions and in 1985 he was recipient of the John H. Lounsbury Distinguished Service Award from NMSA. He was instrumental in the founding of NMSA and held many positions in the Association including serving as President in 1987-88. Dr. Toepfer also served as chairman of the Middle Level Council of NASSP and was the recipient of the William Gruhn-Forrest Long Award from National Association of Secondary School Principals in 1986. Toepfer was an influential leader in New York and the New York State Middle School Association (NYSMSA) established the Connie Toepfer Award for Leadership in his honor and he was the first inductee into the NYSMSA Hall of Fame. He was also presented the Service to Youth Throughout the World Award from the NYSMSA and the Louis E. Raths Award from the New York Association for Supervision and Curriculum Development.

Conrad F. Toepfer, Jr. is a highly accomplished professional and scholar who has given sacrificially of his time and talents to advance the kinds of middle level programs young adolescents need and deserve.

Selected Publications

Toepfer, C. F., Jr. (1962). The historical development of curricular patterns of junior high school education in America. *NASSP Bulletin, 271*, 181–183.

Toepfer, C. F., Jr. (1965). Who should teach in the junior high? *The Clearing House, 40*(2), 74–76.

Rosenbaum, D. S., & Toepfer, C. F., Jr. (1966). *Curriculum planning and school psychology: The coordinated approach.* Buffalo, NY: Hertillon Press.

Toepfer, C. F., Jr. (1973). No greater potential: The emerging adolescent learner. *Middle School Journal, 4*(1), 3–6.

Toepfer, C. F., Jr. (1976). The middle school as a multiple school: A means for survival. In P. George (Ed.), *The middle school: A look ahead* (pp. 139–147). Columbus, OH: National Middle School Association.

Epstein, H. T., & Toepfer, C. F., Jr. (1978). A neuroscience basis for reorganizing middle school education. *Educational Leadership, 35*(8), 356–660.

Toepfer, C. F., Jr. (1982). Junior high and middle school education. In H. Mitzel (Ed.), *Encyclopedia of educational research* (5th ed., pp. 898–1000). New York: Free Press.

Beane, J. A., Toepfer, C. F., Jr., & Alessi, S. J., Jr. (1986). *Curriculum planning and development.* Boston, MA: Allyn and Bacon.

Toepfer, C. F., Jr. (1986). Middle level transition and articulation issues. *Middle School Journal, 18*(1), 9–11.

Toepfer, C. F., Jr. (1996). Caring for young adolescents in an ethnically divided, violent, poverty-stricken society. *Middle School Journal, 27*(5), 42–48.

Toepfer, C. F., Jr. (1997). Middle level curriculum's serendipitous history. In J. Irvin (Ed.), *What current research says to the middle level practitioner* (pp. 163–177). Columbus, OH: National Middle School Association.

Lipka, R. P., Lounsbury, J. H., Toepfer, C. F., Jr., Vars, G. F., Alessi, S. P., & Kridel, C. (1998). *The eight-year study revisited: Lessons from the past for the present.* Columbus, OH: National Middle School Association.

Conrad F. Toepfer, Jr.[*]

I became involved with middle level education in the 1950s when I was a junior high school CORE teacher. I was absolutely fascinated by the idea that I could correlate learning among single separate disciplines and provide my students some guidance. I started going to New York State and then national CORE conferences and also to Association for Supervision and Curriculum Development (ASCD) conferences. I was working on a curriculum doctorate and core curriculum was one of my primary interests. In those days, there was nothing special available for junior high school education. I met Bill Alexander at my first ASCD conference. Bill was perhaps the foremost curriculum generalist of his era. We began our shared interest in the middle grades. Later, he frequently came to SUNY Buffalo and did curriculum seminars for our graduate students. In my doctoral study, I came across a dissertation by John Lounsbury on junior high school education. I had met John at CORE and ASCD curriculum conferences and we began our correspondence in the middle 1950s. I focused my dissertation on the historical development of junior high school organization in America. John and I submitted proposals on junior high concerns to educational conferences.

A group of us started to collaborate. It included Bill Alexander, John Lounsbury, Gordon Vars, and Donald Eichhorn who, at that time, was a curriculum coordinator in Upper City Saint Clair, Pennsylvania. We believed that young people in the middle grades were distinctly different. Then, they were called early adolescents. We agreed that terminology didn't jibe with the psychological development. Don Eichhorn was participating in a medical investigation on students' physiological characteristics at the Boyce Middle School in his school district. At that age, students weren't early anything. They were in a unique stage of development not addressed in grade K–8 or 9–12, 7–9, or 7–8 schools. While distinctly different, they were placed in schools with either young children or in secondary schools with more mature students. We felt there was need for a three-level system with schools for children, middle schools for students in their middle grades

---

[*] Conrad Toepfer was interviewed for the Legacy Project in January 2007.

years, and high schools for maturing adolescents. So, we began to advocate this sort of thing. We knew Neil Atkins, an Associate Executive Secretary at ASCD who had been a well-known junior high school principal. We approached him about trying to establish an ASCD study group focused on middle grades curriculum issues. At that time (the early 1960s), ASCD had Councils in supervision, high schools, elementary schools and other areas. We began campaigning for an ASCD Council on the middle educational level. Some favored the term Early Adolescent Learner. We wanted to focus on the transition into adolescence and decided instead on Emerging Adolescent Learners.

ASCD established the Emerging Adolescent Learner Council in 1968. Don Eichhorn chaired it with Tom Sweeny from the University of South Carolina, Mary Compton from the University of Georgia, Jim Phillips from Michigan, Bruce Howell from Oklahoma and me as members. Appointments to ASCD Councils were three-year terms, so we had to accomplish something during that time. We decided to develop a series of instructional filmstrips and tapes. They were funded by ASCD and produced by Educational Leadership Institute in Springfield, Massachusetts. We presented with them at national ASCD conferences and workshops around the country. Don Eichhorn had completed the Boyce Medical Study with Dr. Alan Drash, a leading research pediatrician at the University of Pittsburgh. It identified the nature of emerging adolescent physiological/medical changes and became the subject of Don's filmstrip/tape of our ASCD series. We disseminated these data at educational meetings and conferences. The CORE Association focused on middle grades curriculum integration issues. Harold Alberty had published a book on a high school CORE approach but it never took hold.

As the 1970s began, there was a burgeoning middle grades education movement. There was no national junior high school association. We began attending the fledgling Midwest Middle School Association and persuaded its leadership to expand. Out of that came the National Middle School Association. That's a reprise of how I recall the focus on middle level education emerged. Instead of young adolescents or early adolescents, some of us used two terms Don Eichhorn coined: *transescence,* the middle grades epoch (*trans:* across, and *essence:* substance) and *transescents,* the learners. The first journal that focused on middle school education appeared in 1973. It was a quarterly: *Transescence: The Journal of Emerging Adolescent Education.* I edited it until 1996. It ceased publication when Preston Brown, the founder of ELI, passed away. A champion of middle level education, Preston also published *Dissemination Services of the Middle Grades,* which I also edited. It appeared nine times annually for 24 years.

Recognition increased that (1) middle grades learners had differing educational needs and (2) their school programs should accordingly respond to those needs. A lot of John Lounsbury's work focused on the need for middle level curriculum to become more developmentally responsive. Middle level curricula based on students' developmental nature proved more effective than modified high school approaches. The effort really got into full flow as we passed through the 1970s into the 1980s. Also, NMSA gained increasing visibility through its programs and publications.

While I was working at the University of Georgia, George Melton contacted me at the NMSA annual conference in Nashville. Earlier an outstanding junior high school principal, George had become Associate Executive Director and Director of Middle Level Education of the National Association of Secondary School Principals (NASSP). George asked what I would suggest to help him expand NASSP's middle school services. I said that the ASCD Council on Emerging Adolescent Learners was an important thing that unfortunately went out of existence. He immediately asked, "If we establish one at NASSP, will you chair it?" I agreed and George asked whom I would suggest for the Council. I mentioned two of the newer, established authorities: Al Arth, one of the staunchest advocates for middle level; Howard Johnston, a preeminent middle level education researcher with one of the really brightest minds I'd ever come across; and John Lounsbury, for his perspective and integrity. They were approached and agreed. Later, we added Sherrel Bergmann and Judy Brough, two of the "young, middle level education Turks" and then Don Clark. The Council did three-day Front Line Conferences at four locations around the country and presented at the national NASSP conference. We gave the Council 30 days a year of pro-bono service, except for expenses. We developed the periodical *Schools in the Middle* and authored a five volume monograph series, *Agenda for Excellence in the Middle Grades.*

We were disturbed by unfounded shots the USOE publication, *A Nation at Risk,* had taken at America's schools. Howard Johnson suggested, "Let's develop a Council publication that responds to it." That was *An Agenda for Excellence in Middle Level Education,* the first in the *Agenda for Excellence* series. We asked George to have it printed the same size and in the exact same big type-set and wide margins as a *Nation At Risk.* George retired in 1993, and the incoming NASSP Executive Director wanted the Association to focus on administrative issues. The Middle Level Education Council was disbanded in 1995. I need to say that George earned a special place in my group of heroes. Despite his NASSP deputy executive director's responsibilities, with his passion for middle level education, George also became very active in NMSA. "For the good of the cause," he participated in many

NMSA programs and established important, joint NASSP/NMSA initiatives. Justly deserving, he was humbled when given NMSA's John Lounsbury Award. Then, the standards movement, which went against everything that I believe to be educationally sound, came along.

My belief has been that education should allow youngsters to learn as fast as they can, or as slow as some must. Not all students have the ability to master the same amount of material by the end of specific grades as required in the educational standards rubric. However, the educational standards system expects virtually all to achieve specific progress at common "check points." Punitive and discriminatory, that assumes those not blessed with the abilities of others can pass common tests at the same intervals. Would it not make sense to develop a paradigm allowing all to learn the essential skills and information life will require of them as fast as they can or as slow as they must? That would allow most students to learn what they need to "complete the course." Possible back in the 1970s and 1980s, now such learning and internalizing of facts, skills, concepts, and information have been replaced with teaching for tests.

What or who were your main influences?

I have to give special credit to two people whose names you probably will not know. One is Arthur Kaiser, the professor from whom I took the graduate course, "Junior High School: Meeting the Needs of Youth." He taught that course at the University of Buffalo, where I did my doctorate. It was he who aroused my interest in young adolescents and education in the middle grades. A great teacher, friend, and then university colleague, Art is 87 and we see him quite often. The other was my major Professor Robert Harnack. The other prominent ones were people I previously mentioned. Bill Alexander, John Lounsbury, Gordon Vars, Donald Eichhorn, and later, George Melton, became friends and peers and remain among my idols. Over the years, many good comrades-in-arms shared in the growing middle education cause. It was a wonderful time to be alive. I believed in what I was doing. A host of things were developing that became benefits to young people and their education.

What kinds of middle school literature did you read early on?

I was fascinated by books such as Gertrude Noar's junior high school text. Back then, many of the books on junior high school were not recent publications. Thomas Briggs' 1920 book, *The Junior High School*, was the first one to use that term. In the early 1950s, not much was being written on contemporary middle grades programs because, as an early secondary education unit, the junior high was considered a subdivision of the high school.

When I met John Lounsbury and Gordon Vars at CORE, ASCD, and NASSP meetings in the 1950s, recognition of the need for possible changes in the middle grades programs was just emerging. In looking at those early suggestions we began to think: "Wait a minute, middle grades students really are not early anything." Because of the previous lack of attention regarding possible differences of middle grades students, there had been virtually no recognition that middle grades programs should be separated from secondary education. However, more of us began to agree that middle grades learners were different from both younger children and high school students. We felt they needed more than either advanced elementary school programs or junior editions of the senior high school.

It didn't matter what you called the school, the issue was that programs at that school level needed to respond to the characteristics of the students they served. Again, our group had a common background. Alexander, Lounsbury, Vars, and I all had advanced graduate education in curriculum. We agreed that schools at all levels needed a specific curriculum not an administrative rationale. Unless the curriculum recognized and responded to the characteristics of the students at that school level, the administrative organization didn't matter. So, since he initially viewed things from a curricular point of view, I contend that Bill Alexander rightfully is the father of the middle school. Had a person lacking Bill's perspective considered the middle grades, education at that level might have remained "old wine in new bottles." The four of us, those whom we attracted, and some who studied and earned their doctorates with us, joined in as the middle school movement progressed. In my case, those included Jim Beane and Judy Brough. With preparation in curriculum planning and development, they pursued these kinds of concerns, as well as identifying new and additional ones. It didn't matter how you bottled it. You could bottle it in configurations that local school district circumstances require. That might include grade 5–8, 6–8, even grade 4–8 or 6–9 schools, as local student development allowed. The concern is how best to respond to the unique and common developmental and learning characteristics of students.

What was your primary motivation for becoming involved in the middle school movement?

I guess because, despite my age, I still have a young adolescent outlook about many things. I am out there someplace in youngsters' never-never land and enjoying it. An accident kept me out of school for the second half of my seventh and most of my eighth grade school year. Bedridden a major portion of that period, I missed out on much of the "junior high" kinds of fun my friends were enjoying. Perhaps I have been trying to recapture some things I may have missed. Looking back, I guess I've really never "grown up." I did well in home study and came back to graduate with my eighth grade elementary school class. I always loved baseball and music. I always wanted to either be a musician or teacher. Fortunately, I was able to do the former well into my years in education. I graduated as an English major with social studies and classics minors and was certified to teach. I elected junior high because I felt comfortable with and enjoyed that age group.

The middle school movement began to take hold. Some still wanted to use the term junior high school, but the new middle level school would no longer be a "junior edition of the senior high school." School districts began to replace elementary and junior/senior high schools with a three-level system of (1) elementary schools for children, (2) middle level schools for the transitional epoch, and (3) high schools for maturing adolescents and young adults. Today, I am upset because major educational associations in our nation have not stood up against changes that continue to erode what the middle school movement achieved.

The greatest problem with American education is that it has never been largely research based. Substantially belief and politically based, it remains prone to all manner of outside pressures. An example is that the campaign against middle schools persists, despite the evidence showing that they are more effective for the age group they serve. I have yet to find data that confirms young people do, or will do better, after being put back into elementary schools and secondary-oriented programs. It has not been shown that a two-level school system achieves the success of a three-level one with developmentally responsive middle schools. Again, a large body of research, a lot of it done by Paul George, validates the success of middle schools.

What is primary motivation for your continued involvement in middle level education?

For me it is "was" since I am no longer. In 1999, after 48 years of enjoying my work, problems with arthritis in my hips and right knee stemming from the accident I suffered in seventh grade worsened. I retired in 1999 but continued to teach as Professor Emeritus but by 2001, my tolerance for pain reached its limit. That and decreasing mobility meant I could no longer accommodate going to campus to teach. No one could have been happier in, or enjoyed their work more, than I had been. My most rewarding experience was learning with and from the more than seventy persons who earned their doctorates with me. They included Sam Alessi, Jim Beane, Judy Brough, and Lyle Jensen, each of whom has made continuing, important contributions. They rank with Sherrel Bergmann who learned with Gordon Vars, Paul George who learned with Bill Alexander, David Strahan who worked with Howard Johnston, and Kathleen Wheeler, who worked with Al Arth. Since 2001, three surgeries replaced my hips and a knee and my mobility is better than it was years ago.

How would you describe the early years of the middle school movement around the 1960s and early 1970s?

In the 1960s there was a greater sense of hope in our nation. While some of it may have been naiveté, many felt that the terrible things the world had witnessed in World War II and the Korean Conflict might be over. There was confidence and trust and people seemed to look at things more non-judgmentally. People also looked at educational changes with more open minds. There was a trusting relationship between parents and educators [that is] not there anymore. Today, the public often criticizes schools and faults teachers almost immediately for things they do not understand or with which they disagree. When the middle school movement flourished there was more participatory democracy and tolerance to try new approaches. Educators could more readily try new practices without their being challenged before results could show their value. John Lounsbury would endorse a middle level educational practice if he believed "it would be better for kids." Ken McEwin also used those words in advocating for middle level education improvements.

From my perspective, today's emphasis on school organizational issues focuses almost entirely on form. There is virtually no concern with planning curricula that respond to developmental and learning needs. How can you expect "all God's children" (sorry if that offends) to perform at similar levels at specific times? Research confirms that "all God's children" do not have similar learning abilities. They can't all fit into narrow test boxes. Outwardly, those "little boxes made of ticky-tacky" may all look the same. However, not all students can meet their measure at the same time. Children can learn if they have the necessary readiness to learn what is being taught. I always loved teachers who would say, "You know, I don't think you are quite ready for that yet." However, the educational standards tests expect most students "to be ready for that." This precludes teachers from going slower with students who lack that necessary readiness. What is gained by forcing such students to submit to developmentally inappropriate challenges that are above their capabilities? Poor results inevitably lower their self-concept as learners. Because they could not yet learn what such tests measure, many develop a sense of "learned helplessness." Whether or not they can learn something, subsequently, they make a lesser effort to do so. Instead, they join students of varying levels in trying to memorize information for tests. That has replaced learning and internalizing things possible in the earlier, hopeful times. Then, educators were encouraged to search for better ways instead of praying for good test results. While it is denied, teachers in particular circumstances may be evaluated by students' test performances. When the middle school movement flourished, curricular and program improvement was not prescribed from the top down. A bottom-up flow was essential in organizing developmentally responsive programs. The 1960s into the 1980s were wonderful times.

How has the middle school concept changed since the early years of the middle school movement?

I am not sure it has been a change of kind as much as one of degree. In 1960 we moved into things slowly. The efforts of ASCD's Council on the Emerging Learner efforts led to activities that spurred the beginning of the middle level education movement. Focus was on gathering evidence validating the need for educational programs that better respond to needs of learners as they leave childhood and achieve pubescence. The ASCD Council presentations were to middle grades curriculum workers and teacher audiences. Specific program practices became more common in middle level schools. Al Arth had identified what he considered essential middle level school elements. NMSA established a group to develop a publication dealing with such program components. It was the first edition of *This We Believe*. The writers were Bill Alexander, Al Arth, Don Cherry, Gordon Vars, me, and John Lounsbury as editor. Going through later editions over the years, *This We Believe* remains the flagship publication of the Association.

What was the educational context at the time when the middle school movement began?

When the middle school movement flourished, the attitude was to consider and try things that looked that like they might improve learning. If a new approach didn't work, schools could go back to what was previously done. As I look back, it was a different time, a different era. As the middle school movement falters, student advisory programs and activities have also been curtailed. We never completely implemented the kind of student advocacy recommended by Louis E. Raths. 'Louie' wrote the fundamental works on values education. He profoundly influenced Jim Beane, who took up that area. Jim's work with Dick Lipka on self-concept and self-esteem had substantial impact for middle level education. Self-concept as learner is very important for young adolescents. If they don't see themselves of worth and value, they may not succeed during their formative middle school years. A significant improvement at the time, the loss of that perspective now is tragic.

I chide those who do not oppose dismantling of middle school programs. They continue to (1) ignore the data on which the middle school movement was based and (2) fail to press for data identifying the need to revert to elementary and secondary school organization. I am convinced that, sooner or later, this growing march back to yesteryear will come back to haunt us.

What have been the roles of women and minorities in the middle school movement?

In my three-year term as president-elect, president, and past president, NMSA established working committees on diverse concerns. Involvement of women and minorities on the Association's committees and task forces also increased. To NMSA's credit, it was one of the first major associations to have women in key positions—president, board members, and executive director. While there have been successes, efforts to involve women remain more difficult because, as I see it, the old boy network probably isn't dead yet. George Melton deserves great credit for fighting the old boy network in NASSP. Because of that, we were able to appoint Sherrel Bergman and Judy Brough to the Middle Level Education Council. When George retired, he succeeded in having Laurel Kanthak appointed as his successor. She was the first woman appointed to a high position in NASSP.

While opportunities for women have increased, I remember two particular early advances. Gender and/or race long excluded bright, capable persons in education. When I began teaching, bright women were largely restricted to careers as nurses, teachers, telephone operators, or secretaries. In that era, the glass ceiling limited advancement of women into supervisory or administrative positions. Written and unwritten regulations in education also required that if women became pregnant, they had to resign. Ironically, the opening of more fields to qualified women has created a kind of "brain drain" in education. In the early 1990s, I chaired the NMSA Resolutions Committee for several years. We succeeded in passing proactive resolutions on gay, lesbian, bi-sexual issues and racial middle level concerns.

What are some examples of the way the middle school movement has affected American education?

The middle school movement affected American education by responding to new data that identified traditional middle grades programs that did not adequately address the unique educational needs of young adolescents. It helped parents and communities understand those needs and how the middle school concept sought to address them. During the middle school era, parents knew what middle schools were about and they championed them. Thus, the middle school movement had a grassroots impact.

The middle school era was very transitory, in part, because parents did not pass on their understanding of the value of middle schools. When younger children in large families attended middle schools, their parents could say "I really think the middle school is giving our child something much better than our older children had." Today, parents no longer have children who went through effective middle schools programs. Lacking that experience, they cannot compare the effectiveness of national education standards programs with what middle schools once provided students. As you cannot lose what you never had, you cannot value what you never experienced.

Much of former middle school programs and the ways they were organized and implemented (i.e., like team teaching) are long gone. What has replaced them is, at best, a shallow version of past approaches. Now, primary focus is on getting kids ready for common, standardized tests. Today, parents are not aware of what middle schools once were, and what they could and should be. The middle school era was a very transitory one. Unfortunately, parents did not pass on their understanding of the value of middle schools.

Have particular legislative actions significantly influenced the middle school movement? You can discuss state or national level.

The leadership of Ken McEwin and John Swaim and their work with the NMSA Professional Preparation Advisory Board during the middle school era was critically important. The resultant establishment of national and state teacher certification requirements and standards was a great accomplishment. A persisting national problem is that the United States Department of Education has never recognized middle schools. The USOE still refers only to elementary and secondary schools and lists all of the nation's schools as either elementary or secondary ones. Although young adolescents are neither elementary school children nor high school adolescents, the USOE does not recognize that the middle school movement was based on data showing the need for a three-level school system. Neither NMSA nor the middle level educational field at large has been able to get the USOE to change its anachronistic, misinformed stance. Between elementary schools for young children and high schools for maturing adolescents and young adults, a middle school unit can better address the educational needs of young adolescents. In dismantling what was developed in the middle school movement, the USOE overlooked the data establishing the need for what the middle school movement achieved. In my view, that tragic oversight is obscene, to say the least.

What are some of the ways that the middle school movement has influenced middle level curriculum and instruction?

I think that interdisciplinary teaching and advisory programs were probably the two programs that had the most direct influence on things. Advocating the need to be concerned with self-concept and self-esteem was also important. I believe that state middle school associations have great potential to make changes in their own states. The linkage of state associations with legislators can effectively deal with state middle level issues and needs. Over two decades ago, North Carolina Governor Hunt was a strong advocate for middle level education. With his support, Ken McEwin and Julia Thomason developed a successful state middle school initiative there. North Carolina is the only state I know that has had a middle school advocate at the governor's level. I have never seen the influence of national associations bring about significant middle level educational improvements. Had they been able to do so in the late 1970s through the 1980s, the middle school movement might have persisted.

As middle level educators, how do you think we should respond to the emphasis on student achievement as measured by standardized tests?

People seem to think that if you come out against the standards and the national testing programs, you are anti-achievement. That is neither true nor correct. In that regard, a broader and more specific frame of reference describing effective school achievement is needed. For instance, the growing numbers of people in our nation's prisons have character and citizenship deficits. Those two attributes are not current educational standards and standardized testing initiative achievement targets. Character and citizenship were addressed in effective middle school programs' components along with language arts, mathematical, and other curriculum skill areas. Student achievement during the middle school movement was higher than in current educational standards and standardized testing initiatives. Today, student tests are typically scored in four categories, with one being the lowest. I would suggest selecting a group of youngsters who scored 4 on today's tests. Talk with them about the information on which they were tested. Because they are largely taught to memorize, rather than understand things in context, many students demonstrate significant losses discussing what they can recall. Yet, teachers to whom students go in the next year assume test scores reflect what was learned and can be used. That learning "house of cards" is not valid achievement, but that is the educational standards approach. In the middle school era, teachers discussed individual student test results and passed that information with test scores on to their next teachers. That "intelligence continuum" no longer exists. Back then, next year's teachers could identify that, while a student scored 84 on last year's final test, for example, his or her understanding of verbs or adjectives was inadequate and needed extra work. Multi-graded middle school teacher teams could remain with the same students for grades seven and eight. This provided opportunities to better know students' learning needs, something not possible in today's circumstances.

Teachers require opportunities to communicate with students to identify how well they conceptualize and can demonstrate what they studied, yet the current approach emphasizes memorizing more than understanding information. Improving achievement will require that we can identify what students actually have learned, internalized, and can use. A comprehensive learning approach remains an advantage of European school systems. They progressively test what is taught throughout the school system and can identify the residue of students' learning. That differs from what we presently do in the United States. Middle school programs were more performance-based and identified what students could demonstrate in terms of problem solving, hypothesizing, and drawing conclusions. The educational standards model lacks a comprehensive learning dimension. Thus, there is no indication of how much of what was tested students can demonstrate, apply, and use two, four, six or eight months from now.

In a way, pitching in baseball is similar to teachers working with students. In baseball, pitchers develop "a book" on their hitters so they know what pitches hitters can and cannot hit. The pitcher's goal is to get batters to miss the pitch. However, teachers need to know how to "pitch" things so students connect with and learn them. The goal is to help students learn and conceptualize facts, skills, and information within a context of understanding, something that memorization alone cannot accomplish.

Current emphasis on memorization for standardized tests also fails to recognize and deal with differences in short- and long-term memory. Unfortunately, decisions about students for their following year are solely based on standardized test results. Thus, I believe what is considered as "achievement" in educational standards and standardized testing is often "fool's gold." Previously, middle school programs were more developmentally and conceptually based on how young adolescents learn.

What are the lessons that we still need to learn from the history of the middle school movement?

First, never take anything for granted. Second, don't believe that what is in vogue today will persist on its own. Third, if you think present practice is effective, identify what must be done to insure its continuation. Fourth, provide continuing opportunity to research and develop successful practices and/or refine the effectiveness of what is in practice.

I believe we must learn how to find ways of encoding things into regulation so that if something is established as valid, and effective, that lacking data to the contrary, it cannot be suddenly changed by a 4-to-3 vote. Major evidence has to prove the need to change or discontinue existing practice. Data must be provided as to the advantages of what is being proposed to replace something. As Paul George identified in *Evidence for the Middle School*, no such data were provided in removing and replacing the elements in effective middle school programs with the "clap-trap" of the present national standards and standardized testing movement. Tragically, effective middle schools were jettisoned despite the lack of evidence proving specific shortcomings. Their demise lacked any researched database for dismantling them. What replaced them was not data-based. Abandonment of middle schools was largely based on whimsy, political moves, and the like. As a result, effective middle schools were replaced with something that, in my view, is not working. New for the sake of new has not served young adolescents well. That seems to happen with so many things in education. If there is nothing wrong with current practice, we too often make changes for the sake of change.

How would you characterize the current status of the middle school movement?

We need prayer and help. We need to (1) look at middle level schools and identify those things that are working now; (2) identify those things that merit being preserved, enhanced, and nourished; and (3) identify programs that need to be re-thought, reconsidered, and/or changed. The entire effort must be data-based.

Are there particular efforts that need to be made to help ensure the future success of the middle school movement?

We need to define effective middle school program elements and establish them in state educational regulations. Not providing the latter allowed middle school programs to erode. We cannot allow political judgments and similarly vested interests to determine whether or not school practice is good. Greater respect for middle level educational theory and practice and the professional knowledge authority for middle grades educators is still lacking. If people have cancer, most wouldn't go to their doctor and suggest a procedure. However, most people wouldn't hesitate to tell a middle school teacher what to do with their child or what classroom practice the school should use or disregard. Educators require the same prerogatives given other professions. Had that been accorded educators working with young adolescents, the middle level movement would have fared much better than it unfortunately did. Lack of such professional regard helped dismantle effective middle school programs and practice. As well, public understanding of the difference of young adolescents both from younger children and from high school adolescents would have helped continue the three-level school system initiated during the middle school movement.

Are there any other comments that you would like to make that you have not been asked about in this interview? This would be a good time to mention some other folks also.

I think I omitted Chris Stevenson and John Arnold when talking about such people. Chris's writing and personal witness about middle school programs enabling kids and teachers to make educational decisions was extremely significant. I appreciate the many times Chris did interactive tele-lectures for my graduate students, as did Al Arth and Jim Beane. John Arnold was a real thinker who spoke eloquently and instigated many meaningful activities. The integrity of these people in the middle school movement was herculean. While practically never wrong, if and when they were, they freely admitted it. If someone else had a better idea they would contribute to it and improve educational practice. They were so different from the middle school movement "fair-weather friends" and "summer-time sailors" that rode the coattails and profited from the middle school movement. However, when the waters got rough, they jumped ship to the educational standards movement. I continue to hope the efforts of Chris, John, Jim. Al, and their like can somehow turn things around so that middle level education, as it once was and sorely needs to be, is revisited.

5

Gordon F. Vars

Kids make decisions in ages 10 to 15 that lead to death and destruction, a horrible life, or to a relatively safe life. If we don't do a good job at this age, we may lose a generation. I think it dawned on me slowly that this may be the most important period in a human being's life, other than the first few years.

Dr. Gordon Vars has been a middle level education leader throughout his long and distinguished career. A widely acclaimed expert and an articulate spokesperson for core curriculum, Dr. Vars has provided counsel and leadership for many seminal events in middle level education. He was involved in the creation of the Midwest Middle School Association and in its later conversion in 1973 into the National Middle School Association. He served as the first President of National Middle School Association, was one of the authors of the first edition of *This We Believe*, and was on the Professional Preparation Advisory Board that wrote the first national standards for middle level teacher preparation. Vars is the author of a great many middle level articles, research reports, and books, and he has been a frequent presenter at professional conferences.

The Legacy of Middle School Leaders, pages 71–89
Copyright © 2011 by Information Age Publishing

During World War II, while crouched in a foxhole, Gordon decided that, if he lived through the War, he would work with people and ideas rather than with things. Before that time, he had aspired to be an aeronautical engineer. He graduated from Antioch College in Yellow Springs, Ohio in 1948, then entered the master's degree program at Ohio State University where he took a course on core curriculum taught by Dr. Harold Alberty that fueled his interest in core. Following graduation from Ohio State University, he accepted a position teaching eighth grade core in Bel Air, Maryland. Then in 1952, Vars was recruited to teach eighth grade core in the Demonstration School at George Peabody College for Teachers in Nashville, Tennessee. After teaching three years in the Demonstration School, he became graduate assistant to Dr. William Van Til and developed a professional relationship that continued for many years. Van Til was a respected educator and noted author committed to progressive and democratic educational ideals. Next, he accepted a position at the State University of New York at Plattsburgh where he taught undergraduate courses to university students as well as core courses to ninth graders at the Campus School.

After completing his doctorate at George Peabody College for Teachers in 1959, Dr. Vars joined the Cornell University faculty as an Associate Professor of Secondary Education and participated in the Cornell Junior High School Project. It was during his years at Cornell that he co-authored *Modern Education for the Junior High School Years* (1960) with William Van Til and John Lounsbury. Vars was in the audience when William Alexander made his renowned speech at the Cornell Junior High School Conference where he proposed the *middle school* and was one of the reactors to that presentation.

In 1966, Dr. Vars accepted a position at Kent State University, Kent, Ohio, where again he taught eighth grade core in the mornings and undergraduate courses in the afternoons. He was Director of the Middle School Division of the Kent University School from 1966 to 1976. In 1975, he became Coordinator of the Kent State University Junior High/Middle School Staff Development Project, a pioneering field-based graduate concentration designed to help middle level teachers improve their teaching effectiveness. He retired as Professor Emeritus at Kent State University.

Dr. Vars has received many prestigious awards for his work in middle level education. In 1980, he was named Ohio Middle School Educator of the Year by the Ohio Middle School Association. He was recipient of the highest honor awarded by National Middle School Association in 1987 when he received the John H. Lounsbury Distinguished Service Award. National Middle School Association further honored him by dedicating the 20th Annual Conference to him in 1993.

Dr. Vars dedicated his professional life to teaching, writing, mentoring, and serving his profession in other ways. His pioneering advocacy for the establishment of academically excellent, developmentally responsive middle level curriculum continues to have profound positive effects on middle level education today. In a memoir about Gordon Vars, his colleague and mentor William Van Til stated, "The middle school movement and core curriculum owe much to the energy and insight and persistence of Gordon Vars."

Selected Publications

Vars, G. F. (1951). Problems of a beginning core teacher. *Educational Leadership, 9*(1), 12–16.

Van Til, W., Vars, G. F., & Lounsbury, J. H. (1960, 1967). *Modern education for the junior high school years.* Indianapolis, IN: The Bobbs-Merrill Company.

Vars, G. F. (1965). Preparing junior high school teachers. *Clearing House, 40*(2), 77–81.

Vars, G. F. (1966). Can team teaching save the core curriculum? *Phi Delta Kappan, 47*(5), 258–262.

Lounsbury, J. H., & Vars, G. F. (1978). *A curriculum for the middle school years.* New York: Harper and Row Publishers.

Vars, G. F. (1988). The Kent State University Program. In W. M. Alexander & C. K. McEwin. *Preparing to teach at the middle level* (pp. 34–38). Columbus, OH: National Middle School Association.

Vars, G. F. (1992). Humanizing student evaluation and reporting. In J. L. Irvin (Ed.). *Transforming middle level education: Perspectives and possibilities* (pp. 336–365). Boston: Allyn and Bacon.

Vars, G. F. (1993). *Interdisciplinary teaching: Why and how* (2nd ed.). Westerville, OH: National Middle School Association.

Vars, G. F. (1997). Effects of integrative curriculum and instruction. In J. Irvin (Ed.), *What current research says to the middle level practitioner* (pp. 179–186). Columbus, OH: National Middle School Association.

Vars, G. F. (2000). Common learnings: A 50-year quest. *Journal of Curriculum and Supervision, 16*(1), 70–89.

Vars, G. F. (2001). Can curriculum integration survive in an era of high-stakes testing? *Middle School Journal, 33*(2), 7–17.

Lounsbury, J. H., & Vars, G. F. (2005). Middle level education: A personal history. In V. A. Anfara, Andrews, G., & S. Mertens (Eds.), *The encyclopedia of middle grades education.* Westerville, OH: National Middle School Association and Greenwich, CT: Information Age Publishing.

---

*Gordon F. Vars**

My involvement in middle level education goes way back to 1946. In that year, I decided to switch from the field of engineering to education as a result of having a couple of years sitting in foxholes in Europe in World War II reflecting on what I wanted to do with my life if I got out of that scrap with a whole skin. The first contact with education at Antioch College was with a marvelous educator by the name of Hilda Wallace Hughes. She had studied at Teachers College Columbia—I think she had actually had a course with John Dewey—but she taught the three introductory courses as a core, meaning that the courses were welded together, one interweaving with the other. We students had the opportunity to help plan the course, select the books that we would read, and evaluate ourselves at the end of the course. That was a very heady introduction to the field of education and it introduced me to a concept of education that became the theme of my entire career of over 50 years.

Core curriculum grew out of the progressive education movement, which was at a zenith at that time. In 1949, I graduated from Ohio State University. While there, I had had opportunities to visit and study with the educators at Ohio State University and took some courses with Harold Alberty, probably one of the major advocates of this interdisciplinary, integrative approach called "core" at that time. He had been active in the Progressive Education Association and had been a curriculum consultant to the thirty schools that took part in the Eight Year Study. I took a course in curriculum and a course in the teaching of core with Dr. Alberty.

After graduating, I was hired as a core teacher and taught for four years and enjoyed it very much. In 1952, I became a teacher of eighth grade English, social studies, science, and math at the Peabody Demonstration School, which was affiliated with George Peabody College for Teachers in Nashville. I also began doctoral work with my advisor, Dr. William Van Til, one of the leaders in the field of curriculum at that time. He introduced me to all kinds of opportunities in the field of education, for which I will be forever grateful. After three years teaching at the Demonstration School and simultaneously taking courses, I took a year off from teaching to serve as Dr. Van Til's graduate assistant. It was, I think, during this period that I had the one and only course on the junior high school. Junior high school

---

* Gordon Vars was interviewed for the Legacy Project in November 2003.

was the form of intermediate education that was booming at that time in this country.

One of Van Til's previous students, John Lounsbury, had studied with him just a year or two before. To my great surprise, after working with Dr. Van Til for a while, John and I were invited to join him in writing a new text-book on junior high school education. This provided him an opportunity to introduce his concept of curriculum design, curriculum foundations, and add the historical piece that John had done as his dissertation. I would add the teaching core curriculum piece since it had been the focus of my disser-tation. The three of us started on this long process of getting a big textbook together, trying to put in everything we thought. There seemed to be a need for a textbook on intermediate (junior high, middle school, or whatever you call it) education at that time. After many vicissitudes the book came out in 1961 and was revised and the second edition came out in 1967.

I ended up teaching ninth grade core at the campus school attached to Plattsburg State Teacher's College in upstate New York. At the same time I began my involvement with undergraduate teacher education. At Platts-burg they had a relatively new certification program called the "Early Sec-ondary." It was an extension of high school preparation down to grades seven and eight. It gave colleges an opportunity to introduce some of the special considerations that these young people are entitled to because of their stage in life, the intermediate stage in life. I had a great time teaching core and undergraduate courses at Plattsburg State Teacher's College.

In 1960, the Ford Foundation was very active in trying to solve the teacher shortage. They were giving grants to colleges and universities to develop programs to "retread" liberal arts graduates, give them a concen-trated one year of educational preparation and send them out as certified high school, middle school, or elementary school teachers. The Cornell University School of Education was able to land a Ford Foundation grant for junior high school preparation. It was the only one in the country that focused on the junior high school, which in those days was mostly grades seven, eight, and nine. I worked six years with the junior high school proj-ect at Cornell.

Cornell University, being a "big time" university, offered all kinds of opportunities as a member of the staff of this project. I was invited to give speeches all over the country, which was gratifying to "a young kid on the block." But the project at Cornell was a grant project, "soft money"; the University was not about to pick it up. The president of Cornell also had announced that the School of Education was to be abolished, so that made me think about moving on. Along the way, the association that now is called the National Association for Core Curriculum was moving along. About the year after I went to Cornell I was appointed the executive secretary treasurer of this organization, which had been promoting the integrative approach then called core curriculum ever since 1953. So, a second piece of my professional work in middle level education was becoming stronger and stronger. The place I found where I could teach kids and also teach undergraduate and graduate students who wanted to go on into teaching this volatile middle level age was Kent State University.

Shortly after I arrived at Kent State I was invited to participate in one of the first nationwide conferences on the middle level education movement. It was held in 1967 at the University of Toledo. As I look back on it, that was a wonderful opportunity. For example, I shared the platform with William Alexander, the man they call the "Father of the Middle School" because of a speech he made at Cornell at a conference sponsored by the Junior High School Project. Another notable participant was Donald Eichhorn, whose 1966 book, *The Middle School*, very clearly said that the middle level education movement had to focus on a clear understanding of the nature and needs of this age group, and he spelled them out. Donald Eichhorn conducted some groundbreaking experiments on what actually happens physically, biologically, to young people when they go through puberty.

In 1970, I was elected president of the Midwest Middle School Association (MWMSA). I learned later that a professor and a graduate student at the University of Toledo had put MWMSA together. They invited middle level administrators and professors of education in Michigan, Indiana, and Ohio to a conference to see if it wasn't a good idea to establish an organization supporting middle level education. In the meantime, Paul George had been stirring things up in Florida and had an excellent Florida League of Middle Schools going down there. And in various places in the country, the middle school movement was beginning to get an organizational focus. But there was no organization that was devoted deliberately and completely to junior high school and middle level education.

In 1973, after meeting once in Ohio, once in Michigan, and once in Indiana, the leaders of MWMSA decided, "This is too big for us. We've got to go national." Glen Maynard, the second president of MWMSA, has recalled that Conrad Toepfer of the University of Buffalo made that motion at our business meeting. It was passed and we struggled from then on to convert ourselves from a small regional association to one with national scope and the name National Middle School Association. We had our first NMSA conference in Columbus, Ohio, where I gave the presidential address of about ten minutes. After some difficult early years, National Middle School Association took hold and it's been booming ever since.

My major emphasis or perhaps my contribution to the middle level education movement is my conviction that middle level education has to be designed in such a way that it responds to the unique characteristics, needs, and concerns of young people going through this critical stage in life. If it doesn't do that, it's not good for them. I think this is the essence of what I think my contribution might be to middle level education. At the same time, as Dr. Van Til so eloquently argued, we must be aware of what society expects of these young people. Nowadays what society demands are test scores. And at the same time, we must not ignore but be fully sensitive to developments in the various disciplines of knowledge. If we relate well to the kids and meet the expectations and demands of society, but do it with content that is incorrect or inaccurate (which a lot of it is), then again we are not being true to the expectations of an educator. So it's got to be a balanced, integrated, inclusive approach of: nature of the learner, nature of society, and the nature of knowledge. I consider these the basic "foundations of curriculum."

Who or what were your main influences?

William Van Til. Probably the main reason I ended up teaching at the middle level was that's where core curriculum was most common. I think, my interest in the interdisciplinary core curriculum led me naturally into that age group, and I fell in love with them. They'd drive you crazy one day and two minutes later, you turned around and wanted to hug them. When I was younger, and had more bounce, I could ride with that (their ups and downs) and thoroughly enjoyed it.

What middle school literature did you use to help you with that first book, and then later, what kinds of middle school literature did you use?

William T. Gruhn, a graduate student of Harl R. Douglass at the University of Northern Colorado, conducted a very extensive survey of junior high school principals in the late 1930s or early 1940s, I guess. And from that survey, he formulated a list of what he called "The Functions of Junior High School." Included were such things as guidance, integration, socialization, whatever—not subjects, but functions—things that the school should provide for young people at that age. He and Dr. Douglass published a book in 1947 called *The Modern Junior High School*. It was probably the major text book and model of junior high school education from then on. It went through numerous editions. My guess is that it was one of the books that I read when I was studying with Dr. Van Til in the early 1950s; it was new at that time. John Lounsbury the other night reminded us of Leonard Koos, Bagley, and some of the other early writers on junior high school, beginning in the early 1900s. I probably read some of those, but the particular spin given by Dr. Van Til is probably where I got my major thrust for junior high school education.

Are there particular theorists or writings that have influenced your educational thought?

I have already mentioned Van Til and Gruhn and Douglass. Another would be Harold Alberty. He and Nelson Bossing and Roland Faunce were major writers on core curriculum. Alberty gave me his progressive slant to reinforce what I had picked up in the little bit of curriculum work that I had done at Antioch, so I credit Alberty. I'm an "Alberty core person," really. Dr. Alberty published a list of the six types of core curriculum. But it included "subjects that are required of everybody." That's not the advanced type of integrated curriculum that Jim Beane and I advocate. By calling them all core, he muddied the water. If he had used the word core specifically for those that involved teacher/student planning, then we wouldn't have this continual muddle, I think. I was kind of disappointed when he did that. He later combined five and six into one, so we talked about five levels of curriculum integration. I suppose, considering his background—coming out of the early progressive education movement—they really were using the word core loosely in those early days. And so it's been one of my missionary efforts to clean up the language, the terminology of these various approaches and try to restrict "core" to the ones that are deliberately focused on the needs and characteristics of students and in which the students have a voice in what they learn. The leading spokesman today for this kind of education is James Beane. He makes a very strong case for it in his book *A Reason to Teach.*

What was your primary motivation for becoming involved in the middle school movement?

Number one, as everybody realized, and it was dramatically demonstrated in the first *Turning Points* document in 1989, this is a critical age. Kids make decisions in ages 10 to 15 that lead to death and destruction, a horrible life, or to a relatively safe life. If we don't do a good job at this age, we may lose a generation. I think it dawned on me slowly that this may be the most important period in a human being's life, other than the first few years when we are just trying to stay alive. That happens to be my major motivation.

How would you describe the early years of the middle school movement?

Chaotic. It was kind of fun because of what John or Jim alluded to as a tug of war between junior high versus middle school. That led to some rather unique experiences. One opportunity came to me because I was at Cornell that wouldn't have come to me otherwise. The schools of New York City in the early 1960s were facing reorganization. They had junior high schools with grades 7, 8, 9, and they were proposing to go to 6, 7, 8 middle schools. The junior high school principals said, "No, no, that's not right." And they had big posters, "Junior High School Principals Have Principles" and fought it tooth and nail. I was invited down for a panel discussion at some kind of conference of junior high school principals and others in New York City. We were to discuss the pros and cons of the middle school versus the junior high. I sat next to a principal that said junior high school is the way to go. I was expected to make the case for a middle school. I don't remember all the details, but in between the two of us was a woman representing the NAACP. She was pushing the middle school reorganization to get black kids out of the ghetto faster, to get them out of the neighborhood elementary schools, which were segregated, into a middle school starting in grades six, not waiting until seventh. Starting in the fifth was even being considered. I saw first-hand how part of the push for reorganizing middle school was to desegregate. That was an interesting experience.

How has the middle school concept changed since the early years of the middle school movement?

I don't know that it's changed that much, particularly if you go back to the model junior high school. Read the ASCD pamphlet called *The Junior High School We Need*, which was their position paper on what a junior high school was supposed to be. Compare it with the one they did a few years later, *The Middle School We Need*, which was written primarily by a student of Connie Toepfer. You'll see the thread of commonality from junior high to middle school. Then look at the version of *This We Believe* that came out this year (2003). You'll find similar threads with both ASCD's *The Middle School We Need* and *The Junior High School We Need*. There are persistent threads of Gruhn and Douglass, too.

The way that you organized staff and students in a model junior high school usually included a core or block-time class with one teacher teaching two or three subjects, or occasionally four. William Alexander and Paul George didn't buy that for a middle school. They proposed an interdisciplinary team. People who don't look deeply at the consequences of organizing staff too easily buy the team concept. They rearrange the schedule and think, "Okay. We've done it." But without common planning time and without staff development to get teachers working more closely together, you don't get much integrative curriculum. And so the switch from a one-teacher block of time to the interdisciplinary team has set the whole integrative curriculum movement back, as far as I'm concerned. Ditto the guidance piece, because teacher guidance was part of the core or block-time concept. If one teacher has the same kids for three periods, and a kid walks in all upset, you go put your arm around him and say, "Hey, kid what's up?" But if it's a team, well you've got to get through your social studies so the kids can go across the hall to science. So, I see that as a serious loss for middle school education. People like Paul George and some of the others will argue with you on that, but that's my perspective.

How have middle schools changed since the early years of the middle school movement?

Not much. Very little. You have a few districts that have really gone far with the middle school concept, either the one advocated in *This We Believe* or the one proposed in *Turning Points*. The number of districts that were able to do that is still, I think, pitifully small. Most of them still have a high school bell schedule and they run the kids through a fifty minute or forty minute rotation. So there's no coherence, no opportunity to get close to the teacher or anything. So the schools have a long way to go, most of them. The districts that can afford to build and operate decent middle schools are essentially the wealthy suburban districts. In the cities and in the rural areas they are at the mercy of economics.

How were decisions about the directions taken by the middle school movement made?

Who knows? It's not rational, it's often organizational and it's often driven by economics. I once visited a middle school in Pittsfield, New York that for each of the previous three years had had a different grade configuration at the middle level. They went from 7-8-9 to 7–8 to 6-7-8 purely on the basis of enrollment and building capacity. Unfortunately, that is the way a lot of the decisions are made. I have already mentioned the desegregation issue: reorganize the schools in order to get the kids out of the ghettos faster. That's not an educational decision; it's a political decision. Unfortunately, politics often is the real answer and changes on the basis of a thoughtful, philosophical analysis are rare.

**How were other individuals and groups outside middle level
education involved in the early years of middle school movement?**

The political climate of the times affects everything in education, including middle level education. You were at my talk early this week where I mentioned Sputnik, World War II, and other major political events and even more so it can bring about radical shifts in what you might call a gestalt of American society. When I got into teaching in the 1940s, the war was over; people were feeling pretty good. We were getting back to normal and the Progressive Era, not the Progressive Education Association necessarily, but the philosophy was still common. It was not only in education, but in other things. So there was a sort of warmness, if you can think of it that way, in society's interaction. The country wasn't facing any major problems at that time. So there was interest in humanistic approaches to education or welfare or what not. The New Deal, after all, was a welfare state in some ways and so that permeated the environment.

In the 1950s, during the McCarthy era, things went the other direction. The witch hunt against the Communists, or socialists, or anybody who was liberal, chilled the climate. We went through a very frosty period then and that's bound to affect the schools. Arthur Bester and that crowd lampooned progressive education and said, "They're just coddling the kids, you know. Schools are just touchy, feely places." They ridiculed the things that we were promoting in middle level education. At the local level, schools are at the mercy of voters concerned about taxes and all of that. After Sputnik there was more emphasis on math and science. Core programs often were split up because they had to pull the science out to concentrate on it. Nowadays with *No Child Left Behind*, a punitive "make them learn" emphasis is destroying schools at all levels. I am reminded of an administrative joke, but I think it applies here. Somebody supposedly saw a sign in a building somewhere that said, "The morale in this organization must be improved—or else!" An older version is: "The beatings will continue until morale improves." In this kind of environment it's hard to maintain any kind of human enterprise.

**What have been some of the most significant events, incidents, or
moments in the middle school movement?**

The conversion from Midwest Middle School Association to NMSA to provide a national voice would be one of them. Certain publications like *Turning Points* were significant. Some of the foundations like the Ford Foundation and the Kettering Foundation in Ohio made major efforts to revise both elementary and middle school education through grants and workshops. Our University School in Kent participated in the Kettering i/d/e/a/ project that promoted Individually Guided Education (IGE).

Their model of middle level education is still sound today, but it is largely forgotten. A number of foundations tried to improve education in urban middle schools. Some of those have made significant differences, but not enough difference to justify the millions of dollars that have been spent. They found that the schools are pretty tough to change at any level. Two examples were the Edna McConnell Clark Foundation and the Eli Lilly efforts in Indiana.

Who or what have been some of the greatest detractors or opponents of middle school education?

Politicians, anti-tax groups, ultra-conservatives inside and outside the field of education, state legislatures, since education is largely a state function, and, of course, local politics. The kinds of people that get elected to state legislatures can make or break an educational system. Now, of course, the federal government is playing a major role. We have been trying for years to get middle level education recognized by the federal government even in its statistical reports. We had to struggle to pull out the middle level statistics from their reports that classified schools as either elementary or secondary. And in teacher education, departments on many campuses were either elementary or secondary.

What have been some of the most significant obstacles to the success of the middle school movement?

I think the one I put down first in my reflection could be called "half-hearted implementation." People want the shape of a middle school, but aren't willing to do the hard work of developing staff, students, and parents who support the kind of education that you and I might say is needed. Administrators are too busy to read and teachers are both too busy and too disinterested in many cases. Another major obstacle, I think, has been the way the media have characterized kids at this age. They're all caricatures. The media not only lampoon the age group and education in general, but they also have been part of the major attack on the public schools, trying to destroy the public schools and put education in the hands of private corporations, so they can make more money. Right now a major obstacle of course is the high stakes testing. Standards can be useful if they're applied wisely and appropriately. But the punitiveness and the deliberate setting of goals that are impossible for educators to meet are bringing on a major disaster. We are lobotomizing a generation or two of kids by the emphasis on testing, memory, and regurgitation.

What are some of the mistakes that have been made during the middle school movement that we might be able to learn from today?

The one that I thought of first was failure to require anyone who teaches in the middle grades to have special preparation for that level. I think North Carolina has been the model of a state where they did that and as a result, all of the colleges and universities, I believe, in North Carolina have programs and they have support from the Education Department. Unless teachers have been exposed to at least some of the ideals of middle level education, they are just putting in time. They may eventually get the vision, enjoy the work, and see its possibilities, but it's hard. It's hard on them and it's hard on the kids. As Joan Lipsitz identified years ago in her book, the kids are *Growing Up Forgotten*. That was really a landmark book, calling public attention to this critical age group. In a sense it was kind of a precursor to *Turning Points*. Both were major efforts to focus public attention on a critical age group.

Who has benefited the most from the middle school movement?

I don't think we should be asking "the most." That kind of question forces us into ranking and rating, when we should be exploring how different people benefit in different ways. If I had to choose the most, it would be the kids. There are no guarantees in education, but those who are fortunate enough to have a decent middle level education should benefit for the rest of their lives. They should have avoided the dangerous temptations that surround young people growing up in today's society, and they will face the challenges of later years with confidence born of reasonable success in dealing with life's developmental tasks. Teachers and parents benefit, too. In a good middle school, adults and young adolescents work together to create a wholesome learning environment. Conflict between teachers or parents and youth often arises because they're talking past each other; they don't understand each other. A good middle level school promotes respectful dialogue between and among transescents and the significant adults in their lives.

Who has benefited the least from the middle school movement?

The people in the poor districts are the ones that suffer, not from the movement but because the movement doesn't get to them. Too often, poor districts are staffed with people who are disgruntled, unhappy, poorly paid, poorly prepared, and so forth. So, both inner city and rural areas are paying the price, and minorities of all kinds. Many schools now have many students for whom English is not their first language. Some middle schools have forty different languages spoken by the kids who come through them. Schools dealing with all these problems often lack the leadership and resources to implement a fairly sophisticated concept like the middle school envisioned in NMSA's *This We Believe*. Even the millions of dollars that foundations invested in urban middle schools were not sufficient to make long-lasting improvements.

Who do you consider to be among the most influential leaders of the middle school movement?

I've got to go back and include junior high leaders, of course. I've already mentioned Gruhn and Douglass, William Alexander, Conrad Toepfer, Don Eichhorn, Paul George, and John Lounsbury. Ken McEwin is a really important force in middle level education these days. One significant contribution is his picking up on the work that John Swaim started: to get nationwide standards established for preparation of middle level teachers and administrators. I learned the other night that John Swaim is still on the Board of NCATE (the National Council for the Accreditation of Teacher Education). He and Ken have worked closely to get that whole standards document published by NMSA and to follow through with portfolio review. I think those guys are tremendously important. It is hard to imagine where the middle school movement would be today without John Lounsbury. Who can count all of the ways that he, in his thoughtful, gentlemanly way, has contributed to all of the things that needed to be done in middle level education. I will always be grateful for the opportunities I have had to work with John over the years.

Can you talk a little bit more about your work with John Lounsbury?

Well, in a nutshell, we kind of think alike. That shows up when we collaborate on our writing. We've done that on a number of occasions. The current issue of *Middle School Journal* has our latest collaboration. We haven't had much opportunity to sit down side by side and do it. We use e-mail, fax, and regular mail. However, when the Van Til, Vars, Lounsbury book was under way, we would get together occasionally.

Is there anything else that you would like to talk about?

Here are some more observations about leaders of the middle school movement. Conrad Toepfer was a marvelous public speaker. He could get an audience in the palm of his hand. Another one who's a stimulating speaker and who has done a lot for education is Al Arth. He was chair of the first *This We Believe* writing team. Howard Johnston also is eloquent and communicates beautifully. Howard writes very well, too, and prolifically. Howard was a student of Al Arth's so he probably got the vision from Al. Donald

Eichhorn was another marvelous gentleman. In addition to his groundbreaking book, he has made his mark as an administrator, especially his work with the Upper St. Clair Schools in Pennsylvania. His was probably the only serious effort to group middle level students by "developmental age" rather than chronological age. Most people don't know about, but it's very important. He used the results of the medical study of biological maturation conducted by Dr. Allan Drash of Children's Hospital in Pittsburgh. He used that data plus input from elementary teachers to assign kids to teams when they moved out of elementary into the Boyce Middle School. On one team most of the kids would be relatively immature; the staff knew it and made allowances for it. And then another team might be a mix. Another team might be mostly relatively mature. For years, in spite of horrendous opposition from the community and some parents, he maintained that program and proved that there are some benefits. He told me once that the community was ready to tar and feather him and ride him out of town on a rail. When he left the district, the push behind that system was gone, but Boyce Middle School was still an excellent middle level school when I visited it years later. Paul George is an excellent speaker and writer and really has been Bill Alexander's right-hand man. He has been a great contributor to the middle level education movement and has consulted with middle level educators around the world.

Have there been major debates among middle school leaders focusing on particular issues or beliefs, and if so, what have the debates been about? What was at stake? Which position won out?

We've already alluded to the junior high versus middle school debate, which was organizational. Then there was the curriculum design debate. I don't know if you were active at that time, but Paul George debated James Beane on the pros and cons of integrative curriculum. That issue has been with the group from the very earliest. The people who advocated core back during the junior high school movement had to fight the people who said, No, that will spoil the beauty of English or history or something. Some people don't even like social studies. They want history, economics, political science. This is great at the university level, perhaps, but makes no sense whatever to a ten-year-old.

I wrote in 1966 an article that, in a sense, waved a red flag. It's the only thing I ever got published in *Phi Delta Kappan*. As a matter of fact I had to "ding" on that editor's door for several years to get him to print it. Interdisciplinary teaming was being introduced as the salvation of core. I raised the question and said it in the title of my article, "Can Team Teaching Save the Core Curriculum?" There were people who were saying, "Yes, this is the way to make it really work." And I pointed out that teaming would destroy it, and it's been proven over and over again. The problem is in the logistics that interdisciplinary teams have to work with. Getting four or maybe five people to agree on anything, let alone on some of the subtleties of working with kids is a tremendous task. Then there's the scheduling bit. In other words, the mechanics of operating a group project like that leave little time or energy to develop integrative curriculum. One teacher can do it because you do that all in your head. You'd be out of your mind if you taught kids how to write a decent sentence and then ignored that when they wrote something in a history project or something like that. So, I answered that question, "No."

A more recent debate, which is going on right now (and unfortunately it's going in the wrong direction) is: What is the role of guidance or advisory or advocacy in the middle grades? I argue with Paul George on this, because he pushed the "advisory group" concept. He has wonderful ideas of what could be done with it, and some schools have very good advisory programs. But too often it is poorly implemented. Teachers who don't want it may be required to take an advisory group, whether they have any aptitude for it or not. That destroys the advisory program. I have actually sat in on advisory classes where it was obvious the kids and teacher hated each other. That's no advisory program. My argument has been to let the team decide how they will incorporate the guidance/advisory/pastoral responsibility into their work. Hopefully there may be one or two people on the team who'll say, "I like that. I'll do that piece. I'll be the advisor or the advocate for all the kids on our team. The rest of you can take field trip scheduling or contact with parents or something like that." So you divide up the responsibilities and let the people who have some aptitude or willingness to do it to carry out the advisory part. Then I think you have a possibility of making it work.

Another alternative is to have teachers work in two-person teams. The two-person team has been pushed by John Arnold and Chris Stevenson and some others because two people can work more closely together. They can get past the conflicts between their personalities and they can work together as a team in advising the kids. That may mean working with bigger groups, but that is much better than assigning a group of fifteen or fewer to some teacher they don't get along with. (Remember, a core teacher who works with the same students several hours a day can develop genuine rapport with thirty or more students.)

I think the mechanics of making an advisory program work, especially if all teachers are required to take a group, are destroying the whole concept. I worked with a committee of our Kent Public Schools in designing a middle level program for Kent's middle school back in the 1980s. The guidance counselor who was chair of our particular committee on the guidance piece actually got on the phone with some of the schools that I had worked with in the off-campus KSU Junior High/Middle School Staff Development program. I had a number of teachers and administrators from the Berea public schools outside Cleveland in one of my groups. Berea had already converted from junior highs to middle schools. So I said, "Let's go back and talk to them to see what happened to the advisory program that we talked about in this class." I remember one teacher in particular, in between all the busy things she had to do, said, "Didn't work. A kid doesn't wait until advisory period to have a spat with his girlfriend or to have a crisis come up. The team has to get on it right when it happens, and therefore, it needs to be embedded in the team." That's a tremendous insight that I've tried to publicize in some of my writing. Few people ever heard of it because if appeared in a little newsletter of the National Association of Secondary School Principals. These debates are still going on.

What have been the roles of women and minorities in the middle school movement?

Gertrude Noar, Mary Compton, and Nancy Doda were three women who stick out in my mind as advocates of the movement as a whole. Other people, like Rosalind Zapf and Myrtle Dewey Toops, were prominent in the core movement. But most of the big names in the movement, unfortunately, are men. Sherrel Bergmann is one of the finest contemporary middle level thinkers and doers. She's a marvelous workshop, consultation, or in-service leader. People don't hear about her too much. Receiving the John Lounsbury Award brought her some prominent attention. So, unfortunately, the important women of the movement have not been particularly conspicuous. That's partly an artifact of the male-dominated society that we have in this country.

What educational groups, organizations, and institutions have influenced the middle school movement? And with that, what are some examples of ways these groups influenced middle school education?

The ASCD Commission on the Emerging Adolescent Learner was an important advocacy group. It didn't last too many years, but under Connie Toepfer and Don Eichhorn, it did some marvelous work. NASSP's Middle Level Council, again with Connie Toepfer chairing that committee, I think. For a number of years it brought the middle school message to the secondary school principals of the country. National Middle School Association, of course, though it's gotten so big now that to a person like me it's lost a lot of its "flavor." But that, I guess, is inevitable when you get big enough.

Institutions: University of North Carolina and its branches. There must have been something going on there in North Carolina to make it possible for them to get the kind of state regulations and certifications that made it the model for the rest of us. University of Florida, the home base of William Alexander and Paul George, has had tremendous influence. Teachers College Columbia has been a powerhouse in education for years and was the hotbed of progressive education. It has not, in recent years, produced many big names in middle level education. I looked to that institution and Ohio State for some of the real leadership in the integrative curriculum movement. Those are the ones that occurred to me right off. They have people, and groups, and centers there that promote a model of middle level education.

I should mention National Lewis University in Wheeling and Evanston, Illinois. When it was the National College of Education it was kind of the progressive voice for education for all levels of education. It now has, believe it or not, a center for research in middle level education, but nobody ever hears about it because it's not well supported and isn't very noisy.

As middle level educators, how do you think we should respond to the current emphasis on student achievement as measured by standardized tests?
Fight it tooth and nail any way you can.

Are there lessons we still need to learn from the history of the middle school movement?

1. Watch your politics. Politics will kill you. So you need to educate your politicians.
2. Take the case for middle level education to the teachers, all teachers, not just those in the middle grades. The backbiting between elementary and middle and middle and high school and high school and college is a shame in this education profession.

The public's perception of middle schools or junior high schools has been a continuing problem from the early days of junior high. A middle level school is nicknamed "the zoo." That's where the kids go "haywire." That is where the teachers throw up their hands and let them go. Public perception of middle level education and of the kids at that level has been a problem, so we have to be better at publicity. We have to be better at getting parents on our side, getting kids on our side.

How would you characterize the current status of the middle school movement?

Like all public education, it is being eroded by unreasonable standards and unfair testing and assessment. And I honestly believe that Berliner and his co-author had it right years ago in their book *The Manufactured Crisis*. They said that the "school crisis" was a deliberate conspiracy of the big corporations and the political hacks that served them to destroy the public schools and make it easier for testing companies and test crammers and so forth to make money off the education game. So, the status of public education widely is in trouble and the middle school, as usual, is the whipping boy for a lot of this. Notice that the No Child Left Behind legislation affects children up to grade eight and that's going to hit us hard. It is already hitting us hard.

PART II

*Prominent Leaders
in Middle School Education*

6

John R. Arnold

We've got to work for smallness, and not just small classrooms. I mean small schools, small teams, small policies, small districts, small everything so that you can have relationships that allow teachers to make the decisions and implement the strategies they know they need to engage in.

Throughout Dr. John Arnold's distinguished career, he has been a strong proponent of developmentally responsive middle level programs and schools and a passionate advocate for the education and well-being of young adolescents. He has more than 45 years of experience as a teacher, principal, professor, consultant, and author. Arnold has authored and co-authored five books, including the influential *Teachers' Teaming Handbook: A Middle Level Planning Guide.* He has also written numerous journal articles and other professional publications that focus on adolescent development, exemplary middle school practices, and middle school curriculum. Most of his writing focused on the plight of the young adolescent in society and the great untapped potential that is there, on developmentally responsive curriculum, and on exemplary teaching and projects. He has served as national and international consultant to hundreds of schools, school districts,

The Legacy of Middle School Leaders, pages 93–107
Copyright © 2011 by Information Age Publishing
All rights of reproduction in any form reserved.

professional organizations, foundations, and the National Board for Professional Teaching Standards. Dr. Arnold was a consultant for children's television, focusing primarily upon developmental appropriateness and values, for 23 years. He has had long-term children's TV consultancies with Disney/ABC, Nickelodeon, Hearst Animations, and Evening Sky Productions.

Dr. Arnold received his undergraduate degree from Washington and Lee University, Lexington, Virginia, in 1957. He did extensive graduate work at Yale University Divinity School, New Haven, Connecticut (1957–1960) and at the University of Houston, Houston, Texas (1990–1962). While a chaplain intern at Rice University in 1959–1960, he helped organize Rice and Texas Southern University students in sit-ins to integrate the lunch counters in Houston. In 1979, he earned his doctorate in education from the University of Connecticut–Storrs. After teaching sixth grade in Channelview, Texas, he served as a research psychologist at the National Institutes of Health. He then decided to pursue a career in education. In 1962, accepted a position teaching fourth grade and coaching at Sidwell Friends Middle School in Washington, DC. Five years later, he was named principal of the school. In 1972, he became Director of Advisory Services for the Greater Boston Teachers Center and middle school consultant for the National Association of Independent Schools (NAIS). In 1978, Arnold taught a year at the University of New Hampshire–Durham, then accepted a position at North Carolina State University (NCSU) in Raleigh, North Carolina to initiate and develop the middle grades teacher education program. During his tenure at NCSU, Dr. Arnold was the coordinator for design and development of the Centennial Campus Magnet Middle School located on the NCSU campus. This innovative model middle school focuses on integrative curriculum, extensive student interaction with the university campus and community, the use of cutting-edge technology, and the cultural and social forces that affect young adolescent development. He retired from NCSU in 1997 after serving as professor, middle school specialist, and director of the middle grades teacher preparation program for 19 years.

Selected Contributions to Middle Level Education

- Principal, Sidwell Friends Middle School (1967–1972)
- Founding chair of the National Association of Independent Schools (NAIS) Middle School Task Force (1971–1975)
- Co-author of the first NAIS Middle School Position Paper (1975)
- First middle school consultant for NAIS (1972–1976)
- Director of Advisory Services for the Greater Boston Teacher Center (1972–1976)

- Co-developer of the North Carolina Middle Level Teacher Certification Program (1982)
- President of the North Carolina Middle School Association (1986–1987)
- Editor, co-editor *Journal of the North Carolina Middle School Association* (1988–1994)
- Received the North Carolina Middle School Association C. Kenneth McEwin Distinguished Service Award (1992)
- Board Member, NMSA (1988–1990)
- Member and co-editor NMSA Think Tank on Curriculum (1989–1993)
- Co-developer and Coordinator of Middle Grades Teacher Education Programs, North Carolina State University (1979–1997)
- Received the College of Education Outstanding Teacher Award, NCSU (1985)
- Directed Summer Middle Level Institutes for 25 years (1972–1997)

Selected Publications

Arnold, J. (1982). Rhetoric and reform in middle schools. *Phi Delta Kappan, 63*(7), 453–456.

Arnold, J. (1984, summer). Progressive education and qualitative reform. *Private School Quarterly,* 16–21.

Arnold, J. (1985). A responsive curriculum for emerging adolescents. *Middle School Journal, 16*(3), 14–18.

Arnold, J. (1987). *A celebration of teaching: 100 innovative teaching projects in North Carolina middle level schools.* Raleigh, NC: North Carolina League of Middle Level Schools.

Arnold, J. (1990). *Visions of teaching and learning: Eighty exemplary middle level projects.* Columbus, OH: National Middle School Association.

Arnold, J., & Parker, W. (1992) *Best bets: At risk programs that work in North Carolina middle level schools.* Raleigh, NC: North Carolina League of Middle Level Schools.

Arnold, J. (1993). A curriculum to empower young adolescents. *Midpoints Occasional Papers, 4*(1), 1–11.

Arnold, J. (1993). Towards a middle level curriculum rich in meaning. In T. S. Dickinson (Ed.), *Readings in middle school curriculum* (pp. 63–72). Columbus, OH: National Middle School Association.

Arnold, J., & Beal, C. (1995*) Service with a smile: Service learning programs in North Carolina middle level schools.* Raleigh, NC: North Carolina Association of Middle Level Schools.

Arnold, J. (1997). Teams and curriculum. In T. S. Dickinson & T. O. Erb (Eds.), *We gain more than we give: Teaming in middle schools* (pp. 443–463). Columbus, OH: National Middle School Association.

Arnold, J., & Stevenson, C. (1998). *Teachers' teaming handbook: A middle level planning guide.* Fort Worth, TX: Harcourt Brace College Publishers.

Arnold, J. (2001). High expectations for all. In T. O. Erb (Ed.), *This we believe... and now we must act* (pp. 28–34). Westerville, OH: National Middle School Association.

---

*John Arnold**

A lot of educators have influenced me, but surely Chris Stevenson has been the key. Chris is an original thinker who comes at things from a kid's point of view. He is the best developer of concrete curriculum projects that I know, and he is very adept at developing conceptual frameworks too. Another huge influence was Ed Yeomans. More than anyone, he was responsible for the great influence the integrated day had in the 1960s and the 1970s. Two British educators were particularly important to me. The first was Roy Illsley and the other was Charity James. Don Wells, the middle school head at Carolina Friends School, was another powerful influence. Vincent Rogers, an early, prominent open education advocate, was Chris's and my advisor at the University of Connecticut. Undoubtedly the most concrete influences on my thinking and ideas have come from the multitude of exceptional teachers I have been privileged to work with.

There are many others who have influenced me that here I can only name lest we talk all night. These include Joan Lipsitz, who I worked with occasionally at the Center for Early Adolescence. Nat French, a professor at the University of Massachusetts who worked with me on several task forces and was a wonderful mentor and father figure; Dennis Littky, the mercurial and talented principal of Shoreham-Wading River Middle School; Ross Burkhardt, a great teacher there; Sally Collier, the coordinator of the community outreach program at Sidwell Friends; Roberta Snow, the most gifted teacher I've ever known, who ended up founding Educators for Social Responsibility; Carol Pope, Pat Dalton and Candy Beale, gifted middle level colleagues at North Carolina State University; Kit Laybourne, who turned me on to getting kids to create media; and his wife Geraldine, who has done

---

* John Arnold was interviewed for the Legacy Project in June 2004.

amazing things for kids at Nickelodeon, Disney, and Oxygen and enabled my work in children's television. Later on, when I became a professor and involved with NMSA, other, more "mainline" middle school educators became friends and affected my thinking. John Lounsbury, Paul George, and Jim Beane in particular were influential.

What kinds of middle school literature did you read?

There really wasn't much middle school literature available, and most of it seemed to deal with school structure and administrative concerns. Charity James' *Young Lives at Stake* and *Beyond Customs* were notable exceptions, dealing with adolescents' needs and what types of teaching and learning they imply. I did read some of the junior high material, and of course Bill Alexander's *The Emergent Middle School*, which gave a good "big picture." What I did read a lot of was progressive and open education material. Also, I read a great deal of developmental literature about young adolescents. Joan Lipsitz' *Growing Up Forgotten* provided a treasure of research and opinion about early adolescence. Later as a professor, I read a ton of "regular" middle school literature. I'd say that Paul George's *The Exemplary Middle School*, Jim Beane's *A Middle School Curriculum: from Rhetoric to Reality*, and Chris Stevenson's *Teaching 10–14 Year Olds* and Joan Lipsitz's *Successful Schools for Young Adolescents* were the most stimulating books.

What was your primary motivation for becoming involved in middle level education?

I really got hooked on teaching and the wonder of middle level kids. I was appalled that society, and schools unfortunately, were full of negative, false stereotypes about kids—that they are irrational, hormone driven, argumentative, "crazy," etc. Sure, all kids experience puberty, but this doesn't *have* to be a time of storm and stress. Adolescents' lack of supervision, their isolation from the adult world, the lack of meaningful roles, etc. has a lot more to do with the duress many experience than do hormones. They are a minority group of sorts who need advocates to help empower them. As I was getting started, there seemed little concern about young adolescents, and junior high schools and some of the schools that called themselves middle schools weren't doing much to change their plight. I wanted to make a difference.

How would you describe the early years of the middle school movement (and we have identified those as being around the mid to late 1960s and the early 1970s)?

I think it is important to realize the "middle school movement" is not monolithic. It meant and means different things to different folks to this day.

To some, it was about grade structures and changing junior highs into middle schools. To others, it was about new curricula and methodology. To others, it was about preparing teachers. To others, it was about uplifting kids and being their advocates. To others, it was simply about doing their job in a better way. And I suspect there were many, many divergent and conflicting ideas represented. So using the term will always be ambiguous to some extent. There was a lot of excitement, and the "movement" brought much-needed attention to middle level education. Also, there were many good people involved, people who cared very deeply. On the other hand, on the national level there seemed to be quite a few big egos and a lot of posturing about who was going to "lead." There wasn't the kind of cooperation that there is today. In terms of ideas, I felt that much of what was presented on the national level was much too formulaic. The focus wasn't nearly enough on kids and their growth and learning. In particular, I think the understanding of early adolescent development was often shallow. This hampered progress.

How has the middle school concept changed since the early years of the middle school movement?

I think that our understanding deepened and filled out more. Slowly we've learned more about adolescent development. Based on experience, we have certainly derived a much better idea of teaming and how to establish good teams. We learned a lot about advisories and how difficult they are to establish. Certainly we've learned a lot of tricks about flexible block scheduling. I should add that the development of middle level teacher education programs and certification programs has been a positive force. But unfortunately, progress has occurred more in theory than in practice. I don't want to sound too negative because there are a lot of good schools, but there are tons and tons that have just hung out a shingle that says middle school and have gone right on with business as usual.

I think we've often gotten our priorities confused. In developing middle schools, there are four key questions that need to be addressed, in this order: (1) *Who?* Who are these students we are trying to educate? What are their needs, interests and abilities? This is the developmental question. (2) *What?* What do they need to know now, and are likely to need to know in the future, to meet their needs, interests, and abilities? This is the curriculum question. (3) How? What strategies and techniques shall we use to teach the content and skills that meet the students' needs, interests, and abilities? This is the methodology question. (4) *How can we structure the school experience so that it best facilitates the methods and curriculum to meet student's needs?* This is the school organization question. I don't think many schools have addressed those first three questions adequately, and in fact, they have reversed the order of the questions. They've started with and been preoccupied by the organization question. Once the organization is set, that of course limits what kinds of methods and curriculum you can develop, and then you can only hope that kids' needs will be met. Think of what gets lost, for example, in departmentalized, 50-minute periods with desks bolted to the floor and a teacher up front.

What were some of the motivations that fueled the growth of the middle school movement?

Obviously the insights of developmental psychology, though perhaps not well understood, have been significant, as have new ideas about organizing schools. Also, it was pretty obvious that junior high schools were a mess. Certainly Bill Alexander's work was influential, as was some of the early junior high work before that (some of that stuff is more radical than what you see today). I think Paul George's work has been particularly helpful in helping to institutionalize change. He has had a special knack for gauging how much change can teachers of schools realistically handle and then gearing his work that way. Also, he has been very helpful in drawing on fields outside education and relating the middle school movement to broad social issues.

What was the educational context at the time when the middle school movement began?

It was way more open than it is today. It was very clear that what was being implemented wasn't working well. Many people had felt strongly that education in general had been going downhill, that it was rigid and not meeting the needs of kids. Teachers and administrators were disgruntled. There were the Civil Rights Movement, the war in Vietnam, the war on poverty, and all kinds of social upheaval and unrest.

Absolutely crucial was the fact that we didn't have so much governmental control of education. State legislatures and congress were not nearly as involved as they are today. Testing was not nearly as widespread or intrusive. Significantly, the pendulum of change was able to move back and forth from conservative to liberal positions much more quickly than it is today, or is going to be in the future. It's very hard to change something once it becomes a law. If a problem is due simply to a trend in society, then society can correct things a little more easily. But laws are something different.

Schools and school systems were generally a lot smaller. I'm a great believer in small schools and I really don't believe much in school systems. I believe passionately in public education but I think we'd be a lot better off decentralized rather than huge school systems.

What have been some of the most significant events, incidents, or moments in middle level education and along with that, why did you select them?

Certainly Bill Alexander's original work and the follow-up of it and his work with Paul George. And Don Eichhorn's dissertation and subsequent book because it really called attention to middle level education in a way that nothing else had. Joan Lipsitz' *Growing Up Forgotten* was also very significant, documenting how young adolescents were neglected throughout society. Certainly the establishment of the National Middle School Association was essential, for it provided a focal point for the movement and established an official advocacy group. The establishment of state associations did the same on a local level. The Carnegie Corporation's *Turning Points* was a milestone because it called urgent attention to the need for middle level reform. The development of middle level teacher education programs and certification programs was a big help.

Do you have personal things that have happened in your career— personal accounts related to significant events in middle level education and your involvement in it?

In the early 1970s, I was the first middle school consultant for the National Association of Independent Schools and helped to start middle level programs in numerous schools. I also chaired an NAIS Middle School Task Force. Along with task force member Don Wells (who wrote the final draft), Nat French, Charity James, Peter Cohen, Gene Ruth, and Carol Curry, we developed the NAIS Middle School position paper, one of the first such documents anywhere. We had great fun in writing a really uncompromising statement that made clear kids' development, and not preparing them for Harvard, was what middle schools were about. It caught schools' attention and caused a lot of heated discussion.

I'd like to think that through all the consulting work, workshops, speeches, and papers I and a lot of other people you are interviewing had a significant effect in getting the word out about good middle level education and in helping teachers and administrators develop good schools. I suppose I have worked in at least a thousand schools over the years in one form or another, and led one or two summer residential institutes for each of some thirty summers. Likewise, I hope my writing has been significant. I have focused on mainly two things: the plight of the young adolescent in society and the great untapped potential that is there, and also on exemplary teaching and projects across the country and in North Carolina. As I mentioned earlier, most of what I know and have been able to accomplish is due to having had the opportunity to work with many, many outstanding teachers.

Along with Ken McEwin, John Van Hoose, Wayne Dillon and others, I helped develop the North Carolina Middle Level Teacher Certification and Licensure Program, which I believe was the first or one of the first such programs in the country. Again, the level of agreement and pleasure that we had doing something of this significance was wonderful.

I was a Board Member of NAIS during its years of growing pains, helping the Board to upgrade the state associations. I was also President of the North Carolina League of Middle Schools, one of the first state associations, and was instrumental in developing regional programs and channels of communication. I also wrote several monographs about exemplary school programs for the League.

Of course, I spent the most time as middle school coordinator at North Carolina State University. I came there in 1979 and was in charge of developing and teaching in the undergraduate and graduate teacher education programs. Next to the one at Appalachian State University that Ken McEwin developed, it was the second oldest in the state and one of the few in the country at the time.

Who or what have been some of the greatest detractors or opponents of the middle level education?

I wouldn't want to call them opponents but people who have presented obstacles. These include people who are just locked in to subject matter and disciplines in a very rigid sort of way; people who are control freaks and locked into all sorts of structural things in school; people who don't really care about kids, or if they do, don't show it very well; and people who run schools for the benefit of themselves or the convenience of teachers, to keep parents off their back. Many state politicians and bureaucrats you also can throw into the mix. Also Chester Finn and the "basics" crowd. I'm sure other people have said this, but it's absolutely essential in running good middle schools to ask and say, "Is this for the good of the kids?" If it isn't, then we don't have any business doing it. And where this is done, you have clarity of purpose and little anxiety in the school. Unfortunately, there are too few schools like this.

What are some of the mistakes that have been made during the middle school movement that we might be able to learn from today?

From my perspective, there have been a number of mistakes. First, we've never had a clear enough vision of what we want for kids. I believe we need to embody the progressive education understanding that the aim of education is the development of good people. It's who people are that counts—their character, attitudes, values, integrity. We should value approaches that give students opportunities for taking initiative and responsibility, and for developing self-understanding. We need to foster curiosity and love of learning. We need to believe that young adolescents have enormous potential, and develop environments that foster it.

Second, and related to the first mistake, we have tended to make it seem that adolescent growth and academic excellence are mutually exclusive, an either/or situation. In fact, properly understood, they are mutually reinforcing. Genuine academic excellence involves helping kids to think, to love and value learning, to become curious, to ask questions, to take initiative, etc., things the testing/accountability folks tend to ignore. This kind of academic focus can greatly foster adolescent development, especially intellectual development and the movement into formal operational thinking. It also promotes their overall development and their attempts to make sense of themselves and the world around them. Third, we have been too preoccupied with structures, procedures, administration, policy and the like. A fourth mistake is not valuing the arts nearly enough and creativity—not understanding how important they are in life and in full human development, and how they promote growth, learning and enjoyment.

Finally, one of the biggest mistakes being made today is trying to make the National Middle School Association be all things to all people. I think that as it has grown and become more institutionalized, it has become more cautious. That's the way institutions do, and alas, I think it is sort of inevitable. But I would rather see us have a focused, learner-centered stand with fewer members than be an umbrella organization for anyone/any group involved in middle schools. I would like to see NMSA be a stronger advocate for genuinely good education for kids, and to continuously focus on the items in *This We Believe*. I would also like to see the Association come out with a harder stand against standardized testing and all of the legislated stuff that has very little to do with good education.

So, who has benefited the most from the middle school movement?

People who have taken it seriously: young adolescents, teachers, administrators, and teacher educators. There has been a tremendous energy and enthusiasm in the movement, and it has done a lot of good things that have helped kids and everyone involved.

Who do you think has benefited the least from the middle school movement?

People who haven't taken it seriously—those who are involved in schools that don't care about kids' growth and development and are spinning their wheels. Also those with political agendas who think the middle school movement has been soft on academics.

Who do you consider to be among the most influential leaders of the middle school movement, and why have you selected them?

I have already discussed why the work of Bill Alexander, Paul George and Chris Stevenson has been so important. Don Eichhorn deserves mention because of his dissertation, his general character, and his work with schools. But most of all, John Lounsbury has been influential. John Lounsbury has been the patron saint whose gentle spirit, kind heart, intellect, perseverance, friendship, and just basic goodness have inspired everyone. He has been the heart of the middle school movement. Almost everyone can recount stories where he has gone out of his way to help them and to keep the faith. Jim Beane has been enormously influential too. He has surely done the seminal work and been the chief proponent for integrative learning. Moreover, his understanding that students can best learn about democratic processes by being a part of them and his subsequent advocacy for democratic classrooms are very significant also. There are so many other people—Gordon Vars, Howard Johnston, Ken McEwin—especially for his work in teacher education— Nancy Doda, Tom Gatewood, Tom Dickinson, Tom Erb, John Van Hoose, Sue and John Swaim. I'm sure I'm leaving out a lot of people. Actually, the list of Lounsbury Award Winners would provide a fairly inclusive list of movement leaders.

What have been the major debates among middle school leaders focusing on particular issues or beliefs and related to that, what was at stake and which position won out?

One obvious one involves what grades should be in a middle level school. Grades 6–8 certainly won out over 7–9 junior highs, and that's a plus. Personally, I'm not at all convinced grades 6–8 is better than 5–8, because the latter gives you four years to work with kids. The role of testing is an ongoing one, but I think the protesters are winning this one without much of a real battle. They have the power of the government behind them, and there aren't many people willing to take them on in a serious manner. So sad.

The role of pull-out, isolated program gifted education is another controversial issue. Paul and others have fought the good fight on this one, but I think the pull-out folks are in command. However, with funds so limited, it doesn't seem to be as big an issue as it once was. The status and role of interdisciplinary/integrated curriculum has always been debated, but in practice, unfortunately, I don't think there has ever been a great deal of it.

**What are some examples of ways the middle school movement
has affected American education?**

Certainly it has caused education to focus more on young adolescents and to take their education more seriously. I think it's had a significant effect on interdisciplinary curriculum development, and also on scheduling practices. Its attempts to create smallness out of bigness have influenced the high school house system. It has given a big boost to advisories. The camaraderie and the spirit the middle school movement has engendered I think have spill-over effects to American education in general. It has surely affected clearly the lives of the kids, teachers, and professors involved.

**What education groups, organizations, and institutions have
influenced the middle school movement; and, as you speak about
those, what are some examples of ways that they have influenced
middle school education?**

Obviously NMSA because it's been the rallying point. It has pulled people together. Its publications and services have provided a communication network. Its conferences and conventions were especially important in the early years because that is where people saw each other and could share ideas. The state associations have helped in the same way. NASSP and ASCD have been especially helpful in their publications. I've already mentioned The Carnegie Corporation for their *Turning Points,* a really seminal work that gave status and direction to middle schools. Carnegie also gave birth to the National Board for Professional Teaching standards. The Ford Foundation used to put out a lot of good middle level literature, especially Joan Lipsitz's book. And her already-mentioned services and publications at the Center for Early Adolescence have done a lot of good things. I think states that have developed middle school certification have been very important.

**That might actually lead to the next question. Have particular
legislative actions significantly influenced the middle school
movement at the state and/or national level?**

Quite obviously end-of-year testing programs, No Child Left Behind, the general emphasis on business accountability models that so many legislators feel are appropriate have for the most part had a detrimental effect on education. I do think that they have made schools more serious and accountable for the progress of poor and minority students. That's something highly important, but I think it could have been done in other, better ways. I'm old enough to remember the day when a school could pretty much do what it wanted. And that wasn't all a bowl of cherries either, because you sometimes had a good ole boys club with a principal who would hire and fire randomly, plus a lot of racism and sexism. We need decentralizing strategies that give schools autonomy but at the same time hold them accountable.

State government's advocacy for middle school certification, already mentioned, has surely had a positive effect. There are a number of federal policies that over the years have affected all levels of education significantly. The government-sponsored summer institutes during the Great Society Years, the Teach for America programs are two that readily come to mind.

What are some ways the middle school movement has influenced middle level curriculum and instruction?

I hope it has made it more responsive to the interests of young adolescents. It's certainly boosted interdisciplinary efforts. (As an aside, I wish this weren't thought of so exclusively as a team function. Learning within discrete disciplines, if done well, has a huge interdisciplinary component.) I think by presenting a lot of descriptive material the movement has enabled teachers to see what other teachers are doing. It has provided a forum for teacher sharing, and a lot more could be done with this. And I think state associations could do more by getting teachers together in local communities, not just on a state level, into teacher sharing groups. I also believe the middle school movement has helped people understand somewhat how school structure and curriculum interface: e.g., how knowledge gained in advisories can help tailor curriculum to kids' needs, or how teaming can facilitate curriculum.

Having said that, I think curriculum, outside of the interdisciplinary emphasis, has been one of the most neglected things in the middle school movement. Good curriculum is not about finding some package of the right material. No teacher ever got to be a great one by using a textbook publisher's curriculum guide. Developing meaningful curriculum involves being a good observer and focusing on kids. You never find a really good teacher who isn't a keen observer of kids, who really listens to them and understands. I'm not talking here about their home life or their social life. I'm talking about observing for clues to curriculum, finding at what level kids are functioning, what misunderstanding they are harboring, what piques their interest and curiosity. You have to be an enormously keen observer and create an environment where you can do this observing. We have been too content with direct teaching, ignoring research that shows higher level thinking, problem solving, divergent thinking are fostered much more by indirect teaching methods.

As middle level educators, how do you think we should respond to the current emphasis on student achievement as measured by standardized tests?

Before tackling the intent of that question, I think it important to say that it is an abomination that we use the word *achievement* to describe kids' progress. How did we ever get there? I've used it, and people have used it all along. But we are talking about kids *learning*, we're talking about people *understanding* the world. We're talking about mysteries and marvel and excitement and what makes you a good human being and how you relate to others. That's what education is about. Achievement is about how fast you can run or some honor you won. When we equate true learning with achievement, we are easy prey for the testers.

Simply put, I think we should fight this current emphasis on testing tooth and nail, and constantly—through speeches, articles, books, newspaper articles and letters to the editor, school board meetings, testimonies before government agencies, etc. We should provide an historical perspective, pointing out what real learning is about, the problems and weaknesses of the current approach, and the harm it causes. We need to make clear what the proper role of testing is—what it can do well and what it can't—and offer alternatives.

What are the lessons that we still need to learn from the history of the middle school movement?

Change is not easy. It takes a long time and a lot of perseverance. There are huge resistances out there. It requires a lot of courage and risk taking. We live in a country that despite all its rhetoric doesn't genuinely care enough about children of any age, especially about young adolescents. We need a holistic approach and to collaborate more with other segments of society. You can't look at middle level education without looking at health care and many other issues that affect the lives of kids. Look at parenting and lack of supervision. We've got to keep fighting and to fight harder; we've got to be more politically savvy, and to have more political influence. We need to promote smallness and avoid bureaucracies. I realize that it's very hard for associations to speak out because they may get their money cut off. People withdraw and they lose memberships. It may be better to be smaller and have really committed people than to have a big group who want to belong to something.

What particular efforts need to be made to help insure the future success of the middle school movement and middle level education?

I guess it's all implied in what I said. I think clearly we've got to have renewed focus on kids and a deeper understanding of what that entails. There is a lot written, but it isn't taken seriously on a grassroots level. It's not about getting teachers to know Piaget's Stages or Kohlberg's levels or whatever, but about being deeply interested and observant of kids' intellectual development, kids' moral development, kids' social development, and to develop strategies to help them to grow in those areas. That's always been the biggest issue. If you are doing well you are really empowering kids. There are so many clichés about teaching students to be self-learners, concerned citizens, and so on. They are on target but they are not often taken seriously; people don't really understand what they mean. It's not always explained the right way in classes or in books so it goes by the wayside too often. We've got to work for smallness, and not just small classrooms. I mean small schools, small teams, small policies, small districts, small everything so that you can have relationships that allow teachers to make the decisions and implement the strategies they know they need to engage in.

7

Alfred A. Arth

> *It's interesting, in my career, how many times I've been asked to stand up in front of a group and explain middle school philosophy. I have never heard anybody at any conference be asked to stand up and explain elementary philosophy. When's the last time you ever heard that? When's the last time you heard anybody explain high school philosophy?*

Dr. Alfred A. Arth has carried the message of the importance of developmentally responsive middle schools to a wide range of audiences since the beginning of the middle school movement. His courage to fight for the education and well being of young adolescents and those who teach them and serve them in other ways is extraordinary and long-standing. In the early days of the middle school movement, Arth distinguished himself as one who carried the new middle school message to the byways and highways. He spoke and presented from Alaska to New England, from Saskatchewan to Texas, and nearly everywhere in between, as he gave of his time to spread the fledgling middle school idea. Dr. Arth's role as a mentor is noteworthy. His list of more than 100 publications is particularly noticeable, for his publications almost always involve one or two co-authors, indicative of his

The Legacy of Middle School Leaders, pages 109–121
Copyright © 2011 by Information Age Publishing
All rights of reproduction in any form reserved.

penchant for serving as a mentor, encourager, and collaborator. He has probably assisted more undergraduate and graduate students and practicing educators in becoming active professionals in the middle school cause than anyone else.

Dr. Arth earned his undergraduate and master's degrees from Paterson State Teachers College, Wayne, New Jersey. After teaching sixth grade in Ridgewood, New Jersey, he earned his doctorate in education at the University of Oklahoma, Norman, in 1968, and accepted a position teaching at the University of Virginia, Charlottesville. Four year later, he moved to the University of Wyoming, Laramie, where he pioneered the development of undergraduate and graduate middle-level teacher education programs. After 16 successful years at the University of Wyoming, Dr. Arth became a professor at the University of Nebraska, Lincoln. There, over the next 18 years he taught, was Coordinator of the Middle Level Teacher Education, and developed one of the first doctoral level middle school programs in the United States. He is currently a Professor of Education at York College, York, Nebraska. Arth has been active professionally, primarily with National Middle School Association (NMSA), National Association of Secondary School Principals (NASSP), and Association for Supervision and Curriculum Development (ASCD). Annual conferences of these associations regularly feature presentations organized by Arth and featuring a number of well-qualified practitioners. Fun-loving but serious about the mission of the middle school, Dr. Arth has touched many thousands of middle level educators in all parts of the nation.

Selected Accomplishments and Contributions to Middle Level Education

- Chaired the committee that wrote the first edition of the NMSA publication *This We Believe* (1982)
- A founding member of NASSP's Middle Level Council (1981–1995)
- Received the Distinguished Professional Service Award, NASSP (1981–1995)
- NMSA Board of Trustees member (1988–1989)
- Chaired a national committee for NMSA (1988)
- Received the NASSP Gruhn-Long-Melton Award for distinguished service and leadership in improving middle level education (1997)

- Co-authored *Agenda for Excellence at the Middle Level* for the NASSP (1998)
- Received the John H. Lounsbury Distinguished Service Award from NMSA (2007)
- Received the Network Publication Award: Middle Grades Network, Association for Supervision and Curriculum Development (2007)
- Serves as a member of the *Research in Middle Level Education* Editorial Board, NMSA
- Consultant to Native American tribes in Nebraska

Selected Publications

Arth, A. A. (1971). Decoding the profile of the middle years educator. *Transescence: The Journal on Emerging Adolescent Education, 5*(5), 27–30.

Arth, A. A., & Lounsbury, J. H. (Eds.). (1981). *The middle school primer.* Laramie, WY: University of Wyoming Press.

Arth, A. A. (1981). Renewing the momentum of middle school education. *Education Digest, 46*(9), 38–41.

Arth, A. A. (1984). Selecting appropriate instructional strategies. In J. H. Lounsbury (Ed.), *Perspectives: Middle school education, 1964–1984* (pp. 79–86). Columbus, OH: National Middle School Association.

Arth, A. A., Lounsbury, J. H., Toepfer, C. F., & Melton, G. A. (1987). *Developing a mission statement for the middle level school.* Reston, VA: National Association of Secondary School Principals.

Hornbeck, D. W., & Arth, A. A. (1991). 1990s: Challenge of the century for middle level educators. *NASSP Bulletin, 75*(536), 94–100.

Arth, A. A., Lounsbury, J. H., McEwin, C. K., & Swaim, J. H. (1995). *Middle level teachers: Portraits of excellence.* Columbus, OH: National Middle School Association and Reston, VA: National Association for Secondary School Principals.

Arth, A. A., & Wheeler, K. B. (2005, September). Guidelines for a middle level school visit. *Principal Leadership, 6*(1)32–35. Retrieved from http://www.principals.org/Portals/0/Content/52393.pdf.

Arth, A. A. (2010). Supporting the responsibility of middle school students to constantly ask why. *ASCD Middle Grades Network Newsletter, 7*(2), 1–3.

Arth, A. A., (2010). Working with middle grades students to explore the future. *ASCD Middle Grades Network Newsletter, 7*(3), 1–3.

---

*Alfred A. Arth**

There were two individuals who had major influences on me. One was Don Eichhorn. I started going to Association for Supervision and Curriculum Development (ASCD) and National Middle School Association (NMSA) conferences. I happened to be there when NMSA was created out of the Midwest Middle School Association. Don Eichhorn started presenting and I asked to talk to him. He was the person everybody should have had the chance to meet. And then right after Don Eichhorn was Conrad Toepfer. Conrad Toepfer was also somebody who would sit and talk with you. They introduced me to people, they took me around. Tom Gatewood was writing then. I also got to meet Gordon Vars.

What kinds of middle school literature did you read?

There wasn't anything but *Dissemination Services*. When Eichhorn's middle school book came out, I read it. Then I read Alexander's book on middle school. Then there was Hansen and Hearn who had a middle school book. I suppose I read every middle school book that came out for five or six years. I read a lot of Toepfer's material. I published in *Dissemination Services, Middle School Journal,* and other places. And I started putting pieces together. But I was mostly influenced by Eichhorn's writings. He argued the program had to support student development, and when this occurred they would learn.

Are there particular theorists (or theories) or writings that have influenced your educational thought?

I would say that I was close enough to see the middle school philosophy evolve. In fact some people got nervous because they called it a movement, and that's close to some religious thing, but the theory that we had was that there would be programs that met the special needs of the 10-to-14-year-olds. I looked back at my own teaching career, and I looked at things that worked for me. And I interviewed presenters and when I'd go to sessions and present I'd try and stay later and talk with the people. And we were saying the same thing. I mean middle school people that hadn't met before. It was radical to put them under the same roof at a middle school conference. It was a brand new idea in the 1970s. Middle schools became the caring schools in the nation and that spread. So I was influenced and happened to

---

* Alfred Arth was interviewed for the Legacy Project in November 2004.

be lucky enough to be early enough in this middle school movement when the whole idea was coming together. I was not the first person, but I did get mentored by powerful people who were the first people.

So that's what I believe came from talking to people at the grassroots level; somebody said middle school is the only educational program that has come from the grassroots. That's not totally true because people like Alexander talked about theory and Eichhorn and Toepfer wrote about the possibilities. Paul George later did some initial research and found out that when you named a school a middle school you finally gave identity to teachers, because before that they were upper elementary or lower high school teachers. So all of that drew me in and I found it exciting and I found it highly rewarding, that this thing kept snowballing.

What is your primary motivation for continuing involvement in middle school education?

Teachers who don't care! They shouldn't be there. I get emotional. They were teaching and ruining children and they didn't know it, and getting paid for it. That's why I got into it. I figured that we weren't turning out many people in my small teacher education program in Wyoming, but with my writings and my visitations, I could produce teachers who gave a damn. My goal is to educate middle school teachers, to support teachers. And get rid of people who shouldn't be in there who are hurting young adolescents. So that's my drive. What is motivating me now is excellent middle school teachers. Finding the ones that are out there and telling them how good they are. And producing more good middle school teachers.

How would you describe the early years of middle school education?

How would I talk about the history of middle level education? It was like a circus. It just kept getting bigger and bigger. It was grassroots. One of the major situations happened in 1981. John Swaim was elected president of the National Middle School Association. And John Swaim was an independent thinker. He went before the group (NMSA) and said, we've got a problem. We started in 1974, it's now 1981, and we've never defined middle school. For seven years there have been people in the United States who want to do middle school, but we have no definition. So he commissioned a writing group. And I happened to be lucky enough to be on that commission. We wrote *This We Believe*, which included ten essential principles of middle level education. To this day I understand it's the best seller NMSA has ever had. And so that was the first time in the history of the United States that middle school education had ever been clearly defined.

In 1985 the National Association of Secondary School Principals found out that principals didn't know anything about middle school. Publications started coming out all over the place. University professors who were teaching in master's programs found something new that they could put in their teaching. And teachers started learning about middle school, and when they learned about middle school, they liked it and started talking about it in their schools. They wanted in-service programs, support systems, and a chance to talk about some of these ideas.

And the thing that caught on is teaming. As soon as teachers were allowed to work with each other they jumped on it. Because they were coming out of grades 7, 8, 9 departmentalization that said you just line up with the people in your academic area and you don't need to talk to other people. Well middle school people were sitting there. They were closet middle school people, let's call them that. And all of a sudden they found out they could work with other teachers. And that just exploded into teaming.

Then NASSP steps in and George Melton, who was the deputy executive director of NASSP, wants to get writers because good principals are not always good writers. And George liked Conrad Toepfer. He heard Conrad Toepfer speak, and he said this is one really powerful guy. I want him to chair a council. We are going to call it the Middle Level Council. And he said to Toepfer, "Toepfer who is the other person you want?" Toepfer said, "Eichhorn." At that time Don Eichhorn had some health problems so he had to turn it down. So he said who else. And he said, "Okay, can we get Lounsbury to work with us?" And Lounsbury said, "Sure." And at the same time that Lounsbury and Toepfer got together and said, "Who is this guy out west?" Let's go see what Arth has got. And I was invited in. Then we invited Howard Johnston. And Johnston came in and it was the four of us. It was called the Middle Level Council. And then for almost 15 years we worked for NASSP and NMSA and then ASCD putting together publications. We wrote one of NASSP's top sellers, *An Agenda for Excellence at the Middle Level.*

The final thing, in my estimation, that lit up middle school was 1989 when Carnegie published *Turning Points.* Because that said, not only is early adolescence an area, but it is an area that is critical in the development of the human being. Those three things tied together put middle school on a rocket path into development, acceptance, and progress. And so they were very important things that happened. And I was privileged to be in on two of the three. And the third one, I will just make a point, if you read *Turning Points,* it was extremely well written, but go to the section on teacher certification. The original book, in essence, said, teach everybody arts and science then give them a degree in elementary or give them a degree in high school and then once they are out teaching let them earn a middle school endorsement. Howard Johnston, John Lounsbury, Conrad Toepfer, George Melton, and I read that and said if this goes through, this will kill us because what they are saying is there is no specific middle school teacher education. David Hornbeck was the major author of *Turning Points*. There was a session going where he was speaking. I can't even remember how we came about but we cornered him. And we said to him we were reading pre-drafts and if you let this go through like this and you're not going to get your middle schools because you are saying that middle school is not important enough to have special teacher education programs—special middle level teacher training. And so he listened to us. And we said you've got to do something. And so if you read that book you'll see it goes smoothly and all of a sudden you get to teacher certification and he literally wrote that section at the 11th hour. And he put in there that there needed to be special teacher education programs for middle level teachers.

Hornbeck then got pummeled by the Holmes group. The Holmes group said we don't need teacher education. And the Holmes group was a bunch of deans and presidents that had in mind getting rid of teacher education. Make it arts and sciences. Carnegie Corporation was a part of the Holmes group. And here comes this report saying we need another teacher education program. So Hornbeck got slapped around until about nine months after the publication came out and all of a sudden universities started saying, "Hey, we better start setting up middle level teacher education programs." But that's one of those things in history. Since then, by the way, the Holmes group has done a turn-around and said we need strong teacher education programs. But that was a critical factor in our history. And then we moved on from there, that was 1989. *Turning Points 2000* was written again. Right now there is a book sitting out here that we have to pay attention to and it's called *Breaking Ranks*. It's coming out of NASSP. It has a description of a modern high school. I heard Ernest Boyer speak about a year before that book was written. He said that if the high schools do not look more like the middle schools they were going to cease to exist.

How has the middle school concept changed since the early years of the middle school movement?

The concept has changed because it has become commercialized. Eichhorn, Alexander wanted the academics, the curriculum. Eichhorn pushed the humanist. The two of them made a framework. Most of us could work inside of that. I didn't totally buy Alexander's theory. I bought almost everything of Eichhorn but the two of them were buttresses. They held the idea together. Again listening to Toepfer speak about curricular activities and listening to Lounsbury speak about the human philosophy. And people like Ken McEwin saying that this makes sense, this makes sense in what we're doing. Ken McEwin was the first one, by the way, to ever want to move into really teacher education at the middle school level and push it and push it to the point where people were just saying "oh yeah," but he knew it was the right thing to do. So they built that canopy and then everything evolved under that.

And now that's not there anymore. I don't see it as being a point we're in despair right now. I see some people out there that have a chance to be influential people but I don't see enough people standing up ready to stand for that special something. That's redundant but anyway, there aren't enough people who are willing like the original people to stand up and say, "This is what we believe, this is what we think. If you don't like it, come and challenge us."

How were decisions about the directions taken by middle school movement made?

In the beginning they were made because we had a lot to say and a lot of us said things. And that's the thing I guess I was indicating before. There are not enough people standing up and saying things right now. And back then people could choose. You like what Jim Beane was saying, then you read what Jim Beane had. You liked what Conrad Toepfer was saying, you read that. You liked what Ken McEwin was saying, you became a Ken McEwin groupie for a couple of weeks. And then you read somebody else's stuff. That's not happening now. And so the movement at that time had direction that was almost like a kaleidoscope. It was all coming together, these ideas, these pictures, and people could pick their way through people who were saying noteworthy things. And now it's got a direction but I'm not sure how it's decided. I really don't know.

Who or what have been some of the greatest detractors or opponents of middle school education?

Ignorance. John Lounsbury said some time ago, we were presenting somewhere on a panel, that the biggest problem we've got is "ignorance." People do not know what we are. And that's why the good middle school teacher needs to be able to be educated as a good middle school teacher, but they've also got to help the public understand what we do and that we are one of the best kept secrets in the world. We have the noisiest building in town. We have kids who skateboard through the mall and scare the daylights out of the elderly. And yet inside of that aura is the next congressman, the next person who votes yes on equal housing. *Turning Points* has one major mission for us. They wanted "intellectually reflective students." Can you see if we could do that? In middle school, that's our target—intellectually reflective students. Our teachers can do that if we give them support. If we let them teach the way they know they have to with a kid that they know and want to be with. But intellectually reflective, that's the key.

What are some of the mistakes that have been made during the middle school movement that we might be able to learn from today?

We didn't listen enough to teachers. We listened to them but not enough. There's a whole series of learning modality situations and one is that people learn by talking with each other, they learn by reading, they learn by sitting alone and thinking, they learn by hands-on. The strongest learning modalities I can find in interviewing over 5,000 middle school teachers is they want to learn by talking to others. And they want to learn secondly by reading. And then working alone is not part of what they want to do and sitting alone is not part of what they want. We need to adjust the way we work with middle school teachers so we let them have more time to talk with each other to exchange ideas. That's a mistake we've made. We also have not involved enough middle school administrators.

Who has benefited the most from the middle school movement?

Teachers. I believe strongly in the teacher. I believe strongly in the way teachers teach and what the teachers think. What the teachers believe, that's middle school. You can put me in any building you want. I'm not even worried about that. You just give me the teachers, I'll teach anywhere. You give me teachers who know how to teach, want to teach, are effective, and then put me anywhere.

Who has benefited the least from the middle school movement?

I'm going to take two groups. One, the parents we haven't talked to. They have benefited the least. They have sent their children to us, they trusted us, but we haven't stayed in touch with them. We haven't gone to them. And the other group is the special needs students. Middle school has never seen them as a serious concern. And year after year, I've asked, "Take a look at that conference book and run your finger down the number of special education sessions we offer." This is the second biggest problem I have in my program. The first is to try and get teachers, undergraduates to work with the community. And the second one is to be able to give them enough special education training that they can succeed in classrooms they have never seen before.

**Have there been major debates among middle school leaders
focusing on particular issues or beliefs?**

I think the debates have been about teaming. I think that has been
good. They have been healthy debates. Who's won? I think it was a team
that was supposed to be two people, four people. Those have been good
academic debates. Debates have been about scheduling—block scheduling. One of the debates has been about certification in teaching. I think
we have won because of people like Ken McEwin. We have won as to what
is a well-trained middle level teacher. I think there have been some strong
debates about whether or not middle school should exist. We seem to have
won that. It is now, how do we go back and make it strong?

We have been challenged by the K–8 thing and I think the K–8 thing is
being amply responded to now. Again my argument is I don't care if you are
K–8. Take a look at why you want to be K–8. Is it because you have one less
building to heat? Okay, I can buy that because at the very beginning some
middle schools were created in old high school buildings when new high
schools were built. Hey, we have a building. What are we going to do with it?
I don't know? Let's make it a middle school. They took a high school building and it became a middle school. And so that was it.

**What are some examples of ways the middle school movement
has affected American education?**

I think the whole fact that people can use the word middle school and
it stands for a different level, that's a major, major positive situation. We use
the term now and it stands for something, it stands for a different program.
We've only been around for roughly 40 years for heaven's sake. It's a breakthrough, it's a fantastic breakthrough, it says that there are three levels.
Those things alone are major, major in what's happening in the nation, and
what we've done.

**Have particular legislative actions significantly influenced the
middle school movement at the state or national level?**

Absolutely, the fight that's going on now in some states to get middle
school endorsements. I was very fortunate, when I came to Wyoming there
was nothing, zip, zero. I walked in on an empty slate, and I started creating
a middle school endorsement, and then certification. I hear horror stories,
where states are so close to having middle school endorsements and then
the legislators back off. They're frustrated, and they run back and they try
again. Sherrel Bergmann is one these people who have fought and fought
for Illinois to get a middle level teacher endorsement. They get it partially,
then they lose and she keeps coming back with constant effort. I was very

fortunate in Nebraska, I walked in, and there was nothing there. I could fight from the very beginning and we now have a grades 4–9 teacher certification.

What are some ways the middle school movement has influenced middle level curriculum and instruction?

I think the best example is here. Go downstairs and walk through any National Middle School Association convention in the past four to six years. There are materials for middle school kids. There were none when we first started. There are materials, there are programs, there are people recognizing that teachers need separate involvement with materials, it's been a heavy influence on the curriculum. Then we still have the fight, "What is good curriculum?" That's got to be debated. What is good curriculum for middle school kids? Bottom line in my estimation is that it is designed by the teachers and they can use the materials. That's where good curriculum comes from. Now, do you need certain standards that you have to go with? I have no problems with state and national standards, I truly don't. I have a problem with testing fourth grade and eighth grade for the sake of international competition. You give me a national standard and I'll work it into my program. The only thing is, how far away is a national curriculum, since we have national testing? It is just around the corner. And do we want that in the United States? I don't think so. So I have no problem with having certain things that have to be taught. Sometimes that may mean that curriculum is different in one region of the country over another. Yet you still have the same outcome; you have literate students.

Are there lessons we still need to learn from the history of the middle school movement?

We have to talk more to each other; we have got to get to the community. We have got to get our teacher trainees to get to the community; we have to get middle schools further into the community. The lesson we've got to learn is we must keep pushing teachers to work with the community. Also the other lesson is we've got to look at the materials that are now being sold into the middle school programs; do they fit what the middle school mission is about? Learning about information? Learning how to learn?

How would you characterize the current status of the middle school education?

I think it's in a pause. We're pausing. We've been beaten on the head, but we have enough people coming back. We have people that are finally starting to fight back. I think we are in a neutral gear. We are ready to pull into first gear and start moving ahead again, second gear maybe. I think we have good reason to move on. I think that there is enough confusion to warrant the movement now. There are enough teachers walking around saying, "What the heck is a middle school?" We get enough of those confused people all of a sudden we are going to realize that regional conferences are good again, local. By the way, when you have a regional conference right now what do you do? You teach math. You teach science. You don't teach middle school anymore. I don't hear people even putting it on the agenda. "We're going to talk about middle school." I don't hear that. I hear that this is a math session, this is a science session, and this is how you can raise scores. Eventually, I don't think it's going to be too long, we are going to have teachers saying, "How can we get these kids to learn better?" And that's what middle school does. Well, what are we supposed to do? They are asking right now in small numbers, but I think they are going to start asking across the nation.

Are there particular efforts that need to be made to help ensure the future success of the middle school education?

Yes, we were talking during the break about having sessions where people can talk to each other. I think the National Middle School Association has to look for open forums. We need more of teachers talking to teachers. We need to have the open discussions. We need people disagreeing honestly in public. We need to ask, why can't kids read? I thought every kid can learn. So that's a whole bunch of things that this place (NMSA conference) can do. But it has to listen to the people, and it has to have a direction. The direction has got to be middle school. We pretty much agree about what that is. Supporting young adolescents, continuing learning, challenging all three levels: reluctant learners, average learners, superior learners. NMSA also needs to bring together all the organizations that care about the young adolescents and get them to work more closely together.

Are there any other comments you would like to make that you have not been asked about in this interview?

Yes, maybe two. One, I think this is a fantastic idea, when I first heard about it some few months ago, I said, "This is all I need." I think this is something that has to be done for posterity. I think you need to hear the people; I think you need to hear what they are saying. You have to hear what the people aren't saying. I think this is an excellent endeavor, I think it's something you can be proud of.

The other thing I wanted to say is that middle school came about and has survived because it is right. And anytime I have been attacked, I've always gone back on that. I fought in two institutions to get middle school teacher education programs in. I succeeded in both, but one when I left it, the opposing factors got it back to a two-class endorsement instead of a certification. I literally fight every week to keep the middle school program alive in Nebraska, even though my biggest allies are administrators and teachers out in the field.

So middle school started, has survived, and will survive because it is right. It is philosophically right; it has people who teach correctly. And these are all moral judgments on my part. And it makes kids come out better than they came in, and for that reason, it will succeed and will go on. It may go more rapidly later, but it will succeed. It has a future; it has a positive future. It will not be wiped out. This K–8 movement will not wipe it out. There are too many holes in the K–8 movement. One of them is a glaring financial reason to shifting to K–8, so that's the second thing I wanted to say. All in all what I have talked about to this point is because it's the right thing to do with the right people doing it and the right kids and parents who trust us because we do something special.

8

James A. Beane

Teachers ought to be at the very center of whatever stories are told about the middle school idea. Their work towers over what the rest of us have done.

Widely recognized as an expert on middle level curriculum, Dr. James A. Beane is an influential leader and authority in middle level education. He is a passionate advocate for democratic schools and an integrative curriculum model that promotes personal and social integration through the organization of curriculum around significant problems and issues collaboratively identified by teachers and young adolescents. His negotiated curriculum model uses disciplines of knowledge as organic sources for addressing those issues and problems as well as authentic intellectual projects. Beane is author of more than 200 journal articles, book chapters, books, and other professional publications including his classic book, *A Middle School Curriculum: From Rhetoric to Reality*. He has also spoken at numerous international, national, and state conferences and consulted for educational projects in the United States and elsewhere.

The Legacy of Middle School Leaders, pages 123–147
Copyright © 2011 by Information Age Publishing
All rights of reproduction in any form reserved.

Dr. Beane received his undergraduate degree in English in 1966 from the State University of New York, Buffalo. After teaching in the Amherst, New York Public Schools for three years, he worked at the state education level from 1971 to 1973. During this time period, he completed his doctorate in curriculum development at SUNY, Buffalo, under his major professor, Dr. Conrad Toepfer. While working on his doctorate, Beane's study of the works of early progressive educators was instrumental in shaping his beliefs about democratic schools and curriculum integration. In 1973, he joined the faculty of St. Bonaventure University and became chair of the Department of Administration, Supervision, and Curriculum in 1976. In 1989, he accepted a position in the Interdisciplinary Studies Program at the National College of Education, National-Louis University (NLU), where he was instrumental in planning the Middle Level Curriculum Center. While at NLU, Beane devoted considerable time in classrooms working alongside teachers using democratic and integrative approaches. From 2004 until his retirement in 2007, he also served as a school reform coach at Sherman Middle School in Madison, Wisconsin.

Selected Accomplishments and Contributions to Middle Level Education

- Received the Distinguished Alumni Award from the Graduate School of Education, SUNY Buffalo (1996)
- Received the James E. Stoltenberg Award from the Wisconsin Association for Middle Level Education (1996)
- Received the University Faculty Award for Professional Excellence, St. Bonaventure University, Bonaventure, New York (1987)
- Received the John H. Lounsbury Distinguished Service Award from NMSA (1997)
- Served on the Publications Committee and Lounsbury Award Committee for the NMSA
- Co-edited *Dissemination Services on the Middle Grades*, Educational Leadership Institute
- Served on the Board of Directors of the National Association for Core Curriculum

Selected Publications

Beane, J. A., & Lipka, R. P. (1984). *Self-concept, self-esteem, and the curriculum.* New York: Teachers College Press.

Beane, J. A., & Lipka, R. P. (1986). *When kids come first: Enhancing self-esteem.* Columbus, OH: National Middle School Association.

Beane, J. A., Toepfer, C. T., & Alessi, S. J. (1986). *Curriculum planning and development.* Newton, MA: Allyn & Bacon.

Beane, J. A. (1990). *Affect in the curriculum: Toward democracy, dignity, and diversity.* New York: Teachers College Press.

Beane, J. A. (1990, 1993). *A middle school curriculum: From rhetoric to reality.* Columbus, OH: National Middle School Association.

Beane, J. A. (Ed.). (1995). *Toward a coherent curriculum: The 1995 ASCD yearbook.* Alexandria, VA: Association for Supervision and Curriculum Development.

Apple, M. W., & Beane, J. A. (1995). *Democratic schools.* Alexandria, VA: Association for Supervision and Curriculum Development.

Beane, J. A. (1997). *Curriculum integration: Designing the core of democratic education.* New York: Teachers College Press.

Beane, J. A., & Brodhagen, B. L. (2001). Teaching in middle schools. In V. Richardson (Ed.), *Handbook on research on teaching* (4th ed., pp. 1157–1174). Washington, DC: American Educational Research Foundation.

Beane, J. A. (2005). *A reason to teach: Creating classrooms of dignity and hope.* Portsmouth, NH: Heinemann.

---

*James A. Beane**

I was a pure English Literature major, with the great hope of being an English teacher. My grades in college were not that good. I had no education courses so I applied to get into the English Education Department at the University of Buffalo. They turned me down but told me if I went upstairs in the building and talked to Connie Toepfer, that he had some kind of program for people like me who wanted to be teachers. And if he would let me into his program, I could take a few courses with them and get my full certification. So I went upstairs and interviewed with Connie on a summer afternoon in 1966. After about five minutes he told me I was in the program, and he placed me at a junior high school outside of Buffalo, New York, as a student teacher. Connie was my master's degree advisor. He was my student teaching supervisor and brought me along into the middle school business, which was just getting started then.

---

* James Beane was interviewed for the Legacy Project in November 2004.

What or who were your main influences?

I come out of the general curriculum field which I think was true of a lot of people who have worked in middle level education over the years. For example, Bill Alexander was a general curriculum person as were Connie and Gordon Vars. The early junior high school people were also out of the general curriculum field, but a lot of them aimed their work toward the middle level. So, I was influenced by two groups. One was the great mid-century progressives: people like John Dewey, Harold Rugg, and Louis Raths, who originated values clarification. I would say also that Paulo Freire, the Brazilian educator who wrote *Pedagogy of the Oppressed* had a profound effect on me. I was very interested too in Kozol, Kohl, all the subversives in the 1960s and early 1970s. So that group was very influential as were L. Thomas Hopkins and Harold Rugg. I was influenced by Gertrude Noar, the great junior high school curriculum person. I was certainly influenced by L. Thomas Hopkins, who was the major figure in the field of curriculum integration in the mid-century Progressive Movement. So people like that and lots of general curriculum people who were interested in democratic education were very influential. And then, since I was in on the start of the middle school movement, I was influenced by Connie enormously. But also I knew Gordon Vars in the 1960s. I knew about the core curriculum. I had been in a junior high school that had a problem-centered core program. So I was very interested in that concept. I was influenced by Bill Alexander to some extent. And I knew Don Eichhorn pretty well. And Joan Lipsitz, who, though she was not necessarily in the political "in crowd" in the middle school movement, certainly was enormously influential on me in terms of how she studied young adolescents.

What middle school literature did you read?

I read Hock and Hill's book on the *General Education Class in the Junior High School* as well as works from the Progressive Movement such as Gertrude Noar's great book on the junior high school curriculum. I read Gordon's work on common learnings. I remember that vividly. *The Middle School*, Don Eichhorn's book, which was really the first middle school book in 1966. Ted Moss' book, *The Middle School*, which came out in 1968, in which he coined the term the "muddle school." His point was that if we didn't do something worthwhile we'd end up with "muddle school." So I read all that early middle school literature and I also read all of the pertinent junior high school literature as well.

What was your primary motivation for becoming involved in the middle school movement?

Conrad Toepfer dragged me along. I thought I was going to be a high school English teacher, like a lot of other people. When Connie started me off in the program he put me in a junior high school on an interdisciplinary team. I just sort of went along. It was in the 1960s and because I was on an interdisciplinary team, as a very young teacher he would drag me out to speak at conferences. So I just sort of got into the flow of the middle school movement and stayed interested in it. There was no great epiphany for me that I needed to go into middle level education. It was more, like a lot of people: I found myself there. And as I mentioned earlier, I came to it not through middle level education preparation, but through general curriculum development and curriculum theory.

What is your primary motivation for your continuing involvement with middle school education?

I see the middle level as the ground for the most contentious of curriculum debates. It's the place where elementary and high school come together and becomes contested terrain. It's where the historic curriculum debates take on the most vivid forms: What should all kids learn? How should content be organized? And so on. People have an expectation in elementary schools that there can be some variety and it's not unusual to have units and things like that. At the high school people clearly expect to have a straight, separate-subject program. They are not so sure at the middle level and so it turns out to be tremendous debate. I think my interest in it, aside from the fact that I just really like young adolescents, has to do with the fact that my major field, which is curriculum development, really applies better at this level than at any other level.

How would you describe the early years of the middle school movement (1960s & 1970s)?

They were really hopeful years. You have to remember that in 1970 Charles Silberman, the journalist, in a book called *Crisis in the Classroom* said, after he had toured schools all over the country, that by almost unanimous agreement the junior high school was the wasteland. And then he went on to characterize the junior high school as "the cesspool of American education."

So those of us involved felt that there was something that was about to happen. It was very exciting. We felt that we were actually starting a reform movement because the junior high schools had become pretty dismal places. Exciting too because a lot of it hadn't really been invented or decided on yet. We would be in schools working with teachers, literally inventing curriculum and organizational forms. In some cases I suppose we were re-inventing the wheel, but it all seemed so new and fresh. So it was time, a tremendous time. And it was in the context of times of social upheaval and social hope. A lot of us were not only involved with trying to reform education, but we were involved in larger social reform movements. It was all part and parcel with trying to change the world.

How has the middle school concept changed since the earlier years of the middle school movement?

It certainly is a lot more accepted than it was then. I think people have really come to accept middle schools and to expect them to be of a certain form. I think it is true that it has become more standardized. Despite protests about the litany of characteristics that would make up a middle school, there generally is such a litany. I think when most people talk about middle schools, they mean four person teams, an exploratory program, an advisory program, a block time schedule, and so on and so forth. So, I would say it is now much more standardized than it was then. But, I think the general sense of it, the concept of developmental responsiveness, is still intact, is pretty much the way it was then.

How have middle schools changed because of implementation?

In my recollection there was no sense in the early years of there being any sort of continuum of implementation. And that is because nobody had ever seen one that was really well developed. So, it wasn't as though we were thinking, "Well, we've come this far or that far. We need to do this and that and the other thing." We just sort of kept going down the path. I think now there is a much better sense of that. So, it is hard for me to say, "How have they changed?" because they weren't trying to be the same. Middle school people today, I think, have a sense that there's an endpoint to the thing, that we will get these things and then we are a middle school. Back then we were on the path and we didn't really know where it would take us.

What fueled the growth of the middle school movement?

I think that there are a couple of major forces you can look to in terms of how the middle school movement got started and gained early momentum. Timing is everything in life and in education as well. There is no question that had the baby boom generation not been in place in the elementary schools there would not have been a middle school movement. I don't think I've ever been in a school district where the middle school didn't emerge for reasons other, at the bottom, than administrative reasons: overcrowding at the elementary schools, facilities available, and related issues and concerns. So that certainly was a factor.

A second factor was that, with the possibility of grade change, the middle school became a site for desegregating the neighborhood schools earlier than they would have otherwise. So, in the large urban cities in the North that I was working in, many middle level educators saw the opportunity of getting kids out of the segregated neighborhood elementary schools two years earlier.

Those two factors were in place and then we had this group of people that included Alexander, Toepfer, Vars, Lounsbury, and others who were still around from the progressive days of the junior high school movement who took advantage of the moment and parlayed that whole thing into the concept of middle schools as well. But, I don't think I've ever been in a school where someone said, "We are going to have a middle school because we believe philosophically in it." It was overcrowding. It was desegregation. And then of course in the late 1980s it became more the thing to do, but still it wouldn't have happened had there not been overcrowding; had there not been clear administrative reasons for doing it.

How were decisions about the directions taken by the middle school movement made?

That's a great question. Pieces of the middle school movement came in a couple of ways. One was that they emerged from these people who were holdovers from the days of the junior high school. They tried to carry the best ideas from the junior high school over into the middle schools. They were well respected enough that people accepted much of what they had to say. But, there were also lots of things that emerged from teachers' classrooms to fill out the theories that those people had brought along from the junior high schools. The curriculum work that's happened in the last couple of decades would probably be an excellent example of how the work of teachers in classrooms has shaped the sense of what a progressive and democratic middle school curriculum looks like.

So that was one source or maybe it's all part of the same thing. But it is also true that nothing that's happened in middle schools was purely a part of the middle school movement. There are records of advisory programs, and called "advisor/advisee programs" from decades ago; 1917 is the earliest one that I have seen. There were teams of teachers working in the junior high schools in New York City in the 1920s. Block time scheduling has been around forever.

So, when you think about how the decisions were made you have to think about the middle school as part of the whole historical flow of middle level education—as being in some ways a continuation of the junior high school movement, with this blip in there when we changed the grade levels. I have the feeling I may not be giving the "right" answers but that is okay.

How were other individuals or groups outside middle level education involved in the early years of the middle school movement?

The major group for organizing at the national level was the Association for Supervision and Curriculum Development (ASCD). ASCD had always had an interest in junior high schools. There were always people out of the junior high school movement who were active in ASCD. Bill Alexander had been President of ASCD, for example. Connie Toepfer was enormously active in ASCD. In the mid-to-late 1960s, ASCD had what was called the Emergent Adolescent Learner Council, which involved Connie, Don Eichhorn, Bill—I think Gordon may have been on it as well. They put out a number of publications as well as audio recordings. So, ASCD was very influential and when we used to get together in the 1960s, most of us would see each other at the ASCD conference. That was before NMSA was founded. So, ASCD would be the major one. The Association for Childhood Education International, which is still around and involves mostly elementary people, did have a very active young adolescent group in it for years and years, from the 1930s on. A lot of the old progressives were involved in that.

The National Association for Core Curriculum (NACC) was, of course, the home of Gordon Vars, and the core curriculum movement took place mostly in junior high schools. So, Gordon carried that even though the core movement was not as active by the time the middle schools got going. There were people who were part of NACC who were active in the early days of middle school. NAESP always had junior high school principals in it, but they really didn't come actively into the middle school picture until the 1980s.

One group that's of interest that probably is not very well known, was a group that met in New York City every year starting in the 1950s. It was called the Long Group named after a Professor at New York University by the name of Forrest Long, who every year would bring together graduates of his program, mostly principals, with graduates from the University of Connecticut who had studied under Bill Gruhn who wrote *The Modern Junior High School* along with Harl Douglass.

One of the most, perhaps even for a while *the* most, influential organizations in the Middle School Movement was Educational Leadership Institute (ELI), which was based in Springfield, Massachusetts. They organized weekend workshops around the country and took the middle school message out. I was in on some of them. I remember being in places like Baltimore, Chicago, New York, and St. Louis where, for example on Saturday, Bill Alexander would work in the morning, and Don Eichhorn would work in the afternoon. Connie and I might work on Sunday morning, and Mary Compton or Mildred Wilson, who was a principal from Philadelphia, would work in the afternoon. These were attended mostly by central office and building-level administrators although there were always teachers there. ELI also put out a monthly newsletter called *Dissemination Services in the Middle Grades,* and a journal, which Connie Toepfer edited for years, called *Transescence.* Those really were the major publications on a national level for speaking specifically to middle level education. And those workshops were the way that the word got out, and in a sense I think they were the way by which Connie Toepfer carried the Middle School Movement. I am not saying that other people who were involved weren't great thinkers. But none of them could stand up in front of a group like Connie Toepfer and tell stories and bring people along and invite people in. Connie, literally in my judgment, carried the movement in its early days.

And to belie this notion that the integrated curriculum stuff came on the scene in the 1990s, they dragged me out to those weekend workshops to do two topics. One was to speak to the middle school curriculum. I would stand up and give a talk about developing interdisciplinary and integrated units around problems of living and social problems and social issues. So that was one thing that I did. And the other thing was sessions on how to plan with students. So it was sort of ironic that it was discussed at that time and then emerged again in the 1990s. So, there were groups outside and they were certainly influential and have remained influential, although obviously the National Middle School Association is mainly the center of activity now.

What was the educational context at the time the middle school movement began?

The junior high school was on its last legs. As I mentioned before, Silberman had written that it was "the cesspool of American education." They were desperate places: places of anonymity and hopelessness for a lot of kids. So, that obviously was one kind of context and the other context was of course this general sense of "there is something wrong with education" that was emerging from the progressive critics like Kozol, Kohl, and other

people. It was a good moment in terms of the possibility of change as compared, for example, to the present moment, which doesn't look like a very
hopeful time.

I recall that at the first National Middle School Conference in Columbus, Ohio, the opening speaker was a guy by the name of William Wayson.
He stood up in front of the group and questioned the idea of identifying
and isolating a group of kids called young adolescents. He said, "Well, here
is what people say are the characteristics. And other than going through
puberty, how are those characteristics dramatically different from any other
age group?" There is definitely some room for argument about the whole
idea of isolating young adolescents. I mean it has been good in terms of
trying to do something about middle level schools but isolating them in
a particular place, I don't think has necessarily been a good thing. I think
they are too isolated.

**What have been some of the most significant events, incidents, or
moments in the middle school movement?**

Not in chronological order, I would certainly begin by recognizing
the *Turning Points* report as a monumental moment for the middle school
movement. Lots of things had been going on, but that cast the spotlight
squarely on middle schools and opened the door for a whole new wave of
middle schools and new interest in middle schools. So that was a gigantic
event. The founding of the National Middle School Association was a major
event in terms of organizing people in a central location so that they could
work together and push the whole movement forward.

I also think that Sputnik was a major event because prior to Sputnik
there was still a fair amount of progressive activity in junior high schools. After Sputnik went up, the great core programs ended. Then the junior high
school became a junior version of the high school, and I think that opened
the door and drove the junior high school to the point where it was ripe for
reform possibilities. So Sputnik was influential, the founding of NMSA, and
then *Turning Points,* those are the three big events.

**Do you have any personal accounts related to these events that
might be of interest to others?**

I was in a core program when Sputnik went up, and that was the last
year of the problem-centered core program in my junior high school. I
recognize that very well because I saw the end of the core type program and
the move to the separate subject, junior version of the high school and I saw
what it did to the schools.

With regard to the founding of the National Middle School Association, I remember driving to the first conference with Connie Toepfer and a couple of other folks from Buffalo, New York, down to Columbus, Ohio. I remember how excited we all were. I remember William Wayson's talk that first night. I remember quite well Paul George's talk on the "star system," which was incredible and remarkable because here was a guy who was my age mate standing up in front of this national conference giving this wonderful talk. And it was a very, very powerful talk about the indignities that kids suffered in junior high schools. I remember that well. But most of all what I remember about that first conference was the third speaker, Jessie Stuart, the author of *The Thread That Runs So True.* I was just a great fan of his books from the time I read them in junior high school. So I remember that conference well. I have this picture in my mind of meeting in the basement of the hotel. I don't even think they had us on the first floor of the place. It was a great conference and a great moment, there was a lot of energy.

As far as *Turning Points* is concerned, I was at a conference with middle school people in Wisconsin when it was released and they were angry at the report. Later on we would become excited by the attention it brought to the middle school movement. But they were angry because the *Turning Points* people really did not acknowledge the work that had been done in the previous couple of decades. They acted as though they had invented the idea of core curriculum and team teaching and so forth. So that is sort of the recollection I have about that. But, I also do recollect, the thrill of seeing middle school stuff on the front page of newspapers at that time and thinking, "Somebody's going to pay attention now."

Who or what have been some of the greatest detractors or opponents of middle school education?

There are lots of detractors for middle school education, some people actually inside the movement. But, from outside the movement in particular, certainly the fundamentalist right has not liked the idea of middle schools. In fact in the late 1970s or early 1980s when there were congressional hearings about the whole notion of privacy for kids, some fundamentalist groups managed to get their people in front of the hearings and listed out about seventy-five practices they called "satanic practices in education." Among them were values education, moral education, drug education, alcohol education, guided imagery, and so forth. Also on that list of seventy-five was "middle schools." I think that there has always been opposition from the fundamentalist right to the idea of paying so much attention to the development of kids. And especially advisory programs that would suggest to kids that they have some control over their own destiny rather than having their lives determined by some deity. So the fundamentalist right has been opposed.

There certainly has been opposition from strong conservatives who really do believe that there never should have been anything other than K–8, or K–6, 7–12 schools. I think it's still the case that when people like William Bennett and Chester Finn and people like that speak about schools they don't use the term middle schools. They think about K–6, 7–12 schools or they're talking K–8 schools. So, I think there has been opposition there.

There has been some opposition, although hardly known, from post-modernists and post-structuralists in general educational philosophy and theory, who discredit the work of G. Stanley Hall, that really is the foundation of the concept of a stage called young adolescence. Also there are questions raised on the left about Hall's motives and whether or not the work should stand up. So there's been opposition there. There's certainly been opposition from upper middle class parents and media who don't understand that the road to rigor with young adolescents has to run through relevance. And so they see anything that smacks of trying to be understanding of young adolescent development as being too soft and as somehow ruining their children's chances of getting a leg up on everyone else.

So I think there are lots of critics and I am sure that I am missing some, but it's odd when you think about it. There are so many people who are opposed to so many pieces of what we call the middle school concept, that it's a wonder it's been alive so long. On the other hand, it's also true that the whole movement from the junior high school through the middle school was carved out of a shaky alliance of unusual forces. But we certainly have had our critics and some of them have been pretty vehement. I have this sense that it's very, very easy for educational policy people and academics to criticize the middle level as being somehow soft or un-academic, or whatever criticism they use, without really understanding just how difficult it is to work inside a middle school, and just how complicated early adolescence really is, and how the whole idea for kids of trying to go through early adolescence and deal with the expectations of school is no easy thing. I think most critics and policy makers have no concept of what that's like, none whatsoever. And I can say as a university professor that it's very easy to forget what it's like, too. About three minutes out of middle school and you have already forgotten how difficult it really is.

What have been some of the most significant obstacles to the success of the middle school movement?

Let's use the idea that your assets are also always your liabilities. So the greatest asset of the middle school movement has been a serious, and more than rhetorical, commitment to young adolescents. I really think that today that there are overwhelming numbers of people working in middle level schools who really do identify themselves as middle level educators and one of the identifying features would be that they work with these young adolescents and they enjoy them. On the other hand, the movement itself has, I think, suffered from the fact that it has attempted to elevate puberty to the level of an ideology. I don't think you can carry a movement fully on the back of a developmental characteristic, like puberty. There has to be something more that you are standing for. It's like the old progressive education movement, and in a sense it is a progressive movement, in that it does intend to be responsive to young people. But at the same time, like the largest wing of the old progressive movement, it has failed to take on any kind of a social sense of itself like, for example, democratic education. I think failing to stand for something in a larger societal sense has been an obstacle in the movement.

I'm very sympathetic toward Tom Dickinson's notion of the middle school being in arrested development right now. I think that every movement of any kind always hits a point where it becomes in some ways stagnant. It has a certain period of development and momentum and energy and then it goes into a dip. The question is, can you fight through that dip. Because if you can get through the dip it will accelerate, but if you can't fight through that dip then you have a tendency to stagnate or even regress. I think that in some ways the middle school movement has become too pleased with itself. And it has created a group of people, all of whom play their roles and have gotten into those roles. It is like school, over time people fall into their roles. And if you try to change the school or move it further ahead people have a great deal of difficulty coming out of their roles and will protect those roles to the death, even if they've [the roles] become dysfunctional. I think in some ways that is true of the middle school movement. That is an obstacle for us right now.

I think we're at a point where we are at an absolute stand still. I don't mean to be cynical or pessimistic, but I can't help but think that we've lost a lot of energy and enthusiasm. There really aren't new ideas coming to the fore. We've become less about trying to push ahead and more about trying to comply with external pressures. We have talked about how you can maneuver, for example, No Child Left Behind, but we haven't talked about standing up and saying it is absolutely wrong for young adolescents; it's wrong for our society; it's wrong for our schools. So I think there is an obstacle in the success of the middle school movement. That it had certainly made great progress, but it reached a point where it stagnated. I don't feel the energy, I don't feel new ideas. At this point not only could I not tell you where they might be coming from, but I honestly could not tell you how they could possibly find their way into the middle school movement. I don't think there are any doors open for new ideas. That sounds pretty pessimistic and cynical but I think it is an honest assessment of where we are. I feel like we are not growing.

**What are some of the mistakes that have been made during the
middle school movement that we might be able to learn from today?**

Certainly trying to elevate puberty to the level of an ideology was a mistake, and we need to learn from that mistake. Though, I am not sure people are really aware that it is a mistake, to tell you the truth. But that is something that we need to learn from, that we need to change.

I believe that the door has been opened on two occasions for the middle school movement to take seriously the question, "What should be the middle school curriculum?" One was in the late 1970s when Gordon Vars and John Lounsbury published *Curriculum for the Middle School Years,* and tried to bring back to life the concept of the core program. I remember the publication of that book. I remember how excited I was about it. People I was working with at the time started into curriculum conversations and started debating "Is that how it should look?" and so on and so forth. So that was one moment for a door opening for the curriculum question. The other moment was in the 1990s when the work around the integrated and democratic curriculum got started through NMSA. I think we opened that door, and I think it was a mistake for the Association not to see that as the next move for the whole movement. I don't mean to say, by the way, that the Association should necessarily have opened their arms and coffers to those of us who were doing the really progressive work. But they could have used the work that we were doing as a moment to really do a hard look at the curriculum. We are sitting here, today, in Minneapolis, two days after the Curriculum Committee for NMSA was disbanded. And so we have a middle school association, a professional association, that has always had difficulty with the curriculum question and the door was opened only a decade ago and that door has been closed. It's a professional association about schools that doesn't even have a standing committee on curriculum.

I think that part of that mistake was the emergence of the National Forum to Accelerate Middle-Grades Reform, an organization that grew out of the old Edna McConnell Clark Foundation work with urban schools and a few other groups. I don't have a problem with a group outside the movement, but NMSA, in my judgment, turned itself over to the Forum. And so in a sense the agendas for the two groups became quite similar. The Forum, for example, in looking at the question of equity, as I understand it, spent about two years trying to decide whether they had the guts to say that ability grouping should be ended in middle schools, which tells me also that they will probably never in their history ever get to the question of whether there are curriculum issues that are also related to equity. So I think those are mistakes. I think they are absolutely strategic errors that have gotten in the way of the movement, have prevented it from taking its next steps and reaching what could be a much higher level of activity.

Who has benefited the most from the middle school movement?

There's no question that young adolescents have benefited enormously from the middle school movement. That is so even in the most mainstream middle schools where people haven't really pushed the edges of the concept. I think more teachers than ever are more understanding and responsive to young adolescents. I think there is in schools a much greater understanding of kids than ever before.

I think as well that consultants have certainly benefited enormously from the middle school movement. It is really true. There is a whole industry of middle school consulting. And people who literally make their living off going around pushing the middle school concept, and they've benefited enormously from it.

But I think on the more serious side, that young adolescents have benefited the most. And I should say too that teachers have benefited enormously in the sense that in the dismal days of the junior high school, and still in some of our middle schools, it's almost as if there's a war between the teachers and the kids, or at best a tug of war trying to out-maneuver one another. I think that is very wearing on teachers. It is long duty to be working with a group of young people and having your whole life be about trying to out-maneuver them and survive them. So, I think the middle school concept has brought more teachers into better relationships with young adolescents. And I think it has made their lives better. I think they are happier about being teachers than they would have been had the concept not opened that door for them.

Who has benefited the least from the middle school movement?

I would say exploratory teachers have not benefited from the middle school movement. If there is a single sort of mainstream idea in the middle school concept that has not been even remotely addressed, it's how to bring the exploratory teachers in from the edges of the curriculum. They really are overwhelmingly simply the place where the kids go while the "real" teachers plan. In a lot of schools that I have worked with, the exploratory teachers have been early leaders in pushing the middle school concept, but at the end of the day they certainly don't benefit from it and so a lot of them become pretty cynical about it.

I know that some people say that ninth graders have not benefited from the middle school movement. I would have difficulty saying that, because I am not really sure that's true. In general, I suppose, nobody benefits from going to most of the high schools that we have in this country, but my guess is there are probably ninth graders who have benefited from going over to the high school and getting out of whatever middle level school they were in.

It is true also that poor kids of color in our poorest neighborhoods in cities have not benefited much. But that is a two-way street. The middle school movement as a whole has been largely a white, suburban movement—in fact largely a white, male, suburban movement. So, that has not had a conscientious reach into our inner cities. On the other hand, it's also the case that many of the administrators, central office and others in large urban areas believe, like the general society, that poor kids of color need structure of the sort that is the drill and kill and rote memorization and that's antithetical to what we think of as the middle school concept. So again, it's a two-way street and we have not done a good job of that. There has been some involvement in the National Middle School Association from people of color but it's never been to the degree that it should have been given the percentage of young adolescents in this country who are in urban middle schools. So those two groups, poor kids of color, and their teachers in inner city schools and exploratory teachers in all middle level schools have not benefited from the concept.

Who do you consider to be among the most influential leaders of the middle school movement, and why?

Connie Toepfer! Again I was his student, but I was also his observer. And I honestly believe that there would not really be a middle school movement had it not been for Connie's capacity to stand up in front of a group and invite people into the idea. No matter how well the rest of the folks did their writing and lecturing, Connie was absolutely influential.

Nancy Doda is an enormous figure in the middle school movement. We know her today in terms of this tremendous capacity she has to stand up in front of a group and invite people into the concept. As well, she and Connie have a sense of social conscience and compassion. But Nancy also was really the first widely recognized teacher to emerge in the middle school movement in the Teacher-to-Teacher column in the *Middle School Journal*. So she was tremendously influential.

John Lounsbury has been tremendously influential. Aside from his work in middle level education period, he's done the wonderful work of bringing the publications program to where it is today and making a literature of the middle level. So John is tremendously influential and I think is really getting the kind of respect he deserves from people today.

Don Eichhorn was very influential as a school leader, as was a principal by the name of Mildred Wilson from Philadelphia in the early days. And there were a couple of other principals whose names escape me right now. But they were the people who were in the first middle level schools who could go out and say, "Well you know we are actually doing this thing and here's what it looks like at our schools." So they were certainly influential.

Bill Alexander was a giant figure in the movement. I could go on and on naming people. If you were to look at the curriculum part of the middle school movement, the part that I've been most interested in, I would say in terms of influence the teachers who were doing the work with democratic and integrative curriculum in the 1990s were influential in enormous ways if you think about what was happening in the 1990s at NMSA conventions. These teachers would go into a room to present about the units they were doing or to talk about how they involved kids in planning and assessment and so on. There would be 500 people in those rooms to listen to these teachers talk about what they were doing. And I think they generated a new wave of excitement in the 1990s. And they're certainly receiving some recognition. Mark Springer is being recognized with this distinguished educator award; Barbara Brodhagen has had really good recognition; Carol Smith, who is being written about in a new book about the "Alpha Program" and whom NEA at one time called the best middle school teacher in America. Kathy McEvoy is the incoming president of the National Middle School Association. These people were all teachers in the 1990s, who were doing the work around democratic and integrative curriculum. And again, to the extent to which the movement has at any time taken seriously the curriculum question, those teachers were tremendously influential in that.

I am trying to think whom I have left out. Lots of people have been influential. If you look around at the middle school movement, it was full of role players, people who brought particular things to the movement. You think about Connie bringing social conscience and compassion and the ability to stand up and talk. You think about Nancy Doda in the same way, but also as a teacher who came out of a classroom and could write and speak. And it is not that other teachers couldn't do that, but Nancy played that teacher role. John Lounsbury has played a great role in terms of inspiring people. Ken McEwin in terms of teacher education. I guess I sort of played the curriculum role. Gordon Vars, whom I mentioned earlier, is a most influential person. He carried the torch for interdisciplinary and integrated curriculum from the 1940s in the junior high school movement into the middle school movement and kept it alive. And though Connie was my major professor, Gordon was tremendously influential with me in terms of the curriculum work, guiding my thinking and giving me feedback and so on. In fact I remember, when I wrote the middle school curriculum book, I had said: "Well here it is, this integrated curriculum, that has to do with personal and social issues and integrative themes and democratic classrooms and planning with kids. That's the middle school curriculum and you don't need anything else." Gordon dropped me a note and he said: "Does that mean that kids won't necessarily learn how to play basketball in the middle school?" I said: "That's right, Gordon, we're interested in general education, not in specialized education." "Good," he said. I remember that. He was tremendously influential with me in that way.

Have there been major debates among middle school leaders focusing on particular issues or beliefs?

There've been major debates but they haven't been well publicized. The only debate that was ever well publicized was the one Paul George and I had about the integrative middle school curriculum. That lasted over a couple of years. And there seemed to be tremendous interest in that. Big crowds of people would come out.

It was an error on my part to ever agree to do those debates. I was told before they happened that we were going to talk about the educational issues that were involved in it and that it would all be about the work that we were doing. As it turned out most of the opposition that was raised had to do with the skill of teachers or problems with schedules and things like that. It never really got to be a debate about the organization of the curriculum. So that was a mistake on my part. It hurt deeply because a lot of people who were fearful of the idea of actually standing up for something in the curriculum in middle schools saw that as license to say, "Well, you know, then we don't have to take it seriously. Because apparently there is this other side that NMSA recognizes."

Think about the middle school movement as having two wings, one much larger than the other. The largest one is what I would call the mainstream middle school movement. And that is people who are certainly caring about young adolescents. They speak well of young adolescents and they seem to enjoy young adolescents. But they're mostly interested in structural changes in the middle schools and in a sense, as we used to say with the curriculum work, what they are interested in is trying to find what bait to put on the hook to pull the kids in. So, there is that kind of mainstream group and it is the largest group, and they have been incredibly important and they are extremely well intentioned, and I have great respect for them. And then there is the other wing, to which I would belong, which is the progressive wing of the middle school movement. This wing is trying to be responsive to young adolescents, but also believes that the movement should be addressing larger social issues and obligations. In 1968, in a conversation with Connie Toepfer, he said to me: "You know, the thing about most educators, child-centered educators, is they don't understand that if you really love children you have to hate the things that crush their souls. You have to hate racism. You have to hate sexism. You have to hate poverty." I never forgot that. And I think probably if I were to explain my work in the middle school movement, it wouldn't be about trying to find a way to integrate subject areas, it would be about a search for democratic curriculum and a curriculum with a social conscience.

What has been the role of women and minorities in the middle school movement?

It is like the Marxist revolution: The men were in the front room making the theory and the women were in the back room teaching. The middle school movement has largely involved white men in terms of theory, and women in terms of teaching. Fortunately, in the past two decades, there's been a much more central place for women in the middle school movement, although that is easy for me to say because I am one of those white males. But I think that there are certainly more women visible in central positions than there were, say in the 1960s or 1970s or early 1980s. In fact, Joan Lipsitz was in some sense outside the movement. Mary Compton, who was one of the authors on Bill Alexander's *Emergent Middle School,* a book which many people think Bill wrote alone, but actually four people wrote that book. Mary Compton was one of them, and so she was a huge voice at the beginning of the middle school movement. But, she was not necessarily politically very visible.

The involvement of minorities, people of color, I think does not speak well for the movement. I think that again there's been this problem of the mainstream part of the movement not being able to see itself reaching into our poorest neighborhoods where people of color are generally. And as well, a refusal on the part of many of the cities' central office and administrative staffs being willing to accept the middle school concept, to accept anything other than the "drill and kill" structure that they have. So, again I think there's been the emergence of women in the movement. They are much more visible than they were thirty years ago. But, I think we're probably not doing as well with minority groups as we did fifteen or twenty years ago. I don't think the National Middle School Association has a committee on diversity anymore, or diverse populations. So that doesn't speak very well for us.

What are some examples of ways the middle school movement has affected American education?

To some extent we have brought a lot of attention outside of the middle school movement to young adolescents. Let's face it: people know who we are. They know what we stand for. So I think we've definitely impacted American education.

I wish I could say that we had a larger impact on policymakers. To be honest, I don't think we're always taken very seriously by policymakers or academics. It's interesting that at a lot of large universities where people who do policy and theory work in education are located, very often you don't find much middle level activity going on. I know a story about one large research university that had a meeting of their curriculum and instruction department in the early 1970s to consider whether they should add a middle school section to the elementary and secondary sections of their department. The department voted the proposal down on the grounds that they did not think the middle school movement would last. So, I think we have had some success, certainly people know who we are. Certainly, we're in the newspapers. We've changed the structure of the American school. But I don't think we've been able to impact policy as much as I wish we could have.

Herb Kliebard, who is a curriculum historian, once said that, "the middle school is a movement without an ideology." In a sense, again, it goes back to my notion that, unfortunately people have tried to elevate puberty to an ideology. But it is a movement, seen in policy and academic circles as a movement without an ideology and often dismissed as being another one of those "child-centered" movements that were the bane of the progressive education movement seventy years ago.

What educational groups, organizations, and institutions have influenced the middle school movement?

The National Middle School Association has had a tremendous influence. The National Association for Secondary School Principals also has had a tremendous influence. In the 1980s George Melton formed the Middle Level Council for the National Association of Secondary School Principals. And for a while it almost captured the middle level market. They conducted workshops and put out a series of publications. For that group he had managed to draw in Connie Toepfer, John Lounsbury, J. Howard Johnston, Al

Arth, and Sherrel Bergmann—people who were very prominent. And so they had a tremendous influence.

ASCD has been influential even though in some ways their role dropped once NMSA was formed. They still have done a lot of publishing and videos about middle level education. So they have been influential. The Association for Childhood Education International has been influential. There are people who have moved away from the National Middle School Association and allied themselves more closely with that organization. The Educational Leadership Institute was tremendously influential in their publications and workshop program in the early days of the movement.

The Midwest Middle School Association was tremendously influential inasmuch as the National Middle School Association grew out of that organization. If you think about it, for a lot of people in middle level schools the Movement has been about their state associations. The New England League of Middle Schools has been enormously influential in that area of the country. They still get three or four thousand people at their annual conference. The Wisconsin Association has been very active; the Florida League of Middle Schools. There are lots of very active associations that are the point of identification for a lot of middle level educators who aren't able to get to the national conferences.

And then I would mention too the summer institutes that have been put on by a lot of colleges and universities around the country. The first one that I know of was at Northern Colorado University—organized by John Swaim. And then following that there was one started in 1981 at the University of Wisconsin, Platteville, which in that year had about fifty-five people attending and within five or six years had annual attendance of over eight hundred middle level educators who would come for a week every summer to Platteville, Wisconsin. Not only was it influential just as an example for the teachers in that state, but also as a summer retreat for people who were active in speaking and writing about middle schools, in the sense that they would all come there and participate in the program. The one at the University of Maine has been a tremendous influence in that area of the country. And there was one at Vermont as well. So, while those are not necessarily middle level organizations or professional associations, they had a tremendous influence.

Have particular legislative actions significantly influenced the middle school movement at the state or national levels?

On the plus side, many states took the middle school movement seriously and enacted, if not actual certification, endorsements on elementary or secondary certificates. I saw that as a positive legislative move. In some

states, the state of Wisconsin where I live being an example, the state education regulations look different for the middle level than they do for the
high school in the sense of who is eligible to teach what. So, I see those
things as being on the plus side.

On the negative side, the standards movement which in and of itself may
not have been bad was an absolutely foolish move in that identifying educational standards in the midst of a conservative restoration in the larger society
is very dangerous. And I cannot imagine what people thought would come
of it, but inevitably the standards lead to standardized testing and are now
leading to standardization of the curriculum. More and more districts are
mandating packaged standards-based programs that are scripted and even
worse than the 1960s curriculum packages. So that legislation has hurt us
enormously because working well in any school, including the middle school,
requires a degree of relative autonomy for teachers in the classroom to work
with a particular group of kids. No Child Left Behind, if it stays in place, may
not bring the total demise of public education in general but certainly is going to cause the middle school movement to be so seriously downsized that it
will be a wonder if we survive in any kind of recognizable form.

**What are some ways the middle school movement has influenced
middle level curriculum and instruction?**

The middle school movement has been tremendously influential with regard to instruction. That is to say that middle school classrooms today, more so
than thirty or forty years ago, involve much more hands-on, engaging type activities, to some degree projects, and to some degree interdisciplinary or multi-
subject units and activities. So I think it has been a tremendously positive influence on the quality and nature of teaching and learning in classrooms. And I
think that has been a great benefit to both the teachers and the students.

With regard to the Middle Level movement's influence on curriculum,
again it is a matter of two moments in which doors were opened when the
movement could have finally tried to define itself in terms of what a middle
school curriculum should look like generally, but on both occasions that
door seems to have closed. So it's been influential in terms of instruction, to
a large degree and minimally influential with regard to curriculum.

**As middle level educators, how do you think we should respond
to the current emphasis on student achievement as measured by
standardized tests?**

I think we should stand up and say it's wrong. That it is wrong for young
adolescents as people; that it's wrong in terms of offering a quality educa-

tion to those young people; that it's antithetical to the best of what we know about teaching and learning. One of the problems with the middle school movement is that it has not stood up and said loudly and clearly that it is wrong for young adolescents and we believe that it ought to be stopped.

How about moral outrage? That would be another possible response. One of the things that has happened with the middle school movement because it's been based largely on puberty and has no larger social conscience is that the response to obstacles or hindrances of the years has always been sort of mild. And the movement is incapable of expressing moral outrage, at a time when the most likely response from people who are supposed to care so deeply about young people would be moral outrage. And I think that's a shame. I think that we ought to be speaking for young people and their interests and their rights, and we're not doing that.

Are there lessons we still need to learn from the history of the middle school movement?

There are lots of lessons we should learn. One is that you need to know your critics. And you need to know what they're up to. And you need to be able to anticipate what they might throw your way next. I actually think middle school people, and probably for good reason, spend sometimes too much time talking to each other and not enough time looking at the world outside and anticipating some of the issues that might be coming their way. A really good example is that, had middle school people been listening to right-wing radio shows over the past decade, they might have seen some of the current movements toward turning the clock back coming.

I think we should have learned the lesson that a sound movement for educational reform cannot stand on child-centeredness alone. Child-centeredness is tremendously important, but it is only part of the equation. There has to be some larger societal issue or reason for existing. I wish we would stand for democratic education as an extension of the rights of these young adolescents about whom we supposedly care so much. I think that's a lesson we should have learned. I will leave it with those two.

How would you characterize the current status of middle level education?

I agree with Tom Dickinson's term, I think we are in arrested development. I think we've reached a point where we are stagnant. I read the conference program, I walk around the convention. I read the *Middle School Journal*, I do not see new ideas coming to the fore or even fresh versions of old ideas. So, I think we are in arrested development and I don't know what's going to happen. No Child Left Behind is going to hurt us terribly. And I don't know how we would be moving ahead even if that weren't in place. But I will say that if that particular law and that way of thinking about education is the way it's going to be, I hope that when the movement really begins to hit the end that people stand up and go down in a blaze of glory. Go down screaming, go down yelling in moral outrage and go down speaking for children. It just makes no sense to me that we would limp along trying somehow to comply with rules that are eventually going to do us in.

Are there particular efforts that need to be made to help ensure the future success of the middle school movement?

Let's assume there's going to be a future success of the middle school movement. And on an optimistic side, I think we have to say there have been moments, though never this pervasive, when all progressive ideas have been challenged. But let's say that we are going to get past all this and there will be some positive future for the middle level concept. There is no question in my mind that we need to be doing two things. One is we need to be absolutely certain about what kind of footprints we're leaving. That is to say at a time in the future when people come back to the concept in its fullest version, they need to have access to information and ideas about the things we did well and the things we didn't do well so that they can hit the ground running and move ahead. I think we need to be thinking about what kinds of things we are doing right now as a record that people can use in the future.

The second thing is, we need to be opening the door for more new people to come into the movement. If you come to the National Middle School Association Conference or go to the Forum and read their membership list, or go into state associations and look at their leadership groups, it's the same faces who have been in place for twenty or thirty years. Now that's not necessarily a bad thing, because it means people have been committed over the long haul and what I am going to say is not in any way a criticism of those people. But the fact of the matter is that I don't know how new people could emerge in leadership positions in middle level education. The Forum is a closed group. The National Middle School Association has ended its standing committees. I don't know what the entry points would be. I was lucky Connie Toepfer brought me into the movement, Paul George was lucky that he happened to study under Bill Alexander, Judy Brough was lucky that she studied under Connie Toepfer, and Sherrel Bergmann that she studied under Gordon Vars. There's this group of us who all studied under the people who started the movement. We were brought into it. We had a way in. I don't know how people would get into it now. It doesn't feel, to me, as open as it should be and that's tremendously important because the movement definitely needs new blood, it needs new life, it needs new energy.

In 1976 at the ASCD convention in Miami there was to be a session on middle school. There were four presenters in the session: Connie Toepfer, Paul George, Emmett Williams, and myself. At the last minute Connie and Emmett had to pull out of the conference. So Paul George and I did the program. Now, Paul and I had never met before and we're going to stand up and do a session on middle school at the ASCD conference. It was a large room and it was tremendously crowded. There was a lot of interest at the time. I was talking about interdisciplinary and integrated units and planning with students, and Paul was talking about teaming and advisory programs, and so on. In a sense we were doing in 1976 exactly what we are doing right now. The two of us have played that role in terms of our place in the middle school movement since that time. I suppose it also speaks to some of the roles that were played early on. Bill Alexander did more with structural stuff. Connie did more with the young adolescents. Gordon, whom I knew well, did more with curriculum, so it makes sense that their graduate students would follow them and keep that path going.

Are there other comments you would like to make that you have not been asked about in this interview?

I think that it is worth saying that there has always been a group of teachers who have done the labor of the movement. There would be no movement without these teachers. And, again, Nancy was the first really visible one, but there were others at the time. And there was a group in the 1990s: Barb Brodhagen, Carol Smith, Kathy McAvoy, Mark Springer, Gert Nesin, Dennis Carr, and others who *were* carrying that move on curriculum that we made in the 1990s. People think that I was so influential in that curriculum movement in the 1990s, but the fact of the matter is that my work would still be in the desk drawer if it weren't for those people. Certainly people would come to hear me talk about the design theory, but if you put those teachers in a room to talk about their work, you couldn't get a chair and people would be sitting out in the lobby trying to listen in. I think that those teachers have not gotten as much respect as they should. They ought to be at the very center of whatever stories are told about the middle school idea. Their work towers over what the rest of us have done.

9

Sherrel K. Bergmann

These kids are going to be responsible for the comfort of my old age, and I for one, want them to be responsible, well-educated, caring, and considerate people. These values are instilled and solidified in the middle school years. We cannot lose our focus on their future.

Widely recognized for her expertise in young adolescent development and middle level education, Dr. Sherrel K. Bergmann has been an influential scholar and leader throughout her career. She has authored and co-authored more than 30 journal articles, books, and other professional publications, and has extensive experience as an educational consultant to schools, school districts, state departments, colleges and universities, health organizations, agencies, and other groups. She has made keynote addresses and presentations at several hundred professional conferences and in various professional venues. Bergmann's background and credentials in both education and counseling provided a scholarly and compassionate perspective to her work, much of which focused on young adolescent social and emotional development, advisory programs, middle level guidance, successful middle schools, and family/parent relationships. She has provided

The Legacy of Middle School Leaders, pages 149–163
Copyright © 2011 by Information Age Publishing
All rights of reproduction in any form reserved.

leadership in middle level education at the state and national levels and was a co-founder of the Association of Illinois Middle-Level Schools (AIMS).

Dr. Bergmann received her undergraduate degree in secondary education in 1969 from Central Michigan University, Mount Pleasant, and her master's degree in counseling and personnel services from Kent State University, Kent, Ohio, in 1973. She earned her doctorate in curriculum and instruction from Kent State in 1976. She was a middle school and high school teacher in Michigan and Ohio from 1969 until 1976. Bergmann accepted the position of Chair of the Department of Education at Lake Forest College, Chicago, Illinois in 1976. In 1978, she became a faculty member at National Louis University, Chicago, where she remained until her retirement in 1996. While at National Louis University, she held several teaching and administrative positions including Associate Dean of the Graduate School and Director of the Middle Level Curriculum Center. Dr. Bergmann remains active in middle school education as an author and educational consultant.

Selected Accomplishments and Contributions to Middle Level Education

- Affiliate Representative for AIMS to the National Middle School Association (NMSA) Board of Trustees (1978)
- President of AIMS (1978–1979)
- Co-chair of the NMSA Research Committee (1980–1982)
- Member of the NMSA Professional Preparation Advisory Board (1981–1984, 1993)
- Member of the NMSA Critical Issues Committee (1987–1990)
- Received the John H. Lounsbury Distinguished Service Award from NMSA (1999)
- Received the National Association for Secondary School Principals Gruhn-Long-Melton Award (2001)
- Received the Robert Knight Award from AIMS (2001)
- Member of the NMSA *This We Believe* Revision Taskforce (2002–2003)
- Consultant to Union Pacific Railroad Principal's Crisis Prevention Project for schools and children affected by hurricane Katrina (2006–2009)

Selected Publications

Bergmann, S. K., & Vars, G. F. (1972). The middle school counselor: A teacher perspective. *Midwest Middle School Journal, 3*(5), 38–39.

Bergmann, S. K., & Baxter, J. (1983). Building a guidance program and advisory concept for early adolescents. *NASSP Bulletin 67*(463), 49–55.

Bergmann, S. K. (1986). Making decisions about tough topics in the middle school. *Clearing House, 60*(1), 24–26.

Bergmann, S. K. (1991). Guidance in the middle school: The compassion component. In J. Cappuelluti & D. Stokes (Eds.), *Middle level education: Programs, policies, and practices.* Reston, VA: National Association of Secondary School Principals.

Bergmann, S. K. (1994). Conrad F. Toepfer, Jr.: The jazz man of middle level education. *Middle School Journal, 25*(3), 25–28.

Bergmann, S. K. (2001). Comprehensive guidance and support services. In T. O. Erb (Ed.), *This we believe . . . and now we must act* (pp. 108–115). Westerville, OH: National Middle School Association.

Bergmann, S. K. (2005). Multifaceted guidance and support services (pp. 165–172). In T. O. Erb (Ed.), *This we believe in action.* Westerville, OH: National Middle School Association.

Brough, J. A., & Bergmann, S. K. (2006). *Teach me—I dare you!* Larchmont, NY: Eye on Education.

Bergmann, S. K., & Brough, J. A. (2007). *Lead me—I dare you! Managing resistance to school change.* Larchmont, NY: Eye on Education.

Bergmann, S. K., Brough, J., & Shepard, D. (2008). *Teach my kid I dare you! The educator's essential guide to parent involvement.* Larchmont, NY: Eye on Education.

Sherrel Bergmann[*]

$\mathbf{I}$ can quickly identify my main influences as I became a middle school advocate—Gordon Vars and the experience at the Kent State Lab School. We were the model middle school for the state of Ohio at that time. Gordon also connected me to others with a passion for this age group. I had taught junior high prior to that time in Michigan, so my previous experience helped to solidify my feelings that the middle school was, indeed, a good idea.

What kinds of middle school literature did you read early on?

Everything that was being written about the age group. I proofread a lot of early manuscripts by Gordon and John Lounsbury. I read Tanner, who made a major impact by publishing his research on developmental character-

---

[*] Sherrel Bergmann was interviewed for the Legacy Project in November 2005.

istics. I read Don Eichhorn's *The Middle School* and critiqued it for him from the teacher point of view. I read everything Vars and John Lounsbury had ever written. I proofread for the National Middle School Association because the *Middle School Journal* was just getting started. As Gordon Vars became president of NMSA, I read everything NMSA published, because I was in a position to do a lot of proofing, and they needed help with publications.

Are there particular theorists, theories, or writings that have influenced your educational thought?

I would say John Dewey. I think he influenced the whole middle school as a progressive education ideal. I was also influenced by the writings of Elsie Alberty and Margaret Mead. There is a lot of literature about the development of students that I think had a big impact on the whole young adolescent development arena. I also was very influenced by the work of Krathwohl in affective education. I learned a great deal about teaching middle school kids by applying the work of Benjamin Bloom. The writings of Lounsbury, Vars, Eichhorn, Alexander, Van Til, and Tanner, were by far the most influential to me.

What was your primary motivation for becoming involved in the middle school movement?

I truly enjoy that age group more than any other. It was passion for the age group, especially the at-risk kids, that drove me to learn as much as I could about them. More than anything, I think it was the fact that I was working on the first doctorate specifically about middle school in the country. I was surrounded by the influence and the passion of these wonderful people whose primary focus was the kids of this age. There was such a commitment, such a deep unselfish involvement in bettering the education and lives of children in that age group that you just couldn't help but be brought into it. It was an exciting time as we began to discover and share ideas with all the educators who truly liked this age group. There was new research going on, new patterns of communication, and a sense that what we were doing was important to the kids. For the first time, an organization was actively involving students, parents, teachers, and administrators together for the improvement of education at that level.

What is the primary motivation for your continued involvement in middle school education?

Katie. Katie is my niece and she is in seventh grade this year. She is very smart, very social, and very much at risk because of the neighborhood she lives in. There is always a need to do better things for kids this age. She and others like her need advocates to help them maintain their positive attitude toward school and reach their potential. I think about all the Katies out there in seventh grade and cannot rest until they are safe, secure, and well educated. Middle school is not perfect yet, and the need to get to what we know it can become is a constant pursuit. It's becoming more and more real but there is still a lot of work to be done. I would have to say right now my driving passion is to make sure that Katie has the best middle school experience that she can have, so it's both personal and professional.

How would you describe the early years of the middle school movement around the 1960s and early 1970s?

It's interesting because I got involved in the early 1970s and at that time the Midwest Middle School Association was just getting organized. It was basically curriculum leaders and administrators in Ohio and Indiana—Bob Malinka, Gordon Vars, Hal Gaddis, Lou Tosi, Lou Romano, Nick Georgiady, and a few other leaders. New York was a smaller area with middle school interest because of the work of Conrad Toepfer. The Midwest Middle School Association was gathering research, sharing the data and saying, "Let's make a difference; let's move this junior high concept a little bit further along." Everything that the kids were being asked to do was an emulation of the high school. Everything from curriculum, guidance, extra-curricular activities, and parent involvement needed to change. The junior high was a miniature high school, and the statistics for social problems of young adolescents were beginning to get attention from the media. The leaders of the new middle school movement (who were also major writers and leaders of the junior high) figured that if they really wanted to be effective, they would have to change the name. Maybe that helped, because most of the philosophy was exactly the same but it was not being implemented the same. We had high school curriculum, high school textbooks, high school activities, all in the middle school. We had high school experiences for kids before they were ready. So the concept moved very fast because some practical ideas were offered on how to make the schools more appropriate for young adolescents. From the time that the Midwest Middle School Association went national in Columbus, Ohio, teachers were involved. I was a part of the planning and implementation of the first national conference. It was the first time that teachers had really been invited to a conference that had to do with an age group rather than a content area. When the minds and work of Bill Alexander, John Lounsbury, Bill Van Til, Gordon Vars, Conrad Toepfer, Don Eichhorn, and Mary Compton finally got together and combined their efforts, it was dynamite.

How has the middle school concept changed since the early years of the middle school movement?

For years and years we were able to just focus on the dream and implementing integrated curriculum, advisory, intramural sports programs, and outstanding exploratory programs. We could work with colleges and universities to begin training teachers to work with this age group. Entire degree programs in middle level education were started at numerous universities. Certification policies and requirements were changed to reflect middle school as a separate entity. Now we have to worry about standardized testing, the foibles of No Child Left Behind, and the changing focus from kids to content. So I think it's much more political now than ever in the past.

NMSA has had to focus on the politics of the middle school movement. The rest of us just need to carry forward the concept in the everyday school. There is now more research available to us as to what works and what doesn't. It may not necessarily be called middle school research but we know so much about adolescents and young adolescents now that we didn't know even ten years ago. I think there is less emphasis on students as a central goal right now and more emphasis on test scores. I think a real issue that we have to contend with now in the middle school movement is that by having to focus on the politics we are not spending as much energy as we should on the students.

How have the middle schools changed since the early years of the middle school movement?

Today, I find that there are more flexible schedules and more teachers trained in the middle school concept. I think that's really been a big plus. It's been a struggle, but I think that the teacher certification and the teacher training part of that has made a significant difference in what we have been able to accomplish. The removal of the ninth grade made a big difference in the high school as well as the middle schools. So those are some of the major changes that I've seen. It's interesting, because you can go into a middle school with all that we know about middle school kids, and they are still dealing with the same issues that we were dealing with when we started this whole concept. So the issues for young adolescents are there but the way that we deal with them is different. They are also subjected to much more adult culture than middle school students were in the 1970s. The technology of today has given them access to anything in the world that they want to know or obtain.

**How were the decisions about the directions taken by the middle
school movement made?**

I would say that the members and board of NMSA and the founders
had a big influence. When John Lounsbury and Gordon Vars spoke, people
listened. If something came out from Paul George or Bill Alexander, people
paid attention and became involved in the issues. But primarily NMSA took
the writings of the founding group, Connie Toepfer, Don Eichhorn, Bill Alexander, Gordon Vars, and John Lounsbury, and used those as a set of standards against which to make suggestions and recommendations for what
would be in the middle school concept. Then *Turning Points* came out by the
Carnegie Corporation and that also had a big influence. Then the Center
for Early Adolescence in Chapel Hill opened. When NMSA published *This
We Believe*, it gave schools a set of standards and a philosophy to implement.
So there were all kinds of directions taken by the movement that really had
to do with an expressed need or by the forum that NMSA became. Also,
NASSP began looking at the needs of middle school principals as a distinct
group and formed the Middle Level Council. This group published several
monographs that were read by middle school principals. Those principals
began to make decisions based on the characteristics of kids.

**How were other individuals and groups outside of middle
level education involved in the early years of the middle school
movement?**

I think that NMSA has always been really invitational and so have the
state affiliates. I think through the state affiliates, through NMSA we were
able to reach out. There were individuals outside of middle level education
who were dealing with kids. Elementary and high schools began to take
notice of what was happening in the middle school. There were a lot of
doctoral students and master's students looking for research projects and
so they became involved in middle level education because it was a hot
topic. It was new, it was exciting, kids were loving integrated curriculum,
schools were doing well, there were a lot of good public relations within the
schools, parents were involved because the thing to do was be involved in
your kids' middle school. The national PTA got involved, which was really
helpful. The National School Board Association got involved so they began
writing about the middle school.

**What was the educational context at the time the middle school
movement began?**

It was somewhere between the "let it all hang out 1960s," and "we have
no idea what we are doing." The 1960s were really loose, and so the middle

school was an answer for stability and social response. The educational context was very loose but looking for stability, and schools were free to try new things. We had individually guided education. We had so many projects coming down the line that were fun, and a lot of them involved a social response to some of the issues that adolescents were facing. Sid Simon started the Values Clarification Movement and affective education became popular. The 1960s had spawned some revolutions that parents weren't ready for. So we had parents wanting something different from the schools. There is little room for flexibility now like we had when the middle school first started. Experimentation was welcomed within curriculum. We were looking for broadening the horizon, we were more global. It was more focused on the needs of kids. We could teach like that and we did. There was not so much emphasis on testing and accountability. There were tests and kids did well. We know that because they have become parents now who are doing well. So I think we did some really good things, but it was a very flexible environment for change.

What have been some of the most significant events, incidents, or moments in the middle school movement?

For big moments, events, or incidents in the whole middle school development, I would say the publication of the first journal. That was so astounding to finally see a collection of articles done by middle school teachers. John did such a fabulous job with the journal. There were other little publications like *Transescence* that spread the word. So I would say the most significant events have to be the publication of the *Middle School Journal*, the first NMSA convention, and the Chicago convention, because we doubled in size at that one.

Another major event in the movement was the development of state affiliates. Almost every state is now represented and connected with NMSA. The publication of *Turning Points* was a big event that nationally helped our cause with urban schools. I think that was a big help, because when the Carnegie group spoke, everybody listened. And here was a group that wasn't NMSA publishing a document about how to improve middle schools.

An additional significant event would be the amount of parent and student involvement that was evident in the whole middle school movement locally and state wide. People began to question things. A big moment for me was when people began to question what athletics ought to be for middle school kids. Pediatricians, like Lee Salk, began doing research on young adolescents and their development, and the American Academy of Pediatrics made some statements about what was and wasn't good for kids athletically in the middle school. So we saw a big difference then in competitive sports. We saw a removal of some of the more dangerous sports for middle schools and an attitude towards physical fitness for all students.

I think for me, personally, a really big moment was when we drew in the medical profession to do research on this age group. We saw, particularly at Johns Hopkins, an amazing increase in middle school research on child development. And people saying, "What do we know about this age group and what do we need to know?" They began to do early puberty research, and they began looking at anorexia and all of the social issues. Alan Drash's research at University of Pittsburg Medical Center on nutrition and how often early adolescents need to eat, led to changes in school schedules as snack breaks were allowed. So that was a focus and a turning point. Finally, I would have to say, teacher certification and middle school endorsements. Teachers who taught seventh grade would have to know something about that age group before setting foot in the classroom.

Do you have any personal accounts related to the events you mentioned or any other significant events in the history of the middle school movement that might be of interest to others?

A personal account that would be of interest would be the history of getting the Association of Illinois Middle Schools off the ground. When I went to the NMSA convention in St. Louis in 1976, I had just moved to Illinois from Ohio. I had written and asked to join what was the Illinois Middle Level Principals Organization, and I got back the note that since I was neither a male nor a principal, membership was not open to me. So I did at that time what all good feminists did: I decided that I would start my own organization of middle schools. I was chair of the department of education at Lake Forest College at the time. Gordon had said, "Go forth and spread the good word." So I went to the lower level of the Marriott, and I put a note on the communication board that said anyone interested in starting an Association of Illinois Middle Schools, meet at room 260 at 5:00. Well, there was another note up there with the same message on it that John Hillebrand had written. We had this group of 26 people from Illinois that was so gung ho that we could hardly contain them. The Association of Illinois Middle Schools started that night. We then became a NMSA state affiliate. They were just starting the whole affiliate network and that networking within our own state and with NMSA was powerful. We started something called drive-in conferences, Thursday afternoon drive-ins through AIMS where you could drive in to a local middle school and share ideas on a topic we had selected. We would have boxed dinners, and usually 50 or 60 teachers would come in and just share ideas from 5:00 to 7:00 on Thursdays. It was wonderful networking. And that just grew and grew. So I think that becoming a state affiliate was powerful and that has grown to be a very important part of maintaining the middle school concept.

Who or what have been some of the greatest detractors or opponents of the middle school education?

Conservative politicians, right wingers, Jerry Falwell's group. I don't mind mentioning his name either because he did some nasty speeches about the whole concept of what he called humanistic education. Those have been thorns in the side of a progressive movement, but I was always kind of glad that they were there because it meant that we were making a difference. If no one knew about us then no one would be talking against us. I would have to say the conservatism has been a real problem. Also the fluctuations in the economy. It costs money to have teaming and it costs money to have really good schools. So lack of funding in some states and in some areas has kept the middle school from really developing. I mean how many schools have I been in that said, "Oh yeah, we have teams, but we don't have any common planning time." "We have advisory, but it meets once a month." Or, "We would like to have that curriculum but we don't have any materials." So the economy has been a detractor, at certain times.

What have been some of the most significant obstacles to the success of the middle school movement?

I would have to say the biggest one is the lack of definitive research that it makes a difference. We have a lot of research right now, but early on I would say the biggest obstacle was people would say, "Prove to me that it works. Prove to me that this concept makes any more difference than doing it any other way." I had one school board say to me, "Don't give us theory, give us numbers. We don't want to talk about theory, we want to talk about how it is going to raise our reading and math scores."

And so I would say that the lack of the ability to say, "If you do this, if you implement this, your scores will go up" has been a significant obstacle. I am waiting for a *Time* magazine cover that says, "Middle School makes a significant difference in the lives of kids," but we can't do that today. We can't say that if you implement X program that you are going to raise your reading scores by 10%. I don't know of anybody that gives that guarantee. We need curriculum insurance. If people buy insurance that this program is going to work then we will know. But you can't do that. Wasn't it Benjamin Bloom who said we do all these things right and they send us the wrong kids? Well that is what happens, we get one program ready and we get all new districting. We get rescheduling, we get boundaries moved, so schools change.

I would say that the other thing is the battle that we are fighting right now to keep the arts and exploratory programs in the middle school. There is a lot of research in the music and art fields that says that kids that have music and art do better in school. But that doesn't get publicized as that's why we have exploratory courses in the middle school. So we have not done a good job of providing the proof that those programs are necessary although we know how important they are to students and their future. People always ask me, "Can you prove that advisory works?" "Can you prove that having a student advocate works?" I can say that if you don't have one what happens. Can I prove that it makes a significant difference in the lives 28 out of 30 kids? Probably not. I have not done that kind of numerical research. I would say that the biggest obstacle is not having definitive research on the components. We had the Eight Year Study, and the reissuing of it which NMSA and NASSP published not too long ago. But we don't have a lot of that so when people say to us why should we spend X amount of dollars on teaming, we can hand them proof that it will work. We could prove through the Project Initiative Middle Level Education Study in Illinois that teaming does make a difference in achievement, attendance, and attitude, but funding sources want more than that right now. So that is probably the biggest obstacle. We currently live in a standardized testing world. They want scores; they want numbers. We don't want to know that 88 out of 90 kids became outstanding citizens as a result of the middle school. That is not as important right now as beating Japan in the test score race. I think those are some of the obstacles.

What are some of the mistakes that have been made during the middle school movement that we might be able to learn from?

I think there is one, and that is trying to provide everything for everyone. We have a really good concept based on sound theory about child development. And we know that if it is implemented correctly children strive, survive, and learn. But we are now in this political arena of trying to be everything to everyone. So we are trying to provide for all of the people doing middle schools, the answers to all the questions they have about literacy, and about curriculum and about budgets, and about buildings. I get calls to look at blue prints for middle schools, and asked do I think that would be the best way to organize their building? And we get all of these things to do for schools that aren't related to the concept. But because of the climate that we live in right now, we have a feeling that we really need to do that, so that we don't get criticized for not being responsive. But the reality is that what we are trying to do is be everything to everyone instead of refocusing on what we know is good practice in the middle school. I don't want us to look like an ASCD; that is not our mission. Our job is focus on young adolescents and good practices in schools for them, and I don't like to see us get too far away from that.

What are some of the most important factors that are influencing middle school education today?

I would like to say on a really positive note that I see so many marvelous committed teachers and principals doing phenomenal jobs with kids under the worst circumstances possible, and they are thriving and doing well. They are not getting written about. That is not what is making press. They can do the best job possible yet it's the one school that has problems that gets noted. And so I would say that we need to factor publicity into what is influencing middle schools today. What the public knows and doesn't know about this age group can make or break us. We have a whole new generation of parents to inform and educate and bring into the fold. The parents are little different than they were. Most of the parents that we have today went through middle schools, but the middle schools they went through look a little bit different than what the expectations are right now.

Of course, the political climate is influencing us. We have moved so far away nationally from what we believe is good schooling for kids. Yet I walked into our own local middle school in Michigan last week and the principal was out on the playground with the fifth and sixth graders doing some problem solving and decision making teaching amongst a group that were having some social difficulties. He was so pleased that his parents were implementing a new Character Counts Program. And we chatted on and life was really good in that building. And they were doing middle school every day fifth through eighth grade. We just need to somehow get that word out. That you can do very good middle school and it's still strong in a lot of places.

I think another of the biggest factors that is influencing us today is the whole urban situation. That's been a difficult issue. I worked with the Chicago public schools that have changed administrators I don't know how many times in the last 20 years. They changed administrators, they changed organization, they changed grade level, they have changed philosophy. That's an urban setting trying to solve the problems that are societal in nature. The whole urban question scares people. Detroit gets a lot more emphasis in the newspaper than does a smaller district. So we have to really look at the whole urban issue and say, "What is the best way to educate kids in city schools where the culture, the political culture, is so different?" We have to publicize those urban programs that are making a significant difference in the lives of kids.

I think the baggage that kids bring to school today is different. That is another factor that influences middle school education. What kids come in the door with is not something that we are used to dealing with all the time. The piece of research I just read about is that this is the first year that we can have an identifiable group of crack babies to study in the sixth grade. There is a large enough group that they can be studied as far as their learning abilities or disabilities. That's baggage that comes in the middle school classroom that the typical teacher isn't ready to deal with.

Who has benefited the most from the middle school movement?

The students, by far, the kids. And they will tell you that too. I think those that have been in true middle schools, those who have been part of the focus on them as an age group have benefited through the teaching that has been done. We know some things about them that we did not know before the middle school started. I would say that 10- to 14-year-olds have benefited more than anybody from this because of the research that has been done not just in the middle school but throughout society. But there is still more to be done.

Were there regional differences in the way middle school education was developed or defined in various regions in the country?

We were really fortunate in Illinois because we moved rapidly. We had a lot of strong university connections, we had the state organization, we involved a lot of parents. We coordinated with Illinois Principals Association and coordinated with the Reading Association. We targeted state legislators that had children at the middle school age and began our quest to get middle school certification. While we didn't get an endorsement for five or six years, we kept hammering away at that group and were able to identify the people in the legislature who had seventh graders, and sent them letters and information about middle schools. In the South it moved rapidly in Florida because the University of South Florida opened the National Resource Center for Middle School Education. It also grew rapidly in the Carolinas and Georgia, but in states where people were further apart, Iowa, Idaho, or Montana, it moved more slowly. If your state had a guru, a middle school guru, like Don and Sally Clark in Arizona, or if they had Howard Johnston or Gordon Vars in Ohio, or if they had Ken McEwin in North Carolina, or they had Connie Toepfer in New York, and others like Lou Romano in Michigan, change happened rapidly. If they had somebody in the state spearheading it, it moved real fast. I remember MAMSE [Michigan Association of Middle School Educators] took off in Michigan, because they were looking to make some changes in their configurations in the state at that time, and because Michigan State and Central Michigan took the leadership.

What are the lessons that we still need to learn from the history of the middle school movement?

Connect early. In other words, we spent so much time setting ourselves apart, that what happened is that we lost our connections with the elementary and high schools. So instead of being seen as a transitional school, the middle school became an exciting entity to itself. What had been neglected was now the shining star in education and things were happening and things were good. And we lost our connections to what was going on in the elementary; we lost it as part of the K–12 spectrum. So I think we need to look back and say how does the middle school fit in with what happens to kids kindergarten through twelfth grade.

How would you characterize the current status of the middle school movement?

I think the biggest problem that we have right now is a financial one. We need to get the political support and resources we need for schools to maintain the integrity in programming for this age group. There is a school that I am familiar with in Illinois where everyone teaches reading, has been trained to do so, and has taught reading in the content area for years. Their test scores are at the top of the state of Illinois. Now they have to drop that program because of No Child Left Behind or every one of those teachers has to go out and get certified in reading. In the current status of the middle school movement there are decisions that are being made that affect us, and we have to lobby to maintain our integrity and practice what we know is good for young adolescents.

I know that the middle school concept is working because I see teaming, advisory, exploratory, continuous progress, teachers trained to teach this age group, integrated curriculum and other components of the concept in most of the schools that I visit or consult with. I have watched the transitions over the past twenty-five years and the questions are more sophisticated, and research oriented than they were in the past. The struggle now is to maintain all of those components in spite of financial problems and the restraints of No Child Left Behind.

Are there other comments that you would like to make?

We didn't cover kids at risk. I think there are still kids out there who fall through the cracks for a variety of reasons. And I think those cracks are going to be larger and larger because of issues of which they have very little control in the middle school. I think we have to take a special look at the at-risk group in the middle school because it's really a lot easier to deal with them and help them there than it is when they get to the high school. So I would just say that in the future that we need to spend some time looking at that group of kids who come into the classroom and say, "Teach me, I dare you."

The other thing that we need to talk about a little more is community service. We need to get all the kids in middle schools out developing that concrete compassion that they can develop by helping others. With the over-emphasis on testing right now, we are missing the opportunity to develop some lifelong skills in these kids that aren't in the standards. This is the age where they need to develop the skills of getting along with others, the skills of organizing and decision making, the skills of doing something for another person. I think it is still possible to go all the way through the American school system and never have to do something upon which someone else relies. So I guess we need to spend some time in classes and among schools talking about how to develop good people out of kids. How do we do this in addition to the other things we're asked to do? These kids are going to be responsible for the comfort of my old age, and I for one, want them to be responsible, well-educated, caring, and considerate people. These values are instilled and solidified in the middle school years. We cannot lose our focus on their future.

10

Thomas "Tom" S. Dickinson

We don't have young children who are warm and cuddly and color things that you can hang on your refrigerator or fax to grandma. We don't have high schoolers who are winning state championships or singing wonderfully in a choir. We have kids in beginning band, and that's when people say, "I'm supposed to listen to this?" But, it takes a different kind of person to deal with the beginning band and nurture and shape it so that we get something on the other end.

A former editor of National Middle School Association's *Middle School Journal* (1990–1993), Dr. Thomas S. Dickinson is widely recognized as a distinguished editor and accomplished author. He is author or co-author of more than 60 middle school publications including journal articles, book chapters, books, and research reports as well as a co-researcher for three national studies that assessed the status and progress of middle level education. He was also editor of the influential *Reinventing the Middle School: A Proposal to Counter Arrested Development.* Dickinson was also co-editor, with Tom Erb, of *We Gain More Than We Give: Teaming in Middle Schools,* which is the most comprehensive and authoritative elucidation of middle school

The Legacy of Middle School Leaders, pages 165–178
Copyright © 2011 by Information Age Publishing
All rights of reproduction in any form reserved.

teaming in the history of middle school education. Dr. Dickinson played a key role in the establishment of middle level teacher preparation programs at three universities and has written widely on the topic of middle level teacher preparation and certification/licensure.

Dr. Dickinson received his undergraduate degree in history from Wake Forest University, Winston-Salem, North Carolina, in 1969. After serving in the United States Army, he began his teaching career as a junior high school social studies teacher in 1971 in Hampton, Virginia. He earned a master's degree in social studies education (1976) and a doctorate in social studies education and supervision of instruction from the University of Virginia, Charlottesville (1980). Dickinson was Assistant Professor at Eastern Kentucky University, Richmond, Kentucky (1980–1982), and Visiting Professor at North Carolina Wesleyan College, Rocky Mount, North Carolina (1983–1984), before accepting a position on the faculty of Eastern Illinois University, Charleston, Illinois, in 1987. He then became Associate Professor of Education at Georgia Southern University in Statesville, Georgia (1988), where he remained until he became editor of the *Middle School Journal* in 1990. After serving as Editor of *Middle School Journal*, he was Associate Professor of Curriculum and Instruction at Indiana State University, Terre Haute, from 1993 to 2002. Dr. Dickinson is currently Professor of Education Studies at DePauw University, Greencastle, Indiana.

Selected Accomplishments and Contributions to Middle Level Education

- Founding editor of *The Journal of the Association of Illinois Middle Schools* (1986–1988)
- Member of National Middle School Association (NMSA) Professional Preparation Task Force that wrote the first national standards for middle level teacher preparation (1988)
- Founding Co-editor, *Becoming: The Journal of the Georgia Middle School Association* (1989–1990)
- First Program Review Coordinator for NMSA/National Council for Accreditation of Teacher Education Middle Level Teacher Standards (1989–1990)
- Member of the NCATE Board of Examiners (1989–1992)
- Founding Editor of *Midpoints: Occasional Papers in Middle Level Education*, NMSA (1990–1993)
- Editor of *In Focus: The Journal of the Indiana Middle Level Education Association* (1993–1996)

- Member of the Early Adolescent Generalists Standards Group of the Indiana Professional Standards Board (1994–1995)
- Visiting Fellow, Center for Educational Leadership, Trinity University, San Antonio, Texas (1998–1999)
- Grant Recipient, Lilly Endowment, *Extending Teacher Creativity* (1997–2001)

Selected Publications

Dickinson, T. S. (Ed.). (1993). *Readings in middle school education: A continuing conversation.* Columbus, OH: National Middle School Association.

McEwin, C. K., & Dickinson, T. S. (Eds.). (1995). *The professional preparation of middle level teachers: Profiles of successful programs.* Columbus, OH: National Middle School Association.

McEwin, C. K., Dickinson, T. S., & Jenkins, D. M. (1996). *America's middle schools: Practices and progress, A 25-year perspective.* Columbus, OH: National Middle School Association.

Dickinson, T. S., & Erb, T. O. (Eds.). (1997). *We gain more than we give: Teaming in the middle school.* Columbus, OH: National Middle School Association.

Dickinson, T. S. (Ed.). (2001). *Reinventing the middle school.* New York: Routledge Falmer.

Dickinson, T. S. (2001). Reinventing the middle school: A proposal to counter arrested development. In T. Dickinson (Ed.), *Reinventing the middle school* (pp. 3–20). New York: Routledge Falmer.

Dickinson, T. S., & Butler, D. A. (2001). Reinventing the middle school. *Middle School Journal, 33*(1), 7–13.

McEwin, C. K., & Dickinson, T. S. (2001). Educators committed to young adolescents. In T.O. Erb (Ed.), *This we believe and now we must act* (pp. 11–19). Columbus, OH: National Middle School Association.

McEwin, C. K., Dickinson, T. S., & Jenkins, D. M. (2003). *America's middle schools in the new century: Status and progress.* Westerville, OH: National Middle School Association.

McEwin, C. K., Dickinson, T. S., & Smith, T. W. (2003). Why specialized preparation is critical. *Kappa Delta Pi Record, 39*(2), 58–61.

McEwin, C. K., Dickinson, T.S., & Jacobson, M. G. (2004). *Programs and practices in K-8 schools: Do they meet the educational needs of young adolescents?* Westerville, OH: National Middle School Association.

McEwin, C. K., Dickinson, T. S., & Smith, T. W. (2004). The role of teacher preparation, licensure, and retention in creating high performing middle schools. In S. Thompson (Ed.), *Reforming middle level education: Considerations for policymakers* (pp. 109–129). Westerville, OH: National Middle School Association and Greenwich, CT: Information Age Publishing.

McEwin, C. K., Dickinson, T. S., & Anfara, V. A. (2005). The professional preparation of middle level teachers and principals. *Encyclopedia of Middle Level Education* (pp. 59-67). Greenwich CT: Information Age Publishing and Westerville, OH: National Middle School Association.

---

*Thomas S. Dickinson**

I have had three main influences relative to middle level education. And all of these occurred after I started teaching. My work with young adolescents was in the middle grades and focused in the social studies. So, my influences really came once I started teaching at the university level, and those three influences are rather woven together as three. Probably the first and foremost was Joan Lipsitz and her work that I first came across in *Growing Up Forgotten*. It may be the very first thing that really struck me as a middle grades educator and it was something that continues to have that kind of impact. Secondly was the work that Bill Alexander did. He was a world famous curriculum writer. And the third person is Ken McEwin from Appalachian State University. Ken and I formed a friendship in the very early 1980s and for the last twenty years have been working professionally together particularly in the area of middle school teacher education and research and writing having to do with that. So, those are the individuals who have had the most meaningful impact and it's been a rather synergistic back and forth among the three. I am quite happy now that I know all three and have worked with them. So, I've been fortunate that not only do I have three teachers, mentors, guides, but I've been able to actually work and interact with all of them.

What kinds of middle school literature did you read?

When I started teaching the first middle school course at North Carolina Wesleyan in the early 1980s, I understood young adolescents from a face-to-face teaching context. I understood working in a variety of middle schools particularly as a supervisor. But I was relatively naïve when it came to having a middle school foundation, so it was one of the things I had to practice at when I first started using the first edition of Alexander and George's *Exemplary Middle School*. One of the beautiful things about that

---

* Tom Dickinson was interviewed for the Legacy Project in March 2004.

text all the way through three editions is the resource list at the end of every chapter. I read everything listed voraciously.

There were publications that came out early in the middle school movement that impacted me. One of them is Joan's *Growing Up Forgotten*. Another one is *The Exemplary Middle School* which I have mentioned, then *This We Believe* was another major element, and I started moving backwards into some of the original junior high school materials—Koos, Briggs, Gruhn and Douglass, and Van Til, Lounsbury, and Vars.

Are there any particular theorists, theories, or writings that have influenced your educational thought?

I think a lot of the qualitative work that I've done in the last twenty years has been very heavily influenced by the second book that Joan Lipsitz did, which was *Successful Schools for Young Adolescents*. Joan has had a very significant impact on my career because she's made me look at young adolescents first, foremost, and always. There have been other people that have impacted me. One of them is Chris Stevenson. And Chris has had a particularly positive impact about thinking about curriculum.

What was your primary motivation for becoming involved in the middle school movement?

Really I didn't have any. I got handed a middle school course at Wesleyan. And at that point, I was a social studies educator. I perceived myself as a social studies educator. I wasn't looking to do anything outside the social studies. And I found myself drifting over to the middle grades. I went to my roots relative to what I do with something new, which is to read, and I found out that, number one, I had a context to understand what people were writing about because I had taught these kids and I had supervised in the classroom, so it made sense. I had a practical connection with them, but I didn't have any motive. I didn't have any agenda or a grand design.

Ken's and my friendship and professional relationship resulted from my finding myself at Eastern Illinois University and having to design a middle grades teacher education program. So, immediately, I started looking at the teacher education material and as anybody that's done anything in twenty years would find out, Ken's name pops up. And so we started talking together and we presented together at a conference. I didn't even have any designs to go into teacher education. It was one of those harsh realities that I had to get a program approved by the State of Illinois. So, I went into that area. So, it's been rather serendipitous.

How has the middle school concept changed since the early years of the middle school movement?

I don't think the concept has changed at all. I think we have stopped paying attention to it. Matter of fact, I don't think that; I know that. And I have indicted the profession in a recent publication because we have forgotten that. There is nothing wrong with the original middle school concept. That's one of the things that people get into with the whole idea of presentism. The original foundation of the concept is still valid. And one of the things that happened that was just plain chaos is that a lot of people, not everyone, but a lot of people, lost sight of the intellectual validity, and the criticism [that] has been leveled is that we did not challenge young adolescents as much as we should have.

But the concept never said that we shouldn't challenge them, you can't have three curriculum writers like Alexander and Vars and Lounsbury and not see the richness of the curriculum proposals that came out of their writing and speaking. So, if there's anything that's changed is we have gone blind in one eye, on occasion, to what the concept was really all about. And anybody that's ever worked with a young adolescent knows that intellectually they are capable of tremendous amounts. And yet that's one thing that we have been indicted for because we lost that, but the concept never said "We ought to have a school just focused on social development."

You've answered part of this, but how have middle schools changed since the early years of the movement?

Well, if you think about educational movements, this is a very significant movement on a number of levels. While everyone might not have known exactly what they were doing in the transition from junior highs to middle schools, one of the things that we have accomplished is that people understand that this is a school focused on development. That's one of the success stories. One of the things that has changed is that we've made a significant change in grade organization. To move from junior high schools that were seventh, eighth, and ninth grade to an organizational change of sixth, seventh, and eighth and in a lot of the southern states grades five through eight, was not a small change. Moving the ninth graders out was no small task; the ninth graders were the tail that wagged the dog in the junior high school. They were the Carnegie Credits. They were the reason we had competitive athletics, competitive cheerleading, competitive band, subject matter orientation, and to move that out to another school organization and move in a perceived elementary grade from the sixth grade or elementary in the middle grades with all the protests of "oh, no we can't have these little sixth graders around eighth graders." We've profited across this country from sixth grade teachers and their child-centered focus and their richness of instructional abilities coming into the middle grades. That's been one of the really positive things that has happened and I think that's impacted the instruction positively in more middle schools than all the in-services anybody has ever done.

What were some of the motivations that fueled the growth of the middle school movement?

I think there are probably three motivations. One comes out of the junior high school, which I think almost everyone realized became largely unsuccessful. And I think that was because we had a school that was dominated from the ninth graders down and that really needed to be changed. I remember early on, people used to argue if we move the ninth graders out, then we can concentrate on this group of kids.

A second motivation that I think has been going on, and to me it has been a failure up to this point, is finding an appropriate curriculum for this age. I would offer, as Jim Beane has written and spoken about eloquently, that the separate subject curriculum organization is inappropriate for young adolescent thinkers. It's antithetical to where they are in their larger thinking and their developmental orientation. I think that is something that a lot of people don't argue with any more, but I think we're also in a period of time where we have high stakes testing, and we have a climate and culture that wants to know how Johnny or Susie scored on their history test, rather than what is their thinking about humanities topics.

The third one is the motivation to make the school what it has always aspired to be. And I think a lot of that goes back to some fundamental things with *Turning Points* and the gap between vision and reality. I think that was fueled tremendously and positively by *Turning Points* and *Turning Points 2000* focusing our attention back on where we should be and what we should be doing.

How were decisions about the directions taken by the middle school movement made?

This movement has attracted some of the very best minds in education. It's also attracted some self-serving individuals who saw it as an opportunity to garner financial reward, garner press for themselves, and garner positions of power. So you've got people that if you look at the movement across thirty, forty, fifty years you see people float in and out and do things and then disappear from the radar scope. And then you see people come in consistently and work in the vineyard and continue to work in the vineyard.

So, you've got both a chaotic situation with people serving any number of purposes other than young adolescents and then you've got people coming in that are making long-term decisions, but overall this movement has been rather chaotic.

There's a particular parallel if you look at the National Middle School Association. The Association was really established by the foundational thinkers: the Gordon Vars, the John Lounsburys, the Ken McEwins, the Tom Gatewoods, the Don Eichhorns. And you get the early years of the middle school movement and the early years in NMSA, very, very rich in the thinking and the writing and the speaking and the work out in the schools, and then it's almost as if "Okay, we've gotten to this point," and other people see that this very much can be a power position, and so now you look at the leadership in NMSA and there aren't any writers, researchers, thinkers. I mean, they might be practitioners and I'm not condescending to practitioners and their importance, but it's almost as if the movement has turned a page and said, "Well, we don't need any theoretical people. We don't need any writers. We don't need any broad thinkers. We need people that administer schools day after day." So we've gone through several phases. That is why if you want to look at some of the richest literature, you read the early founders.

How were other individuals and groups outside of middle level education involved in the early years of the middle school movement?

There is a whole thread of psychological research. Jeanne Brooks-Gunn is one that comes to mind and Jacquelynne Eccles comes to mind, ones who have never been part of the "middle school movement," but who have done tremendous amounts of research outside of the mainstream educators. Yet their work is really what we base all of our work on. The psychologists and the researchers have been primary in giving us a knowledge base to stand on. Then there are others and you have to look to places like the Center for Early Adolescence with Joan Lipsitz. You have to look at the different foundations: Carnegie, early-on Ford, Pew Charitable Trust, and others, which were really repositories of a lot of very thoughtful creative people who supported a lot of what went on in middle grades. And there are some parallel tracks out there and only every now and then when you have a group like now the National Forum to Accelerate Middle Grades Reform do you see the cross-over and broad participation. Early on there were a lot of parallel tracks, but they didn't mix and that was to our detriment.

What was the educational context at the time the middle school movement began?

When Bill Alexander called for a new school in the middle in the early 1960s, we were still in the post-Sputnik situation. At that point we had come out of the really horrible days of the Cold War, the Cuban Missile Crisis, Berlin, and the context was, I think, very propitious for what Bill did because it was turned around psychologically that change is possible. If he'd tried to propose a new school in the middle, maybe five years before, I think politically in this country, there was still this whole cloud of nuclear Armageddon hanging over our heads, that I don't think it would have made it possible; but in this period of time when Kennedy was elected there was a sense of feeling of possibilities, the U.S. Office of Education and National Science Foundation were pouring money into the schools and I think that there was in essence, in the broadest cultural sense, a very positive "We can do this." We can put a man on the moon. We can educate people.

What have been some the most significant events, incidents, or moments in the middle school movement and why did you select these particular events?

Let me talk about the one that began it all. Bill Alexander's plane was late and this is the old story and I happen to have been blessed enough to be able to hear the grand old man tell me the story himself. Bill was going to the Cornell Junior High School Conference and he was going to speak on the dynamic junior high school. Well, there wasn't one. You know, they asked him to speak on something and he wrote a speech, and he's there at LaGuardia and the plane is late and he sits back and he thinks about his speech and he re-writes it. And he calls for a new school in the middle. Now first of all, that's pretty bold, but it was something that, I think, even Bill would admit a number of people had been thinking about—we're in this situation and things are just not working and something's got to be done. And Bill, if you read his own history and background, had been thinking about middle grades kids all of his life. Now he had been working in the curriculum field, but he'd been thinking about middle grades kids, and here it was—it all came popping out. I don't think you can underestimate the impact of a foundation. We happen to be blessed with one of the best curriculum minds in this century—as the father of our movement. Now that goes a long way to give us legitimacy from the early 1960s on. He spent the rest of his career and even after his retirement educating people about middle grades and what it should be.

The second thing that I would probably point to has to do with curriculum, and that's Jim Beane's work on integrative curriculum. If there's one indictment of the movement it is that we did not pay attention to the curriculum as we should have because we had an inheritance from the junior high school with the separate subject curriculum, which we should have looked at as part of our organizational changes. We didn't; we just kept on with the same divisions. And what Jim did, I think, struck some particular notes for some people. I think one of the things that he said was that there was a reason to have a different curriculum.

The whole thrust of what middle school education is about is very much a Deweyan progressive democratic school. And the secondary subject matter, separate orientation, does not match up with that well at all. I mean, everything is sliced and diced and organized and laid out and it's almost "swallow it now, and chew it later" in certain manifestations. So, one of the things that Jim did was to remind us of our philosophical roots with integrated curriculum as a school that is supposed to be about the democratic ideal of helping these children develop and develop who they are, which means we need to be responsive and flexible and that an interdisciplinary and integrated curriculum can do that. So I think Jim's publication of his small volume on middle school curriculum was just a real powerful bell that got rung.

Now, it ran into the conservative restoration and high-stakes testing and separate subject reporting and many other things since then. I think a lot of people don't understand the "small d" democracy orientation of the middle school. I don't think they understand where it came about at the turn of the century and what it was intended to deal with. I don't think they understood the whole focus of the original junior high school founders. I don't think they understood the implications. If you tease out the middle school concept and implications, you very much change the relationship of teacher and taught. You very much change the relationship of teacher and taught to knowledge. And I don't think people have teased that out. And I think that's one of the things that Jim's work and his writing did, and then work that followed up from Chris Stevenson, John Arnold, Ed Brazee and others. I think that those have been very, very powerful. Do I think it's going to come to fruition? No. I think the window's already shut. I think things have happened in the broader culture that are literally not going to permit it. So we'll have pockets of success with Watershed and other examples. And we'll have teachers in their own two-person teams that go about an integrated year and we look at those with pride, but they are only islands in the stream.

I think the third element was *Turning Points*. And I mean by that, the original *Turning Points* because I think *Turning Points* riveted our attention back to where we were supposed to be. I think it turned our attention back to the concept fundamentally. *Turning Points* is in and of itself. It's pretty straightforward and well-known.

What have been some of the most significant obstacles to the success of the middle school movement?

I don't think you can underestimate the problems and difficulties that have been visited upon this movement by the lack of across-the-board, across the 50 states, separate and distinct teacher preparation and teacher licensure standards. You cannot create and sustain any educational endeavor without appropriate preparation. And throughout the history of this movement teachers that teach in it have been prepared for other developmental ages, or prepared differently for subject-matter orientations rather than a combination between children and knowledge. And it's been one of those handicaps that continues to revisit itself. You'll have certain states like North Carolina, Ohio, or Georgia that will be in the vanguard and then you'll have other states.

I don't think anymore that it's really a problem with the universities and deans and provosts. At one time it was, but it's not now. Now it's with a cadre of people at the state levels who are on licensure boards, who are in political power positions, that don't want to have anything but the flexibility to put a warm body in front of a classroom, regardless of whether they are qualified or not. And I think that's where we are and I find it shameful.

There are other terms that Ken McEwin and I have used, including "malpractice." And it really is; if you prepared to teach young children, you should teach young children. If you prepared to teach older adolescents and separate subjects, you should do that. We shouldn't be all in the middle in the dumping ground. And I think that's one of the big problems that continues to haunt us even to today, despite a large number of people's best efforts.

The second thing is the search for an appropriate curriculum. I've done enough curriculum work to know that in this century every curriculum design that's ever been proposed is in existence. We have integrated, we have interdisciplinary, we have separate subject, and we have everything. I've never felt like we got to the point of argument between the purists on integrated curriculum, and people that maybe are a little fuzzier in their thinking on interdisciplinary. I never thought we got to the point where that was even a major point. I'd like to just put those two parties together and we'll argue about it one day down the road.

Who do you consider to be among the most influential leaders of the middle school movement and why did you select each of them?

I'd have to put Paul George at the very top. And I've already said enough about Bill Alexander so, you know, to me Bill is an icon as well as a founder of the movement. But I don't think any movement has been as well served by a single text as it has by *The Exemplary Middle School.* It's the only middle school text that I've used for twenty years, and I know everything that's out in the field. It puts us at ground level at exemplary schools and uses example, after example, after example and what the book says is, "Yes, you can." The book talks about ultimate possibilities because it talks about the concept.

I am going to put Ken McEwin in there. I made Ken laugh one time because we are of a particular age. When I grew up, old style windows had a sash and a weight inside with this rope, and when you'd lift the window the weight would go down and it would hold the window open. Now one of the things that would happen in older houses was the rope would break from use, and the weight would fall down inside, and the problem was the window wouldn't stay open, and so the window would fall down. Okay, now, there are plenty of people around that don't know about this. I've explained this to my daughters when they were at their grandmother's and you know, they couldn't understand why the window wouldn't stay open. They kept opening it, it'd slide back down. Sometimes it slams back down. And I use that analogy because what Ken McEwin did was, he opened a window and he put a stick in it and that's what he did with teacher education. If Ken had been alive sixty years before, who knows where the junior high school would have gone. Because if the junior high school had established teacher education for the junior high school, it might have gone and would have gone a different direction. Whether that would have been positive or not, who can tell. But, what Ken did was he opened a window and like you do with one that has a broken weight rope, he put a stick in it to hold it open. And that stick's been in that window now for twenty plus years.

There are people now in teacher education who don't know who opened the window, but it's not necessary because the window's open. For every program we have out there, we have publications, consulting speaking that Ken has done or that other people that have studied and worked with Ken have done, all the way up and down the line. He is very much like Paul. And the linkage between Ken and Paul is also very instructive too, because that's a history that goes back many years to the founding of this movement in the middle grades as well. Both of those are people that knocked dominoes over. And the dominoes are still falling. The dominoes for both of those men are going to fall for a good number of years still and we're going to be graced with their presence. Those two have given us a really solid foundation.

What have been the roles of women and minorities in the middle school movement?

One of the tragedies is that for minority members of the population, we have not as an overall movement on a national level had that many visible minority people involved at the college level, at the schools, at the central office level. There have been a large number of minority teachers and administrators, particularly in districts and in school systems that are large and urban and represent the minority population as well, but we haven't had minority participation in a lot of the leadership roles. I don't know why that is. Women have participated very heavily and we've had minority women much more than minority men in some of those situations.

What are some examples of ways the middle school movement has affected American education?

I think it's been a very visible, a very tangible progressive education organization. You can't have a school oriented towards a child and focus on their needs without calling it a progressive school. I mean, it just is. If you want to have an essentialist middle school, it would be a different design.

There are a lot of ways to do schools, but I think middle schools say, "Hey, this is a progressive idea. This a progressive school in the best sense of the word. This is school oriented towards kids and their needs and they're not going to be passive recipients here. They're going to be part of the program. We're going to take them into account. We're going to change things and augment them towards their needs. And we're going to study things, yes, but there are lots of ways to study things." That's the beauty of what the school does. It takes the best ideas of what Dewey is talking about with experiences and it makes them flesh. And the good schools that do that day in and day out are perfect examples of what progressive education can be.

One of the tragedies in this movement is we haven't made enough allegiance with our kindred folk. The longer I've been around the more I understand that the early childhood people understand very well what developmentally responsive middle schools are without even knowing middle schools; they know it from an early childhood orientation. And people that have pushed the orientation of true early childhood, the Montessories, the Lillian Katzes, the others, understand middle school very well because they are part of that whole developmental thrust, and we haven't made enough connections, we haven't made enough bridges there.

**Are there lessons we still need to learn from the history of the
middle school movement?**

Our predecessor failed. We have fewer than 500 junior high schools
anywhere around. Another twenty years going down this road not paying attention to things, as people have said in your interviews, we could find ourselves to be a relic. The current drive to change in some big cities' schools
like Philadelphia should not be seen to change as they're going from middle schools to K–8 schools, that should not be seen as an oddity and the
movement should not turn around and look at that and say, "Ah, they're
really stupid." There are some lessons there. If we don't pay attention to the
tenuous nature of a progressive democratic school that's oriented towards
development in the midst of a cultural sea that doesn't prize that necessarily as the best. And if we don't make the connections with the other schools
and the other players, we can find ourselves a dinosaur. And the idea of it
tomorrow is going to be like today. See, this is what happens without the history. This is what happens without the programs to teach the teachers about
the history, to go out and be a realist about what you do. This is vulnerabil-
ity. People think teacher education and separate licensure has to do with
only certain parts of what we do, instruction and adolescent development.
It has a much bigger function than that, a much bigger function.

**How would you characterize the current status of the middle
school movement?**

I already have. The book is called *Reinventing the Middle School.* I made
the comment that the majority of middle schools that are out there are in
a stage of arrested development, and I began the book by saying one line:
"There's nothing wrong with the middle school concept." So it's not the
concept; it's the application of it. And so I will stand by what I said there
and say, "It is right there."

11

Nancy M. Doda

> *The larger assumption of the middle school movement was that every single child should have a first-class seat. That there should be equal educational access and opportunity to the best curriculum, the best teachers, the best resources, the richest learning opportunities we have.*

Widely recognized for her devotion to improving the lives and education of young adolescents, Dr. Nancy M. Doda has provided middle level consulting services in all 50 states as well as in Canada, Europe, the Far East, and Australia. She has conducted thousands of workshops, professional development experiences, and institutes. Well known for her engaging and inspiring speeches, Doda has also contributed significantly to professional literature including the Teacher-to-Teacher column in the *Middle School Journal* from 1976 until 1980, co-authoring NEA's long-time bestseller, *Team Organization: Promise, Practice and Possibility,* and a similarly long-standing publication for the National Middle School Association (NMSA), *Treasure Chest.* In addition to publications suited for practitioners, she has written several research publications including an anchor essay on Middle School Equity in *The Encyclopedia of Middle School Education,* as well as a case study

The Legacy of Middle School Leaders, pages 179–194
Copyright © 2011 by Information Age Publishing
All rights of reproduction in any form reserved.

collection, *Transforming Ourselves: Transforming Schools.* Numerous articles and forewords complement her written contributions. Dr. Doda is a well-known and highly regarded consultant who is in great demand as a conference speaker and workshop leader. Her passion for teaching, her love of children, and her commitment to the improvement of middle schools has made her a household name among middle school educators.

Dr. Doda received her undergraduate degree in English education from Wake Forest University, Winston-Salem, North Carolina in 1974, and began her career teaching language arts and reading on a team at Lincoln Middle School in Alachua County Schools, Gainesville, Florida. It was in these early years of the middle school movement that she developed an understanding of and strong commitment to the middle school concept. She earned her master's degree in middle school education and reading in 1978 and her doctorate in curriculum and instruction/teacher education in 1984 from the University of Florida, Gainesville. In 1985, she became an Assistant Professor at Virginia Polytechnic Institute, Falls Church, Virginia, before accepting a position as Associate Professor at National-Louis University based in the Washington, DC area, where she taught until 2007. Dr. Doda continues to be active as a professional development facilitator, workshop leader, and author.

Selected Accomplishments and Contributions to Middle Level Education

- Delivered the first keynote address given by a teacher at NMSA Annual Conference in 1977 and gave keynote addresses in 1984 and 1989
- NMSA Board of Directors (1987–1992)
- Received the New England League of Middle Schools Distinguished Service Award (1989)
- Received the Connecticut Association of Secondary School Principals Special Recognition Award (1990)
- Received the Virginia Middle School Association Distinguished Service Award (1996)
- Charter member of the National Forum to Accelerate Middle Grades Reform (1997–2002)
- Received the John H. Lounsbury Distinguished Service Award from NMSA (2001)

Selected Publications

Doda, N. M. (1981). *Teacher to teacher.* Columbus, OH: National Middle School Association.

Doda, N. M. (1984). The generics of middle school teaching. In J. H. Lounsbury (Ed.), *Perspectives: Middle school education, 1964–1984* (pp. 87–97). Columbus, OH: National Middle School Association.

Erb, T. O., & Doda, N. M. (1989). *Team organization: Promise, practices, and possibilities.* Washington, DC: National Education Association.

Doda, N. M. (1992). Teaming: Two novices find success. In J. H. Lounsbury (Ed.), *Connecting the curriculum through interdisciplinary instruction* (pp. 81–86). Columbus, OH: National Middle School Association.

McLaughlin, J., & Doda, N. M. (1997). Teaching with time on your side: Developing long-term relationships in schools. In J. Irvin (Ed.), *What research says to the middle level practitioner* (pp. 57–71). Columbus, OH: National Middle School Association.

Doda, N. M., & George, P. S. (1999). Closing the gap between exploratory and core: Two worlds of middle school. *Middle School Journal, 30*(5), 32–39.

Doda, N. M., & Thompson, S. C. (Eds.). (2002). *Transforming ourselves, transforming schools: Middle school change.* Westerville, OH: National Middle School Association.

Doda, N. M. (2005). The challenge of middle school equity. In V. A. Anfara, G. Andrews, & S.B. Mertens (Eds.), *Encyclopedia of middle grades education* (pp. 25–34). Greenwich, CT: Information Age Publishing and Westerville, OH: National Middle School Association.

Doda, N. M. (2006). Creating socially equitable middle grades schools. In S. C. Thompson (Ed.) *The handbook on research in middle level education* (pp. 65–84). Westerville, OH: National Middle School Association and Greenwich, CT: Information Age Publishing.

Doda, N. M. (2010). What every good middle school principal should know. *Middle Level Leadership,* National Association of Secondary School Principals. Retrieved from http://www.principals.org/Content.aspx?topic=60545

Nancy M. Doda[*]

The folks who had the most influence on me are really many and varied. Certainly Paul George, my doctoral chair and my advisor at the master's degree level, was most instrumental in encouraging and supporting me. He invited me to show my work, my teaching, to the larger community. I had

---

[*] Nancy Doda was interviewed for the Legacy Project in June 2005.

never in my wildest dreams thought about doing anything like that, and I probably wouldn't have had Paul not been involved in consulting work with public schools and demonstrating how that could be done. And Ken McEwin with his invitation to present at Appalachian State University summer institutes allowed me a place, a forum, to do that work. And so in the very early years that was a way in which I was able to grow. And John Lounsbury has always been a mentor to me.

In the mid to later years, Jim Beane has been the most influential of all of my collegiate relationships among middle school educators. Jim challenged me to think much more deeply than I ever thought before about the social justice agendas of middle schools, about the curriculum question, what should we be teaching young adolescents, not just how should we be teaching them but *what* is it that we should be teaching them and who decides what's worth knowing.

There are so many other people who have been influential. I served on the National Middle School Association Board of Directors for five years as the chair of the Resolutions Committee. That committee was formed by Connie Toepfer. Connie was always very concerned about democratic, participatory governments. We did some serious work around developing resolutions using the membership voice to tackle some really tough political issues—gender rights, for example, came as one of our resolution issues and others that were very controversial. What was wonderful about that experience and Connie's influence on me is that it allowed me to sort of get to know the National Middle School Association and the role of that association in our movement. It allowed me to serve in a way to advance social justice in the organization. So Connie was very powerful in helping me move forward.

I would say that in various other ways there have been individuals, teachers, state organizational representatives, and people within the community of that early group of middle school educators who really were helpful and influential, and there was mutual respect among all of us even though we weren't always of like-mindedness in our thinking about middle school. One of them was John Van Hoose and another was Tom Moeller, both of whom have passed away. Both of those individuals were always, I would say, the enthusiasm of middle school. George White was another person who has been consistently supportive and helpful for me in my work. And Sue Thompson has been a phenomenal influence, and Sue and I worked as far back as 20 years ago. I'm grateful for opportunities like working with Walt Grebing at the Nuts and Bolts Summer Institute for many years. And there are individuals like that that have opened doors for me in many ways.

What kind of middle school literature did you read?

I followed the *Middle School Journal* faithfully, especially since I was writing a column. Certainly all the NMSA publications were on my bookshelf. I remember reading *The Exemplary Middle School.* And I read Chris Stevenson's early work which wasn't all that early actually, it was *Teaching Ten to Fourteen Year Olds.* And John Van Hoose's work, *Promoting Harmony,* was influential in my thinking. Jim Beane's *Affect the Curriculum.* Jim Beane and Dick Lipka's work on self-esteem/self-concept was very important to me. But as a new middle school teacher in graduate school I was immersed in a pretty rigorous academic program which wasn't just middle school. We certainly ventured into lots of middle school literature. We even looked at historical texts from the junior high school, you know, all the way up. So we were definitely influenced by some of the folks that had written about the junior high school in comparison to the contemporary middle school. And it wasn't until much later that I was nudged to read more about curriculum in middle school, surprisingly enough, but that would be commensurate with the time period because in the 1970s and 1980s people were in the restructuring rather than reculturing. They were in the question of "How do we organize schools in the middle?" versus "What do we teach kids in the middle?" and so it wasn't until later that I began to read curriculum issues and curriculum books so getting into that came much later for me. So I guess those were some of the significant pieces. *This We Believe* obviously was extremely important.

Are there particular theorists, theories, or writings that have influenced your educational thought?

One of the things that really affected me in my work in the inner city school was a book written by Melvin Kohn, *Class and Conformity.* The other was a classic called *Schooling in Capitalist America.* But in a unique way that entire school of thinking which really challenges the meritocratic system that we have in America led me to be very skeptical about our nation's educational system and its capacity to educate fairly all children from all walks of life, from all classes and from all races. So that really sort of catapulted me into a lot of thinking about social justice issues, and that's when I became very passionate about detracting American schools and particularly about eliminating rigid ability grouping and exclusionary star systems and competitive norms that pit one child against another and programs that track groups of students by race and class inadvertently and so on. Those early works led me into work with Jeanie Oakes' *Keeping Track* and Anne Wheelock, a lot of the work around the issue of tracking and the ability grouping and social justice. So I would say that those were very important parts of my early social justice thinking. Then

I got into the curriculum area where I really theoretically began to understand the progressive educational movement.

I often talk to Jim Beane about this question. I said, "You know, I thought the middle school movement had an ideology. I thought the middle school movement was about democracy in education. I thought it was a progressive educational movement." I didn't know that folks out there weren't entirely convinced that we're in the middle school movement, and that we're advocating for it as more than just a cure for perils of puberty. I mean it was more than just a school that was developmentally responsive. I always thought that it had to have multiple layers in the agenda. Yes, it was developmentally responsive, but every good school is developmentally responsive. But it was supposed to offer kids this incredible juncture in their life, a chance to become respected individuals and treated as serious young people with ideas worthy of our attention. I took it for granted that others shared that progressive vision. And part of the reason that I did that was because I was in a school that was really progressive at the time and I just assumed that since we were an exemplary middle school and people acknowledged us as an exemplary middle school that what we were trying to do was it.

What was your primary motivation for becoming involved in the middle school movement?

I think probably more than anything else when you see something work and it really is effective, you want to tell other people why, how, what has happened here. So I was fired up. And we had the wonderful Lincoln Middle School these years. We kept the kids three years. After having the same children for three consecutive years, the eighth graders would line up at the end of the school day and with tears and hugs and this magnificent display of affection, but at the junior high school just down the road the kids would be racing out the door. And people were always just stunned by that because they wondered, "What are you doing with those children?" And you know, we loved them, and we were committed to them, and we knew that we were more than facilitators of academic learning. We knew that we were committed to the whole child and we took that very seriously. And I think above all in the middle school movement what separated us from some of the early other schools who were still wedded to the notion that teachers teach content, and we were teachers who teach people, but that was really how I got involved in the middle school movement and what kept me going. And to be surrounded by so many other fellow educators who work in hormone heaven and have this enormous shared mission was such a professional gift. It was a gift to be able to sit around the table and know that we all are working on the same huge agenda.

**How would you describe the early years of the middle school
movement, around the late 1960s and early 1970s?**

It was a grassroots movement, when you think about it. Really it was
individual educators who rallied and had this passion around young adolescents. It was a high-energy, highly passionate, love-filled kind of movement,
and it felt as if we were part of this incredibly noble, soulful child-centered
movement. I think anyone that participated in those early years would say
that it was a professional joy to be a part of the collegial network and energy
that surrounded the middle school movement. And there were lots of folks
out there, you know there's all new territory so we all had opportunities to
expand our work and to reach out and rally the troops if you will. There
was almost a missionary zeal at that time, and I am so grateful in my professional lifetime to have been a part of that because I can't imagine, maybe I
would have found another niche, but I think that for a lot of young people
who enter the field they don't have that sense of being a part of something
grand, something great. And it was a wonderful time.

**How has the middle school concept changed since the early years
of the middle school movement?**

We've kind of become arrested as Tom Dickinson has said and the development I think is arrested for a lot of different reasons: One, because we
never had a clear ideology and two, because we didn't push the teaching
and learning piece as fervently as we should have. Three is because it is
just really hard to change schools, and professional development models
were horrendously inadequate to engage faculty in significant introspective
kind of work, and finally we have an educational system that is still wedded to what I would call ordinary, usual, or traditional practices that have
never been reexamined. I mean the separate-subjects approach is taken for
granted [in] K–12, the fact that we use letter grades is taken for granted,
that punitive assessment, or punitive measures of control are still taken for
granted, that the basic fundamental life in schools hasn't changed. So the
middle school finds itself challenged particularly because of the many reasons previous to the NCLB movement and the accountability movement.

And one thing that is really interesting is all this is in the name of closing the gap between rich and poor students in the United States, and what
we know is that our most vulnerable students are the very students in middle
school who need heightened affiliation, heightened intimacy, heightened
connection with human beings, long-term accountability relationships with
adults and other kids. They need environments that are extremely safe and
trusting circles of friendship and security, and we've diminished the emphasis on that in the name of test accountability, and so ironically in the

short term while things may shift and appear to be favorable for test scores, ultimately it will bottom out and those children who have needed those wonderful elements of middle school, the strong affiliation focus, will suffer, and the gap will widen again.

I keep hoping that people will get it, that they will get the connection between affiliation and academic accomplishment that it will become eminently clear that if you want to make a difference in the lives of children you have to let children be an incredible interruption in your life, which means that children have to be a part of the middle school experience, and we can't just *do* school to them, and I do think that there are people out there that do get that and maybe the contrast is becoming clearer as there is less and less of that good stuff, and problems start mounting in schools that people will become, like in the Columbine post window of time, a little bit more aware that you can't create good middle schools without that kind of affiliation.

Who or what have been some of the greatest detractors or opponents of the middle school movement?

There has always been a dynamic tension with the gifted and talented educational organizations and part of the tension has been resolved at times and resurfaced at other times. Fundamentally I think some folks would argue that there is a consensus about gifted and talented education, but it is far from what we see in practice. But that dynamic tension is huge, and I think it has challenged the middle school movement and it's also held us back in some respect because the larger assumption of the middle school movement was that every single child should have a first-class seat. That there should be equal educational access and opportunity to the best curriculum, the best teachers, the best resources, the richest learning opportunities we have. And we know that when you sort and separate children by ability or as we've argued to the middle school that the company you keep is every bit as important in determining educational opportunity as the books you read, so if you sit next to children who consistently fail in school and who have been less successful, just the discourse alone will be less rich than the discourse in a classroom of children who have been successful. And that educational discrepancy is unacceptable in my mind in the middle school philosophy. And yet that tension continues.

I think the second sort of force that's been difficult for the middle school movement has been the most current accountability movement, which is really not new. It's a movement that has been with us for a long time; it's just been continuing to emerge. And you know its focus priority is on academic acquisition. And the tendency to lean heavily towards content knowledge acquisition, I think, and so it's the process/content debate that I think is not an either/or, it's not a polarity, but there's this tension between how do we best serve citizens of the future, and in the middle school, we've argued that at this age and stage in life for children that we should err on the side of developing learning-to-learn skills, that content is important but ultimately children ought to be able to be successful learners. And I would think that's been somewhat reconciled by the rich literacy work that's going on these days. And I'm really impressed with some of what I do see in the field of development so we've broadened it a bit, but like the whole language versus the phonics issue that's contemporarily tugging us, it's not an either/or; it's a balanced approach. And I think that the middle school has struggled to find balance in its process, content, or affect.

What are some of the mistakes that have been made during the middle school movement that we might be able to learn from today?

There are so many traps that we fell into, I think. One of the things that I'm struck by as I look back on those early conversations in middle school is that we were so caught up in this passion to bring feeling and heart to the middle school, to the institution, to the lives of children. So desperate to create school in which whole human beings could be celebrated and valued, that children would be honored as human beings as well as students. And all that remains very critical in education, but because we were so passionate about that part of the story, we didn't articulate as clearly as we should have the connection between that affect and academic achievement in learning. And I think that the public then could, and did, interpret that middle schools were really just soft, warm, fuzzy places that really weren't about deep intellectual learning.

The second one is that we fell into the trap of creating an impression about young adolescents that misrepresented that intellectual capacity. Part of this was our infatuation with "hormone heaven" as the term has been called here in my own state or the perils of puberty. And so there were lots of sharing and commiserating around the funny nature of young adolescents and sometimes even obnoxious characteristics of kids at this stage and less emphasis on the wonderful, rich, beautiful, intellectual, philosophical, and spiritual side of development. I think the middle school movement really made a mistake in that sense because we weren't portraying this whole child. So I would say I also think it invited us to be vulnerable to all kinds of criticism.

The third thing is we didn't talk about race, we didn't talk about class, we didn't talk about gender very much. And you know the middle school movement was a white movement, and ethnicity was not reflected in our early work. And so I think that was a huge deficit in our movement and, it was, it sort of isolated the work we did, and urban schools were not privy to that. Even to this day I think our least-well-served population in terms of understanding middle schools is the urban community. And what I'm observing today is that the shift away from the original middle school concept which focused on affiliation and inclusion and are leaning more towards test score achievement and accountability is really pushing the urban schools to dismantle middle schools even though they are dying for affiliation; those children are desperate for inclusion. And if we create schools that are based on test preparation, which is what is happening, they are becoming test prep centers, then we really, we could see why some of the places would go to K–8 as a desperate attempt to try to rally around something called affiliation, and I would say that that is a big part of the mistake.

And the other was that our version of professional development was very narrow. But this was not just for middle school. We were notorious for falling to the consultant trap of having a bunch of us come out into the field and do workshops that were very inspirational and even practical, I hope. At least I always thought mine were practical, but at the same time we didn't have that larger vision of professional development which is, "You've got to sustain this, you've got to do coaching, you've got to have learning communities in your building working on these big ideas and practical implications," and that's not the fault of the middle school movement; that was, I believe, symptomatic of our time. I don't know that any of us knew what we know today about good professional development. We should have been more vigilant about finding ways to craft professional development in those years that got down to the deeper levels of understanding, what it meant to have a child-centered place.

Who has benefited the most from the middle school movement?

Unfortunately not always, but the children have benefited because if I look over the big picture of the past, my own children included in that, when my first son who is much older than my second child went to middle school, he was really in a traditional junior high. And my younger son went to a middle school, and there were changes that were very favorable. He was suddenly a member of an interdisciplinary team. If I wanted to have a parent conference with the faculty, I could sit with all of those teachers as opposed to how it was with my first son. I had to go to each teacher in each department, and it certainly was clear in those different contexts that my second son in the middle school was known better by the faculty that shared a team planning time and had the opportunity to talk about that child and other children. Certainly as a parent observing my two children going through the junior high and middle school, there were tremendous changes in that decade window, and I would say that across our times from the 1960s to today mark that we've really done a tremendous job of changing the climate of buildings. I don't think their classroom experiences are deeply changed. But I would say that we have multiple benefits and maybe actually to answer your question if I were to just have to make a choice I would say that teachers have benefited. I wonder what they would say, but my sense is that teachers have benefited the most because they have been recipients of lots of new learning.

Who has benefited the least from the middle school movement?

To me it's hard to answer these questions because it's not quite so black and white or clean cut. But I would say probably the students overall. That hurts me to say that, but I would say that if we were to do as we have, shadow studies, we would still see a lot of practices that are not giving us the student benefits we have hoped for. I think a lot of middle school kids begin middle schools with great dreams for their futures and many end up with diminished visions of their future, and that's not the way it's supposed to be. So if that is the case, then we simply have not achieved what we should have achieved. And I would say that they benefit the least. Needy students, particularly students of color and poverty, still fall through the cracks.

Who do you consider to be among the most influential leaders of the middle school movement? Why did you select these?

I would say Paul George is probably one of the most prolific, articulate, thoughtful, and certainly vibrant middle school leaders in the field. He has always appealed to practitioners and leaders. He's been provocative in stretching his ideas out in points of dynamic tension. He has certainly been an advocate for leaders in the field and provided leadership training. But his collection of writings and his, just his sheer volume of work, has certainly left him as one of the great leaders of the middle school movement. I would say James Beane and his work on curriculum integration, it stands out for me as the profoundly important of all of the contributions to the middle school movement, and I would acknowledge his work as seminal. I would say John Lounsbury, and he of course stands out as a model voice for the middle school conscience if you will. He's always been our moral compass in the leadership circle, but he has also been a very influential speaker and writer and leader, very articulate about the higher ground if you will, the higher moral ground that we should be taking in the middle school movement. And Connie Toepfer had an influence on me as well in those early years, and I would put him out there as one of the early leaders in the middle school movement. These are also individuals, all four of them, who had state-level and national-level influence and international influence, but I would say that they have been instrumental in networking and creating networks and forging alliances and partnerships and fashioning opportunities for other educators, opening doors for other educators, and I think that's for me one of the definitions of great leadership is that capacity to open doors for others. I think those are probably the ones I would list, but I would also acknowledge contributions from many of my colleagues. I can't begin to tell you how many—it would be unfathomable to try and even list them, but I think of people like Ed Brazee and his work at the Maine Institute. I think of folks like John Swaim who organized institutes in the early years. I think of individuals like Sherrel Bergmann, who was instrumental in her work and Cynthia Mee in her work on *The Voices of Kids.* You know it would be impossible for me to name them all, but I would say those for me are the most significant.

What have been the roles of women and minorities in the middle school movement?

There hasn't been a significant representation from African Americans, or people of color or from women actually in the movement. I think, there were three Lounsbury Award Winners, Sherrel Bergmann, Joan Lipsitz, and me. Joan remains very influential and continues to be a very important person. I think Ann Wheelock has been an important leader. Both in her book *Crossing the Tracks* that I think became her first middle school book. Her second work was *Safe to Be Smart* which is phenomenally important and challenged all of us to think about race, class, gender. She brought those issues into the conversation of middle school and continues to do that work in her work in policy studies. The issues of gender came up on the Resolutions Committee when I served as a chair of that committee. And we talked about sexual orientation and acknowledging with sensitivity children in middle grades who struggled with sexual orientation and sexual identity issues. We really didn't just deal with gender, but that was one of the issues we began to look at that was extremely controversial and we did pass a resolution to the effect that the middle school organization should be very sensitive in helping young people avoid discrimination around sexual identity issues.

As for young adolescent girls, Mary Pipher has been a leader in that field in general, and she has been invited in as a speaker to the National Middle School Conference. Her book, *Reviving Ophelia,* references the perils of young adolescent girls and the difficulties they face fashioning positive images of themselves and their futures. So at what points that entered our conversation in our history, I don't know exactly, but I think it's certainly thanks to folks like Mary and others who do work in that particular area that conversation has become a part of our conversation. It's still not a dominant topic of conversation and I think it needs to be more fully addressed. But I think some of the work we've seen regarding math and girls is important. I think one of the best organizations which has recently become more involved but has always been at this work is the Educational Development Corporation, EDC. And I would say recently *Turning Points* and Center for Collaborative Education out of Newton, Massachusetts, has this wonderful work in which they keep the focus on equity and that focus is not as dominant as the National Middle School Association's level of conversation. I would like to see that be an issue we tackle more fully. I would say it's not been sufficient in our history for sure. Those are issues that have been underplayed.

What are some examples of ways the middle school movement has affected American education?

I think the middle school has sort of been the "wedge between" in the K–12 continuum. I think that although we've learned a tremendous amount from the elementary school in terms of understanding pedagogy for example and even the benefits of intimacy and affiliation in school and learning environments. I would say that we've pushed and begun to nudge the American high school with the National Association of Secondary School Principals' *Breaking Ranks I* and then again in *Breaking Ranks II.* There has been a clear invitation from the middle school that there needed to be change at the secondary level, and now with the small schools movement and the Gates Foundation's monies devoted to reforming the American high school, it's no surprise to me that much of the high school reform could be traced back to the early developments in middle school and then the later invitation through *Breaking Ranks* and other documents to rethink the high school model.

Have particular legislative actions significantly influenced the middle school movement?

Certainly Title IX has changed some of our thinking. If you go way back in terms of young adolescent girls and athletics. Certainly the IDEA and associated special education legislations have tremendously impacted middle schools in that they really affirmed our invitation for inclusion and have supported our work in providing least restrictive environments for all children. So it really gave us impetus to move from interdisciplinary teams, where the special-needs children were pulled out to be served, into models now of co-teaching and collaborative inclusion and team teaching, and partner teaching. Those models now are commensurate with the legislation that exists. So I think it has really advanced our work and been very helpful for the most part. The current NCLB legislation is the one I find is most problematic for middle schools, but I would say that's probably true for K–12 schools in general, but particularly true for middle schools.

What are some of the ways the middle school movement has influenced middle level curriculum and instruction?

Certainly the middle school movement has brought into the conversation a more teacher-friendly translation of constructivist philosophy. I think when I look back on classroom teaching in general, many of our early middle school teachers were high school trained and trained poorly at that. I would say that middle school has really advanced the level of sophistication in terms of teachers being able to take a classroom of 25 children and engage them in collaborative learning, for example, project-centered learning, inquiry-based learning, there's been certainly an infusion of authentic assessment, portfolio assessment. I've seen a tremendous change in classroom practice in terms of evidence of student voice being embraced, choice being incorporated, and that's not to say that there's still not a lot of old-fashioned, probably not best-practice teaching going on, but I would say that the middle school movement has nudged that agenda, and it has been a very powerful change initiative. We've done much more on instructional change than curriculum change, but I would say we've advanced instructional change. Maybe it's because I'm older, but I look back and I think I had a lot of fortunate intuition to lead me in that direction, and I did have a phenomenal undergraduate degree at Wake Forest University. I would like to think that teachers are prepared better today to teach in ways that reflect best practices. I do think that there's evidence that people are rethinking curriculum. It's a smaller number than we would like, but there are folks out there rethinking curriculum and certainly the work on curriculum mapping has changed things. People are beginning to look at when we teach, what we teach, even if they haven't really challenged themselves to think about the content of the curriculum and student voice in that content. They are definitely thinking about the organization of the curriculum and its delivery. And so that's been helpful and powerful. Also I would say that folks are exploring alternative ways to assess student learning, and that's been really helpful. There are still folks that are slapping a C on a paper, but most folks are using rubrics and defining expected performance, and they're talking about what good work looks like, and that's been a very positive benefit.

As middle level educators, how do you think we should respond to the current emphasis on student achievement as measured by standardized tests?

I think we all know that best-practice teaching will yield more learning. That if we have students engaged in meaningful, powerful, unforgettable learning, regardless of what tools we use to measure their outcome and assessments, whether it be standardized tests or other tools or instruments that they would perform better than they otherwise would. So the focus should really be on providing rich learning experiences that are academically stimulating for all children, and I often say to teachers: The test should be set aside. Alfie Kohn has said, "You know we may have to do these tests, but we don't have to celebrate them." We don't have to give them any special notice, and we shouldn't be spending weeks and weeks on test preparation. We shouldn't sacrifice the larger, powerful work of interdisciplinary studies just because we think we can't cover curriculum. We should rethink *how* we cover curriculum.

It scares me when I hear kids saying, "Well I got good grades, but I didn't learn anything." So I would say that's what we need to do. Martin Haberman, who wrote a powerful book called *Star Teachers of Children of Poverty*, is very influential in my work these days. Haberman tells teachers to feed bureaucracy just enough to keep it out of their way. And that's my philosophy with the testing movement. Although I must tell you it's more convoluted than that. Be political. Get out there and voice concerns and collect your own data so you have data to document what you do works.

Are there lessons we still need to learn from the history of the middle school movement?

Progressive education is really tough to do. That is one lesson. And that number two, the larger political context has deafening implications for what can occur in public schools. And three, we have to involve parents and community, and we have to educate them better than we do about best practices. And we can't forget to include student voice. We can't just talk about it so much that we forget that we're not doing it. We really need to do it; we need to take kids seriously and invite them into the conversation. And I think last of all, we need to collaborate, and we need to model what we believe and become a professional learning community ourselves, those of us who are involved in this work need to learn from each other and learn together and to constantly continue that learning process so that we're growing as a movement of educators as well as a model of education.

**How would you characterize the current status of the middle
school movement?**

It's so hard for me not to be hopeful, but I am feeling a bit defeated,
I have to confess, and I would say that we are sort of in a window that feels
like a plateau and we've lost ground. There's a beautiful story told by one
of my friends who claims this is a story her Jewish grandmother told her
that is a great way to think about the middle school movement. During
the Holocaust many of the Jewish people had lost a great deal of their life,
their hope and they talked about having this quilt, and they said, "When
someone takes the quilt apart you should save a piece so that when the Oc-
cupation is over you could rebuild the quilt; you can stitch it back together."
And I feel like in some ways, that's a good metaphor for the middle school
movement. That you know we have these pieces of wonderfulness in our
movement, and the quilt has been somewhat dismantled, but maybe down
the road we'll be able to re-stitch the quilt, you know rebuild the quilt, and
it would look different from the original quilt but that it would be a version
of some of the old same good truths that we knew were really important and
really were wise and really were compatible with research so that I think all
of us have to think about the future. That way, that we could build this new
quilt, and I hope that's true because I would like to be remembered in my
life and profession as having been a part of something great and not have
on my grave that I raised test scores, but that I actually raised the dignity of
life, the quality of life for young people and for the schools in which they
found themselves.

12

Thomas "Tom" O. Erb

A conundrum our society faces is that what counts may not be easily measured and what is measurable may not really count for much. If education is about addressing the learning needs of a rising generation, then it has got to be dealt with in a developmentally responsive way. You cannot just up the accountability with a big test and expect the learning problems to be solved.

As editor of the *Middle School Journal* from 1994 to 2009, Dr. Thomas Erb took National Middle School Association's (NMSA) flagship publication through expansion and improvement. He is also author and co-author of more than 90 professional publications including journal articles, book chapters, books, research reports, monographs, occasional papers, and columns. Much of his published work focuses on middle level teacher preparation, interdisciplinary teaming, and middle school curriculum. He has also presented at several hundred national and international conferences and served as consultant to more than 200 school districts, higher education institutions, policy-making groups, agencies, and other groups. A scholar, researcher, writer, philosopher, advocate, curriculum specialist, administra-

The Legacy of Middle School Leaders, pages 195–211
Copyright © 2011 by Information Age Publishing

tor, and first and foremost, a teacher, Tom Erb's dedicated service to middle school education and the NMSA has been both extensive and significant.

Dr. Erb received his undergraduate degree in history from DePauw University, Greencastle, Indiana in 1967, and his master's degree in history and social studies education from Northwestern University, Evanston, Illinois in 1968. He earned his doctorate in curriculum and instruction from the University of Florida, Gainesville, in 1977. Erb began his teaching career as a middle school core teacher in Wilmette, Illinois, where he taught for four years. In 1971, he accepted a position at the University of Chicago Laboratory School where he taught sixth grade social studies. Then from 1972 until 1974, he was a core and exploratory teacher at *Escola Inglesa de Luanda*, Angola, West Africa. Erb was a faculty member in the Department of Teaching and Leadership at the University of Kansas, Lawrence, Kansas from 1978 until his retirement in 2005. During his tenure there, he directed middle level teacher preparation programs, taught undergraduate and graduate middle level courses, conducted middle level research, and served as Chair of the Department of Curriculum and Instruction from 1989 until 1991. Upon his retirement from the University of Kansas, he was awarded the title of Professor Emeritus of Teaching and Leadership. Since then, Dr. Erb has served two terms as Distinguished Professor of Educational Studies at DePauw University, Greencastle (2005–2006 and 2009–2010) and remains active in middle school education.

Selected Accomplishments and Contributions to Middle Level Education

- Received the Michael A. James Award for Outstanding Service to the Kansas Association for Middle Level Education (KAMLE) (1982)
- Member of the NMSA Board of Directors (1983–1986)
- Editor, the *Journal of the Kansas Association for Middle Level Education* (1987–1994)
- Chair of the NMSA Professional Preparation Advisory Board (1990–1994)
- NMSA Manuscript Review Board for *Research in Middle Level Education* (1991–present)
- Received the Kamelot Award for Outstanding Contributions to Middle Level Education from KAMLE (1993)
- Honored by having KAMLE establish the Thomas O. Erb Award for Excellence in Teaming (1993)

- Edited the NMSA Founders Series for the *Middle School Journal* (1990–1994)
- Received the Career Teaching Award, School of Education, University of Kansas (1994)
- Ex-officio member of the NMSA Publications Committee (1994–2009)
- Received the Faculty Achievement Award for Service, School of Education, University of Kansas (2002)
- Designated a Distinguished Alumnus of Fort Wayne South Side High School (2007)
- Received the John Lounsbury Distinguished Service Award from NMSA (2008)
- Served as a Hampton and Esther Boswell Distinguished Professor of Educational Studies, DePauw University, Greencastle, Indiana (2009–2010)

Selected Publications

Erb, T. O. (1981). Eighth grade classrooms in theory and practice: The gap persists. *Journal of Early Adolescence, 1*(1), 11–25.

Erb, T.O. (1987). What team organization can do for teachers. *Middle School Journal. 18*(4), 3–6.

Erb, T. O., & Doda, N. M. (1989). *Team organization: Promise, practices, and possibilities.* Washington, DC: National Education Association.

Erb, T. O. (1991). Preparing prospective middle grades teachers to understand curriculum. *Middle School Journal, 23*(2), 24–28.

Erb, T. O. (1995). Teamwork in middle school education. In H. G. Garner (Ed.), *Teamwork models and experience in education* (pp. 175–198). Boston, MA: Allyn & Bacon.

Dickinson, T. S., & Erb, T. O. (Eds.). (1997). *We gain more than we give: Teaming in middle schools.* Columbus, OH: National Middle School Association.

George, P. S., Renzulli, J. S., Reis, S. M., & Erb, T. O. (Eds.). (1997). *Dilemmas in talent development in the middle grades: Two views.* Columbus, OH: National Middle School Association.

Erb, T. O., & Stevenson, C. (1998). Requisites for curricular reform. *Middle School Journal, 30*(2), 68–71.

Erb, T. O., & Stevenson, C. (1999). From faith to facts: Turning points in action—What difference does teaming make? *Middle School Journal, 30*(3), 47–50.

Erb, T. O. (2000). Do middle school reforms really make a difference? *The Clearing House, 73*(4), 194–200.

Erb, T. O. (Ed.) (2001). *This we believe ... And now we must act.* Westerville, OH: National Middle School Association.

Erb, T. O. (2001). Transforming organizational structures for young adolescents and adult Learning. In T. S. Dickinson (Ed.), *Reinventing the middle school* (pp. 176–200). New York: Routledge Falmer.

Erb, T. O. (2005). Enacting comprehensive middle grades reform. In T. O. Erb (Ed.), *This we believe in action* (pp. 1–10). Westerville, OH: National Middle School Association.

Erb, T. O. (Ed.). (2005). *This we believe in action.* Westerville, OH: National Middle School Association.

Erb, T. O. (2006). Middle school models are working in many grade configurations to boost student performance. *American Secondary Education, 34*(3), 4–13.

Tom Erb[*]

I learned middle grades education from the ground up from Yvonne Kuhlman in Wilmette and Mary Williams at Chicago Laboratory School. These mentors and our colleagues were implementing the rudiments of good middle school practices that were just then, in the 1960s and early 1970s, being articulated by educational leaders. When I started teaching in 1967, William Alexander had given his Cornell address four years earlier and Don Eichhorn's *The Middle School* had been published in 1966. However, these materials, as I recall, were never discussed in any formal sense in the schools where I taught.

But many of the elements that we have come to associate with middle school such as the advisory concept, inclusive intramural programs, exploratory curriculum, and interdisciplinary teaming were in place in when I taught in Wilmette, Illinois. The elements were there; I just didn't understand what they meant. These practices sure seemed to make sense. I moved to the Chicago Lab School and I got a broader perspective on middle school and teaching young adolescents. Then, Karen, my wife, and I took those ideas to *Escola Inglesa* in West Africa, which was a very eye-opening experience because it was such a small school that had only 110 students in grades K–8. About 40 of those students were in the middle grades (5–8)—compared to 900 in Wilmette (6–8) and 375 at Chicago Lab (6–8). That was the foundation for some of the practices that I later came to associate with the middle school concept. However, at that time, we were dealing with fifth,

---

[*] Thomas Erb was interviewed for the Legacy Project in November 2005.

sixth, seventh, and eighth graders, even though the term "middle school" hadn't permeated the lingo yet.

How did you get from your days as a middle school teacher, doctoral student at Florida, and professor at Kansas to being editor of the *Middle School Journal*?

At some point in my life I decided that I wanted to pursue the *Middle School Journal* editorship. I had been editing things since my high school days in Fort Wayne, Indiana. Shortly after moving to Kansas, I became the second editor of NMSA's *Middle School Research: Selected Studies*. About five years after that, I founded a journal for the state middle school association in Kansas, which I edited for eight years, the last two of which overlapped the editing of the Founder's Series for Tom Dickinson in *Middle School Journal*. Becoming the editor of the *Middle School Journal* was a happy event, for me. I like writing, I have a background in middle level education so I thought that becoming the editor would be a good way for me to serve middle level education.

What was your primary motivation for becoming involved in and continuing to be involved in the middle school movement?

I did not have my life planned out beyond planning the next step as it emerged. However, middle level education, centered on teaching young adolescents who were in the most interesting stage of human growth and development, kept pulling me back time and time again. As far as getting a first teaching job, I took what was available, which happened to be an eighth grade position. About three years into my first teaching experience, I developed a commitment to what I was doing at that time as a middle grades teacher and no longer had a desire to teach high school. I no longer harbored any thoughts at all that I was taking second best by focusing on middle grades teaching. I was happy to be doing what I was doing. However, as a young man, I had desires for more adventures and new challenges. When I got to the point where I was looking for a doctoral program, I was really looking for a challenge in African studies or comparative education that would take advantage of my work abroad. Again, serendipity played a role as I wound up at the same university as Paul George and William Alexander.

How would you describe the early years of the middle school movement, especially regarding the 1960s and 1970s?

I think that it was clear in the late 1970s that the education of young adolescents was the most underdeveloped area of K–12. In 1977 Joan Lipsitz published *Growing Up Forgotten*, which documented how researchers and most institutions really did not understand young adolescents very well and were not serving their needs. She reinforced the notion that early adolescence was the most critical period of human development after the neonatal period.

Early adolescence is an intriguing time to encounter learners. This realization kept me intellectually interested in middle school education. How could we do this better at a time when the larger society was not all that interested? Although with the beginnings of the middle school movement, there was a growing awareness of the developmental needs of this age group. Being part of that seemed to be an important thing to do, even a noble thing to do. The middle school really was a kind of dumping ground. People did not quite know what to do with it, where to place it, or what kind of programs would work best in it. For historical reasons we had elementary teacher education programs and secondary teacher education programs both funneling teachers into the middle grades without adequate preparation. While this situation has changed somewhat over the past 30 years, it is still too common today.

By the late 1970s, what kinds of middle school literature were you reading?

By the late 1970s, I had discovered the junior high literature from the 1920s to the 1950s as well as the early middle school curriculum writings of Gordon Vars and John Lounsbury, whose *Curriculum for the Middle School Years* came out in 1978, and Alexander's seminal work *The Emerging Middle School* (1968). In 1977 NMSA's very first monograph *The Middle School: A Look Ahead,* edited by Paul George, was published. Soon to follow in 1977 was Joan Lipsitz's *Growing Up Forgotten.*

Reading the junior high literature, I began to see how the middle school movement in many ways gained its intellectual heritage from the junior high movement of earlier decades in the 20th century. Alexander's Cornell address articulated some of the changes that were evolving in the 1960s as we learned more about early adolescence as a developmental stage and as societal factors changed the context of middle grades education. But I do not think that there is a sharp departure from what had been advocated during the junior high era, because the junior high movement was designed to meet the needs of young adolescents. Both movements grew out of continuing efforts to apply our growing knowledge of early adolescence and of societal changes to middle grades education. However, that effort had grown somewhat stagnant. Alexander's Cornell address jumpstarted a rejuvenation of middle grades education. We better understood that young adolescents needed something different than what was offered to older adolescents in high schools.

**How has the middle school concept changed since the early years
of the movement?**

There are two ways to look at this question. First of all, one can look
at what philosophical or intellectual changes have occurred among people
who understand the evolving middle school concept. Second, one can look
at what has actually happened in middle schools to change their curricula
and practices. For example, since the enactment of No Child Left Behind
and various budgetary cut backs, we see teaming beginning to disappear.
This phenomenon has not occurred because of a change in the middle
school concept. On the contrary, we now have a pretty strong research base
to support a theoretical basis for interdisciplinary team organization in
middle schools. This is a better way to organize the delivery of core curriculum in schools for young adolescents than are separate, uncoordinated
classes. Yet we know that many schools are steering away from it.

We have argued for a number of years, with increasing evidence to support our position, that the more a curriculum can be integrated the better
it is, because you involve students in learning activities that are more natural
and more meaningful. Consequently, students tend to learn various skills
and knowledge based in different disciplines that enable them to perform
better academically by solving integrated learning problems. Yet virtually all
the standards are written from a separate disciplines perspective. Standards
are written by discipline, and universities educate their teachers by disciplines. How are teachers to become aware of and skilled in interdisciplinary
or integrated approaches to curriculum and instruction? Part of the answer
might be found in the application of interdisciplinary teaming. In this type
of organization, teachers with different backgrounds, different knowledge
specialties, could coordinate their work with the standards from different
disciplines to create integrated instructional units. I have not seen a better
plan for organizing middle schools than what we have documented and
created over the years in the middle school movement. However, there are
political and economic forces that are preventing interdisciplinary teaming
from being more widely implemented. At the same time the supports for
disciplinary curriculum are being strengthened, the supports for interdisciplinary curriculum are being weakened.

**What have been some of the most significant events, incidents, or
moments in the middle school movement?**

The articulation and application of the word "middle school" in 1963
by William Alexander was critical. We saw also in the 1960s, Don Eichhorn's
book *The Middle School* and Alexander's *The Emergent Middle School* in 1968.
Joan Lipsitz's *Growing Up Forgotten* in 1977 added fuel to the fire by assem-

bling much of the extant research from several disciplines, not just education. This documented the current state of affairs. The creation of the National Middle School Association in the early 1970s, with the *Middle School Journal,* its regional and national conferences (which soon came to include the research symposium and a research journal) played a seminal role in advancing the middle school movement.

NMSA articulating the principles of middle level education in *This We Believe* was a significant event. First set forth in 1982, these principles were revised in 1995, and again in 2003. *This We Believe* has been a living document of the fundamentals of middle grades education, inspiring changes in *Middle School Journal* practices, and inspiring several publications and conferences to flesh out these cohesive principles. I think the discussion in 1996 at the NMSA Annual Conference between James Beane and Paul George on integrated curriculum was important for improving understanding of the nuances of this sophisticated concept and its application to school settings.

Who or what have been some of the greatest detractors or opponents of the middle school?

In some areas of the country, middle school education got caught up in the larger "culture wars" that have defined American politics in the past quarter century. In the early 1980s, I encountered this phenomenon in Kansas. It was to be a prologue to the evolution–creation science controversy that surfaced at the State Board of Education level in the late 1990s and still affects state level curriculum and educational policy decisions. In the early 1980s, the Kansas Association for Middle Level Education, the Kansas State Department of Education, several universities, and some school districts were working together to institute middle level teacher certification. We found opposition to the proposal at several public hearings where we heard that the middle school movement was really "ungodly." Some Christian fundamentalists were arguing that advisory programs were being used to manipulate the minds of children by imposing "secular humanism" using a relativist values clarification approach that was antithetical to "family values" and Christian religious teachings. To this agitated minority, the middle school was seen as an evil idea. We are still fighting some of this type of opposition to what goes on in the middle school movement. Some people who believe these things vote for school board members and legislators who give political legitimacy to these ideas, which in turn can affect educational policy making. So, while we in middle level education look at what we are trying to accomplish as a kind of moral imperative to do what is best for young adolescents, others hold to very different perspectives that actually demonize what we are trying to do.

On the other hand, there has been another source of opposition to the middle school concept, resulting in the debates that we have had with advocates for the gifted that ironically has had the long-term effect of strengthening middle schools. I think we have within the movement become more sensitive to the fact that when we say we are trying to educate *all* children, we mean it and that includes precocious and high achieving students, not just those who struggle or display other forms of diversity. We had an equity/excellent debate, which I hope we are growing beyond. This represents another of those false dichotomies that often plague educational debates. By bringing together the work of Joseph Renzulli and Sally Reis with that of Paul George and Carol Ann Tomlinson, NMSA has developed the theme of integrating differentiated instruction with interdisciplinary curriculum as a viable framework for effectively addressing the learning needs of a wide range of young adolescents.

We have a lot of work to do to maintain our integrity and the integrity of effective middle school programs, at the same time, not being so rigid in our thinking about what has to be done that we become irrelevant. The struggle continues over what is the central core of a good middle school that cannot be compromised and what is negotiable that may need to be compromised to preserve the core. As conditions change, there is no final answer. It has been an ongoing discussion since the early 1980s. The debate continues over the extent to which middle school "education" overlaps the broader concept of "adolescent development."

As middle level educators, we are saying if we are going to have developmentally responsive programs, we do have to ask what type of cognitive, social, and values development is appropriate for schools. The debate is about what is central to middle schooling and where are we going to direct available funding? Legislators are currently trying to redefine what is a basic education so that they can eliminate some things that they do not want to fund like physical education, the arts, even social studies in some cases, because these are not being tested.

In the first decade of the 21st century a debate is occurring around the question of whether a separate middle school facility is even a good idea at all, or should young adolescents be housed in a K–8 school? If they are in a K–8 facility, what happens to the programs for sixth, seventh and eighth graders? Currently, several large urban districts are turning away from separate middle school buildings. What does that mean? We better figure that out and address those issues. Some people are concluding that the middle school concept is not working. We need to re-examine our core. We have a body of research growing out of the *Turning Points* model of school reform that suggests that when you implement the middle school concept, it does make a positive difference for young adolescents. There is much evidence to document that. Ironically, however, we have been so successful in marketing the term "middle school" that many schools are called middle schools that do not really follow very many middle school practices. Consequently, they do not do a very good job of serving a broad range of young adolescents. Then the middle school concept gets unfairly blamed for being a failure.

That is not how I read the research on the middle school concept. Now, it may appear to be true if you pick something like grade level test scores that look at *all* middle level schools and show low test scores among eighth graders generally. However, that is not evidence that the middle school concept is not working. One would have to compare true middle schools to other school organizations that house young adolescents to accurately assess the effectiveness of the middle school concept for educating youth.

What have been some of the most significant obstacles to the success of the middle school movement?

No Child Left Behind is currently the elephant in the room. It is having a profound impact. There are some positive elements in NCLB; however, the devil is in the details—in how it is applied. We need to be alert and responsive to stay on top of NCLB's influence. Working in conjunction currently with NCLB in a harmful way are the budget problems that the states are facing. Education is becoming problematic as a priority for the larger society. Dealing with political priorities is a critical issue as we enter the second decade of the 21st century.

There is another thing that I think has not been adequately discussed that is affecting education. It is having a big impact, not only on middle schools, but on public education in general. That "thing" is a public shift from the notion that education is a public good, that society should support public education because democracy requires an educated population. I think that idea was more prevalent in the 19th and early 20th centuries. Now, I think there are strong political forces that believe that education is like any other marketable commodity. You can buy what you can afford at market prices. If you cannot afford a good education for your children, well, that's life! The ideal that a market economy can solve most societal problems better than democratic public control is influencing our perception of what education is. This shifting change is not only a factor in education. I think this thinking is permeating many other aspects of our society. Is education a public service and a public good or is it just another marketable commodity like an SUV that you go out and buy if you can afford it or settle for a bicycle if that is what you can afford? I think we are facing that debate right now. I am not sure most of us are clearly aware of it. Will that have an impact on middle schools? You bet it will! There will be powerful middle schools for people that can afford it, and there will be warehouses for 10-15 year olds whose parents cannot afford it. That debate, often not argued in clearly defined terms, is something that we need to pay attention to.

Who has benefited the most from the middle school movement?

I would like to say young adolescents. They now have scholars and educators and organizations that are focused on their stage of development. There is some evidence from the research that has been done in recent decades to suggest young adolescents are benefiting from middle school principles applied with integrity.

Who do you consider to be among the most influential leaders of the middle school movement? Why did you select these particular leaders?

A good place to start would be the individuals whom the NMSA Board of Trustees has selected as Lounsbury Award winners. Many of them were active long before I got involved in middle level education. William Alexander was already nearly retired when I was at the University of Florida. His curriculum writing was pivotal in launching the middle school movement. John Lounsbury, the energizer bunny of middle grades education, is incredible. I suppose overall he has had more influence than any other individual. His contributions have occurred over such a long time and been so central to what has happened—all the way back to the work he was doing with Van Til and Vars in the 1960s, right up to today—without a break. He has had such great focus and passion over the years. Then there is Gordon Vars, now retired, who, as far as curriculum integration is concerned, has been the most persistent advocate. Vars has been the major influence on core curriculum being integrated into junior high school, a notion that has morphed into middle school curriculum practices. By the 1990s, James Beane (*Middle School Curriculum: From Rhetoric to Reality*) took up the curriculum integration mantel as its most articulate spokesman. He has also been the leading voice for democratic schools and classrooms at the middle level.

Joan Lipsitz's *Growing up Forgotten* (1977) and *Successful Schools for Young Adolescents* (1984), as well as her work at the Center for Early Adolescence at the University of North Carolina and the Lilly Foundation in Indiana, have been very influential. Howard Johnston is one of the best thinkers we have about young adolescents and their needs and what teachers should do to address those needs. Tom Dickinson is one of the most creative thinkers the movement has had about the fundamentals of middle grades education—teacher education, curriculum, and school organization. He has been so successful in bringing together the best work in recent years as reflected in his *Reinventing the Middle School* (2001), and his taking the lead on *We Gain More Than We Give* (1997). Looking at the development of middle school critical issues, Ken McEwin's work on teacher education and middle school practices makes him the single most knowledgeable person in the country on middle grades teacher education. Sue Swaim's leadership over the past couple of decades in the National Middle School Association has come at a very critical time for reaching out to other political and professional associations to engage the very dynamic larger environment in which middle level education exists. Her work has built on foundations previously laid to expand the influence of advocacy for educational justice for young adolescents. Paul George stands tall as one of the most influential middle level advocates over the past 40 years. There are also many powerful practitioners out there. They may not write as much, but they have had tremendous influence, if not national recognition for their successes.

Have there been major debates among middle school leaders focusing on particular issues or beliefs?

One that comes to mind is the curriculum integration debate between James Beane and Paul George that occurred at the National Middle School Association annual conference in 1995. These two influential thinkers argued the nuances and subtleties of curriculum integration. However, much of what happens in schools has little to do with what James Beane and Paul George said to each other. While their discussion, featured in the following September's *Middle School Journal*, was a seminal event in the 1990s curriculum dialogue in middle grades education, and is being continued in middle schools around the country, much of it is constrained by budget decisions which have led to discontinuing interdisciplinary teaming and funding for professional and curriculum development not directly connected to raising test scores. The support system for curriculum integration has eroded as teachers are having a harder time getting together to coordinate curriculum planning. Integrated curriculum is hard to carry out in a specialized environment where teachers are responsible for different subjects and cannot easily communicate with each other across departmental lines. Consequently, the fate of integrated curriculum is determined more by outside factors than by any debate about its educational merits.

What have been the roles of women and minorities in the middle school movement?

Women and minorities have been very prominent in middle grades education. Looking at the leadership of NMSA through the years, one sees that in the very early years there were mostly males in leadership roles. However, if you look past the first seven presidents of the association, there has been a gender balance, slightly favoring women presidents. Lounsbury Award winners in the early years were all males. In recent years several prominent females have won the award: Joan Lipsitz, Sherrel Bergmann, Nancy Doda, Barbara Brodhagen, and Sue Swaim. If you look at NMSA's board and committees many members are female and/or minority. As of now, NMSA's Distinguished Middle Level Educator Award has been split evenly between males and females. I have a sense that among national institutions in this day and age that NMSA is a fairly gender- and minority-friendly association.

What are some ways the middle school movement has influenced middle level curriculum and instruction?

Well, it revived the notion of the integrated and interdisciplinary curriculum from the progressive era. Both of these concepts have been kept alive by the middle school movement and its thinkers and practitioners who have implemented practices based on this idea for organizing curriculum—the notion, too, that there is to be exploratory curriculum, that students ought to have choices, they ought to have a chance to explore their talents and interests and not be shortchanged by being foreclosed prematurely. For example, educators should not be just picking the ten best students to be the cheerleading squad to the exclusion of all others. Instead, many middle schools provide opportunities for as many girls and boys who want to be involved. That is part of the middle school concept. If it is a good activity for young adolescents, then everybody who wants to ought to be able to do it. There is a curricular concept that there is more to curriculum than just mastering subject matter. Curriculum is connected to other things—it is dependent on relationships between students and teachers and between students and their environment. The National Forum to Accelerate Middle Grades Reform has identified a three-legged foundation for middle grades education consisting of academic rigor or excellence, developmental responsiveness, and social equity. But unless you have all three of those elements working together you really cannot have a good curriculum. That is clearly fundamental to the middle school concept. NMSA continues to promote that concept and others in the living document *This We Believe.*

**As middle level educators, how do you think we should respond
to the current emphasis on student achievement as measured by
standardized tests?**

There are a couple of things to keep in mind; one of the positive things
is the NCLB mandate to disaggregate achievement data to expose differences among various student groups. Schools cannot just focus on raising
their overall average scores. Educators need to focus on subgroups of students. What is laid bare is what is happening to ethnic minorities, English
language learners, and students with learning disabilities. However, what to
do with that data is not revealed by NCLB mandated test scores, but it does
cause us to face up to the fact that not all kids are being educated well. That
is a good thing to know. Because I have worked with middle school facul-
ties where half the students were getting failing grades, half the students
were on free and reduced lunch, and the faculty more or less said, "Well
that's the way the world is." They did not say it that bluntly, or in so many
words, but the way they responded to the information they had was basically, "Well, that is the way it is." NCLB would not let educators take that
attitude. We have to live up to what we say about educating *all* students.
However, there is no one-size-fits-all solution to helping various subgroups
improve their performance—certainly not just more test-prep that aims at
fixing test scores by bypassing learning.

What my fear is, though, is that the very schools that are currently not
doing very well are going to suffer, and the very children who are not being
served now are not going to be served any better by alternatives. We may
wind up ultimately perpetuating the current system and not really solving
the learning gap. However, the problems are more visible, and that gives
me hope. Because of this visibility, I think we will get more attention focused on how to address the problem. What kind of learning modifications
do we need for English language learners? What do we need for various
types of learning disabilities? What do we need to do to relate to students
from different ethnic backgrounds to develop different ways of delivering
curriculum? So it could open up a wide range of possibilities for doing a
better job of educating the diverse students that we have in our society. I
think that is a potential positive outcome. It depends on how it plays out,
it depends on how political forces work. At the same time, I find it strange
how we hear from politicians and the larger society about improving student performance being such a high priority, yet we are cutting back on
school budgets. That is a strange way to deal with priorities. If this is really a
priority, then why are we not finding ways to systematically focus resources
on the problem? Whereas NCLB offers quite the opposite way to solve the

problem. You have a problem? Well, take money away from it and let it die. That is how we solve it under NCLB!

Are there lessons we still need to learn from the history of the middle school movement?

If education is about addressing the learning needs of a rising generation, then it has to be dealt with in a developmentally responsive way. You cannot just up the accountability with a big test and expect the learning problems to be solved. Tests may document the existence of a problem, but they do not offer much guidance about how to solve the problem. We in middle school education put a focus on addressing developmental characteristics, and we are somewhat unique among the levels of education in this regard. It was not so much true of elementary education or secondary. Both of those levels of education were developed in the 19th century, before modern social sciences (psychology, sociology, and anthropology) helped educators to more fully understand, not only how human beings develop, but also how they develop in societal contexts. Middle school education came into being in the mid to late 20th century, and it focused on how we can address early adolescent development in social contexts and in flexible organizational structures. We share that perspective with early childhood education, which also has developed more recently. Ultimately, we have that powerful developmental perspective to perpetuate into the future and perhaps spread more into both elementary and secondary education.

When the standardized testing movement came upon us we found that we could not easily test much of what is in the standards—especially not higher-order process skills. What you can easily test is information students can recall and simple, isolated skill sets—whether students know where to put commas or not, and causes of historical events and pieces of information that can be tested rather quickly and scored mechanically. We can write some questions that require some analysis in order to respond to them, but they are more difficult to create and to score on standardized tests. Use of standards generally expands and deepens education. However, the actual standardized testing technology in use today tends to narrow and restrict what students are taught. What counts in the end is the score on the test, not the broad range of academic standards. We often refer to educational standards and standardized testing in the same sentence. While these two influences may have come along at the same time, they are mostly opposing forces, not reinforcing ones, regarding the content of middle school curriculum.

How would you characterize the current status of the middle school movement?

There are powerful challenges, as I have already suggested, created by fundamental changes that may be occurring in our view of the historical role of schools in a democratic society. They present tremendous challenges for both middle schools in particular and public education generally. However, I think it is an exciting time to be alive. Middle school advocates have much to offer to the national dialogue about the role of public education in a liberal democracy. We have an increasing body of sound research documenting the impact of applying middle school principles to the education of young adolescents. We have evidence-based talking points to support what we are trying to do for the education of 10- to 14-year-olds. There are other factions that do not see it exactly the same way. Consequently, we need to expand the arena for our teaching to become educators of not only young adolescents, but members of other constituencies beyond the membership of our own associations in order to respond to critics and educate the public on behalf of young adolescents.

Are there particular efforts that need to be made to help ensure the future success of the middle school movement?

Yes, I think we probably need to have better communication with people who are making political decisions from the federal government to local school boards. If we look at the bigger picture of what we would like to have happen with young adolescents as they grow and develop, there are many commonalities across the political spectrum. We need to look for that common ground by listening to others and not holding rigid positions leading to shouting at each other. We need to keep the debate open and not be afraid of open discussion. I think we are definitely on the right track as far as defining sound educational practices for educating young adolescents. The National Forum's three-legged platform is a powerful one that needs to be widely understood. Many people only see the academic rigor aspect as they look to interpret test scores. They need to be helped to understand that academic rigor does not exist in isolation. If you are not being developmentally responsive, you are not going to create academic rigor. You may influence test scores, but that does not necessarily demonstrate academic rigor. It is the same for social equity. If you are not delivering a good education to a broad spectrum of learners, then you are failing to do the job of sound middle school education. A sound education is based on developmentally appropriate academic rigor being provided for *all* students in the school.

Are there other comments you would like to make?

In the continuing discussion on how best to educate young adolescents, we need to listen as well as talk. We need to study what we are doing in relationship to the larger environment, which continues to change, resulting in the fact that the world young adolescents are growing up in is not the same as it was 30 years ago. What young adolescents face today—socially, technologically, economically—is different from what most of us faced at their age and different from what they will face in their own mid-lives. Foundational as it is, education exists as part of a larger society. We must always interface with that larger society if we are going to be effective in what we do. One of the last things we want to be doing is to morph into a kind of little cult that exists apart from the larger society. Getting the complexities of our message out will be a challenge in a sound-bite culture, increasingly characterized by cable TV shouting matches, 140-character tweets, and information overload in general.

13

Thomas "Tom" E. Gatewood

> *The very fact that the middle school has survived over the years and is where it is today, that it is recognized as widely as it is, that we have as vibrant a national movement as we have, shows that when good ideas are held onto and are believed in and are supported unswervingly by people over the years, they will survive.*

As one of its founders, Tom Gatewood played a key role in efforts to establish the National Middle School Association (NMSA) in 1973 and to help it thrive in its early years. He was the first editor of NMSA's *Middle School Journal* and the fifth President of NMSA (1975–1976). Gatewood has authored more than 60 journal articles, books chapters, books, research reports, and other professional publications. One of his most influential middle level publications, co-authored with Charles Dilg, was *The Middle School We Need*, which was published in 1975. This seminal publication helped shape the nature of middle schools in the early years of the middle school movement and contains recommendations that remain valid for contemporary middle level schools. He has also served as middle school consultant

The Legacy of Middle School Leaders, pages 213–228
Copyright © 2011 by Information Age Publishing
All rights of reproduction in any form reserved.

to more than 300 school systems in the United States and in Asia, Europe, South America, Bermuda, and the United States Virgin Islands.

Gatewood received his B.S. in geography from Illinois State University, Normal, and his master's degree in secondary education from Southern Illinois University, Carbondale. He earned his doctorate in secondary education from Indiana University, Bloomington, Indiana, in 1970. From 1964 to 1970, he was a public school educator in Illinois and an instructor at Indiana University. He joined the faculty of Central Michigan University, Mount Pleasant, in 1970. In 1980, he accepted a position at Virginia Tech (Virginia Polytechnic Institute and State University), where he remained until his retirement in 2006.

Selected Accomplishments and Contributions to Middle Level Education

- Co-editor of the *Midwest Middle School Journal* (1971–1973) which later became the *Middle School Journal*
- Chair, Working Group on the Emerging Adolescent Learner, Association for Supervision and Curriculum Development (1975–1976)
- Received the President's Award from NMSA (1979)
- Inducted into the Michigan Association of Middle School Educators Hall of Fame (1981)
- Member of the NMSA Board of Directors (1989–1991)
- Executive Director of the Virginia Middle School Association (VMSA) (1987–1995)
- Founding editor of *VMSA Newsletter: Crucial Link* (1987–1997)
- Received the VMSA Lifetime Achievement Award (1994)

Selected Publications

Gatewood, T. E. (1971). What research says about the junior high versus the middle school. *North Central Association Quarterly, 46*(2), 264–276.

Gatewood, T. E. (1973). What research says about the middle school. *Educational Leadership, 31*(3), 221–224.

Gatewood, T. E., & Mill, R. C. (1975). Teacher education's most neglected area: Middle school teacher preparation. *Contemporary Education, 46*(4), 253–258.

Gatewood, T. E. (1975). What research says about the middle school. In R. Brandt (Ed.), *Middle school in the making* (pp. 13–16). Washington, DC: Association for Supervision and Curriculum Development.

Gatewood, T. E., & Dilg, C. A. (1975). *The middle school we need: A report from the Association for Supervision and Curriculum Development working group on the emerging adolescent learner.* Washington, DC: Association for Supervision and Curriculum Development.

Gatewood, T. E. (1977). A less than optimistic view of the middle school—1977. In P. S. George (Ed.), *The middle school: A look ahead* (pp. 7–16). Columbus, OH: National Middle School Association.

Swick, K., & Gatewood, T. E. (1978). Developing a learning climate which is both affective and accountable. *Middle School Journal, 9*(2), 10–11.

Gatewood, T. E. (1981). History and philosophy of the middle school. In A. E. Arth & J. H. Lounsbury (Eds.), *The middle school primer* (pp. 3–5). Laramie, WY: University of Wyoming Press.

Gatewood, T, E., & Evans, P. (1985). Successful home/school interaction. In J. Myers (Ed.), *Involving parents in middle level education* (pp. 12–20). Columbus, OH: The National Middle School Association.

Gatewood, T. E., Cole, C., Rottier, J., McVetty-Vars, A., & Vars, G. (1986) Preparing teachers for the middle grades. In *Professional certification and preparation for the middle level* (pp. 9–12). Columbus, Ohio: National Middle School Association.

Belli, G., & Gatewood, T. E. (1998). Readiness for formal learning in the middle grades: A study of predictors for success in eighth grade algebra. *Journal of Early Adolescence, 7*(4), 441–451.

Gatewood, T. E. (1989). Caution! Applying brain research to education. *The Clearing House, 63*(1), 37–39.

Gatewood, T. E., Cline, G., Green, G., & Harris, S. E. (1992). Middle school interdisciplinary team organization and its relationship to teacher stress. *Research in Middle Level Education, 15*(2), 27–40.

Evans, P., Gatewood, T. E., & Green, G. (1993). Cooperative learning: Passing fad or long-term promise. *Middle School Journal, 24* (3), 3–7.

Gatewood, T. E. (1998). How valid is integrated curriculum in today's middle schools? *Middle School Journal, 29*(4), 38–41.

Thomas E. Gatewood [*]

Bill Alexander had a major influence on me as I got involved in the Movement. I learned a lot about the work he had done before the middle school came along. He and some others persons I'll mention in just a moment were discontented with the junior high and what the junior high had

---

[*] Tom Gatewood was interviewed for the Legacy Project in June 2005.

become by the 1950s. Their belief was that junior highs needed a major overhaul, so I read a lot of Bill's work like his classic speech where he proposed the middle school for the first time. He proposed the middle school name, a concept and a great organization and that led me to Gordon Vars. Gordon was one of the few people writing on this topic of the middle school versus the junior high. I thought Gordon had some of the clearest thinking with regards to that particular question. I also read John Lounsbury. Some of John's writing spoke to me very loudly. Another great influence was Don Eichhorn, who at the time was a young middle school principal in Upper St. Clair, Pennsylvania. Don had done his doctoral research on the middle school age group and their developmental characteristics. And he drew on the work of a man from England by the name of Tanner who had done a lot of research on early adolescence. He used students in his school district in Upper St. Clair to gather a lot of medical data to confirm that this age group really is unique physically, intellectually, and socially. He wrote *The Middle School* that summarized his research. Don Eichhorn's work was very powerful in shaping my thinking in what middle school could be and should be.

What middle school literature did you read?

At that time there were no middle school journals. About the only organization producing good material for middle level was ASCD through *Educational Leadership* and some of their monographs. The famous first shadow studies that ASCD sponsored back in the 1960s was a good example of some very good material. Phi Delta Kappa through their publication *The Kappan* gave some attention to the middle school and of course we soon had some very good books that were written back in that time. Alexander's *The Emergent Middle School* and Don Eichhorn's book were available. There was also *Modern Education for the Junior High School Years,* by Gordon Vars, John Lounsbury, and William Van Til.

What was your primary motivation for becoming involved in the middle school movement?

My early, brief experience teaching sixth graders and the good fortune I had working with a middle level specialist, Dr. McGlasson, at Indiana University and then my dissertation, which led me to decide to make a lifetime commitment to middle school. So when I graduated from my doctoral program in 1970, I sought only positions that would enable me to work with either undergraduate or graduate middle level programs, but that was not easy because there were very few of those available back at that time. I took my first position at Central Michigan University because it did give me an opportunity to develop a graduate level program for teachers and a chance to work with undergraduates preparing them for middle school. I think it was in the late 1960s that I saw the excitement of the new movement and I believed that there was great potential in it, and I loved a lot of the ideals and philosophy that went with the concept.

What is your motivation for continuing to be involved in middle school education?

Well, what started in the 1960s has ended up being a 42-year career in education, and I've continued because I still feel as I did in the late 1960s that this concept is critically important for early adolescents. For years before middle schools came along, they weren't served well by junior high schools. School systems were too often attached to the high school model. Now, as then, I still believe we have to keep the focus on a unique program for this age group. That still excites me as much today as it did many years ago. I love this age group—sixth, seventh, and eighth graders—primarily young adolescents; it's just a wonderful age group.

How would you describe the early years of the middle school movement around the late 1960s or early 1970s?

I would say that the middle school movement from an organizational perspective really started in the early 1970s. I walked right into a situation in Michigan and the Midwest that just happened to be there at the time that I was starting my career, and I became involved in it. I looked for an organization to join as a middle level educator and the only one I could find in 1970 was a small organization called the Midwest Middle School Association. Midwest Middle School Association was a tiny organization made up of only college professors and school administrators. So, just out of curiosity I attended one of their conferences. It was the only thing going at the time.

Gordon Vars was part of that organization, and I had been looking for an opportunity to work with people like Gordon. They had an annual conference; they started a little journal called the *Midwest Middle School Journal.* Since it was so small, just about everyone who took an interest in working immediately was tabbed to do something. The editor of the *Midwest Middle School Journal* was not interested in doing it any longer, so he asked if I would take it over, which I did in 1971 and became editor of the *Midwest Middle School Journal.* At that time it was literally something that was cranked out on something like a mimeograph machine. It was often made up just of reprints from other journals, and very little original material. So I started working with the journal, and we started soliciting manuscripts and trying to develop it into a journal where middle level educators could submit articles that we could publish. We were trying to create the first journal in the country that I'm aware of for middle level.

After a couple of years of working in that original organization, it was obvious we were struggling. We weren't attracting a lot of new members, probably because we couldn't get some of the officers to budge off this exclusivity of not allowing teachers to be members. Some of us were expressing frustration about that to the point that we either needed to change this organization, make it more open and inclusive, or we just need to close it down. There was no National Middle School Association at the time. So some of our conversations began to be about if we change this organization why not make it the National Middle School Association. Now that was pretty tall talking back then because we probably didn't have $200 in the bank, and we were lucky if we had 200 people show up at a conference; we were just struggling along as this little Midwest organization. But we started talking about the concept of the National Middle School Association.

My memory may not be real firm on this, but it is that in 1972, in Toledo, Ohio, we had a board meeting of the Midwest Middle School Association. Hal Gaddis was a professor at Wright State University and was one of the officers in the Midwest Middle School Association. And we had been debating this question about what to do with this organization. Hal and I talked and said you know we need to go back and really put this before the board very, very firmly. And as I recall we went back with the plan that we should either move to be the National Middle School Association or we should disband. But we weren't willing to put that out as a formal action. So we went back in and put the idea on the floor, and that kind of intensified the debate a bit more. I don't think the decision was made at that meeting, but I think that was the beginning of our finally moving to a charter organization called the National Middle School Association.

In 1972 we had a conference in Detroit of the Midwest Middle School Association. And at that conference we had some discussions with our very small membership about doing this. A lot of people were excited about it. They saw that this organization was going nowhere fast, and that if we were going to continue, we needed to do something bold like that. As our discussions continued, and we decided in 1973 to have a conference in Indianapolis, but instead of calling that a Midwest Middle School conference we called that the first National Middle School Conference.

We wrote a constitution for something called the National Middle School Association. We knew conceptually where we wanted to go; we knew that we wanted to create an organization first to be inclusive: anyone interested in middle school could join. Anyone—parent, teacher, administrator, college professor, college student—anyone could be a member. And we would continue producing a journal that we would call the *Middle School Journal*. And we would have an annual conference that we would try to make a national conference. And we would try to broaden our membership by creating national regions.

In 1973 we had a conference we called the first National Middle School Conference. But we really hadn't gone to our membership to ask for approval of this yet. At the Detroit conference we had kind of kicked the idea around, but we didn't do anything official. So at the 1973 conference in Indianapolis we probably didn't have two to three hundred people that attended. And they mostly were out of the old Midwest Middle School base. We had a business meeting and we put the question to our membership to approve a new constitution and a new charter and they approved it. So at that meeting in 1973 was really the official beginning of the National Middle School Association.

The next year was a very interesting year. I was on the board at that time and we weren't sure where to go next because first we had no money. So what could we do to establish a national office? At that time the major university support came from Wright State University and Kent State. Gordon Vars was at Kent State. He had a colleague there, Glen Maynard. And Hal Gaddis was at Wright State University. They got their universities to provide a bit of infrastructure support. Kent State provided support for the journal. We started publishing the journal there, and Wright State provided support for what was the beginning of an organizational office. And Hal Gaddis became somewhat of an executive secretary director. But all of us were still working full time; we had no full-time employees. We hired a part-time secretary as I recall, and my memory may not be real crisp on this, but I recall we hired a part-time secretary at Wright State University, and she became our office. She processed the memberships and helped with the annual conference, and whatever money we had was pretty much there. And we continued doing the journal that we published through Kent State.

We talked about our next conference because the next conference we really wanted to bill as a national conference. We wanted to advertise it nationally and really wanted that conference to be a big event that really unveiled this new organization nationally. So we decided to go to Columbus, Ohio, because Columbus was kind of in the center of where most of our leadership was at the time. I think we had about 300 or 400 dollars in the budget. So we decided to book a hotel in Columbus, Ohio, and to sign the contract at a hotel for this conference in the fall of 1974. We had to sign contracts committing ourselves to maybe up to $10,000 of expenses and, since we had no money, the members of the board signed off on the expenses for that first conference. We estimated we needed about 400 people to show up to pay the fees to break even. About 400 registrants showed up so we just barely broke even.

There was a lot of excitement at that conference. I recall that we had Paul George as our first keynote speaker. Paul did a wonderful job. We attracted some people from around the country. I remember meeting Ken McEwin for the first time at that conference. I believe John Wiles came from Florida. So there was a lot of energy at that first conference. A colleague of John Lounsbury's from Georgia invited us to hold the next conference in Atlanta, Georgia. We accepted and that conference attracted about 800 people; we doubled.

I was president in 1975 and 1976, and when I became president I had to give up the editorship of the journal. So the board was faced with the problem of finding an editor for the journal, so they asked me for suggestions and one name that I recommended was John Lounsbury. So I called John and John jumped at it. He said, "Tom, I've been looking for something like this." He said, "I love what you're doing with the National Middle School Association." He said, "I really think you're on to something here." And he said, "I would like to take this on." So if you ask me my greatest contribution to the middle school movement, it would probably be my insight in recommending John Lounsbury to be the editor. The rest is history, what John did with the *Journal* and how he developed all the publications that the National Middle School Association continues to this day. John, of course, is still very active with publications with the National Middle School Association, and here we are almost 30 years later.

It's been a very long answer to your question, but those were very exciting years. They were very challenging because most of our universities didn't give us a lot of support to travel to these meetings, so we often paid our expenses out of our own pockets. The Midwest Middle School Association and the new National Middle School Association didn't have enough money to pay us so we just basically donated our time and services. We didn't have the money, but we had faith that this thing would just take off and go. And it's just so wonderful now to see where the National Middle School Association is and seeing where it came from and those early years and how things could have gone one way or another.

How has the middle school concept changed since the early years of the movement?

The middle school concept hasn't changed a bit. It is still the same concept we started with. I would say the middle school concept was pretty much in place by the 1920s. If you go back and read some of the historical literature, a lot of the original concepts and thoughts were basically in place back at that time. I think the concept that we follow today was probably best articulated by Bill Alexander. But I don't think that concept has changed at all since the early days. It's always been a very basic concept focused on providing a special education program for this unique age group of youngsters. That's always been and is still our focus. The only thing that has changed over the years is how we deliver the program. I'm not sure we still have reached a clear consensus in the movement about the type of program to provide for those youngsters. I think we reached consensus early on that we should organize teachers and teams and that we should begin to break down the barriers between and among the content areas through interdisciplinary teaming, integrated curriculum, and teacher advisory programs. But unfortunately, clear models have not evolved, particularly in the curriculum area and with teacher advisory programs over the years. There are still some troubling issues about the delivery of the middle school model. However, the basic concept has never changed.

What have been some of the most significant events, incidents, or moments in the middle school movement?

I think Alexander's call to arms was perhaps the biggest. Another was the publication of The *Emergent Middle School,* which included the first major study that documented the emergence of the middle schools in the United States by showing the number of middle schools and documented the types of programs that were in them. The publication of Don Eichhorn's work in the mid 1960s in the book called *The Middle School,* but also the groundbreaking applications of his work in Upper St. Clair, Pennsylvania, were also significant. The beginning of the National Middle School Association in the early and mid 1970s and the evolution of the *Middle School Journal* as the preeminent publication in the middle school movement were very important. In addition, there was the growth of NMSA's continuing leadership over the years. The publication of *The Middle School We Need 1975* by ASCD is the first real national publication that laid out the philosophy of middle school in a popular way. The development and publication of *This We Believe* by NMSA in the early 1980's to establish a clear conceptual model for the middle school was one of those landmarks. I think the publication of *Schools in the Middle: Status and Progress* that Ken McEwin and Bill Alexander did in 1988 was also a landmark event, because it is a chronicle of the most significant years in the development of middle schools nationally. It updated Bill Alexander's study from 1968 that was published in The *Emergent Middle School.* The *25 Year Retrospective* established a chronicle of the status of middle schools and how they had changed since 1968. It also identified some major lingering issues by the early 1990s. The work of the Carnegie Foundation, their publications starting in the late 1980s and continuing in the early 2000s, had an impact.

I think it's interesting that I don't think we've seen anything in the last 10 years that has taken us to a new level, I think the movement is probably ready for another. The NMSA has revised *This We Believe*, but perhaps we need something of national stature that says, "Here is where we are today. Here are the major issues and here is where we need to be going." Why would I say that? Because some of these lingering issues are still with us. We are still debating curriculum, we are still debating grade levels, organization, we're still debating some major components of the middle school model. That's why we probably need something now that would kind of take us to that next level.

Who or what have been some of the major detractors or opponents of middle school education?

The greatest detractors over the years have been state departments of education and a lot of local superintendents who have fought efforts to create special teacher certification requirements for middle level educators. The result has been that we still don't have a lot of institutions that are preparing teachers for the middle level. We have always had a diluted concept of teacher preparation, which has always been connected unfortunately to the high school model. And that has been caused by the lack of enlightenment at state levels in state departments of education, and a lot of local superintendents have been some of our biggest enemies. Some have been some of our greatest supporters, but in general they have been some of our greatest detractors.

Secondly, we have a conservative movement in this country that believes that all schools should fit a very narrow philosophical agenda, but unfortunately has been connected to middle schools. Over the years we have had a lot of false claims made that middle schools are soft on the basics and discipline, that the middle school concept is just interested in enhancing self-concept. These claims are just a lot of nonsense, but a lot of that has reached the level of dogma by some state and national organizations that have had the ear of the public, who have had the ear of national publications like *Education Week*, and have had the ear of governors and state departments of education.

What have been some of the most significant obstacles to the success of the middle school movement?

I have just mentioned teacher certification. I believe Gordon Vars said that he believes one mistake that we made in the early years of the middle school movement was not concentrating enough on teacher certification, and I think he's absolutely right. I believe we became sidetracked in forming a national organization and creating publications, and having big meetings and promoting certain forms of programming in schools, and we didn't pay enough attention to the political agenda. We didn't pay enough attention to this and I think it's come back to haunt us many times.

What are some of the most important factors that are influencing middle school education today?

I think the accountability movement is something being fought in every state. I don't think there is a middle school in the country that is not finding some way to balance a proper focus on teaching middle level kids and at the same time preparing them for state exams and being caught in a high stakes accountability effort. So a lot of schools are unsure about how much emphasis they can still give to the pure components of the middle school concept and still at the same time meet legal and political requirements. Preparation of teachers is still a huge issue. We still do not have enough teachers prepared specifically to teach middle school.

This whole conservative effort to destroy middle schools is still out there. There are people who would like to do away with middle schools, period, and just roll the middle school students into an elementary model or make them part of a high school. There are a lot of folks who see no legitimate reason at all for the middle school concept, and it troubles me that we are still battling that. We apparently have failed in selling the idea at the national, state, and local level to the extent that the community will fight for the middle school. The ones who fight for it are those of us who are still in the Movement. We're the ones who still continue to try to hold on and to provide some line of defense. Will it remain an issue 10 or 15 years from now? I don't know. That's why I said I think we are at a point in our movement where we need another breakthrough. We need another Bill Alexander, we need another person, we need another major publication, we need something that comes through and energizes the movement, that provides a clear vision of where we are and where we need to go. Otherwise I think we are going to continue to fight these battles.

Who has benefited the most from the middle school movement?

I think students and teachers have benefited the most. The teachers have benefited greatly by being involved in teaming communities. I think clearly our greatest success organizationally has been the embracing of interdisciplinary teaming. Great majorities of middle schools nationwide use a teaming model, and this allows teachers to work collaboratively and to plan in ways elementary and high school teachers can't even remotely do. So I think teachers have benefited enormously.

Students have benefited because they have been treated as they should be treated at their age level in schools that have the middle school concept. So I think my children benefited by being in good middle schools, in schools where the leadership believed in the middle school concept and philosophy, where teachers were there because they wanted to be there. I think it provided a very special foundation in their lives for what came afterwards, but most importantly I believe just allowing them to be treated as youngsters who are no longer children, or yet teenagers, but have their own unique needs. It is very special to them and I think that has been repeated thousands of times across the nation. So I think many, many students have benefited by being in good middle schools.

Who has benefited the least from the middle school movement?

Probably those persons who have not had the good fortune to be in schools that have made a commitment to the middle school concept. There are school systems around the country that either have never really had good middle schools, or had good middle schools and then lost them. So those people who unfortunately were there when the concept never developed or had gone downhill have not benefited. So I think those who have not benefited have been those who have not had the good fortune to be part of a good middle school.

Who do you consider to be among the most influential leaders of the middle school movement and as you tell us those, why did you select these particular leaders?

Well, we are fortunate that some people who were there in the early days are still with us. John Lounsbury is still very vital. John still provides a strong leadership role in the publications of the National Middle School Association, which I think are better now than they have ever been before. Gordon Vars is still involved with his National Association for Core Curriculum which was there long before the National Middle School Association as an organization. The National Association for Core Curriculum is still there and it's still a voice. I think he is still having an impact. In terms of people who have come along in more recent years, you'll interview Nancy Doda this afternoon. But When I first met Nancy she was a young middle school teacher in Gainesville, Florida, in the mid 1970s. Over the years it's been wonderful to see Nancy emerge as one of our top speakers and writers in the middle school movement. Nancy is still very vibrant and very active.

Tom Erb is doing a wonderful job as the editor of the *Middle School Journal*. Tom has developed a strong voice through the journal that reflects a lot of his philosophy. I certainly consider him one of our top people today. Sue Swaim and her long-term executive directorship of National Middle School Association is notable. Paul George is still writing, still speaking, he is still very active. I think Paul always has been one of our best thinkers and writers. Rick Wormeli has become a voice for teachers. Ed Brazee has always been a very pure voice for integrated curriculum. Jim Beane—Jim and I have disagreed often on the delivery of curriculum. We've debated it both in print and at the National Middle School conference, but I have the utmost respect for Jim, and I'm glad that he is still active. He's still writing, speaking, and carrying this very pure concept of integrated curriculum to the movement.

I particularly want to identify Ken McEwin, whom I first met in 1974 in Columbus, Ohio. I've had great admiration for the work Ken has done at Appalachian State, the work he did with Bill Alexander over the years to bring Bill to Appalachian State and to collaborate with Bill in some great works over the years including the 1988 *Retrospective Study*. Ken's leadership of this project that you are involved in now shows that he's trying to chronicle where things are and where they need to go. I think Ken is still providing a vital national role.

What have been the roles of women and minorities in the middle school movement?

I think NMSA can be proud of its record with women and minorities. I can recall from the early days that the old Midwest Middle School Association I would say in a lot of ways was very sexist. It was nearly all males, college professors. It was school principals, school superintendents, kind of an old boys' organization, so when we moved to a National Middle School Association, it was intended to be an inclusive organization. And by inclusive we meant everyone. No one would be excluded, no one left out. The Association would need to be based simply upon merit, upon interest, upon enthusiasm, upon purely human qualities that have no racial or gender boundaries. So from the very early days we've had some key people. So I would say that its record has been quite good—if you look at the presidents of NMSA over the years we've had many women, we've had minority presidents, we have had different ethnic groups represented on the board and at the presidency level. NMSA has been an open organization; I think Sue Swaim is very much an inclusive individual. We've always been very inclusive, very diverse.

What are some examples of ways that the middle school movement has affected American education?

I believe the greatest contribution that middle school has made to American education is legitimizing an organization in the middle grades that is truly unique. I think despite all the controversy that continues to swirl around middle schools about whether they should continue to exist, what they should be, I don't think there is any question now that middle school is now a part of the education establishment. I think it is clearly accepted. I think that the public has accepted middle school as a school, as an organization. I think there is a general feeling that it needs to be different from elementary, different from high school but it's a necessary, separate entity of its own. I think another contribution made is the organizational structure. The teaming community, that organizational approach in the middle school, still continues to be unique.

What are some of the ways the middle school movement has influenced middle level curriculum and instruction?

I'd like to say that there has been a lot of influence, but I think in curriculum we have had little movement. I think we do have more of an attempt to break down boundaries now between and among content areas. There have been some reasonably successful attempts at integrated curriculum, although not in the pure sense I think that Jim Beane would like to see. I think within the context of interdisciplinary teams a lot of interdisciplinary projects, units, and things of that sort have occurred. While instruction is still primarily teacher-directed, I believe in general we have seen a shift toward approaches that are probably more constructivist, more problem-based, more reflective of what students need cognitively. I think there is a dawning awareness of readiness at the middle school level. I think more schools are sensitive to the shift from concrete to formal level thinking and try to reflect that to some extent in how they admit students to algebra, but not nearly enough. But I think we have more of that than we did several years ago. I don't believe the movement has influenced curriculum and instruction nearly as much as it should have or that we envisioned in the early years that it would.

As middle level educators, how do you think we should respond to the current emphasis on student achievement as measured by standardized tests?

I think we need to hold firm and attempt to articulate the middle school concept and philosophy. And I don't believe that we should compromise too much. I don't think we should throw in the towel. At the same time, if schools are to be punished and teachers are to be held accountable for test results, we have no choice but to participate in those dilemmas. But I think we've seen here in Virginia that good teachers and good schools can still carry the middle school concept forward and still meet the needs of state accountability. So I believe that is our best response that we hold firm to the concept, that we don't throw the towel in, that we don't overreact, but we stay firm to what we really believe.

Are there lessons we still need to learn from the history of the middle school movement?

I think that what we have learned is that good ideas, good philosophies will endure. I remember a time when a lot of critics said that middle school was just a fad, just a phenomenon and it would just pass away. My dissertation research was focused on that question. Are new middle schools different from junior highs? Are they really carving out an identity for their own? The very fact that the middle school has survived over the years and is where it is today, that it is recognized as widely as it is, that we have as vibrant a national movement as we have, shows that when good ideas are held onto and are believed in and are supported unswervingly by people over the years, they will survive. So this great idea that Bill Alexander had for the middle school concept is still with us today and a lot of people said it wouldn't survive the sixties. A lot of people said it isn't going to last, that junior highs are too strong. So I think that we have learned that when good ideas exist and if enough people believe firmly and are willing to devote their lives and careers to them, if they are not willing to compromise but fight the good fight to keep these ideas alive and keep them moving forward, they will endure. The middle school movement is testimony to that. Something that was perceived as just a temporary fad, when fads were coming and going quickly in the sixties, is where it is today.

How would you characterize the current status of the middle school movement?

It's vibrant, it's alive. The middle school is here. It's not going away despite what I see as a temporary attack on the middle school organization. I believe the middle school has established itself. It is here to stay. I believe the National Middle School Association is here to stay. I believe the state organizations are here to stay. I think we will continue to have wonderful publications. We will continue to have conferences, I think all these things will endure. I'm still concerned, however, that we haven't resolved some of these long-standing issues about curriculum and instruction, and about grade organization structure. I believe that's why we are at that point again where we need to jump to the next level of our evolution. I think all movements stand the danger of closing in on themselves if they don't confront the issues that are still present and then attempt to evolve to the next stage.

I can remember something about Bill Alexander many years ago. I recall going out to one of those ASCD working groups' early adolescent conferences that we had out in Boulder, Colorado. Bill and I were among some others that were on the staff of that institute. I bumped into him at the Denver airport and we rode the bus up to Boulder. It was a great chance to talk with Bill in a way that I hadn't before. I remember asking him that question: "Bill, we are just starting this National Middle School Association. What do you think is the danger?" "Well," he said, "the danger is that any movement can become too institutionalized. It can become too orthodox and too wrapped up in itself. I'm worried about middle schools for the same reason. If we over-institutionalize middle schools, we may create enemies for middle schools themselves. And if we over-institutionalize this national movement, it may become a movement unto itself, and in a few years could begin to lose its steam and its dynamic energy. It could lose quality." I think Bill was very prophetic. I think that is where we are right now. I think there are some indications that we are not moving forward but that we are kind of at a peak. We could be starting down the hill the other way unless we confront some of these big issues. And I'm not sure how that is going to be done, I don't have that kind of wisdom. Perhaps it is through a person, perhaps it's through a new direction of the NMSA, perhaps it's through another Carnegie Foundation *Turning Points* publication, and perhaps it's through something that we can't even imagine right now, perhaps through our response to a national crisis. I'm not sure what it is, but I think the middle school movement needs something. It needs a shot in the arm, some kind of propulsion that builds on the past but moves to the future. That future is just simply going to have to resolve some of these nagging issues that are continuing to stay with us year after year after year.

14

Paul S. George

I think . . . the middle school concept is a wonderfully grand idea based on all of the good things about human beings and education. It is an idea that has light and that light isn't going to be put out by challenges. It has persistence. It has strength and it will continue.

Dr. Paul S. George is nationally and internationally renowned for his expert knowledge and passion for middle level education. He is widely recognized as an authoritative author, speaker, consultant, scholar, and researcher. He is author and coauthor of many middle level books including the influential *The Exemplary Middle School,* which he wrote with his colleague William M. Alexander, and *The Handbook for Middle School Teaching,* co-authored with Gordon Lawrence. George is author of more than 100 journal articles, book chapters, and books. He is also the primary or featured presenter on more than 20 professional development videos.

Dr. George has served as middle school consultant to schools, school districts, policy makers, and other stakeholders in all states in the United States and in many other countries including Japan, Greece, Germany, Canada,

The Legacy of Middle School Leaders, pages 229–246
Copyright © 2011 by Information Age Publishing
All rights of reproduction in any form reserved.

Mexico, and Kenya. Widely recognized as a powerful speaker, a top scholar, and prolific writer on middle level issues, Dr. George's work on the international scene has been especially noteworthy. He is noted for having the courage of his convictions as well as for having creative initiative. He has put his stamp on numerous middle school activities, projects, and resources.

Dr. George received his undergraduate degree in history from Westminster College, New Wilmington, Pennsylvania, his master's degree in history from Kent State University, Kent, Ohio, a second master's degree from Vanderbilt University, Nashville, Tennessee, and his doctorate in curriculum and instruction from Peabody College (Vanderbilt). After teaching junior and senior high school social studies for nearly ten years, Dr. George taught at Belmont College in Nashville, Tennessee and Monmouth College in Monmouth, Illinois. In 1970, he joined the faculty at the University of Florida where he remained until his retirement in 2007. Dr. George is Emeritus Distinguished Professor of Education at the University of Florida.

Selected Accomplishments and Contributions to Middle Level Education

- A founder of the Florida League of Middle Schools (1972)
- Received the Educator of the Year Award from the Florida League of Middle Schools (1993)
- Honored by the Florida League of Middle Schools as its first executive director (1995)
- Received the John H. Lounsbury Distinguished Service Award from National Middle School Association (1998)
- Referred to as the "foremost expert on middle schools in the country" by the American Association of School Administrators

Selected Publications

George, P. S. (Ed.). (1977). *The middle school: A look ahead.* Columbus, OH: National Middle School Association.

George, P. S. (1981). The middle school century. *Principal, 60*(3), 11–14.

George, P. S. (1992). Four phases in the life of a team. In J. Lounsbury (Ed.), *Connecting the curriculum through interdisciplinary instruction* (pp. 57–65). Columbus, OH: National Middle School Association.

George, P. S. (1992). *How to untrack your school.* Alexandria, VA: Association for Supervision and Curriculum Development.

George, P. S., Stevenson, C., Thomason, J., & Beane, J. (1992). *The middle school and beyond.* Alexandria, VA: The Association for Supervision and Curriculum Development.

George, P. S., & Shewey, K. (1994). *New evidence for the middle school.* Columbus, OH: National Middle School Association.

George, P. S., Renzulli, J. S., Reis, S. M., & Erb, T. (1998). *Dilemmas in talent development in the middle grades: Two views.* Columbus, OH: National Middle School Association.

George, P. S., Lawrence, G., & Bushnell, D. (1998). *Handbook for middle school teaching* (2nd ed.). New York: Longman.

George, P. S. (1999). A middle school if you can keep it: Part II. *Midpoints Occasional Papers.* Columbus, OH: National Middle School Association.

George, P. S., & Lounsbury, J. H. (2000). *Making big schools feel small: Multiage grouping, looping, and schools-within-a-school.* Westerville, OH: National Middle School Association.

George, P. S. (2001). The evolution of middle schools. *Educational Leadership, 58*(4), 40–44.

George, P. S., & Alexander, W. M. (2003). *The exemplary middle school* (3rd ed.). Belmont, CA: Thompson Wadsworth.

George, P. S. (2009). Special series: Renewing the middle school: The early success of middle school education. *Middle School Journal, 41*(1), 4–9.

George, P. S. (2009). Special series: Renewing the middle school: The manufactured crisis. *Middle School Journal, 41*(2), 55.

George, P. S. (2010). Special series: Renewing the lesson of Hansel and Gretel for middle schools. *Middle School Journal, 41*(3), 49–51.

Paul S. George[*]

I got involved in the middle school movement when I was a teacher in Nashville, Tennessee, in a junior high school that reorganized in 1967 to be a middle school. I was teaching in the ninth grade and the reorganization of the school was something I paid a whole lot of attention to. At the same time, I was involved in a graduate level course on middle school education at Peabody with Gordon Lawrence, who later did more work in the area of middle school.

---

[*] Paul George was interviewed for the Legacy Project in November 2003.

Who or what were your main influences?

Gordon Lawrence and Bill Alexander. When I moved to the University of Florida thirty-two years ago, Bill Alexander was the director of several programs there and already recognized as the "Father of the American Middle School." I worked directly with him there, so he very much provided mentoring to me and influenced what I was doing. I would say those two fellows were probably the most influential.

What literature did you read and are there particular theorists or theories or writings that have influenced your educational thought?

The most important early reading that I did was Bill Alexander's book *The Emergent Middle School,* published in 1968, which was right around the time I was finishing my doctoral work and teaching in the school that was reorganized. That was really foundational literature. There also was a middle school book by Ted Moss (*Middle School*) who taught at New York State University at Oswego that was not very well known but influenced my thinking a whole lot just because of the clarity with which he pursued the whole concept of middle level education, and so those two books were important. Then there was Don Eichhorn's work published in 1966 as one of the very first books on middle school education. Those three books probably got me started in middle level education sooner and better than anything else.

What was your primary motivation for becoming involved in the middle school movement?

I saw the middle school movement as the embodiment of values and ideals that were important to me. I spent most of my time as a junior high and high school teacher and it wasn't really the young adolescent that attracted me the way it has so many other people in the commitment to the young adolescent. It was what the middle school concept embodied and it was the principles and the values and vision of the middle school concept that attracted me more than anything else and still does thirty some years later. It is not that young adolescents and their needs are unimportant; it's that in my mind the middle school concept goes way beyond young adolescents.

I see the middle school movement as the continuation of really 500 years of enlightened ideas about human beings, their purposes and their education. I think you, if you wanted to, could trace the contemporary movement in middle school education back through the progressive education movement in the 1930s all the way back, really, to the Enlightenment in post-dark-ages Europe and the ideas that were rejected and the ideas that were affirmed by the Enlightenment, by the Renaissance, and by right-thinking people and educators from Rousseau through Pestalozzi down through Carl Rogers and A. S. Neil to Bill Alexander and other people who were a part of the middle school movement. The middle school movement is today's version of enlightenment for education and it goes far beyond reorganization of grade levels.

How would you describe the early years of the middle school movement?

Tumultuous. The early years of the middle school movement were characterized, among other things, by a group of early adopters who were zealots really. And the very first National Middle School Association Conference thirty years ago was held in Ohio in a little motel outside of Columbus, Ohio, and there were 250 people there and they were all on fire with the whole idea of reform and reforming the junior high school, which had really gotten lost. And those early adopters were the people who really caught other people on fire and they were really voices in the wilderness, courageous people who were really working by themselves and it was those people, people like John Lounsbury and Gordon Vars and then important practitioners who were involved early on who rode that wagon train, if you will, through all kinds of other important changes like desegregation, which had a phenomenal impact on the middle school movement. Most people don't realize that half the middle schools in America in the 1970s and the 1980s were created as a response to school desegregation and to judges' orders that made it possible for a middle school to be a school district's answer to segregated schools. The judge would accept the school plan that allowed for neighborhood segregated elementary schools if the middle schools were integrated. These were all over the South certainly. Middle schools were created as a response to desegregation. That was an incredibly tumultuous time and was difficult for middle schools because people couldn't blame poor black kids for their problems so they blamed the middle school concept.

And it is a tribute to the strength of the middle school concept that it overcame those objections. I was asked to leave several school districts that later went on to embrace the middle school concept with fervor because it worked. So the school desegregation effort was on the one hand a great energizer for middle school and it was also a challenge. In the 1970s and 1980s there were population demographic shifts that propelled middle schools even further. A lot of people don't realize there were schools in Minnesota, let's say, where they didn't want to close the high school because closing a high school is tantamount to losing your job as a superintendent. So superintendents with schools with district enrollments that were declining, it's almost hard to believe that now, but in the 1980s school district enrollments were declining all over the country and eventually school superintendents figured out that you could move the ninth grade out of the junior high school and increase high school enrollment by 25% and you didn't have to close the high school. And then you could move the sixth grade out of the crowded elementary schools and you wouldn't have to build elementary schools. So, a whole new wave of middle schools was created as a result of shifting enrollments all across the country. Behind the wave of middle schools that came through segregation was a wave of middle schools that came as a result of dislocation demographically, and people were angry about that too, and saw the middle school as the culprit.

Then of course, in the mid-1980s we had the *Nation at Risk* report now widely discredited but at the time tremendously influential, and one of the things that it did was cause virtually every state legislature to pass laws to strengthen high school graduation requirements and that reached down to the ninth grade and it made the ninth grade even more of the high school year and so having a high school year off in the junior high and the rest of the high school over here didn't make a whole lot of sense and so districts that hadn't changed because of desegregation or because of demographics changed because the state legislature made laws that made it reasonable and efficient for them to move the ninth grade to high school. Then of course there was a fourth wave that rode on the experience of people who had adopted the new middle school early on and later when people realized that the middle school concept worked.

That fourth wave really completed the reorganization of American schools along middle school lines, and those four waves really had nothing whatsoever to do with the young adolescent except the last one that created an incredible series of eruptions, really almost earthquakes, that brought about this change that would never have come about had it been advocated simply as something good for young adolescents. It came about because educators had other reasons for making changes that the middle schools rode in on the coattails, so it was a tremendously challenging and difficult time fighting off being the whipping boy, fighting the fact that there was virtually no training provided for teachers in many cases. A school district with thirty-four middle level schools would change to middle schools over night. It was an amazing time and it is amazing really that the middle school concept is still here when it came about as a secondhand rose almost every single place without any training of staff, without any support, without any financing and here we are with 8,000 people attending the 30th Anniversary of the National Middle School Association. It's miraculous, really.

How has the middle school concept changed since the early years?

I once attended a conference of the Florida League of Middle Schools where the director of teacher certification for the state of Florida stood up and said, "What is a middle school, really?" and what he meant by that was nobody knows what a middle school is. And in the early 1970s, nobody did. It was an unclear, unformed, nebulous concept that was focused on doing the right thing for young adolescents, even though we weren't exactly sure what that meant. A lot of people thought, for example, that teamwork meant team teaching. I can't tell you how many school districts I worked in where they thought that what that meant was that we were all going to exchange lesson plans every day and teach from each other's lesson plans and a lot of teachers still have bad tastes in their mouths because of what someone told them a component of the middle school was supposed to be.

It took a long time before we began to understand that the middle school concept is not as much about school organization as it is about curriculum and instruction. Before, we understood that the middle school concept was about how the teachers are organized to deliver instruction and interdisciplinary team organization clarified and grew from that. We understood that flexible scheduling and the control of those teams of teachers was very important and all kinds of things were unclear and we burned up a lot of hours spinning our wheels because we weren't clear about what the middle school concept meant. We thought it meant a change in the curriculum and then everybody went back and taught what they had always taught. We thought it meant a change in instruction. Back in the 1970s it was the heyday of individualized instruction and people engaged in hundreds and hundreds of workshops all across the country on individualizing instruction all summer long and then everybody went back and taught the way they had always taught. So it wasn't until probably ten years into all of this reorganization that the basic components of middle school began to become clear in people's minds and the big difference between the middle school today and the middle school thirty years ago is that we have a nationwide, really an international consensus in many ways, on the basic components of what works for young adolescents, and we also have a growing support base of evidence that shows that that national consensus has validity when it comes to measuring things like increased academic achievement. So it's been a tumultuous and long and curving road to wind up where we are. If we knew in the 1960s what we know now, it would be a dramatically different experience, but we grew and we learned as we reorganized and as we built new schools.

How have middle schools changed since the early years?

Well, I think in many ways middle schools have changed but probably more than any other single way is the change from departmentalized organization of teachers to the interdisciplinary team. That is, if you could point to one big difference between schools for young adolescents today and schools for young adolescents thirty years ago, it would be the understanding that teachers that share the same students make more sense than teachers that share the same subject when it comes to the education of young adolescents and no one anywhere, until maybe recently with No Child Left Behind, quarrels with the idea of interdisciplinary team organization. No one advocates a return to departmentalized instruction, and the high school has begun to take that same page forward with more and more academic teaming and less and less departmentalization. So that's the big difference.

How were decisions about the directions taken by the middle school movement made?

I think they were made by expediency more than deliberate attention to what's best for young adolescents. I don't think that was always the case. In the school district where I live and work, simply because Bill Alexander was there when the school district was reorganized, there was great care given to talking and thinking and planning about what makes the most sense for young adolescents. But even then, our experience was so limited and our knowledge was so limited that our effectiveness was also limited. We opened open space schools, for example, because we thought that would facilitate team work and individualized instruction, and open space schools were a disaster almost everywhere, and they were also cheap, so it made it appealing in a lot of places, but we made lots of mistakes and lots of those decisions were made by expediency. That is, somebody had to save the high school so they moved to middle school; somebody was under a court order to desegregate so they moved to middle school. Somebody was reacting to the new law so they moved to middle school. It was an expedient decision where middle school served the decision rather than being served by the decision.

How were other individuals and groups outside middle level education involved in the early years of the middle school movement?

I think there is one organization that was powerfully important and that was the Association for Supervision and Curriculum Development. In the 1960s and in the early 1970s, before there was a National Middle School Association, it was the Association for Supervision and Curriculum Development [ASCD] that carried the ball. In the early 1970s I made dozens of presentations at ASCD on "What is a middle school, really?" and hundreds of people flocked to those presentations because they were under the gun to change to the middle school and they didn't know what it was. ASCD published all the things that were written about middle school education. They had a national task force on middle school education; in fact, they had several national task forces on middle school education under Gordon Cawelti's leadership. The Association for Supervision and Curriculum Development really did Herculean labor on middle school education that nobody remembers.

What was the educational context at the time the middle school movement began?

It was the 1960s and it was a time of liberality in education and the freedom that came with the 1960s led to the expansion of the whole idea of individualization and importance of the individual outside education and inside education and that's why we had such a powerful emphasis on individualization of instruction in middle school education and independent study. Bill Alexander wrote a book on independent study in the 1960s and so it was a 1960s kind of a school and it was a 1960s kind of motivation to change the world through education. It changed a lot in the 1970s when the back to the basics movement hit really, really hard. And then it changed again later on when the *Nation At Risk* report came out. So there have always been these forces in our society that reverberated in the middle school education movement, and you can see, I think, those direct influences like individualized instruction and teamwork and then interdisciplinary curriculum and then a tremendous attempt to get back to the basics right around the same time as mistrust spread throughout America in the 1970s and people began to mistrust the government and president and they also began to mistrust the schools, so innovation became a dirty word in American education and exploration became something that one didn't do. One went back to the basics and so you can see this all along the line and here we are in the early years of the 21st century and schools are again being impacted by national movements of political and social nature. That is the way it is.

What have been some of the most significant events, instances, or moments in the middle school movement?

Two that I can think of in addition to some of those I have spoken about earlier. One was the idea to form state and regional middle school associations. We had all of these early adopters out there who were really alone and they needed company. They sought similar people who were doing similar things, and that resulted in state associations like the Florida

League of Middle Schools which was founded in 1972 actually before the National Middle School Association was founded. North Carolina Middle School Association, New England League of Middle Schools, Midwest Middle School Association, those organizations gave solace and support to people who were on their own prior to that time. And then the formation of the National Middle School Association was a powerful solidifying force for middle school educators and still is. Those organizational efforts were probably as important as anything else that happened.

Do you have any personal accounts related to those events that might be of interest to others?

Bill Alexander was influenced by John Goodlad. John Goodlad had written a lot about professional development and school change, and Goodlad talked about and tried to establish leagues of schools that would support each other in attempting to bring about change, and Bill Alexander really liked that idea. So when I came to the University of Florida in 1972, I was charged with taking that idea and making it happen, so the University of Florida basically gave me the time and the freedom to create the Florida League of Middle Schools about thirty-two years ago and it was a wonderful experience. In the early years of the National Middle School Association, I got to give the keynote address at the first National Middle School Association because Bill Alexander was on Fulbright in Iran and Don Eichhorn's father was sick so he couldn't do it. I was the only one around who people thought about so I got to do it. There are lots of little stories like that but those are the ones that come to my mind.

Who or what have been some of the greatest detractors or opponents of middle school education?

Early on there were people in connection to those movements that I spoke about earlier. There were people who attacked middle school education, not because they were opposed to middle school education but because middle school and the middle school movement and the reorganization of schools were challenging things they cared about. In the South, it was conservatives who did not want to desegregate their schools, who fought tenaciously, often against middle schools. I have been in situations where sometimes I felt personally threatened by people who were very much opposed to desegregation but couldn't say it and so shouted down the middle school concept instead. I think there were people who were very much committed to the junior high and very much against change who were early detractors and critics of the middle school concept. People who simply didn't want to change and when the middle school came and the junior high was threatened, they became very critical of the middle school concept. Since 1983, the biggest threat to middle school education is from people who see the world and the world of education very differently from the way most middle school educators do. I believe that ultraconservatives in America are opposed to the concepts and the values that lie at the heart of middle school education and that those people are doing basically everything that they can to drive out the kinds of things that middle school education stands for, and we are in a tremendous struggle certainly for the rest of this decade, maybe forever, to try and keep the middle school concept alive and to keep the light of middle school education on during a period that I perceive to be growing darker and darker with people whose views about human nature are dark—people whose views about human potential are dark, people who believe in accountability, people who don't trust, people who want to monitor and supervise and test. Those are the people who threaten the middle school concept in 2003 and beyond. Those are the people who don't believe in integrating the academic disciplines. Those are the people who don't believe that curriculum can actually spring from the needs of young adolescents themselves. Those are the people who believe that curriculum needs to come from on high somewhere. That people who have already learned and taken power should decree what young people need to know for the future. Those are the threats to middle school today.

What have been some of the most significant obstacles to the success of the middle school movement?

One of the most important is the difficulty in establishing middle school teacher education programs. We don't have comprehensive, careful, and complete training of middle school teachers. Most teachers enter middle school teaching without really ever having heard the word middle school in their teacher preparation programs. They take jobs in middle school without ever being in an exemplary middle school. They take jobs in middle school still without wanting to be in middle schools. And so I guess I would identify one of the biggest barriers is having been the failure to establish middle school teacher education the way we should have, and I am as guilty of that as anybody else is.

Are there any other obstacles that you would like to talk about?

Funding is obviously an obstacle. The history of middle school education is the history of being funded at a lower level than either elementary or high school. Virtually every state in the country provides less money to funding young adolescents than it does for young children or young adults, so middle schools have been crippled all along by being literally less money per child than other levels of education. That's a big part of it. The third part is not communicating clearly what middle school is to people outside the middle school movement. Most people still think of the middle school concept as fuzzy, as new age, as muddled thinking. They really don't understand; and fourth, I think there are people, as I mentioned earlier, that are dramatically opposed to those concepts. Who don't believe that children are basically good. Who don't believe that human beings can be trusted to do the right thing. Who don't believe in cooperation. Those are significant barriers.

What are some of the mistakes that have been made during the middle school movement that we might be able to learn from today?

The first mistake was that we thought we should have great middle schools before we should spend our time on teacher education. I made that mistake. I thought that since most of the evidence was that placing good middle school teacher education candidates in poorly formed middle schools would result in those teacher candidates losing what they had been taught that it didn't make much sense to spend much time on middle school education until we had the fully functioning middle schools ready to receive them. I think that was a mistake. I think we should have done those things parallel and worked harder on that. I think the advisory program was doomed because we haven't given up on the idea that teachers need to be mentors and guides and experts and advisors, but we never have done it in a way that was palatable to teachers. That was a mistake. Team teaching was a mistake in the sense that, I explained it earlier. We made lots and lots of mistakes, but those mistakes were honest mistakes and they were mistakes in the learning process and in the process of developing experience. The middle school concept has survived and surmounted those mistakes. I think because the middle school concept is a wonderfully grand idea based on all of the good things about human beings and education. It's an idea that has light and that light isn't going to be put out by those challenges. It has persistence. It has strength and it will continue.

What are some of the factors that are influencing middle school education today?

The standards-based reform movement is the biggest challenge to middle school education, locally, statewide, and nationally. State standards-based reform programs and the No Child Left Behind Act to me are the embodiment of all of the negative thinking that we could possibly summon about the capacity of human beings and how they should be educated. Middle school educators need to join the ranks of the rising angry left. We need to join Al Franken and Michael Moore and Jon Stewart and Bill Maher and throw up the window and say we are mad as hell and we are not going to take it anymore. We need to be as loud and as angry as the conservative critics have been. It's worked for them. They need to get some of their own medicine back.

Who has benefited the most from the middle school movement?

Joycelyn Elders today mentioned that there are 20 million young adolescents in middle school today. If you multiply 20 million by 30 years, I think you can say that by any means the last two generations of young adolescents have been the direct recipients of innovative education and benefited from it immeasurably far more than they would have had the middle school movement not been there for them, so for me it's easy. Of course people like professors and teachers who have been caught up in the middle school movement and who have found in that middle school movement a way to move forward things they deeply care about have been direct beneficiaries as well. It's kept a lot of us alive and energized and enthused for a long, long time.

Who has benefited the least from the middle school movement?

I would like to think that the middle school movement has kept alive the best about human beings and the best about children and the best about education, so we have at least held at bay the forces that represent anger and hostility and mistrust and darkness.

Were there regional differences in the way middle school education was developed or defined, for example New England versus the South?

The South where I live and work was primarily influenced, as I said earlier, by desegregation. Other school districts weren't quite impacted the same, and for a long time the middle school movement was an east-of-the Mississippi movement. It wasn't really until the mid 1970s that the middle school concept really leaped across the Mississippi and made it all the way to California. So, in many ways people who were late adopters missed the struggles that dealt with desegregation and missed the struggles that dealt with changing enrollments and missed the struggles that dealt with *A Nation at Risk*. So they really had an easier time of it because they missed all those struggles, and they were beneficiaries of two decades of growth and experience in middle school education. So that today, when you open a middle school, it is ninety percent easier than it was thirty years ago because we know what we are doing and we have a national consensus that it makes good sense.

Who do you consider to be among the most influential leaders of the middle school movement and why did you select them?

Bill Alexander would be number one and John Lounsbury would be number two. John Lounsbury has personified the middle school movement for forty years. When I was in graduate school in 1960, John Lounsbury published an article on changing the junior high school. Nineteen sixty, that's forty-three years of attempting to influence the education of young adolescents. Don Eichhorn is tremendously important because he was one of the very first people to do it. To take those ideas and make them work, and the schools in Upper St. Clair, Pennsylvania, are still quality middle school places as a result of that influence he put forward thirty-five years ago. People like Gordon Vars were important and Connie Toepfer, the list goes on and on. The middle school movement has benefited from the concentrated and lengthy attention of some very bright people.

Have there been major debates among middle school leaders focusing on particular issues or beliefs?

There have indeed. You know the middle school concept is a cauldron of ideas and that's one of the things that has kept me interested all these years is that we keep unfolding what the middle school means and so, for example, people like James Beane and I have had several popular debates at annual conferences and an essay on the topic of the integrated curriculum and its centrality in the life of middle level education. Joe Renzulli and I had a debate on the way the middle school concept and the education of the gifted should get together. In fact, Joe and I wrote a book for the National Middle School Association called *Talent Development: Two Views,* and they were two widely divergent views. We are still friends, but the middle school concept and the advocates for gifted education are still at odds because I believe the middle school concept advocates educational excellence for all students, not for a particular group. And there have been other debates of course. We are still debating the whole issue of standards-based reform and its value for middle level education. All of this is good. We don't have enough debates. We used to debate things, we even had debates over whether or not the young adolescent's brain spurted or plateaued, during those young adolescent years. The middle school has been fertile because it has been open to debate. In fact, Bill Alexander's first book on middle school was titled *The Emergent Middle School,* and it was an awkward term and for a long time I didn't understand why he insisted on that term, the emergent middle school, and I still teach a course at the University of Florida called The Emergent Middle School and nobody notices that word anymore, but Bill was absolutely convinced that for the middle school concept to thrive and succeed that it had to be constantly emerging, that the day the middle school concept was fixed would be the day that it started to die, and I think he was right, and I think we need to do our best to keep tinkering, keep tweaking, keep challenging, keep debating, and keep it alive as a consequence.

What have been the roles of women and minorities in the middle school movement?

I suppose you could say that the roles of women and minorities in education parallel the roles of women and minorities in society in general. In the middle school movement, women and minorities have played a central role. In many ways the middle school concept has strong feminine qualities and I think as a consequence it appealed to women early on and to men who were more than coaches and more than athletic directors. Teamwork, for example, focusing on the needs of others, individualizing, differentiating. In many ways those are all feminine concepts and of course minority people attached themselves early on to the middle school concept because it strongly spoke for equity and for involvement and for equal participation and for every child, and so for many years the middle school concept has been—to use a political phrase—a big tent, and it still is. I think if you look carefully you'll find that there probably is more diversity involved in the middle school movement than many other places in education.

What are some examples of ways the middle school movement has affected American education?

The first thing that comes to my mind is the impact it is having now on high school education. We have a generation of middle school people who have moved to high school and have carried with them what they have learned in middle level education leadership positions. And they face problems at the high school level, similar to those that they faced at the middle school level; they reach for middle school solutions. So one of the things I think we are seeing around the country, although high school people don't often admit to it, is a tremendous influence on the high school of concepts like academic teamwork and advisory and integrated curriculum and softening the influence of departmentalization. That's been a tremendously important influence of the middle school on education, and I think middle school has been a liberalizing force in the best sense of that word and continues to be in the face of tremendous challenges from ultraconservatives. Those are the two things that strike me as the most important influences at the moment anyway.

**What educational groups, organizations, and institutions have
influenced the middle school movement, and what are some
examples of ways they have done so?**

I have mentioned ASCD and the state leagues and middle school associations and the National Middle School Association. Those organizations
probably influenced middle school education positively. On the negative
side, universities have not been kind to middle schools. Middle school education and middle school teacher education has not yet found a home
firmly and naturally in colleges and universities around the country. We
still provide teacher education for elementary and secondary, and middle
school falls almost always through the cracks. State departments of education and their certification rules have not been a beneficial influence on
middle school education. National level learned societies have not always
been helpful for middle school education. The math, the science, the English, the social studies, those people are so focused on academic disciplines
they can't attain a broader vision, and so they tend to be so defensive about
their own territories that they put up barriers that make it difficult for integrated curriculum, for example, or for teachers to teach more than one
subject area. I think the impact of specialization is often negative in American life in general, but in education the downward reaching of academic
specialization into the departmentalization of elementary schools has been
a disastrous influence. The idea that I am a science teacher and I've got a
coffee cup that shows I am a science teacher and I don't do anything else,
couldn't possibly teach anything else than that, is a very sad state of affairs.

**Have particular legislative actions significantly influenced the
middle school movement at either the state or national level?**

Yes, and I think I've mentioned most of them. The legislation that followed the *Nation at Risk* report, the legislation that is coming out of No
Child Left Behind. We've really had twenty years of disastrously conservative, anti-middle school legislation, and currently the No Child Left Behind
with its mystical interpretation of highly qualified teachers is making it very
difficult for states to produce teachers who can teach more than one subject. We're jumping way back to highly specialized, disciplined boundaries
that nobody can cross and it's a giant step backward.

**What are some ways the middle school movement has influenced
middle level curriculum and instruction?**

I think our influence on what the curriculum has been is far less than
what our influences have been on school organization like teaching, team
organization, and flexible schedules and that sort of thing. I don't think

the curriculum is very different than it was when the Committee of Ten laid it out in 1890–91. I don't think there's much evidence that teachers teach very differently from the teachers who taught them, and we do have pockets of excellence in the curriculum, we have cutting edge programs in integrated curriculum, and cutting edge efforts at differentiated instruction but those are very few, very small, and very isolated. We have yet to really make a major change in what we teach and how we teach it, simply because those things are very difficult to change and it's not anyone's fault, it's simply we really haven't been given the resources to make those changes.

As middle level educators, how do you think we should respond to the current emphasis on student achievement as measured by standardized tests?

I think we should reject it, reject it, reject it, and reject it, and I think we should do it loudly and angrily and publicly.

Are there lessons we still need to learn from the history of the middle school movement?

I do think we need to keep it alive and we need to learn our history, and I think this project that you are involved in is important in that regard. I do sense as the reorganization of American middle level schools comes to an end that as some of you have spoken about, that the middle school movement may lose momentum as a consequence. In our state, for example, the people who were involved in the start-up of the Florida League of Middle Schools thirty-two years ago are still the people who are running the Florida League of Middle Schools thirty-two years later. It is difficult to find young educators who are willing to get involved beyond their school. Somehow, thirty years ago, it was a mission that everyone caught on to, but today it's very difficult so I think what you're doing is very important. We've got to keep that history alive, but you know what, even if we don't, the middle school movement will stand out historically as the most comprehensive, complete, and successful liberalizing influence in the history of American education. It's already been a complete success.

How would you characterize the current status of the middle school movement?

I think we're in a defensive mode and we've got to shift to an attack mode. We've got to take the offensive. We've got to stand up and shout out the principles that underlie the middle school movement. Otherwise, the darkness is going to overtake us, so we really need to be active. We need to be militant. We need to be out there. We can't apologize. What we are doing in the middle school movement, I believe, is saving the best of American education during a difficult time.

Are there particular efforts that need to be made to help ensure the future success of the middle school movement?

We've got to find a way to save middle school teacher education. You of course know that teacher education is under attack nationally and wholly. There are people in the national government and surrounding the national government who have found the favor of the national government who would very much like to do away with traditional teacher education as a whole, and they are making tremendous progress. They may win. So one of the battles we've got to fight right now is to hang onto as much of quality teacher education as we can. We've got to change a lot of the things we have done poorly because a lot of people don't support traditional teacher education. So fighting for middle school teacher education is a very important part of it. We've got to continue to work together at state and national levels. We've got to get political. We've got to support candidates who understand and support quality and enlightened education rather than narrow, punitive, negative, and hostile approaches to education. More than anything else, we have to understand that as individuals we have to keep clear in our minds what is important and make sure that we live our lives in ways that exemplify that because ultimately each of us is what middle school education is all about. So we have to live out that meaning in whatever way we can as a teacher, as a principal, as a researcher, we've got to keep those principles in mind, and as an earlier Texan old pioneer Sam Houston once said, "We've got to do right and damn the consequences."

15

J. Howard Johnston

A lot of what is being considered to be innovative practice for high school reform has been going on in middle schools for thirty years. Smaller communities; student advocates; a focused, interdisciplinary hands-on curriculum; lots of real-life experiences—it's all there. . . .I think we have raised the bar for all school reform efforts in this country.

Dr. J. Howard Johnston is widely recognized and respected for his commitment to young adolescents as well as his leadership in middle level education. He is a sound researcher and author of more than 100 journal articles, research reports, book chapters, books, and other professional publications. He has delivered keynote addresses and provided professional development at middle level conferences in all 50 states as well as in Europe, Asia, South America, and other regions of the world. His interests include school achievement and productive behavior of learners, the diversity of the American population, the need to structure schools for success, and the use of technology in challenging environments. Johnston is a brilliant teacher, a much sought-after mentor, and an eloquent speaker. He has been recognized for his manifold and valued services to the cause of young

The Legacy of Middle School Leaders, pages 247–263
Copyright © 2011 by Information Age Publishing
All rights of reproduction in any form reserved.

adolescents and their education, whether expressed in writings, oral presentations, consultations, research studies, scholarly treatises, or classroom teaching, all emanating from a personhood of decency and quality.

Dr. Johnston received his undergraduate degree in English, anthropology, and secondary education in 1969, and his master's degree in English and social studies in 1971, from the State University of New York at New Paltz. In 1974, he earned his doctorate in curriculum and instruction at the University of Wyoming, Laramie. Johnston began his career as an English and social studies teacher at the junior high and high school levels in Wappingers Falls, New York in 1969, and served as a demonstration teacher at Laramie Junior High School, Laramie, Wyoming, from 1972 until 1974. He accepted a position as professor in the Department of Curriculum and Instruction at the University of Cincinnati (UC), Cincinnati, in 1974. He held several positions at UC including chair of the Department of Curriculum and Instruction and Associate Dean for Graduate Studies and Research. In 1990, Johnston became professor and chair of the Department of Secondary Education at the University of South Florida (USF), Tampa, Florida. He served as department chair until 1995 and is currently professor of secondary education at USF.

Selected Accomplishments and Contributions to Middle Level Education

- Founder of the column *What Research Says to the Middle Level Practitioner* in the *Middle School Journal* (1979)
- Member of the National Association of Secondary School Principals (NASSP) Council on Middle Level Education (1981–1996)
- Lead author for NASSP's *An Agenda for Excellence at the Middle Level* (1984)
- Received the NMSA Presidential Award (1985)
- Member of the NMSA Board of Trustees (1987–1989)
- Received the NASSP William Gruhn-Forrest Long Award for distinguished service and leadership in middle level education (1996)
- Charter member of the National Forum to Accelerate Middle Grades Reform (1997–2000)
- Team Leader for the High School Principals' Partnership sponsored by Union Pacific (2001–Present)
- Received the John H. Lounsbury Distinguished Service Award from NMSA (2003)

Selected Publications

Johnston, J. H., & Perez, J. M. R. (1985). Four climates of effective middle level schools. *Schools in the Middle: A Report on Trends and Practices.* Reston, VA: National Association for Secondary School Principals.

Johnston, J. H., & Lounsbury, J. H. (1985). *How fares the ninth grade?* Reston, VA: National Association of Secondary School Principals.

Johnston, J. H., & Markel, G. C. (1986). *What research says to the middle level practitioner.* Columbus, OH: National Middle School Association.

Johnston, J. H., & Lounsbury, J. H. (1988). *Life in the three sixth grades.* Reston, VA: National Association of Secondary School Principals.

Johnston, J. H. (1990). *New American family and the schools.* Columbus, OH: National Middle School Association.

Johnston, J. H., & Borman, K. M. (1992). *Effective schooling for economically disadvantaged students: School-based strategies for diverse student populations.* Norwood, NJ: Ablex.

Johnston, J. H. (1992). School transitions and their effects on social membership for at risk students. In J. H. Johnston & K. Borman (Eds.), *Effective schooling for economically disadvantaged students: School-based strategies for diverse student populations.* Norwood, NJ: Ablex.

Johnston, J. H. (1992). John H. Lounsbury: Conscience of the middle school movement. *Middle School Journal, 24*(2), 45–50.

Johnston, J. H., & Hines, R. H. (1997). Fostering achievement for all students in middle level schools. In J. Irvin (Ed.), *What current research says to the middle level practitioner* (pp. 109–119). Columbus, OH: National Middle School Association.

Williamson, R. D., & Johnston, J. H. (Eds.). (1998). *Able learners in the middle level school: Identifying talent and maximizing potential.* Reston, VA: National Association of Secondary School Principals.

Williamson, R., & Johnston, J. H. (1999). Challenging orthodoxy: An emerging agenda for middle level reform. *Middle School Journal, 30*(4), 10–17.

Johnston, J. H. (2001). *The history of the middle level school.* Online internet-based video training module. Reston, VA: National Association of Secondary School Principals.

Berson, M., Cruz, B., & Johnston, J. H. (2004). *Social studies on the Internet,* (2nd ed.). Englewood Cliffs, NJ: Prentice-Hall.

Williamson, R. D., & Johnston, J. H. (2005). Leadership in the middle school. In V. A. Anfara, G. Andrews, & S. B. Mertens (Eds.), *Encyclopedia of middle grades education* (pp. 45–57). Greenwich, CT: Information Age Publishing and Westerville, OH: National Middle School Association.

J. Howard Johnston[*]

There were a number of individuals who influenced me. Al Arth certainly got me started with middle level education and Gene Cottle really rooted me in the literature of the progressive movement in education. There are others: Connie Toepfer, superb mentor and good friend; John Lounsbury is, I think, everyone's mentor, and I am pleased to count him among my friends. Also, there was Don Eichhorn; I read a tremendous amount of his stuff and really enjoyed my relationship with him. The list goes on: Gordon Vars, Bill Van Til, and George Melton, who was really a superb human being and a consummate organizer of professional activity. They're all just tremendously influential people.

What kinds of middle school literature did you read?

Gene Cottle had a library of everything that had ever been written about the junior high school, and he started me at one end of it and said, "When you're done, come back and we will talk about what you have read." And some of the very early stuff was very good; for example, I was reading about G. Stanley Hall and the child study movement. His first book on adolescence as a phase of childhood was in 1904. I read Leonard Koos, which is not a name that a lot of people run across in contemporary literature. I read extensively, of course, Van Til, Vars, and Lounsbury, and Gruhn and Douglass on junior high education. In the middle grades I read everything, I think, Conrad Toepfer wrote. I know I read everything Don Eichhorn wrote. Obviously, John Dewey and a lot of those people were included. Also, I read a lot of the critics of junior high and progressives.

What was your primary motivation for becoming involved in the middle school movement?

Curiosity. I have a very short attention span, but I'm very curious about things. And, initially, I was curious about the sometimes very unusual behavior that young adolescent kids engage in. I've always been fascinated by how people make sense of their world, and I've always been particularly interested in how kids make sense of their world. Al Arth kept insisting to me that most behavior is purposeful. It's designed to fulfill some need. I'm always intrigued by trying to understand the purposes that are fulfilled by some of the things people do. So, in studying middle school kids, I've

---

[*] Howard Johnston was interviewed for the Legacy Project in November 2003.

always just been intrigued by them. I mean they are just absolutely the best interview subjects there are. They'll tell you stuff you don't want to know. And so for an anthropological approach to research, which is what I have done most of my life, they're the ideal research collaborators. Really, they are mostly just interesting.

How would you describe the early years of the middle school movement?

This is an interesting question because I noticed in the interview protocol you specified that the earlier years started with the 1960s and 1970s. My concern about starting there is that, and certainly my memory doesn't extend back any further except to my own junior high experience, we're really in danger of losing the long view. What I mean by that is that middle schools have always been at the center of controversy—always. And if you look at the patterns that existed at the turn of the last century, we had a huge dislocation of workers, a massive realignment of what it meant to work, as people moved out of agriculture and into the industrial setting. We had a tremendous migration within the United States, from the southern states to the northeast and to the west. We had, between 1880 and 1920 I guess, about 20 million immigrants enter the United States. They spoke a variety of languages and they came from an incredible variety of backgrounds. The school dropout rate was skyrocketing. The parallels with our own age are amazing. From those conditions at the turn of the century, 1892 in fact, arose NEA's Committee of Ten, followed by the Commission on the Reorganization of Secondary Education in 1918. They all had such ghastly dull titles and wrote in such awful prose that nobody ever reads them anymore, but it remains very interesting because, in fact, what existed then were largely the same conditions that exist now. The need for "reform" is what brought about the junior high—which was replaced by the middle school in the early 1960s, largely because of other external conditions. Sputnik, racial tensions, poor performance by U.S. students on international comparisons and all kinds of other things led many to conclude that the junior high was a failure. Ironically, it was seen as a failure by both the political left and the right. It was seen as a failure among progressives who saw that it hadn't lived up to its promise of providing a progressive education and the transition between elementary and high school. And it was also seen as a failure by the traditionalists who saw it as a softening of academic standards. Arthur Bestor and James Bryant Conant wrote scathing indictments of the junior high school. And so, the middle school sort of evolved out of that.

Here we are at the turn of the next century, with massive realignment of work environments, massive immigration, economic dislocations, and enormous complexity in terms of the diversity that exists in the United States. We all know about the demand for higher and higher standards of performance to meet international competition. It's interesting, we often talk about what motivates change in education and I think it's like there's a bunch of "big I's" out there: things like industrialization (or de-industrialization in favor of an information-based economy), immigration, and internationalization. To illustrate, in 1957 the Soviets shot Sputnik into space and threw American education into a crisis because we weren't producing enough scientists, and our programs weren't producing the kind of graduates who were going to compete with the Russians. That's the era in which I grew up. But then, in 1999, the TIMSS study, the Third International Mathematics and Science Study is released and became the information age Sputnik. Here we are—failing to compete once again!

I think if we truncate our sense of history too soon in looking at how any education institution evolves, especially the middle school, we fail to understand that they're always born in turmoil and the middle schools always existed in the center of a storm of controversy. Sometimes more shrill, sometimes less shrill, but nevertheless, it has always been there right smack in the middle of it. So, I guess the bottom line answer is when you ask what influences how I think about the early years, I think our understanding of the early years aren't early enough. Once you start to understand that a pattern exists, it becomes more predictable and a little less frightening and more acceptable to accommodate some of the demands that are placed on the institution by the society that created it.

How has the middle school concept changed since the early years of the middle school movement?

I think the concept has certainly adapted to changing conditions. And I think that the early years of the middle school were characterized by these sorts of lists of features that comprise the institution, and if you had the right list of features, you were doing okay. I think the emphasis now has shifted, rightfully so, and in the last dozen years or so the emphasis has been on how all of these things come together and how they work. I also think there's also a fair amount of interest in alternative ways of organizing things for middle level kids.

So I think that one of the things that has changed is the declining importance of procedural orthodoxy and the move toward a much stronger focus on creating an institution that serves directly both the needs of the public that supports it and the needs of the children who are in it, in a humane and sensible way. So a middle school has really evolved from a list of practices to being a commitment, I think, to produce high achievement, to be developmentally responsive, and to promote social equity. Those are the commitments, and the way you choose to do it is pretty much a matter of local decision. I think the other thing we have learned is about the non-transportability of schools. A school that works in suburban Ohio may not work in rural Georgia or inner city Florida; indeed, the practices that work in those places may be absolutely bizarre in another setting. So I think we've really expanded our procedural notions about what the schools are, but intensified our commitments to really important outcomes—and to innovative approaches and to research-based best practices.

How have middle schools changed since the early years of the middle school movement?

I think they are relying less on external definitions about what they should be. I think I'm seeing more and more internal initiative by teachers and staff to come to terms with what their purposes are—what their community expectations are, and how they can best muster their resources and expend their energy to make those things happen. I think it's become less of a design model and more of a commitment to make certain outcomes occur. And we've moved to accepting accountability for those outcomes. The bottom line is that I think there has been a lot more local decision making about the way things ought to be.

What were some of the motivations that fueled the growth of the middle school movement?

I'd like to say they were all noble and just, but probably they weren't. I suspect that in some respects it emerged during the school construction boom in the late 1960s and early 1970s, fueled partly by a baby boom going through the system. They're cheaper to build than high schools and they're more efficient than having a bunch of elementary schools. So in one respect, it's a much more efficient way of housing kids. It also makes more efficient use, I think, of the distribution of time.

I think middle schools were also seen as a way of making an earlier intervention in desegregation issues. It was an attempt, I think, to bring about a greater integration a little earlier in the system than might otherwise happen, because, obviously, if you move from a K–8 system to a middle school system, K–8 schools tend to be relatively smaller, and demographically homogeneous. Middle schools are somewhat more diverse, so I think there was some initiative in that respect.

I think there was also sort of a bandwagon effect. If as suburb A grows and puts in a middle school, when suburb B grows, it looks like the thing you ought to have is a middle school—so we built them. I think that, combined with a growing professional consensus on the need for special treatment for young adolescents, created this mixture of motivations and that's what produced the schools themselves, the physical plants. Then, of course, the programs tend to grow into physical spaces. I think we had some of that phenomenon as well. But I think it was a combination of professional commitments, research outcomes, and demographic pressures.

How were decisions about the directions taken by the middle school movement made?

I suspect that in the early years they were made largely by professionals, the early years being in the 1960s and 1970s. When a community got ready to open a new school or reconfigure a school, there was typically some sort of community decision made about what they wanted to have; then, basically, professionals took over and designed these programs and facilities. I think what's changed in recent years is it has been direct community input. There have always been legislative inputs in the form of teacher certification and funding, and capitation formulas for elementary versus middle school versus high school and so on. But, ultimately, I think, the decisions about where the rubber meets the road were made by professionals. That's changed in the last few years, and I think by changing the accountability structures in states and by changing certification requirements, the legislature has started to intervene much more directly in the day-to-day affairs of schooling. They don't do so necessarily by prescribing precisely what it is you must teach, although *de facto* that occurs as a result of testing.

Who were other individuals and groups outside middle level education involved in the early years of the middle school movement?

There were a lot of them. Not always positively either. I mean there were certain groups that saw the rise of the middle school and the growing independence of the middle school and middle school professional organizations as a direct challenge to their supremacy in the profession. There were fairly bitter contests among some principal groups where the introduction of the middle school was seen as perhaps diluting the programs that were offered for high schools. I think there was some very, very enlightened leadership in NASSP a number of years ago with Scott Thompson and George Melton, both of whom were originally middle level people. They saw this as just a huge part of their mission to serve leaders, all school leaders.

What have been some of the most significant events, incidents, or moments in the middle school movement?

The demise of the junior high school and the rise of the middle school really began before Sputnik. I think around that time the work of John Lounsbury and Bill Van Til and Gordon Vars got a lot of attention. Gordon worked primarily on the core curriculum area, which really became the most widely accepted curriculum model that people endeavored to attain with the middle school. I'm not sure it was ever entirely successful, but certainly their work articulated a vision that was extremely important to people that were laying plans for the middle school.

The very first Elementary and Secondary School Authorization Act was passed in 1964, I think, and provided direct assistance to districts for things such as reading intervention and special education and other services—compensatory services for disadvantaged children and people living in poverty. It was one of the first attempts by the federal government to redistribute resources in an effort to equalize educational opportunity. All of those were extremely powerful influences.

All of this activity produced a certain amount of resources, but it also produced a certain amount of wholesomeness about the mission of the schools and of teaching. I think that was something that motivated people of my generation who began working in the middle schools in that era. There was a certain nobility of purpose—a belief that our work was focused on and dedicated to equalizing opportunity. You know, we probably weren't any more successful with that than anybody else ever was, but it gave our work a certain importance and a certain dignity. And I think that's one of the things that people my age tend to rebel against when confronted with some of the high stakes testing initiatives. Somehow those goals seem so crass by comparison with some of the other things that education strived to do in the past, and that, I think, is kind of a sad outcome. But the education context was highly charged and certainly intimately connected to the social and political context of the middle of the 20th Century.

Who or what have been some of the greatest detractors or opponents of middle school education?

Let me start with a premise that is a very important one for me because it's increasingly how I try to live my life. I honestly believe that people act out of what they consider to be the best intentions. I believe that people do and say what they do because they believe that it is in the best interests of our world *as they see it.* Now I may disagree with what they do and say, and I may disagree with their view of the world and what our best interest is, but, with the possible exception of true psychopaths, I honestly think people operate from good intentions. So, when I talk about detractors I'm actually going to talk about people who may have proposed alternatives that are more problematic for us.

It started almost a hundred years ago. One of the first major critiques of the junior high school was published, and it was a blistering indictment of the watered down curriculum and this ludicrous notion that everybody could possibly learn all of this stuff. The true mission of schooling was to prepare people for college, and anything else was a waste of time and public resources. The purity of that goal was all but eradicated by this rogue institution—the junior high. But, I think more recently, the middle school has come under fire for a variety of other reasons. Progressive education was always critiqued for venturing into areas where the schools had no business—actually, where the state had no business and *ergo* the schools had no business there either since they're instruments of the state. So that discussion has been going on practically forever, the dispute over who is responsible for things like the development of morals, ethics, and values, the investigation of values and moral issues, and the treatment [or non-treatment] of religion. The list goes on and on.

I think that a lot of criticisms have been leveled by people who see personal development as an area that the state has no legitimate interest in. And what we call the "religious right" or the conservative religious movement in the United States, have deep concerns about what many of them consider to be the "public religion" of the United States, secular humanism, which they see being taught with a vengeance in middle school. So I think there's one whole issue around that.

And by the way, I don't think we've even begun to see the beginning of religious controversy in schools. Interestingly enough, for over 200 years, when we talked about religious differences in the US, we meant variations on Judeo-Christian religions and more conservative or liberal interpretations of a relatively common stream of religious beliefs. That's not true anymore. The new immigration into North America comes largely from Africa, Latin America, and Asia and those are not necessarily places where spiritual life was shaped by Judeo-Christian traditions for the most part. So for all of the turmoil that we've had in dealing with the issue of religion in schools for the first 200 years of our history, I believe "We ain't seen nothing yet." And I think that it is going to continue to be a major issue for us.

The other major detractors have been people who have concerns about the intellectual vacuousness and lack of academic rigor in the middle school. Again, this is hardly a new criticism, but it is better organized. It's coming largely from relatively conservative foundations such as the Thomas

B. Fordham Foundation, and people like Chester Finn and Diane Ravitch. Although Ravitch seems to be much more of an academic traditionalist than she is a moral traditionalist. There is also the whole Alan Bloom phenomenon—the prescriptions for what your child needs to know at the age of 6, 7, 8, 9, 10, 11, 12, and so on. Those are not new positions; those are positions that have always risen and fallen. In 370 B.C. Socrates drank hemlock because he was teaching unauthorized stuff to the young men of Athens. It's the idea of the transmission of traditional knowledge versus the creation of independent thinkers. It's not a new one; it's been going on forever. So I think we're going to continue to see that. I think those are the two big issues from which everything else evolves. Direct instruction, high stakes testing, assaults on multicultural curricula, all seem to come from a "stick to the business" stance by many of our critics. Don't mess around with all this other soft stuff, stick to the academics, stick to the teaching. And I think there are going to be bigger curriculum wars in the future.

What have been some of the most significant obstacles to the success of the middle school movement?

I would have to say that it is our inability to articulate a compelling vision for middle schools that the public understands and accepts. Very quickly, our conversations about middle schools deteriorate into technical language and programmatic issues, and I don't think we've ever gotten the public fully hooked by what a middle school is and can be. And when I talk about the public I am not just talking about the parents. In 1960 about 70% of U.S. households had school-age children. In the last census only about 18–21% of U.S. households had school-age children. So, even if we convince every single person who has a kid in school that middle school is the best idea since sliced bread, we're still missing 80% of the population. I just think that we've never really fully articulated or captured a vision that can be expressed in a sentence. If you stop somebody on the street and ask them what an elementary school is about, they will tell you it's about skills and naps and cookies and stuff like that. And what's high school about? High school is about subjects and getting ready for college or work or something like that. Ask somebody what a middle school is about, and they can't tell you. In fact, you could probably walk around this [National Middle School Association] conference and ask people that question and get a whole collection of non-succinct answers about what it is. So, I think that's been one of our major problems.

The other major problem is that when you promise much, and we do, if you fail to deliver on those promises you become the target of criticism. And in some respects we promise too much, I think. We're going to take care of the kids' self-esteem, we're going to make them literate, we're going to make them smart, we're going to make them well-adjusted decent human beings, we're going to make them functional members of society, we're going to make them good neighbors, we're going to make them contributing members of their communities. Man, that's a tall order! You run the risk of having such a long shopping list of promises that if you don't do any of them well or even if you do 80% of them well, you're still not doing everything you promised you were going to do.

And, lastly, I think, middle schools have been unfairly targeted as the weak link in the system. Oh, some of the stuff that people say about it now is truly astonishing. The institution has never caught the imagination, or the commitment, of the American people to the extent that it deserves.

What are some of the most important factors that are influencing middle school education today?

I say there are three. Accountability, accountability, and accountability. There are probably five. Accountability, accountability, accountability, teacher preparation, and funding. And those probably would have been the same list that I would have given you ten years ago as well. The reason I said accountability three times is that there really are three kinds. There's accountability to the public to achieve the standards they have set for us, whether we like them or not, and in the format that they've established for us whether we like it or not. I'm not usually this law abiding, but that's the law. A school in Florida cannot opt out of FCAT; it's against the law.

Second is accountability to assure that we are achieving equity both in our treatment of kids and in the outcomes. And this kind of accountability deals with things like the achievement gap, the digital divide, the opportunity gap, and all of the other things that divide us. I think that really is a major one.

And the third one is accountability to our own professional canons and ethics, accountability to engage in best practices as research tells us what they are. It's the accountability to do the best job we possibly can. We all know that there are times when we simply don't do the best we can do. That is the nature of the human beast. But even though we know that we're flawed people, as an institution, we have to commit to doing the very best we can do just as often as we can possibly do it.

The other two big issues are teacher preparation and money. One of the great difficulties that we face now is only going to get worse—the effect of essentially unregulated access to the profession. This isn't a call for more colleges of education, but I think, as a minimum, the state is obligated to provide a competently trained person for the classroom. But we have a history of abandoning preparation standards when they become inconvenient. We had a teacher shortage during and following World War II, and we had basically the same admission standard we use now—if you want to teach, well come on! And as a result of that recruitment strategy in the 1940s and 1950s, we wound up with was a very, very challenging set of circumstances and the investment of tens of millions of dollars in public money through NDEA and other programs to get people up to speed to teach the stuff they were supposed to teach. Unfortunately, I think we are headed down the same road again. Some of the people who come to us through alternative routes are absolutely wonderful teachers and some of the ones who come to us through traditional programs aren't all that good. But I think that simply opening the gates to fill classrooms with people who may be well intentioned but may lack skill or knowledge about kids or content will create more difficulties in schools than they resolve. Unfortunately, alternative program people are very often the ones who leave after a short period of time creating more turmoil for the kids and more difficulty for faculty teams and community relations. So, I honestly think that's a really critical issue. I know that it is one that Ken McEwin has been working on for many, many years.

The last one is money. We are going to continue to be asked to do more with less; that's the nature of contemporary life. It's the nature of globalization. That's the euphemism we use for budget reductions now. It's become some noble objective; doing more with less is somehow supposed to be a good thing. Certainly we can work smarter and I know there are things we can do to reduce costs. But there are things you just can't do without money.

Who has benefited the most from the middle school movement?

I honestly think that middle schools have benefited the vast majority of kids. I honestly believe that middle schools are better for kids than any other alternative that I've seen at that age. To me a middle school is one that has three deep commitments at heart: high achievement, developmental responsiveness, and social equity. So when I talk about a middle school or middle level school, I am talking about a school that is devoted to the interests and the welfare of young adolescents. I honestly believe that schools with that focus produce very positive results for kids. But it all starts with a commitment to serve middle level children in a unique and supportive, compassionate environment.

Who has benefited the least from the middle school movement?

I don't know that anybody has not benefited because of the middle school movement. I suspect the people who benefited the least from it are not people who are harmed by it, because I don't think that happens, but I think there are people who are less positively affected. My guess is that very high-performing kids would be very high-performing kids no matter where you put them. So maybe that's one of the reasons middle schools are always in a little bit of trouble. It doesn't maximally advantage the kids who are already sort of maximally advantaged. Or it doesn't further advantage the kids who are already maximally advantaged. But I don't know that.

Who do you consider to be among the most influential leaders of the middle school movement?

That's a hard one. It's hard because it's a long list of people, and there are so many people that have worked so hard and done so much. You can't begin that answer without starting with John Lounsbury. John is amazing. John provides something that's intangible but essential. He provides a sense of soul and continuity. There's something about him that brings a level of wholesomeness to this enterprise. To me, that's really very appealing and very attractive. It's a good thing to be associated with a movement that has a John Lounsbury in it.

There are so many other good people. Ken McEwin, he's probably done more to influence teacher education at the middle level than anybody I know. Jim Garvin is one of the most dedicated and articulate proponents of a child-centered program. Al Arth is one of the people who is relentless in his pursuit of a developmental and responsive school. Connie Toepfer has written articulately about curriculum. So has Jim Beane, a former student of Connie's who writes with courage and conviction. Paul George is like the dean of the middle school. He knows about everything, and is probably the most widely quoted person in the field. Don Eichhorn, whom we really miss, began the articulation of solid developmentally based education. Sherrel Bergmann is a remarkable professional. What I love about Sherrel is she has always dealt so toughly with the soft side of middle level education. She's the one who has always unabashedly faced the tough issues, like sexuality, drug use, and adolescent disruption and disability.

The list just goes on and on and on. Hayes Mizell. Hayes calls himself a critical friend of middle school. And he has been. Sue Swaim, of course, has piloted this organization through a number of very tumultuous years. Judy Brough in curriculum. Don and Sally Clark working in leadership along with Ron Williamson, who has probably brought more of a leadership focus to this organization than anyone else. These are the people who are writing and talking, and, putting their money where their mouth is, I guess. John

Van Hoose, my late friend and colleague, is really missed. He was one of the people that brought such a level of decency to this movement that he dignified all of our work.

I must have given you twenty and I think there must be a hundred more. And the strength of the movement isn't so much about people who are most influential, but people who are influential in different ways, like Cecil Floyd, who puts on one of the largest middle school conferences every year in Texas. It has become legendary. It's about people who work so hard in their own state to sustain their organizations, because that's where the work gets done. That's where things really happen. Somebody is going to go tweak the North Carolina Legislature to do the right thing . . . and it's going to be a North Carolinian. So, when you talk about influence, real hardhitting, on the ground, practical influence, I think, there are thousands of people I could name.

What have been the roles of women and other minorities in the middle school movement?

I'd say that, with the possible exception of reading, there are probably more women in leadership positions in this group than virtually any other. In fact, I think NMSA has gone out of its way to really make a place at the table for people of color and for women and for other underrepresented people. It has gone to the point of changing its government structure in an attempt to give voice to a lot of folks who have been excluded before. I am very proud of being associated with NMSA for that reason. I think it has been deeply committed to justice.

What are some examples of ways the middle school movement has affected American education?

I think it's really done it in a number of ways. Interestingly enough, I work now extensively in high school reform initiatives, and a lot of what is being considered to be innovative practice for high school reform has been going on in middle schools for thirty years. Smaller communities, student advocates, a focused, interdisciplinary hands-on curriculum, lots of real-life experiences—it's all there. John Lounsbury and those guys were writing about that stuff forty years ago, and I think it's had tremendous impact on what we expect of our schools. I think we expect them to be whole-child focused and compassionate, and we expect them to be developmentally responsive. And I think we have raised the bar for all school reform efforts in this country.

What educational groups, organizations, and institutions have influenced the middle school movement?

Obviously NMSA. But so has NASSP [National Association of Secondary School Principals]. In the 1980s NASSP formed a council on middle level education, which persisted for almost fifteen years. It was their action arm regarding middle level education and middle level leadership. ASCD has continued to do work on issues related to middle school, although they don't really have a very active middle school focus. But they do a lot of work on small learning communities and student mentorships and so on. The National Staff Development Council, Dennis Sparks and Stephanie Hirsh, do a great job with authentic school-based staff development as a way of restructuring and improving middle schools. The special middle school interest group at AERA [American Educational Research Association] has contributed a lot of research. The American Psychological Association has continued to be influential for adolescent education. The guidance group is a big player, too. It has long been an advocate of solid middle level programs. Even the American Red Cross and UNICEF have sort of dipped their oars in the water. And a number of foundations have as well: Edna McConnell Clark, Champion/International Paper, Carnegie, Kellogg, and Disney. I think it's about as comprehensive a movement as you could possibly find.

What are some ways the middle school movement has influenced middle level curriculum and instruction?

I think one of the things that it did, quite frankly, was pay attention to what a middle level curriculum ought to be. It had typically been either sort of a scaled-up elementary curriculum or kind of a dumbed-down high school curriculum. Starting with people like Gordon Vars and John Lounsbury, it was the first time that there's ever been clear attention given to this separate entity. I think there's also been a lot of attention paid to what makes it unique and what the right functions of curriculum really are.

How would you characterize the current status of the middle school movement?

Under assault! I think some of that is our own doing, but it has also been unfairly targeted as the emblem of school failure in the United States. I think it's because of the volatility and difficulty of the population we serve. From a public point of view, it's nobody's favorite grade level; nobody remembers fondly the middle grades. And because we have not articulated a positive and compelling vision about what we are doing, I think we are a target of convenience for many school critics.

Are there particular efforts that need to be made to help ensure the future success of the middle school movement?

Yes. I think we really need to invite our communities into deeper and more sustained conversation about what they expect and what they want from their middle school. And I'll tell you, the first thing they're going to tell you is they want high test scores. But the second thing they're going to tell you is they want a place where their kid wants to go to school, they want a place where their kid feels safe, where their kid feels involved, and can develop as a person. They want a place where their kid can learn to make good ethical decisions. These people aren't the opposition; they're pretty much like you and me—regular people concerned about their kids and their community.

And we may not like where they put high test scores, which is going to be at the top of the list, but right after that, comes all the stuff we've been saying middle schools are all about. I think that once we invite parents into the conversation, and then work collaboratively with them to create the kinds of schools that produce those results, I think our future is golden.

16

Joan S. Lipsitz

How do you teach this very diverse group of kids in the same place at the same time? It's an unresolved theme all the way through the decades, that no matter how much we value diversity of ability, there's a limit to organizational elasticity, and there's a limit to how much heroism we can count on from ordinary people. And it's ordinary people who have to educate the next generation. We can't count on heroism. Counting on heroism is not good public policy.

The career-long advocacy of Dr. Joan S. Lipsitz for the education and well-being of young adolescents transformed the way they were perceived. Her work fostered an authentic understanding of the uniqueness and importance of this age group. After beginning her teaching career in 1960 at the high school level, Lipsitz accepted a middle level teaching position and found the transition to teaching young adolescents challenging. This was when she first discovered that there were few resources available that addressed teaching young adolescents. From 1972 until 1978, Dr. Lipsitz was a Program Associate for the Learning Institute of North Carolina which provided her opportunities to become involved in public school reform.

The Legacy of Middle School Leaders, pages 265–281
Copyright © 2011 by Information Age Publishing
All rights of reproduction in any form reserved.

Her classic book, *Growing Up Forgotten: A Review of Research and Programs Concerning Early Adolescence* (1977), provided a national wake-up call regarding the neglect of young adolescents by society including educators, youth agency personnel, medical professionals, and other people and organizations serving them. She is also author of many other influential professional publications including the widely acclaimed *Successful Schools for Young Adolescents* (1984).

Dr. Lipsitz received her undergraduate degree in English from Wellesley College, Wellesley, Massachusetts, in 1959, and her master's degree in English from the University of Connecticut in 1964. She earned her doctorate from the University of North Carolina, Chapel Hill (UNC-CH) in 1976. In 1978, she founded the Center for Early Adolescence at UNC-CH. This was the first national center to focus on supporting young adolescents in their homes, schools, and communities by providing training, technical assistance, and other services and resources to those who served them. In 1986, she left the Center for Early Adolescence to develop a Middle Grades Reform Initiative funded by the Lilly Endowment that she directed for nine years. An additional major contribution of Lipsitz is her role in founding the National Forum to Accelerate Middle Grades Reform (the Forum) in 1997 and the Schools to Watch program sponsored by the Forum in 1999. The Forum is an alliance of over 60 educators, researchers, national associations, and officers of professional organizations and foundations committed to promoting the academic performance and healthy development of young adolescents. Schools to Watch is a reform program aimed at improving middle grades education by identifying specific criteria that define high performing middle level schools and selecting schools that meet the criteria to serve as models and learning sites for other schools. Dr. Lipsitz serves on several governing boards, and she remains active in her advocacy for young adolescents.

Selected Accomplishments and Contributions to Middle Level Education

- Received the Phi Delta Kappa Award for Outstanding Research (1977)
- Faculty member, Bush Institute for Child and Family Policy, University of North Carolina, Chapel Hill (UNC-CH) (1980–1985)
- Research Associate (on loan from UNC-CH) at the National Institute of Education (1980–1981)

- Received the John Lounsbury Distinguished Service Award from NMSA (1994)
- Received the C. Kenneth McEwin Distinguished Service Award from the North Carolina Middle School Association (2004)
- Received the Purpose Prize for older social innovators solving society's tough problems, for Schools to Watch (2006)
- Received the National Forum to Accelerate Middle Grades Reform Schools to Watch Program Joan Lipsitz Lifetime Achievement Award, which is named in her honor (2006)
- Member of the College Board Commission on Precollegiate Guidance and Counseling
- Served on the governing boards of the Hershey Trust Company and the Milton Hershey School
- Consultant to the Carnegie Corporation, the National Science Foundation, the United States Department of Education, the Foundation for the Mid South, and many others foundations, agencies, and organizations

Selected Publications

Lipsitz, J. S. (1977). *Growing up forgotten: A review of research and programs concerning early adolescence.* Lexington, MA: D. C. Heath and Company.

Lipsitz, J. S. (1979). *Barriers: A new look at the needs of young adolescents.* New York: The Ford Foundation.

Lipsitz, J. S. (1980). Public policy and early adolescent research. *The High School Journal, 63*(6), 250–256.

Lipsitz, J. S. (1980). The age group. In *Toward adolescence: The middle school years—The seventy-ninth yearbook of the Society for the Study of Education* (pp. 7–31). Chicago, IL: University of Chicago Press.

Lipsitz, J. S. (1984). *Successful schools for young adolescents.* New Brunswick: Transaction Books.

Lipsitz, J. S., Jackson, A. W., & Meyer, A. (1997). What works in middle-grades school reform [Monograph]. *Phi Delta Kappan, 78*(7), 517–556.

Lipsitz, J. S., Mizell, M. H., Jackson, A. W., & Austin, L. M. (1997). Speaking with one voice: A manifesto for middle-grades reform. *Phi Delta Kappan, 78*(7), 533–540.

Lipsitz, J. S., & West, T. (2006). What makes a good school: Identifying excellent middle schools. *Phi Delta Kappan, 88*(1), 57–66.

---

*Joan S. Lipsitz**

I was not part of anything that happened with middle schools in the 1960s. It was in the 1970s that I started reading, and I think the first book on the subject that I read was Charles Silberman's *Crisis in the Classroom*. Silberman said that the junior high school was the cesspool of American education. That got my attention. And then John Arnold told me to read the works of Charity James, a wonderful British writer. She wrote *Young Lives at Stake* and *Beyond Customs* in the 1970s. She had a totally different way of looking at who kids were and how they should be educated. I just adored her work. Then I found the work of John Hill, and met John and started working with him on some projects. I was very influenced by his approach to adolescent development and his attempt to de-dramatize the age group. That was the word he would always use. "How can we *de-dramatize* this age group? How can we de-stigmatize it?" I was also influenced by the work of Gisela Konopka, who was a researcher at the University of Minnesota doing work on girls' development. Here I was in Chapel Hill, where Glenn Elder, a great sociologist, was looking at one point in his career at the research on adolescence and wrote a chapter called *Where Are the Girls?* Well, Gisela Konopka had done work before Carol Gilligan on where the girls are, who the girls are, and on a lot of the myths about adolescents, some of which were myths about girls because they hadn't been studied. Then I started reading Piaget. I think those were the major influences as I started to think about the age group.

After that I read Seymour Sarason, because once I thought I knew about the age group, my question was, "So what do we do in the schools?" I read Sarason, who was saying that our chances of getting a lot done with these kids without changing the institution of the school are about zero; I became very interested in the nature of this strange institution that we teach in. So my interest started with adolescent development and progressed to organizational development. I didn't read middle school literature.

Are there particular theorists (or theories) or writings that have influenced your educational thought?

Without a question, Piaget, Erikson, and Dewey were at the core. It was definitely the developmentalists who influenced me. There were also some people who wrote about organizational theory who influenced me. But I was unaware about most of the writing about middle schools from the 1960s.

---

* Joan Lipsitz was interviewed for the Legacy Project in September 2004.

**What is your primary motivation for continuing involvement in
middle school education?**

I think we are at a really interesting point now in middle school education. We have a broader base of people involved in it. We finally have an in-
tersection between practitioners and public policy. I don't think we can get
away anymore with being a small club of people who "own" middle-grades
education. The middle grades have been taken over just like everything else
in K–12 by public policy. That fascinates me, because we need to figure out
how to maintain the best of what has been done in middle schools while entering that mainstream of K–12 public education. I think it's an enormous
challenge to us, and it fascinates me.

**How would you describe the early years of middle school
education?**

When I left the classroom—trying to figure out who knew what, and
where about young adolescents—that became a book called *Growing Up
Forgotten*. When I was preparing that book, which was in the mid 1970s, the
work of people in what was being called "the middle school movement"
was barely on the national policy screen. What was important in the larger
picture at that time was dissatisfaction with the junior high school—a feeling that something was going wrong. Junior high schools had been started
to deal with what people called "leakage" in the early part of the twentieth
century. "Leakage" was the dropout phenomenon after eighth grade. So,
that was one issue. Junior highs being grades 7, 8, 9 were, on the one hand,
an attempt to stop a dropout problem that occurred after grade 8 in a K–8
school. Junior highs were supposed to get kids over the eighth grade hump
and into high school.

When I look back at key people who were working on middle schools in
the worlds of foundations, government, and public policy, "middle-school
movement" people weren't on the screen. So, I have a somewhat idiosyn-
cratic view of this history, because I know that a lot work was being done
about the failures of junior high schools at that time, but it wasn't influencing me or a lot of other people I was working with.

For me, and this history is completely autobiographical, I was asked in
the mid-1970s by some foundations to run a series of regional conferences
around the country on "who's doing what, where for young adolescents."
The focus was not only on schools. It was on juvenile justice, community services, health, family supports, and so forth. We held six conferences around
the country. I wrote the proceedings from the conferences, called *Barriers*,
supported by the Ford Foundation. One of the barriers that participants
identified in five of the six conferences was that there was no central place

where they could go to find out about early adolescence, to get training, to get information, to advocate for public policy. They wanted an institute, a central place to go. The Mary Reynolds Babcock and the Ford Foundations asked me if I would start what became The Center for Early Adolescence, housed at the University of North Carolina in Chapel Hill. It was founded to be a national center that did research and gave technical assistance and information services to people across institutions and across sectors, like schools, health, recreation, and so forth. The work that we did was often school-based, but never in isolation of other institutions that have an impact on kids' lives. We tried to think about how a kid makes his or her way through a day, and what institutions that kid's life touches, and then ask what the Center for Early Adolescence therefore needed to contribute. We wanted to know what value added would there be because of our work.

How has the middle school concept changed since the early years of the middle school movement?

That's a really important question because the middle school has taken lots of hits for being touchy feely. The issue always is, when you're trying to reset the pendulum, how you keep what was good in what you're resetting. So, it was right and proper for people to be concerned that there was a terrible lack of fit between the institution that we put young adolescents in for so many hours a day and their developmental needs. We wouldn't tolerate a kindergarten that was institutionally wrong for young children. It would be perverse. The problem is when you're fighting for what I call developmental responsiveness, and that's all you say, you're perceived as being touchy feely. I've never understood what's wrong with touchy feely, incidentally. We all want our kids to be in a good touchy feely environment. But you're perceived as doing that to the exclusion of academic standards and excellence, and to the exclusion of social equity issues. I think the problem was that in the middle school movement, people forgot that they were trying to *add* a vital component, which was developmental responsiveness—understanding the nature of development and therefore changing the nature of the school day and instruction and curriculum. They didn't strike forth as aggressively and energetically for high standards, for revised curriculum. I know in the work that we were doing at the Center for Early Adolescence, and the work that I did looking for effective schools for young adolescents, that I felt even the schools that I was identifying as being effective needed to take a new look at their curriculum. The curriculum was often weak. The middle school movement was forced to start paying attention to academic standards, and that pressure came from the outside in, when it should have been a powerful voice from within the movement all the time.

How were decisions about the directions taken by the middle school movement made?

I found it like watching two themes of a story on two screens simultaneously. There were decisions that were made from within the movement by what became the National Middle School Association, and then there were decisions that were made on this other screen among researchers and public policy people and foundation officers. It was like action occurring on two separate tracks, and every once in a while one influenced the other. What's interesting now is how much more together they are than they used to be. I can't answer the question of how it was done from within, because I was not a part of that. I think that while the National Middle School Association and others were paying a lot of attention to improving practice within the growing number of middle schools, there were people on the outside who were getting foundations and people in government to pay attention to the age group, both in practice and policy. We needed both.

What was the educational context at the time the middle school movement began?

For me, the context was a personal feeling of failure. After my first year teaching in a junior high, I had realized how many kids in my classroom were functionally illiterate, even in a community like Chapel Hill, North Carolina. I promised myself that I would not return to the classroom until I had learned how to teach functionally illiterate young adolescents how to read. Now by functionally illiterate I meant kids who could not handle the curriculum that I was supposed to be teaching. I gathered catalogs from all over the country, looking for courses I could take during the summer that would help me to teach these kids how to read. And I couldn't find anything. There was nothing for young adolescents. I shouldn't say nothing, because I might have missed it someplace. But, I had fifty to sixty catalogs from around the country, and I couldn't find it. What I could find was Reading for Comprehension for Adolescents and the like, but nothing for the problem that I had of kids reading at the third or fourth grade level in the eighth or ninth grade, needing to handle whatever they were handling in my classroom, let alone whatever they were reading in history and other courses. So, the absence of teacher preparation classes for this age group was a fact. It was just a given.

That for me personally was the context. The context was that I needed help teaching reading to my kids, and I couldn't get that help. Another context was that the South at that time was under the supervision of the Office of Civil Rights for desegregation. We could not have re-segregation within the school, which meant that we could not have ability grouping in a place like Chapel Hill, where you had the children of professors, and the children of farmers, and the children of janitors, and they were racially identifiable. So we had to teach everybody together in the same classroom, and that was a real shock for me coming from Connecticut, where we had tracking. So, here I was in this part of the country that was desegregating schools and insisting also on desegregating within each classroom. I went to my mentor teacher and I said, "How do you teach such a diverse group of kids at one time, in one place, in the same classroom?" I think that was the second week I was teaching here. She said, "Damned if I know." And that was the total amount of professional development that I got. So that for me is the context of what *wasn't* there.

When I wrote *Growing Up Forgotten*—which was not just about schools, it was about the age group and what was available for this age group across different domains—early adolescence was a non-field. So whatever was happening in education—or was not happening—was also not happening about early adolescence across the board in other fields. In all of the United States and Canada combined in the early 1970s there were 15 residencies in adolescent medicine, period. That just says it all. It was stunning to me that this age group was a non-field. It wasn't just about what was going on or not going on in schools; it was about what wasn't going on or not going on for a completely pivotal age group in the lifespan. It was amazing to me that you could have an age group that everybody knew was important and that nobody was willing to pay attention to.

What have been some of the most significant events, incidents, or moments in the middle school movement?

I think it was significant when the middle school movement acknowledged that it needed to be responsive to its critics about academics, about having a stronger curriculum, about figuring out how to incorporate the standards movement into the middle-grades movement instead of fighting it. To me that was a seminal moment, because then the movement became relevant to the lives of kids in poverty, whom we educate least well.

Why did you select that as the most particular event?

I've always been very struck by the fact that the middle school movement leaders had a lot of trouble being inclusive, being inclusive of women, being inclusive of people of color. I don't think their sense of exclusivity had anything to do with anybody's individual values. I think it had to do with the formation of a kind of adult peer group, and people from the outside viewed the peer group insiders as being exclusive or even irrelevant. You look at the beginning leaders of the middle school movement and you don't see major urban educators, and yet you know that the vast majority of the kids that we're struggling with are in the urban centers. You don't even see some of the major rural leaders. The leadership was ex-urban, suburban, and white. You can't have a movement that serves people who most need to be served without having the key players from the rural and the urban areas.

The standards movement started as an equity effort. For better or for worse, the standards movement started because people looked at the data and saw that there are too many kids who predictably fail. There are too many schools that predictably fail. How do we stop this predictability? Some kids are always going to fail. I'm not a utopian about this. It's the predictability of the failure that is so discouraging and immoral. The standards movement people said, "We are going to make sure that the school inputs are equalized." Now No Child Left Behind says that we must make sure the outputs are equalized, without adequate attention to the inputs. These are two radically different but not mutually exclusive approaches to improving schools. They are both, at the core, equity arguments that predictable categories of kids will not fail, that we must break that stranglehold of predictability. So for me, when the middle school movement started saying, "We can't fight them, we need to join them, we need to let them in under the tent, we need to start saying what *we* mean by standards, we need to start saying what *we* mean by collecting data. We need to start saying what we mean by ALL, that all isn't some, that to me is a seminal moment."

Do you have any personal accounts related to these events that might be of interest to others?
My personal account comes from my experiences at the Lilly Endowment. When I left the Center for Early Adolescence at the end of 1985, I went to the Lilly Endowment in Indianapolis, and I was made program director of K–12 education. The Lilly Endowment is a very wealthy foundation, so it has the ability to think big. At one point the president said to me about some proposed youth work, "Think no small thoughts." That's such a different environment from the one we're usually in, where we're used to having budget drive policy and practice. Here, he was saying, "Give me the policy and practice and I'll give you the budget." So, just as an example, when people started talking about the National Board for Professional Teaching Standards, I was in a position to think a big thought, and say, "Let's get them started programmatically, now that the Carnegie Corporation has gotten them started organizationally. We'll get them started on early adolescence (a novel idea at the time), and let's get the right people, who know about young adolescents, working on setting the professional

standards." That kind of grantmaking is an indirect way of having considerable impact. You are in charge of giving three million to the National Board for Professional Teaching Standards, and you make a few suggestions about how it organizes its work. You suggest, for example, that there not be an elementary and a secondary division of the Board, which is what had been proposed, but that there should be an early adolescence, or developmental, division to the work. You suggest that they don't get tied to the institution, but rather organize around age groups. Well, for me that was an opportunity to get right in there at the moment the policy is being set and influencing it in ways that we believe it should be influenced, rather than reacting to it after the fact. So, that, for me, is one of the significant moments in middle-grades education.

I had the opportunity to make a grant to National Council for Accreditation of Teacher Education. NCATE asked for some money from the Lilly Endowment. I was able to ask what we know about young adolescents, about the nature of good middle schools, and therefore about the necessity for changes in higher education teacher preparation. I explored what the Endowment could do in a partnership with NCATE to make the teacher preparation process better for young adolescents. There are these moments that change the way people have a conversation. Then at Lilly Endowment we were in a position to get the National Board and NCATE to talk to one another, which they hadn't been doing, and that had the potential to be the beginning of helping align the improvement of teacher preparation and the quality of teachers in the classroom.

I think another critical moment is the formation of the National Forum to Accelerate Middle Grades Reform. At that moment, you have the tent really opening up and you have the major organizations concerned with middle grades, the major researchers, the major policy setters, the major educators coming together under one tent to say that they have a vision for what middle grades education should be. That vision is not owned by any particular interest group. It's owned by a forum that speaks with one voice. That started in 1997 because of conceptualization and funding from the Edna McConnell Clark Foundation. To me that's a major benchmark.

What are some of the mistakes that have been made during the middle school movement that we might be able to learn from today?

I think that the tent has to be big and wide and open. Sometimes when you start something, you need for it to be protected and small and in a hothouse. But after that, if you really want to have impact, you have to ask not who the true believers are, but who the true believers need to be and how you can make that happen. Otherwise you don't have enough impact.

In the end, I think, there could have been greater impact early on had a more strategic set of alliances been forged into the world of research, into the world of public policy setting, into the major political forces in urban education. It was a boutique movement for too long.

What are some of the most important factors that are influencing middle school education today?

I don't think there's any question that the emphasis on a particular definition of accountability is the major influence. If middle schools are going to be closed, then schools are going to go back to K–8 structures. It's going to happen because the data will convince people that middle schools can't make good on their promise. And that promise right now, in the public arena, is academic scores. I see that as the one biggest threat to middle schools. I think we spent much too much time saying we were doing the right thing, when the data didn't necessarily support that assertion. Or we spent too much time saying we were not going to look at the data, because we thought the measures were wrong. Well, the measures won. If you have to plow with the mules you've got, and you do, then you have to show not only that you're excellent on that very narrow measure, but also show how much else you do excellently. The good schools are doing this. We need to be willing to say that some schools are not. We need to be critical instead of self-congratulatory.

Who has benefited the most from the middle school movement?

I like to the think that the kids who have gone through the best of these schools have benefited the most. I mean, in the end this isn't about adults. This isn't an employment program for adults. I believe that there are tens of thousands of kids who have benefited from going to good middle schools that are developmentally appropriate *and* academically excellent *and* socially equitable for all kids.

Who has benefited the least from the middle school movement?

The kids who didn't get that opportunity. I think you know that I like to study high-performing schools, and when I do that, I ask myself, "What is everybody complaining about? Look at this fabulous school! I would put my child in this school. I would put my grandchild in this school. I mean, this is just wonderful! These are great people doing wonderful work. Look how happy the kids are." (And I happen to think that one of the outcomes of school should be joy. You walk into a school and there's this incredible joyousness. It's palpable. You actually can measure it. You can measure smiles and you can measure laughter. It's not something we tend to measure, but we could. Every one of us who's a parent knows that we intuitively know whether a school is a happy, joyous school or not, right?) So, I start saying, "Schools are wonderful. What's the matter with people? Why are they complaining?" And then, somebody will say to me, "OK, Joan, get real. You've gone native. Go see such and such a school." And I go to that school and it's sullen at best, solemn, dark. No smiles, no joy, no adult–kids interaction, no energy. I'm not saying that terrible things are happening, but wonderful things aren't happening. It's just a turn the crank kind of school.

Who do you consider to be among the most influential leaders of the middle school movement?

I'm going to talk about more contemporary people than others might mention, because I think that in the 1990s several foundations became leaders in middle grades education. You had the W.K. Kellogg Foundation, the Carnegie Corporation, Lilly Endowment, and the Edna McConnell Clark Foundation as the four key funders of middle grades reform, whether at the individual school level, at the state policy level, at the district level, or even the national level.

One key event was the publication by the four program officers from those four foundations of an article called *Speaking With One Voice: A Manifesto for Middle Grades Reform*, which was published in *Phi Delta Kappan* in 1997, just before the formation of the National Forum to Accelerate Middle-Grades Reform. The publication was unprecedented. Foundations don't play well in the sandbox together. Four foundation officers sat down together and asked what they had learned as a result of their funding middle-grades reform. Instead of being competitive, they asked, "Where have we failed?" They were actually willing to be honest with one another, and then wrote the article together, saying, "Look, folks! We've been funding you. We know what's going on here. Everybody is poised for major reform. Do you have any idea how long you've been poised? Isn't it time to stop being poised and take the next step to actually do the work you are poised to do? Here are some lessons we have learned about what helps people to move off the dime and take that next step. Okay, you've got teaming, you've got houses, you've got scheduling down pat. You've worked on school culture, so it even feels good to be in some of your schools. Now you have the infrastructure for doing the work. When are you going to do the work that has to be done on curriculum and instruction? We've been spending close to a decade on middle level reform. We're not going to continue this funding forever. Get your acts together. Here are lessons learned. Get busy." That was powerful. It was a really important moment. It also helped lead to the beginning of the National Forum. Through the National Forum, especially through the state level Schools to Watch programs, which I'm so excited about. I think there is a much more strategic and diverse group of leaders, which is very healthy.

Have there been major debates among school leaders focusing on particular issues or beliefs? If so, what was at stake? And then, if there is a position that has won out, can you talk about that?

There have been major arguments about grouping by ability and about No Child Left Behind and testing. Because it's a contemporary debate, it's hard to say if there's a position that has won out. What's at stake is important. If you take the grouping by ability issue, there are some people who believe that under no circumstances should children be grouped by academic ability in middle schools—that we can individualize instruction, group and regroup based on interest and skill level, and work deeply enough that we never have to have more structured grouping by ability. There are other people who believe that there is a limit to organizational elasticity. They believe it's absolutely true that very talented, committed heroines (it's almost always women) can figure this out. It goes back to that question that I asked the beginning of my career: "How do you teach this very diverse group of kids in the same place at the same time?" It's an unresolved theme all the way through the decades, that no matter how much we value diversity of ability, there's a limit to organizational elasticity, and there's a limit to how much heroism we can count on from ordinary people. And it's ordinary people who have to educate the next generation. We can't count on heroism. Counting on heroism is not good public policy. So, some would say that at some limit you have to have cutoffs. Now, the limits don't have to be manifested as five ability tracks, which is what I saw in one New Jersey school in the 1980s. Five! The hubris was amazing. They actually thought they knew enough to segment kids into five ability groups. The argument I think is about where you set some limits that recognize where organizational elasticity and human capacity may break down, for instance in the form of professional burnout. So, the argument is not a values argument; it's about whether to recognize that there are practical limits or to find successful practices to broaden those limits—or both. The good news is that nobody wants tracking. Do you know what I mean? It's a question of whether there is a practical limit to heterogeneity in the classroom. Some people say there can't be, and others say there has to be.

The second issue, about testing and accountability, and how much you yield, and how much you do not, and how true to your values do you stay—again, it's a very important issue, because you don't want to lose what's essential, what you see as being the core of your vision of middle-grades education. At the same time, you have to figure out how to live in the real world, where school boards, principals, and teachers are accountable in a relatively uninformed public arena. This country is in danger of losing its commitment to public education. What's at stake is very real and crucially important. It's the Jeffersonian ideal of taking children from all quarters, and using the public coffers to educate them. So, we have to figure out no matter how pure we are about middle schools, how public schooling is going to cohere, and how we are going to be accountable to the public for what is in essence involuntary incarceration. Because that's what compulsory schooling is. And we have to be able to show the value added of those kids' having been involuntarily incarcerated. And that value added has to be both for the individual and for the cohesion of our democratic society. We have to figure that out. The issue about testing is not a small technical issue. It's an enormous question about public accountability.

Have particular legislative actions significantly influenced the middle school movement at the state or national level?

I think that the career education movement in the early 1970s definitely influenced practice, because it codified what was a good fit between what we thought needed to happen in expanding the curriculum and the experiences we wanted all kids to have. It changed our preoccupation with "occupations" to "careers," which meant that the flow of money ensured that every kid was going to learn about the world of work, not just the kids who couldn't learn Shakespeare. Legislation like that has been influential. Certainly, now we have an emphasis on testing for accountability with No Child Left Behind, which is an undeniable influence on what's happening directly in the classroom.

Earlier, there was Title I, as part of the "War on Poverty," which openly and publicly acknowledged the fact that some children, whom we wanted to be invisible, were extremely poor and therefore at a disadvantage in school. We acknowledged through public policy that schools with large percentages of poor kids needed additional resources. That was a major influence, especially on elementary education. It needed to have greater impact on the middle grades, but many school systems decided to spend the money exclusively on the early school years. In those places where the middle schools did have access to Title I money, there were stronger reading and family-based programs. If you used to go to a middle school meeting, like a National Middle School Association meeting, you rarely heard anything about upcoming national legislation. This is just now beginning to change. We should all be advocating for legislation to improve middle-level schools. We know that major national bills like Title I and No Child Left Behind reorient our schools. They deflect us for better and for worse onto a different trajectory.

What are some ways the middle school movement has influenced middle level curriculum and instruction?

I think we spent a lot of productive time asking, "*Where* do we teach?" And we changed the nature of the school building—literally, we changed how it's configured in order for us to do a better job teaching this age group. We created houses, we created places for teams, and for teaming teachers to plan with one another. The nature of the use of space has changed radically. I think that we took a long look at *whom* we are teaching. And we said that given the nature of the young adolescent, we needed personalization, interpersonal relationships, guidance, and so forth. I think we even looked at *how* we teach. We thought a lot about instructional methodology, making things more experiential, constructing things, and getting concepts across through concrete instructional methodology. I'm still waiting for us to take a good look, in subjects other than math, at *what* we teach. Why do we teach *what* we teach at this level, in this day and age?

How would you characterize the current status of the middle school movement?

I think it's shaky, and I think it's always going to be shaky. Young children are adorable. We all love them. We know how important early childhood development and early childhood education are and how critical the early years of the elementary school are. We will always care about those children. We know we have to wake up again and pay attention when kids are in the last years of high school. We attend to the inputs and the outputs. We keep track of whether high school students pass military exams. We keep track of where they go to college. Although we do it inadequately, we pay some attention to those last years of compulsory schooling. But I think that it's always a struggle to get people to pay attention to the middle.

But I think we're in a bad time right now in addition to that because the middle grades aren't blowing the lid off the tests. And we have the same trouble we have always had of not enough people being prepared to teach, not enough schools of education caring about this age group, and not enough resources going to the middle grades. In addition, we now have the fact that the kids aren't blowing the lid off the tests. We know when we pay attention, they do. We have to figure out how to make the case for these schools based not on ideology, but based on outcomes, based on the value added of the middle school experience.

I've never been somebody who took a stand on grade organization. In fact, I've steadfastly refused to, because I believe whoever the kids are and wherever they are, we have to teach them. I don't want to give anybody an excuse, "Oh, we didn't have the right grade organization, so I couldn't teach them." The question is how and what you teach kids. To think that you can change the grade organization of a school and thereby have an impact on outcomes without changing your approach to the culture of the school and the curriculum and the instruction, is just diversionary. The issue is what we do in those schools with those kids, whatever the grade organization.

Are there any other comments you would like to make that you have not been asked about in this interview?

I want to say why I have been so hopeful about the National Forum to Accelerate Middle Grades Reform, otherwise known as the Forum. It's not exactly a catchy title. But the title is important, because it's national, it's a forum for bringing people together, and the key word is "accelerate." You know, we have been trying to improve schools for young adolescents for such a long time. It's time to accelerate. And then of course there's the word "reform." We're not talking about working around the edges here. So, even though it's a very ungainly title, people really spent time thinking about those words. This organization grew organically. It wasn't created externally as a complete entity. It grew organically because of the efforts being made by key foundations, because of their coming together, sharing their experiences and asking one another what they should do next. The idea of creating this big tent was actually Hayes Mizell's, from the Edna McConnell Clark Foundation. What I like about the Forum is that it is a big tent, it is a diverse group. The only thing that isn't diverse about this group is that everybody cares about young adolescents and is professionally situated to be able to have an impact on what happens.

It took this group six months to come up with a vision statement. Every word has meaning. Then we realized that while we had this vision and could articulate what we stand for, people were going to ask us to describe what exemplifies this vision. And so again, and this happened organically, we realized that we had better talk about the characteristics of high-performing middle-level schools. We came up with criteria about developmental responsiveness, academic excellence, and social equity for what would we expect to observe in such schools. When we finished, we realized that now people were going to say, "Show me." We needed to go out and look at schools, and pick some we would recommend for people to visit and emulate. We didn't want to call them "exemplary," for a couple of reasons. First, there's no such a thing. Every school can improve. Second, there's something perverse about all of us. If I tell you this is an exemplary school, you will go in looking for what's wrong with it. I want you to go in looking for what you can learn from it. So, instead of saying "exemplary," we say, "Schools to Watch." That way we acknowledge that yes, some aspects of this school aren't going to be great. Don't get caught up on that. Instead, watch and learn from the school's positive trajectory towards excellence.

Then, after selecting four Schools to Watch, we made a major decision, which I think was a great decision, to take this program to the state level. Our intent was not to host a Miss America contest through recognizing schools. We were not interested in a beauty contest. The point was to figure out how to infuse good practice into increasing numbers of schools' classrooms through articulating the vision and the criteria. We realized it would be powerful to have people at the state level actually using these criteria and self-monitoring, going into schools in their states and recognizing schools that were on the trajectory to high performance, and even more importantly, helping those who were not but wanted to be. I think that this is an important practice-based school-reform effort. I'm very excited about it.

Some of us have been talking about high performance as consisting of developmental responsiveness, academic excellence, and social equity for many years, but this is the first time that we are talking about it collectively, speaking with one voice. We're insisting that developmental responsiveness is not enough. We're saying that academic excellence is not enough. We're saying that social equity is not enough. You have to do it all. And we know that some schools can do one of these or even two. For instance, you can be developmentally responsive and academically excellent for a subset of kids. But no, to be a School to Watch, you have to do this for all. Or you could take all comers and be developmentally responsive. But how about academic excellence for all? And then we look at whether a school has the necessary organizational and leadership supports to sustain the positive trajectory towards high performance. To me this is such a powerful and practical vision of what middle grades should be that I am very excited about its potential to become a national middle level school reform movement.

17

C. Kenneth "Ken" McEwin

We all need to continue to be active. Simply thinking about things or quietly speaking to others about how things are not the way they ought to be doesn't serve anyone well. We all have to be activists. We need to continually be out there, even if people get tired of listening to us. Simply liking young adolescents and thinking the middle school plan is a good idea just won't cut it. We really all have different roles to play, and we need to play them in concert with each other.

Dr. C. Kenneth McEwin is recognized as the leading authority in middle level teacher preparation. He has conducted many research studies on teacher preparation and written extensively about the importance of specialized professional preparation for teachers of young adolescents. For more than 20 years, he has served as National Middle School Association (NMSA) coordinator for the national review of middle level teacher preparation programs seeking national recognition as part of the National Council for Accreditation of Teacher Education accreditation process. McEwin provided leadership for the development of specialized middle level teacher preparation programs at Appalachian State University, Boone, North Carolina, and in 1975 the un-

The Legacy of Middle School Leaders, pages 283–298
Copyright © 2011 by Information Age Publishing
All rights of reproduction in any form reserved.

dergraduate and graduate programs there were among the first middle level preparation programs in the nation. Dr. McEwin served as the coordinator for undergraduate and graduate middle grades education at Appalachian State University for 22 years. He is currently Professor of Curriculum and Instruction and Coordinator of Graduate Middle Grades Teacher Preparation at Appalachian State University.

Dr. McEwin received his undergraduate degree in elementary education in 1963 and his master's degree in elementary school administration in 1966 from Texas A and M Commerce. He earned his doctorate in elementary education and school administration from the University of North Texas, Denton. He is the author or co-author of more than 150 journal articles, book chapters, textbooks, research reports, and other professional publications focusing on middle school education and including a book dealing with the issue of middle school sports. McEwin has been a consultant to schools, school districts, universities, and policy-making groups in over 80 North Carolina school systems and in school systems and state departments of education in more than 30 other states, as well as in Germany, England, and Belgium. In 1988, the North Carolina Middle School Association (NC-MSA) awarded its first Distinguished Service Award to McEwin and designated it as The C. Kenneth McEwin Distinguished Service Award.

Selected Accomplishments and Contributions to Middle Level Education

- A founder of the North Carolina Middle School Association (NCMSA) (1981)
- First Executive Director of the NCMSA
- First editor of the *NCMSA Journal*
- President of NMSA (1983)
- Received the John H. Lounsbury Distinguished Service Award from NMSA (1989)
- Member of National Board for Professional Teaching Standards Committee that wrote the first Early Adolescence Generalist Standards
- Member of the National Forum to Accelerate Middle Grades Reform (1997–2008)
- Member of the National Association of Secondary School Principals National Task Force on Middle Level Leadership (2005–2008)

- Presented at many professional organization conferences including the National Middle School Association, Association for Supervision and Curriculum Development, National Association of Secondary School Principals, and the European League for Middle Level Education.

Selected Publications

Alexander, W. M., & McEwin, C. K. (1984). Solving the dilemma: Training the middle level educator—Where does the solution lie? *NASSP Bulletin, 68*(473), 6–11.

Alexander, W. M., & McEwin, C. K. (1989). *Schools in the middle: Status and progress.* Columbus, OH: National Middle School Association.

McEwin, C. K. (1992). William M. Alexander: Father of the American middle school. *Middle School Journal, 23*(5), 33–38.

McEwin, C. K., Dickinson, T. S., & Jenkins, D. M. (1996). *America's middle schools: Practices and progress, A 25 year perspective.* Columbus, OH: National Middle School Association.

McEwin, C. K., Dickinson, T. S., & Jenkins, D. M. (2003). *America's middle schools in the new century: Status and progress.* Westerville, OH: National Middle School Association.

McEwin, C. K., Dickinson, T. S., & Smith, T. W. (2004). The role of teacher preparation, licensure, and retention in creating high performing middle schools. In S. Thompson (Ed.), *Reforming middle level education: Considerations for policymakers* (pp.109–129). Westerville, OH: National Middle School Association and Greenwich, CT: Information Age Publishing.

McEwin, C. K., Dickinson, T. S., & Anfara, V. A. (2005). The professional preparation of middle level teachers and principals. *Encyclopedia of Middle Level Education* (pp. 59–67). Greenwich, CT: Information Age Publishing and Westerville, OH: National Middle School Association.

McEwin, C. K., & Swaim, J. (2007). *Clearing the hurdles: Issues and answers in middle school sports.* Westerville, OH: National Middle School Association.

McEwin, C. K., & Greene, M. W. (2010). Results and recommendations from the 2009 national surveys of randomly selected and highly successful middle level schools. *Middle School Journal, 42*(1), 49–63.

McEwin, C. K., & Greene, M. W. (in press). Programs and practices in America's middle schools: A status report. In G. Andrews (Ed.), *Research to guide practice in middle grades education.* Westerville, OH: National Middle School Association.

McEwin, C. K., & Smith, T. W. (in press). The professional preparation of middle level teachers. In G. Andrews (Ed.), *Research to guide practice in middle grades education.* Westerville, OH: National Middle School Association.

C. Kenneth McEwin*

I do not think there were any particular theories or theorists that influenced me early on. I never really thought of the middle school reform movement as a theory because it is based so much on what we know works well, what young adolescents need, the way schools need to reflect what we know about young adolescents and how they learn, but of course, I certainly have been heavily influenced by William Alexander. He was my mentor for 14 years, he came to this campus for 14 summers, and we became close friends as well as colleagues, and later, co-authors and co-researchers. So he had had the strongest influence on me. Also, I worked with Paul George, John Lounsbury, Gordon Vars, and Don Eichhorn. They have greatly influenced me, as well as other people nearer my age and now, much younger, such as Howard Johnston, Sherrel Bergmann, and Nancy Doda—I could give you a long list of people who have influenced me. But also, I have to mention young adolescents and their teachers who have inspired me, and continue to do so.

What was your primary motivation for becoming involved in the middle school movement?

I really wanted to teach young adolescents from the very beginning. I didn't want to teach young children, and I did not really want to teach at the high school level; the middle level always appealed to me. That has led my whole career in that direction. It's just simply been my career from the beginning, and I don't believe there is a more important age group to work with, or a more neglected group, so it's like a cause. If you are a true-blue middle school educator, it is a real cause, and you know that your work is going to be worthwhile. So, I still feel that way after all these years. Two thousand three is my 41st year in middle level education.

What is your primary motivation for your continuing involvement in the middle school movement?

The answer is the same. I feel like we have accomplished a lot, and some people don't understand how much we have accomplished because they don't know what happened in the early years of the middle school movement. But I feel like, in a way, we're just getting started. Our knowledge base is growing, our research base is growing, we have larger numbers

---

* Ken McEwin was interviewed for the Legacy Project in October 2003.

of principals and teachers and others who understand what middle schools should be and can be, and there is strong momentum, and I don't want us to lose that momentum, especially with some of the current legislation at the federal level. So, I intend to stay a few more years, and I feel like there's still plenty of work for everyone to do.

If you think back, how would you describe the early years of the middle school movement, especially regarding the 1960s and 1970s?

I graduated from college in 1963, so I haven't personally experienced the early 1960s as an educator, but I was very active in the middle school movement during the 1970s and still am today. So, when you ask the question I think primarily about the 1970s. I came here to Appalachian State University in 1973 when the middle school movement was just getting started. Certainly, middle schools were the exception rather than the rule. Of course now the middle school is the traditional school in the sense that you find we have over 14,000 public middle schools all across the country. So, one of the big changes was that the middle school was more of an idea. There were a few early middle schools that could serve as examples, but there was very little literature. *The Emergent Middle School* came out in 1968, and Don Eichhorn's pioneering book in 1966. That is one example of how things have changed. The middle school concept itself hasn't changed, in my view, but there is wider implementation.

How have middle schools changed since the early years of the middle school movement?

I think middle schools themselves have changed. We're still fighting the battle of trying to move away from the traditional miniature high school model in middle schools. That battle hasn't been won, but we certainly have made progress. As I think you're aware, Bill Alexander and I repeated his national study of programs and practices in middle schools that he did in 1968. We repeated the study in 1988 and I have continued to do status studies on up until today. So, one of the first things you think about is one of the major changes has been the wider implementation of what we would call middle school practices or programmatic kinds of issues. For example, interdisciplinary team organization was very rare when I started doing consultant work with middle schools. I was trying to talk people into at least considering the idea that teachers might need to work on teams, that there would be benefits from that. We have a long way to go, but the bottom line is middle schools are more fully implemented than they have been in the past.

How were decisions about the directions taken by the middle school movement made?

The first thing I thought of when you asked the question was, the middle school movement, from the very beginning, has been a grassroots movement. So the reason it's a difficult question, but a good question, is that those decisions were made almost exclusively at the school district level. So it wasn't that Bill Alexander could make a nice proposal, and he did, and one that made a lot of sense, but he couldn't make the decisions at all the district levels and at the individual school levels and in some cases at the state levels. The decisions were made by school boards and other policy-makers across the country. Also, some states passed a special legislation, this was later, not in the mid-1970s but into the 1980s. States such as Georgia and Florida passed legislation that offered special funding for schools that implemented middle school practices and programs.

What have been some of the most significant events, incidents, or moments in the middle school movement?

Certainly the establishment of the National Middle School Association. I know we would not be where we are today without the National Middle School Association. The context was that people scattered all across the country were trying to do things individually. They were looking for literature, they were looking for information, they were looking for models, and there was almost nowhere to find it. No Internet or anything like that. So what NMSA offered was the opportunity to get together, share expertise, knowledge, and frustrations, and find your other colleagues across the country. Middle school was a new kid on the block, and junior high school was the kid on the block that no one liked, I suppose.

There was a terrible set of stereotypes about these "wild and crazy" young adolescents that went to junior high school. I still remember reading one article many years ago that still irks me. They called the junior high school the "educational parking lot." I don't remember who wrote it, but you get what I mean by that, I believe. It was where teachers parked until they could be promoted to the high school and get a *real* teaching position. So that was some of the context, also, and that still exists to some extent, but nothing like it did then. Now people will proudly say "I'm a middle school teacher." People at my institution, for example, can now major in middle grades education, and that's true across the state and in many other states, so that is a part of the changing context.

I think *The Emergent Middle School* that Bill Alexander and his students wrote made a major contribution. Part of *The Emergent Middle School* reported on the status of middle schools in the country. It gave people something to hold in their hands and read and learn from, and it described the components that he had recommended at the Cornell University conference. So, that was significant. The timing was good, it was easy to read and understand, and most practitioners and university people and others could really understand that a middle school did not have to be a miniature high school. It got people thinking; it gave them things to rally around, so certainly that's an important one.

The establishment of affiliate organizations with NMSA was very significant. The North Carolina Middle School Association was one of the earlier ones, but now there are now over 50 affiliate organizations. The European League for Middle Level Education as well as Canadian organizations are also affiliates of NMSA.

I don't know if you call an increasing research base an occurrence or not. I guess it is in a sense, it didn't happen at one time or on one day, but certainly the growing research base that we have now is extremely crucial, especially in these times of high-stakes testing and student achievement scores and No Child Left Behind. So that's another thing that is very positive. I should mention at least one more, and that's that we've gone from three states to seven states to 28 states to 32 states to 46 states having some form of middle grades teacher licensure. That is a change that has happened over a long period of time, but is very substantial. And as a result, we have hundreds of middle level teacher preparation programs now across the country. That's another thing that has happened that is extremely important.

Do you have any personal accounts related to these events that might be of interest to others?

Since I had a chance to know and work with Bill Alexander for so many years, I would like to tell you about something he said. We were in the car going to the airport, and I asked him when the thought of having a separate middle school occurred to him. I was surprised to find out that it happened when he first started teaching. Incidentally, he did not intend to be a teacher. He was a person that was going to go into banking, but when he graduated from college it was during the Depression so he decided to teach awhile, and he was really glad he did. He told me many times it's the best thing that ever happened to him. So he got a job in McKenzie, Tennessee. He taught at the elementary school in the morning and the high school in the afternoon, walking between the two schools, and when he got to the high school, he was a high school teacher. So he said he couldn't help noticing that the high school and the elementary people weren't working together. There was no transition. So that was the first time that he started thinking that something needed to be better at the middle level. That's something that people might be interested in.

I know you talked a little bit about being involved in the start of the affiliate in North Carolina. Is there anything about that you'd like to share?

I was attending the second National Middle School Association Conference in Atlanta, Georgia. I was on the planning committee that John Lounsbury chaired. At that conference I asked John if he would, when he got up to make his keynote address, ask anyone from North Carolina to please come to my room—202 or whatever the number was. I thought maybe we should start a state association, and I didn't know anyone there, so I just thought I would see if anyone would come. About eight or ten people showed up, and we decided to get back together when we got back to North Carolina and organize the North Carolina League of Middle/Junior High Schools. [The name was changed many years later to North Carolina Middle School Association.] We met in Greensboro about a month later and had our first state conference 90 days after that. That's how North Carolina Middle School Association got started. Also, we thought we probably needed some money in the treasury, and we didn't have any. I believe the dues were $10 or $20 per district in the beginning. We took the money we had left at lunch and I went down to the bank and opened an account. That's how we started, and I was what they called the "expediter," which meant Executive Director, and Appalachian State University funded a lot of the cost of the early North Carolina Middle School Association. It's grown and been very effective since that time, in fact, we're about to have our 30th anniversary conference next year [2004].

Who or what have been some of the greatest detractors or opponents of middle school education?

I cannot think of anyone that I would put into the category of being an opponent. Certainly we've had persons who were negative influences for education in general that would also apply to the middle level, but I really don't know of any detractors. I'm fully aware that there are people across the country that don't support the middle school plan, but usually it's not the plan they are against; it is consolidation or some other issue. For example, in some rural districts where there are large numbers of small schools, one way that the districts have solved that problem is that they have gone to middle schools. So the community may be against middle schools, not because they're middle schools, but because they may be closing small schools or they're concerned that small schools would be closed or their children will have to ride further on buses. Those are the kinds of things that detract. Also, not so much now, but in the 1970s some of the biggest detractors were individual teachers, and in some cases, individual principals. I don't think they were detractors because they were bad persons or didn't care about what they did; they simply didn't understand what the middle school concept was all about.

I have said for many years that our biggest problem in middle level education is ignorance, and I certainly do not mean stupidity—just a lack of knowledge. We still fight that battle with the severe teacher shortages now in many states. I am afraid that battle is going to have to be fought again because we have many hundreds, and in some cases thousands, of teachers entering middle schools, not only without any middle level teacher preparation but with no professional preparation at all. So, ignorance is still our biggest battle, and the best way to overcome that is to find as many people as possible and share as much as you can with them. I've found it's almost impossible to be against the middle school concept if you go down element by element and think about it the opposite way. Teaming, the opposite way would be that teachers don't need to work together; two heads are not better than one. The opposite of a flexible schedule would be a rigid scheduling: "We're teachers and we don't want to make any decisions about time." So you could go down that road. In fact, I talk about it that way sometimes in my classes. The middle school concept is a proven set of programs and practices, not really a theory. We know about the age group, and we know what kind of school serves them best.

I have tried to be patient over these years, and I'm still working at it. We know what to do. We just need to do it. And we know how to do it, and we're doing it better than we used to do, but every time young adolescents walk into a classroom of a teacher with no special knowledge of that age group or how he or she should be teaching them, then I think it's almost a crime. It's a shame, to say the least. So many people just don't understand that; they think any teacher will do. If we really want to change American education, including middle level education, then the best way to do that is to help teachers be well prepared and knowledgeable. They already care about young people. They already have degrees. They are already smart persons. But just loving a kid is not enough. They need that special knowledge, including content knowledge, of course. You cannot teach what you do not know, but just knowing the content alone is not enough.

Who has benefited the most from the middle school movement?

Young adolescents, and right behind that would be their teachers. I think most of the time we think only about the young adolescents, but there have been a lot of teachers out there struggling over the years. The last 30 years I have taught teachers who are currently teaching, so I couldn't help but notice that putting people into middle grades classrooms without the proper preparation and experience is not only difficult for young adolescents, but also for the people asked to teach those young adolescents. I've seen many teachers who are very competent and caring become very frustrated because their preparation was for kindergarten and second grade, or tenth and eleventh grade honors mathematics or something like that. And they end up being assigned to teach seventh-graders and are not sure how to do so effectively.

Were there any regional differences in the way middle school education was developed or defined?

If you're talking about the middle school plan itself, there weren't any major differences. Certain parts of the country did seem to be ahead of other parts of the country as far as the number of middle schools and levels of implementation. Many of the early middle schools were in the South. Also, many of the early middle schools were in suburban areas. However, there have always been rural middle schools as well. Now middle schools are in all kinds of districts: urban, suburban, and rural. Part of the good news about middle schools is that the middle school plan works in all kinds of areas for all kinds of young people. Small schools, large schools, old buildings, new buildings; new buildings are nice but are not required. It's not like you need one kind of middle school for urban kids and another kind for rural kids and another kind for suburban kids. That's the good news about middle schools. We don't need 10 or 15 different models.

Bill Alexander used to remind me of this quite often. He said we had to be really careful and not standardize the middle school. One of the problems with the junior high school was that it became the same everywhere; it became standardized. So while there are certain essential elements that ought to be in every middle school, how those are implemented depends on the students and teachers and the community. For example, there are all different ways to do teaming, and one way has not been proven to be better than the other. What we do know is that it's very important to have teaming at a school; among other things, it raises scores on standardized achievement tests. That's not the most important thing, perhaps, but it's certainly important for us to be able to document that you can have advisory and teaming and flexible scheduling and all those kinds of things, and young people will still learn and score high on their tests. In fact, they will score higher at middle schools that are more intensely implementing what some people call "authentic middle schools." The bottom line, to put it in colloquial terms, is "the more middle school the middle school, the higher the scores."

Because your area of expertise is teacher preparation, can you think of any regional differences in teacher preparation in middle level education programs?

There are regional differences as far as licensure is concerned. Most of the states with early middle level licensure plans were in the South. Not all, but the leading states have been in the South. For many, many years hardly anything was happening in the western part of the country. That's now changed, but there are still several states, like Idaho, that don't have a middle level license. Most of the states that don't have a middle level licensure now are very rural states, ones with very low student populations.

Who do you consider to be among the most influential leaders of the middle school movement?

William M. Alexander, John Lounsbury, Don Eichhorn, Gordon Vars, Paul George, Howard Johnston, Tom Dickinson, Sherrel Bergmann, John Swaim. I'm just saying these as they come to me; I will leave out some very important people, I am sure. Tom Erb, Mary Compton. I won't go all the way to modern day because then I would have really a long list of people to talk about. So many people have influenced the movement. Sue Swaim, executive director of NMSA, is another example. She has been a middle level educator and been a part of the middle school movement for many years. Chris Stevenson and John Arnold are also good examples.

What are some examples of ways the middle school movement has affected American education?

Paul George, John Jenkins, and I wrote a book called *The Exemplary High School.* What does that have to do with this question? Well, the reason we wrote that book was because we started noticing that some of the most successful high schools in the country were following the "middle school concept." We decided to gather information from highly successful high schools all across the country. Because of that project and other things, we know that high schools are beginning to learn from middle schools. They are beginning to understand that adolescents need to be known well by at least one teacher; that high school teachers can do a better job when they know each other and work with each other and when they know their students. So, one influence is that the "middle school plan" has been so successful that it is now moving to the senior high school level, at least in some states and in highly successful schools. The middle school movement, in my opinion, learned a lot from elementary schools. The first publication I wrote was in the *Middle School Journal* and was titled "What Middle Schools Can Learn from Early Childhood Education." So now I guess we need to write something about what high schools can learn from middle school education. It is hard to ignore success. When you see achievement scores rising, and when you see students more pleased with middle schools and parents more pleased with middle schools that are operated the way they should be operated, it's hard for people not to think things should be done differently at the senior high school. Also, there's a rather intense dissatisfaction these days with the American high school, so they are looking for models and looking for better ways to do things.

What are some other educational groups, organizations, or institutions that have influenced the middle school movement?

Before we had NMSA, the Association for Supervision and Curriculum Development had some pretty significant publications and some sessions at conferences that were important. One of the first conferences I attended was at ASCD. I think of that immediately when you ask that question. They had a little book earlier called *The Junior High School We Need* and then later they had a book called *The Middle School We Need*. So those are two examples of publications from ASCD that were important. Also, at the major conferences they would have sessions for middle and junior high school people. Also, the National Association of Secondary School Principals has played a role in the middle school movement for a long time. Significant numbers of their members are middle and junior high school principals, so at their conferences they always have sessions for middle school and junior high school principals. I have done some of those over the years. Alfred Arth— he is a person I did not mention earlier but who has been working with the middle school movement for a long time—but Al and I have done presentations at NASSP over the years, along with others. The *NASSP Bulletin*, which has been around for many, many years, has had middle school articles in it over the whole 30 years that I have been associated with the middle school movement, and, to some extent, the National Association of Elementary School Principals has been involved.

Another important incident that happened is when NMSA became a constituent member of the National Council for Accreditation of Teacher Education. Once NMSA became a constituent member, that put representatives from NMSA at the table. It also led to the writing and approval of NMSA/NCATE-Approved Middle Level Teacher Preparation Standards. And those standards have greatly influenced the nature of middle level teacher preparation programs across the country. So that was another development that is important and is still having a positive effect.

Have particular legislative actions significantly influenced the middle school movement?

I mentioned No Child Left Behind, and so far, at least that has had some influence on middle level teacher preparation. In fact, it has had negative influences on teacher preparation. It is not that middle level has been singled out, but in the early publications that came from No Child Left Behind, middle school was not even mentioned; everything was elementary and secondary education, so that gives you one clue. One of the main concerns as far as No Child Left Behind is concerned is that all the emphasis should be on content knowledge and nothing else is important. If you read that legislation, that's about what it says. For example, "highly qualified teacher" is defined as a teacher who has a degree in something, does not have a criminal background, and can pass a state-approved content test. So, it really irks me to hear "highly qualified" being defined as those very minimal criteria.

In many states now, if you look at curriculum, or the state course of study, curriculum is divided into elementary, middle school, and high school. So, although that is not a mandate, it carries the message that there are three distinct levels in American public education. Also, many of the state departments now have people who are assigned specifically and exclusively to work with the middle level. So that has been a policy change, although not a legislative change. I guess the most important legislative change has been when the legislatures have approved a separate license or certificate for middle level teachers. That certainly has an impact. You know as a teacher educator, if you want to change teacher preparation, you change licensure requirements. If you want wholesale change, whether it should be the case or not, it should be understood that teacher preparation programs follow the state requirements. If those requirements include a separate area for middle level teachers, then those programs get more widely implemented.

What are some ways the middle school movement has influenced curriculum and instruction?

As far as curriculum is concerned, I believe we are now finally to the point where knowledgeable middle school teachers expect to at least do some interdisciplinary teaching and serve on an interdisciplinary team. Certainly, the large majority of middle schools have not moved to the level where I would say they have integrated curriculum, but it's become more common for teachers to better understand and implement lessons and units and smaller components of the curriculum that are integrated. Also, just the fact that we have so many interdisciplinary teams at least increases the likelihood that there will be more integration. It doesn't guarantee it, of course. Teaming doesn't guarantee good teaching, but there's an extremely high correlation between schools that use teaming and students who learn well and score high on tests and have high self-concepts and fewer behavior problems.

As middle level educators, how do you think we should respond to the current emphasis on student achievement as measured by standardized tests?

We have to stay the course. We know what we are doing is right. We have to stay the course because young adolescents are too young to take care of themselves, too young to lobby. We know what we need to do and have to do it. We have to help educate policymakers, and our colleagues in some cases, and make sure that they understand that when you "stay with" the middle school concept, positive things happen. One of my fears is, out of ignorance, some decision makers will go backward. They will say, "Well, we really think the middle school plan is a good idea. We really think you ought to integrate curriculum. We do think that young people are different, but we cannot do it." I have always tried to get my students, and others who would listen to me, to watch out for the "it." I will explain: "We tried to do it, but 'it' didn't work; we tried 'it,' but somebody would not let us keep doing 'it'." People are always talking about the "it" instead of "*we* failed." We have to be willing to say, "*We* tried to implement this and *we* failed at it, so we need to try again," instead of backing away and saying "it" didn't work. It is easier to blame it on the "it," that's not a good explanation, and "it" is a real enemy. So, No Child Left Behind is an "it" which we can overcome. I am not pessimistic about the middle school movement. And when I say "movement," I think that the sense of a "movement" may be over because we've basically already reorganized the country. Most school districts, but not all, now have three tiers: elementary, middle, and high. So that part of the movement may be over, but the part of the movement that is not over is trying to make schools be authentic and serve young adolescents and their teachers well. That part of it we are still working on.

Are there lessons we still need to learn from the history of the middle school movement?

There are always lessons to learn from the past. Even if you think about yesterday, there would probably be something to learn. I don't know if there is anything that I haven't already talked about, but to reiterate a little bit, we need to continually look at curriculum and instruction. We need to look at all the areas that you would look at within any school level. We have to focus on teacher preparation; and I know I am pounding on that that, but I believe if you really want to change schools then you support and empower teachers. Who is making those daily decisions, minute-by-minute, even second-by-second on some days, all year long? What kind of preparation do middle school principals have? Well, if you have middle school principals who have been a middle school teacher and taught on a team and really understand the middle school, it's more likely they're going to be supportive of an "authentic middle school plan," when they become principals. If you continue to hire people without middle level knowledge and without middle level experience, they may be very well-intended, good persons who do care about kids and want to do a good job, but they may not know what to do. Also, it is good to have a really strong teaching force who understands what needs to happen for the middle school plan to be authentically and systematically applied, so that when a new principal does come in he or she can be trained quickly, as far as what really needs to happen in the school, if that person is not already knowledgeable.

How would you characterize the current status of the middle school movement?

I am cautiously optimistic. I believe we have made great progress. There are a great many barriers that we will have to continue to either jump over or knock down. There is a real hope, and hope, I think, comes from the teachers. Even the ones who haven't been through a special middle level teacher preparation program, I believe will, through experience, come to understand that young adolescents are different. They have different needs; these needs can be served. So, it is not that we need to make a radical change. I have thought that several times over the years, "I wonder if someone like Bill Alexander needs to make a new proposal?" and the answer is "no." I went back recently and read his proposal again. The very things he proposed are just as current today as they were in the 1960s. A colleague that I already mentioned, Tom Dickinson, has a book called *Reinventing the Middle School*, and he says in the introductory part of that book that we do not need to reinvent the middle school. He writes about the middle school having gone into what he calls "arrested development"; in other words, we have plateaued. He's advocating, not that we need new ideas, but we just need to do a better job of implementing the things that we already know about.

**Are there particular efforts that need to be made to help insure
the future success of the middle school movement?**

We all need to continue to be active. Simply thinking about things or quietly speaking to others about how things are not the way they ought to be, does not serve anyone well. So I think we all have to be activists. We need to continually be out there, even if people get tired of listening to us. Simply liking young adolescents and thinking the middle school plan is a good idea just will not cut it. That is a prerequisite to some other things, but we really all have different roles to play, and we need to play them in concert with each other—not everybody out doing his or her own thing independently.

18

Christopher "Chris" Stevenson

Pay careful attention to the children and get them to tell you about them-selves and listen to them and believe them and trust them and build your program to a large extent around your best knowledge of those children. Then you are going to begin making real progress.

Former students, colleagues, and others who know Dr. Chris Stevenson describe him as the quintessential teacher. Throughout his distinguished career, he modeled the kind of instruction he hoped his students would use in their own teaching. He also served as an exemplary role model and mentor for his students and colleagues. Stevenson has been involved in the education of young adolescents throughout his adult life, serving as a teacher, coach, teaching principal, parent, professor, and researcher. His advocacy for young adolescents is evident in all aspects of his many contributions to middle level education, including his influential textbook *Teaching Ten to Fourteen Year Olds*. Stevenson is an acknowledged middle school curriculum expert who values young adolescents and strives to ensure their active voice and involvement in the learning community. He also has strong beliefs about the importance of schools implementing curriculum, programs,

The Legacy of Middle School Leaders, pages 299–312
Copyright © 2011 by Information Age Publishing
299

and practices that are developmentally responsive (e.g., partner teaming, curriculum integration, and quality student–teacher relationships). Dr. Stevenson has served as consultant to more than 400 schools in 38 states and several other countries, authored more than 150 professional publications, and presented at more than 250 professional conferences. He teaches by who he is and how he relates to others as much as by what he knows. His influence on curriculum and instruction has been substantial, and his work will continue to have an impact well into the future.

Dr. Stevenson received his undergraduate degree in psychology from Birmingham-Southern College, Birmingham, Alabama, in 1960, and his master's degree in psychology from Furman University, Greenville, South Carolina, in 1962. He earned his doctorate in Education, Supervision and Curriculum Development from the University of Connecticut, Storrs, in 1979. From 1960 until 1976, Stevenson taught at the middle level in Greenville, South Carolina; New York City; Atlanta, Georgia; and Cambridge, Massachusetts. From 1976 to 1980, he was Teacher Center Advisor and Lecturer at the University of Connecticut. In 1980, Dr. Stevenson became Professor of Education at the University of Vermont, Burlington, where he remained until his retirement in 2001.

Selected Accomplishments and Contributions to Middle Level Education

- Received the Phi Delta Kappa Award from the Harvard School of Education (1973)
- Received the Phi Kappa Phi Award from the University of Connecticut (1979)
- Received the New England League of Middle Schools Distinguished Service Award (1993)
- Received the Connecticut Association of Schools Award for Distinguished Service (1995)
- Had a book written in his honor, *Living and Learning in the Middle Grades: The Dance Continues: A Festschrift for Chris Stevenson* (2001)
- Received the Vermont Association for Middle Level Education Distinguished Service Award (2001)
- Received the National Middle School Association John H. Lounsbury Distinguished Service Award (2002)

Selected Publications

Stevenson, C. (1986). *Teachers as inquirers: Strategies for learning with and about young adolescents.* Columbus, OH: National Middle School Association.

Arnold, J., & Stevenson, C. (1998). *Teachers' teaming handbook: A middle level planning guide.* Fort Worth, TX: Harcourt Brace College Publishers.

George, P. S., Stevenson, C., Thomason, J., & Beane, J. (1992). *The middle school and beyond.* Alexandria, VA: Association for Supervision and Curriculum Development.

Stevenson, C., & Carr, J. (1993). *Integrated studies in the middle grades: Dancing through walls.* New York: Teachers College Press.

Stevenson, C. (1993). You gotta see the game to see the game. In T. S. Dickinson (Ed.), *Readings in middle school curriculum* (pp. 73–82). Columbus, OH: National Middle School Association.

Erb, T. O., & Stevenson, C. (1999). From faith to facts: Turning points in action—What difference does teaming make? *Middle School Journal, 30*(3), 47–50.

Stevenson, C. (2001). Curriculum that is challenging, integrated, and exploratory. In T. O. Erb (Ed.), *This we believe and now we must act* (pp. 63–68). Westerville, OH: National Middle School Association.

Stevenson, C. (2002). *Teaching ten to fourteen year olds.* New York: Longman.

Stevenson, C., & Bishop, P. (2005). Curriculum that is relevant, challenging, integrative, and exploratory. In T. O. Erb (Ed.), *This we believe in action* (pp. 97–112). Westerville, OH: National Middle School Association.

*Chris Stevenson**

My father was a very effective teacher and had a major influence on me. Beyond that I don't think I really encountered many other teachers that I was really impressed with until I began to work in an experimental school where there were a few truly gifted teachers. I became more and more aware of how many different ways of teaching effectively there could be. I recognized that there is an authentic "craft of teaching" that influenced my values and understanding about working successfully with young adolescents. The first book that I read that really set me on fire was ASCD's 1962 yearbook, *A New Focus for Education: Perceiving, Behaving, Becoming.* I

---

* Chris Stevenson was interviewed for the Legacy Project in June 2005.

think that book is still ASCD's all-time bestseller. It included chapters by Abraham Maslow, who was one of the important references in my thinking, and Arthur Combs, whose writings were similarly influential.

Are there particular theorists, theories, or writings that have influenced your educational thought?

In 1968 I had an opportunity to go to England to study British schools during the era of what was called *open education,* and while there I met some interesting teachers and principals, and I asked the same question of them: "What has really influenced you?" And so they told me. I came home with two shopping bags filled with books. There were some real treasures in those. Two that particularly stand out were by Charity James, whom I was lucky enough to get to know later through John Arnold, who worked with her at the Greater Boston Teachers Center. She had some truly extraordinary insights about what it was like to be a young adolescent. She asked them questions and listened to what they had to say and took their answers seriously. So those were important books, but later on I was also influenced by some of John Goodlad's writing. Of course philosophically John Dewey was an important reference in terms of personal values I had about the purposes of education, and portions of his writing complemented the work by Abe Maslow. It was through Dewey that I came to realize that schools as we generally know them are more about carrying out political mandates than they are about really educating children in the purest ways possible.

Once I became aware of the middle school literature, I read everything John Lounsbury had written and have grown to know him well and consider him a close friend over the years. I think John has always been right on target. Then colleagues of my generation, like John Arnold, who is the most profound influence I have encountered in terms of understanding the ideal purposes of schooling and also all our responsibilities toward our children. Countless courageous Vermont middle level teachers who were generous enough to let me work with them were very inspiring. They, more than anyone else, gave me the courage to continue pushing the envelope. Paul George, Jim Beane, Dick Lipka, and Tom Erb were very influential as well. I'm reluctant to name names because I know I will leave out people.

What was your primary motivation for becoming involved in the middle school movement?

The primary motivation for my becoming involved is that I found that schooling as practiced in the 1960s simply didn't work very well. It seemed to, in general, reward the successes of children who came from healthy, stable families and who enjoyed a lot of support and motivation from their parents.

But it didn't seem to do much for children who weren't school-oriented in their basic nature. So dissatisfaction with a public tolerance for that kind of masquerade of schooling was a major motivator. Later on, I learned about the National Middle School Association and in that formal movement, I recognized people whose motivations, goals, and values were consistent with my own. So I wanted to be around them and learn from them and find a way to contribute in my own way to that movement because I remain today as firmly convinced as I was the first year I taught, that schools do a poor job of matching up to the way that young adolescents are. And we could do ever so much better if we could get past the naysayers to make it happen.

How would you describe the early years of the middle school movement?

I wasn't a part of the very early years of the national movement. I've read about it, about the existence of an association in the Midwest that was growing and catching on, and I think Paul George may have told me a little bit about those early years, but it was a sort of natural coming together of people who had common values about the education of young adolescents. I think Bill Alexander was a central figure in that era.

I joined the middle school movement in its own early adolescent years. Perhaps there is a certain propriety to that coincidence, but during those first years there was a fair amount of uncertainty about the future of the movement. What I do remember from those early years was the exuberance of so many practitioners about what they were doing. To attend a middle level conference was an opportunity to hear a half dozen presentations a day being given mostly by teachers, often in schools and communities where there was not a lot of support for changing school practices. In those early adolescent years of the movement I drew energy from exemplary practitioners and conversations with people whose work I had read like John Lounsbury, Connie Toepfer, and Gordon Vars—people I knew only in the abstract and through their writings until I went to the conferences. Once I got started I didn't miss any NMSA or New England League of Middle Schools conferences, because I really needed and looked forward to the stimulation of being there. It was a rich time, and I always came home with renewed energy and ideas to explore on my own and with colleagues in Vermont public schools.

How have middle schools changed since the early years of the middle school movement?

I'm sad to say not nearly enough. There are schools that have made remarkable progress, but they are too few in number. I've wondered myself how sustained the innovations have been in those schools that were part of the *Turning Points* research. But the bulk of the schools even in Vermont that I knew well remained for the most part pretty traditional schools, not terribly different from the one I attended back in a small town in Alabama in 1950. But Vermont was a place that had, if not a tolerance, a celebration of progressive teams. There were some teams in several schools that did exceptional, even exemplary work, and they stand as certain evidence of how viable the values that NMSA and *Turning Points* advocate. In fact those teams were comprised of youngsters who do fine on their standardized achievement tests but more importantly who are infinitely more interesting, well-developed thinkers, and mature children and citizens than most of their counterparts in conventional school settings where there are six or seven teaching periods a day and all the mandated but disconnected separate subjects.

What were some of the motivations that fueled the growth of the middle school movement?

You don't have to be a rocket scientist to figure out that the way most middle level schools work is pretty much the same as how a high school works, which is pretty much the way a college works. There are some structural differences, of course, but they basically emphasize direct teaching of preconceived and mandated curriculum content. Looking beyond the conventional paradigm has proved to be very difficult, and for most schools getting beyond it has proved impossible. The last schools I was in, not in Vermont but the last schools I have been in have been dreary places. I don't know why anyone—child or adult—would want to be there except to be with their friends. I haven't seen much in the way of inspiration and intellectual stimulation. It seems to me that, on the whole, middle level schools haven't changed appreciably in my lifetime with the notable exceptions of some select teams and schools.

Who or what have been some of the greatest detractors or opponents of middle school education?

It is difficult to address that question without going off on a political diatribe. There is a condition in our country and especially in my community and other communities I've lived in which I refer to as a modern day Tory mentality, Tory in the sense of the perspective of the American Revolution. No matter what happens, you stick to tradition and you don't seek to change things without the permission of the rulers. This mentality is particularly dominant right now with regard to child-centered changes in schooling practices. The few schools I have visited recently are oppressive to the kind of educational programs and practices that I know to be valid and badly needed. The foolishness of the No Child Left Behind Act is an example. When political authorities are satisfied that high-quality education is reflected in paper-and-pencil test scores, the orders come down to drill kids in content on the assumption that their test scores will go up, making them and the teachers and the school appear to be of high quality. I was in a middle school recently where teachers were so afraid and anxious about their kids' performance on tests that all they were doing was drilling and grilling them to come up with correct answers. Privileges and punishments were meted out based on the numbers of questions answered correctly. I found it so consummately degenerate in comparison to what is possible and infinitely more appropriate with young adolescents that I excused myself and left as quickly as I could. My friend John Arnold refers to this syndrome as a preoccupation with getting kids to memorize answers to questions they haven't asked.

Integrated curriculum at the middle level entails building curriculum around the questions and curiosities and interests that children have. That is how to arouse the cognitive processes that are instrumental to learning and growing in healthy, productive ways. I'm afraid that I'm not very optimistic about public education just now. Since high test scores can be so easily marketed to the general public as indicators of quality education, I've concluded that schools are not really about education first, they are about politics first and then if you can slip in a little education while accomplishing your political goals, that's all well and good. But what appears to always come first are political goals that have little or nothing to do with raising our children well.

What are some of the mistakes that have been made during the middle school movement that we might be able to learn from today?

The major mistake that jumps to my mind is the belief among teachers and parents that the only way you can change a school is a little piece at a time. I'm convinced that overhauling a traditional school to move it in the direction of the middle level concept must be done in large strokes with lots of preparation for teachers and communication to and with parents. Kids seem to handle big changes easily, and in my experience they generally welcome them. Carnegie research supports this principle as well. I first assumed that you'd start out by establishing advisories and then after a couple of years re-organize a few teachers into teams and then introduce one integrated curriculum unit a year. The logic of making changes incrementally seduced me. But further personal empirical experiences confirmed that central to the change process is a clear vision of what the school must move toward. When that vision drives everything, big-time changes come much more easily.

What are some of the most important factors that are influencing middle school education today?

I think the influence of far right neo-conservatives are the biggest deterrent. There is an arrogance of authority that isn't interested in what has been referred to as the whole child or the whole person. Their preoccupation is with their own political success and power. Such people have no real knowledge of the remarkable change process humans experience in adolescence. The spiritual humanity and the cognitive part and the physical part and the social part that evolve so rapidly together in early adolescence constitute a remarkably rich opportunity for enlightened schooling. There is a great deal to be learned from the successes youngsters will have during these years if we just give them opportunity and thoughtful guidance. If political people committed the kind of energy and determination that *No Child Left Behind* has received, imagine what might be accomplished. But they haven't signed on because it doesn't lend itself to the kind of measurement politicians think they can use. My friend Judy Carr told me that she doesn't refer to *No Child Left Behind* anymore; she refers to it as *No Child Left Untested.* It's about testing, and it is psychometrics masquerading as science.

Who has benefited the most from the middle school movement?

I think people like me—teachers and administrators who've been in school situations that were friendly to the kind of initiatives we wanted to take. We've built careers, we've written books, and we've developed professional identities that we have benefited from. And I think along the way other people have benefited as well. They've drawn understanding, inspiration, and encouragement to take bold steps. Beneficiaries also include that small portion of our population of children that have developed and learned and grown in nourishing, supportive, stimulating school circumstances. It is too bad that all children in this country haven't had equal opportunity for that kind of education.

Who has benefited least from the middle school movement?

It is risky to make a generalization in responding to your question. I suppose that children, 10- to 14-years-olds who are struggling to figure out who they are and make their way in the world but who have not had the advantages of a high-quality middle school are the biggest losers. But that's a big generalization, and as I think further about it, I must quickly add that countless children have benefited from exceptional teachers in ordinary circumstances. I think the important point here is that we must continue to work to reform middle level practice so that increasing numbers of young adolescents are making solid progress as students and as responsible, moral young people.

Who do you consider to be among the most influential leaders of the middle school movement, and why did you select these particular leaders?

I'm worried about leaving someone out because I have learned from so many colleagues in our profession. But I will begin with John Lounsbury. My father, who as I said was an enormous influence on my thinking about schools and education, died a long time ago. In some ways John has been a father figure. He's somebody I can look at when I'm remembering my father, and I see qualities and attributes alive in a man as strong and as insightful as John is. He is also a man of great personal faith as well. Someone that is not known in the middle level community but had great influence on me and John Arnold was Ed Yeomans. He actually introduced John Arnold and me, and our great friendship has thrived since that time. Ed was a hard-nosed, resilient progressive educator who was Headmaster of Shady Hill School in Cambridge for many years. He was a special mentor in the early part of my career, and he had a great deal of influence in bringing me to the experimental school in Cambridge. Ed was a wonderful, progressive educator from way back.

There are so many writers. Abraham Maslow was very powerful in shaping my views. His work gave important direction to my life in my twenties when I was trying to get a grasp of what I wanted to preserve in my own life and perpetuate in others. There are more contemporary people who are colleagues and who have become friends. Ken McEwin has been a great friend and colleague in projects for NMSA for a long time. And although we don't see each other very often it's a very easy and natural thing to pick up immediately when we are together. Paul George began as a colleague and has become a close friend along with his wife, Reisa. They are remarkably bright, committed people, and I have great affection and respect for both of them and the work that they do. Judy Carr, who was originally my graduate student, is really an amazing woman with a phenomenal mind.

Ed Brazee at the University of Maine has been a steady, committed, and a generous colleague and friend working for the same things for which I've worked for years. And Sandra Caldwell, who was principal at the Middle School of the Kennebunk, did a phenomenal job of transforming that school along with the undying support of the core faculty of that school. And in New England, Jim Garvin who was the director of the New England

League of Middle Schools for a long time. And there were so many of the teachers, and principals and professional colleagues who were active in that community.

I'm not going to name Vermonters because I would inevitably leave some out. But first and foremost influences in my professional life are teachers and principals in Vermont who were good enough to let me come into their schools and courageous enough to join some initiatives that were really important. Many of them were participants in various projects I started, and their names appear often in pieces I've written about our work together. *Dancing Through Walls* identifies some of them, but there are many, many more.

I think of Tom Dickinson, whose quick mind and sharp wit have always been stimulating and provocative to work with. John Swaim who has such eternal good humor and is yet just gullible enough that you can have fun with him and do good work with him at the same time. Nancy Farmer in North Carolina. John Van Hoose and Dave Strahan are great examples, I think, of the best of American professional educators—learned, generous and kind and long-sighted and never seem to lose sight of the goals. Dennis Litky has been inspirational. Ross and Diane Burkhart are great teachers that I got to know both professionally and as friends. I have benefited from close association with so very many superb people in middle level education.

There's one other thing I would like to say about this. I don't know if engineers, bankers, physicians, or other professionals who have colleagues have the opportunity to have the same feelings about their colleagues that I have, but every person that I have named and so many that I haven't named are people that I genuinely love. And I think what I love about them is that we have common ground and we care about many of the same things even though we may be getting at it in different ways. It has been an enormous blessing in my life to have all these associations, and I don't have any idea that I've contributed anywhere near as much to them as they've contributed to me. But I just feel an enormous satisfaction in having been associated with all those people. But especially I must acknowledge the Vermont teachers and principals who were so generous, courageous, and loyal to our common values about the raising and educating of young adolescents.

What have been the major issues debated among middle school leaders? Have they been resolved?

I think teacher advisories is the best idea of all that have been a part of the middle level movement. But they have also been the most poorly and insufficiently accomplished. I think the debate has been about whether teachers are there to teach content and skills or to be adult advocates for children as if those functions are in conflict. Of course they are not in conflict. But no amount of evidence in support of their effectiveness persuades many teachers. So we have had a lot of failures with teacher advisories in most schools. There are exceptions, but it's been a major disappointment because it is such a magnificent concept and needed service to kids.

A second issue I will address and I'm going to be brief because we could talk for days about this is the matter of what kind of curriculum for the middle grades. I think it has been falsely posited that it's integrated curriculum versus separate-subject curriculum because it's often easier to debate things when you can create two straw men and pit them against each other. However, through the process of integrating children's questions, ideas, concerns, priorities, and personal goals into curriculum decisions, we are personalizing the learning experience and I know in the long run contributing much more to its durability than if we did not involve children in planning curriculum. I'm not talking about interdisciplinary curriculum here; I'm talking about integrated curriculum in the same way Jim Beane and Gordon Vars have helped us to understand it. Those are two more people whom I did not name as treasured influences on my thinking. They are both valued influences in my career and also great personal friends.

A third issue is about how we go about providing for what used to be called "gifted" children, but now I think we're at least most appropriately referring to as accelerated or advanced learners. The crux of the debate seems to be around whether or not they should be in pull-out programs or separate track programs versus the customary school classroom, whatever the nature of the school might be. One of the great things about the middle level concept when it is fully instituted as I've seen in some teams in a few schools is that the truly advanced learner or accelerated learner is kept busy by his/her sort of optimal level of learning activity, and it happens at no price to anyone else. And in a democratic society I think that carries the day in terms of deciding how children should be grouped. Carol Tomlinson has important insights about this issue.

Have particular legislative actions significantly influenced the middle school movement at the state and national level?

Yes indeed, and at present they are choking the movement to death. This neurotic obsession with paper-and-pencil test scores is very destructive of any initiative that isn't committed to politicians' pledge of "raising test scores." I am amazed that any enlightened person really believes that test scores reflect educational quality. I simply can't wrap my mind around it. It's a really absurd premise, and the resulting political pressures have done enormous and incalculable damage to schools and teachers, and in particular the teachers I think who are not becoming the teachers they might have become because they are not pursuing those directions that have been identified as the viable directions for middle level education to go.

What are some ways the middle school movement has influenced middle level curriculum and instruction?

I think of the influences here as being reciprocal. Advances in understanding of curriculum and pedagogy in turn affect the middle school reform movement. Through innovation and integrated curricular programs we've been able to demonstrate that organic learning is a real thing and it can be seen and understood and it is in evidence when conditions are changed to truly integrate curriculum. I'm speaking of "integrated" in Jim Beane's terms. There are many brilliant examples of such fabulous curriculum work. Judy Carr and I put together a project with Vermont teachers that resulted in a book, *Integrated Studies in the Middle Grades: Dancing Through Walls.*

That's the kind of work that has taught me beyond any shadow of a doubt that we can create learning experiences at school that children will thrive in, that they will mature rapidly through, and through which they will grow into better citizens and better human beings for themselves and others. When we get the conditions right in our schools, amazing things come to pass. But as long as we shuffle them in there for forty minutes of thrill-packed instruction in whatever the preconceived subject matter may be, we're deluding ourselves, our students, and the public. The assumption that they will get answers right on tests is a just a sad, false hope.

As middle level educators then, how do you think we should respond to the current emphasis on student achievement as measured by standardized tests?

Oh, I could weep over this question. I've talked to so many teachers who tell me that if they could afford to they would leave the profession because they are suffering so much, having so much personal anguish. They find their schools boring and tedious and the children are being oppressed, and they are feeling culpable as if they are committing a crime against children. Your question triggers a whole set of emotions in me that I find discouraging and disappointing at the least and disheartening at the most. I guess keeping the faith that better days will come keeps people moving along; that's the Pollyanna version. Surely we're not going to live forever with this flawed mentality of what schools should be.

What are the lessons that we still need to learn from the history of the middle school movement?

All that you read and hear people talk about can be very interesting and intriguing, maybe even seductive, but what you can trust, and I'm talking to teachers here or young people who want to become teachers, what you can trust for sure is the actuality of what happens each day that you are engaged in this profession. They should certainly draw from whatever promising and trustworthy resources there are available, but they must pay careful attention to the children and get them to tell about themselves and listen to them and believe them and trust them and build your program to a large extent around your best knowledge of those children. Then you are going to begin making real progress. And that's kind of a testimony because when I started out, it took me a few years to gain the realization that I really didn't know much about what it meant to be twelve or younger or older. I needed that kind of information from them. And I began to trust the actuality that if I asked a twelve-year-old to tell me about it, they would, and they would be candid and I should believe them, and the more I did that and the more I listened to them the more, what I called inquiry and shadow studies, the more of that sort of thing that I did, the closer my understanding of them and their priorities moved closer to their actuality. If I'd never read a book about education but had done that, I think I would have done all right as a teacher. I liked being a teacher and the one thing I miss since retirement is interacting with students on a daily basis. I take advantage of any opportunity that comes my way to spend time with students because I do enjoy it. It nourishes me, and it challenges me all at the same time. I think that's a kind of mentality or point of view—a game plan perhaps—that I would advise every teacher now or person planning to be a teacher to carry into their work if they want to progress as teachers and maybe progress as human beings themselves.

Will you tell us a little bit about the origin of archiving of middle level documents and other things at the University of Vermont?

As National Middle School Association has grown, Sue Swaim is the first person I remember who had the vision to say that we need to start keeping an archive of our materials. They are all over the place. It might have resulted from a conversation with John Lounsbury and Sue Swaim, but some other university, and I don't remember which it was, had been identified as the probable site for storing these archives. Something happened that the university wasn't able to comply, so I immediately went to our dean and the head of our library system with the proposal that the University of Vermont, which already has the Dewey Center which preserves a lot of archival material related to progressive education, would be a logical place to house the middle school archives. To their everlasting credit the librarians and the dean of our college at that time, Jill Tarule, agreed. We would be happy to house the NMSA archives, so I asked if she would write a formal letter of invitation. So NMSA formally accepted the invitation from the University of Vermont. We began to receive things, and then since NMSA had been collecting some papers and publications for quite a while those were sent. Now these materials are in the Special Collections section of the library at the University of Vermont as the Middle Level Archives. The challenge now is that we need more materials. I know in a gesture of great generosity Gordon Vars has committed the archives of the National Core Curriculum Project to that collection. And other individuals who have been writers in the middle level have said that they will send their papers as well. So we have something started that I hope will expand and become an increasing resource to scholars interested in the origins of the middle school movement.

19

John H. Swaim

Some people have the old coaching philosophy, that the best way to get ready for the game is to practice it. So to get ready for high school, you practice high school. I think the people that believe in that type of push-down theory of education, that elementary's sole purpose is to get them ready for middle school, middle school's sole purpose is to get them ready for high school, and high school's sole purpose is to get them ready for college, don't tend to have a developmental perspective on education.

While Dr. John H. Swaim was president of National Middle School Association (NMSA) in 1980, he realized the need for having a comprehensive clarifying document that defined this new middle school. He, therefore, appointed NMSA committee to develop a position paper. The work of this committee led to publication of the first *This We Believe* in 1982. This historic and influential document has since been revised and released in1995, 2003, and 2010. Swaim was also a pioneer in the advocacy of specialized middle level teacher preparation and middle level teacher certification/licensure. The middle level teacher preparation program he developed at the University of Northern Colorado, Greeley (UNC-G), was one of the first middle level

The Legacy of Middle School Leaders, pages 313–326
Copyright © 2011 by Information Age Publishing
All rights of reproduction in any form reserved.

teacher preparation programs in the nation and served as a model for many other early preparation programs. During his tenure as professor at UNC-G, Dr. Swaim provided leadership for establishment of the first campus organization for prospective middle level teachers. This led to the development of the Collegiate Middle Level Association, which became an affiliate member of NMSA in 1989. He also served on the NMSA task force that wrote the first national standards for middle level teacher preparation—The National Middle School Association/National Council for Accreditation of Teacher Education Approved Middle Level Teacher Preparation Standards.

Dr. Swaim earned his undergraduate degree in social studies and mathematics in 1967 and his master's degree in teacher education in 1969 from Kansas State Teachers College (Emporia State University). He was a graduate assistant at Kansas State before moving to the UNC-G in 1974 to teach and coach at the UNC-G Laboratory School. He also served as principal of the middle school portion of the Laboratory School. Swaim received his doctorate from UNC-G in curriculum and instruction in 1976. He left the Laboratory School in 1983 to join the faculty of the UNC-G College of Education where he was instrumental in establishing middle school undergraduate and graduate programs. Dr. Swaim left the faculty of UNC-G in 1994 and was awarded the title of Professor Emeritus. He then accepted the position of Professor of Education at Otterbein College, Westerville, Ohio, where he helped design and implement successful middle level teacher preparation programs and provided leadership in the establishment of middle level teacher certification in the state of Ohio before his 2007 retirement from Otterbein College.

Selected Accomplishments and Contributions to Middle Level Education

- Authored or co-authored many professional articles, research reports, chapters, and books
- Presented at more than 100 national and international professional conferences
- Served as consultant to schools, school districts, institutions of higher education, and policymaking boards
- Chaired the founding committee for the establishment of the Colorado Association of Middle Level Education
- Served as the first president of CAMLE (1976)
- Co-chaired the National Middle School Association (NMSA) Conference Committee (1977)
- President of National Middle School Association (1980)

- Provided leadership for the establishment of middle school teacher licensure in Colorado (1983)
- A founder of the Western Regional Middle School Consortium (1984)
- First Faculty Sponsor of Collegiate Middle Level Association (CMLA) (1989)
- Received the John H. Lounsbury Distinguished Service Award from NMSA (1995)
- Served on several National Council for Accreditation of Teacher Education Boards and chaired the Special Areas Studies Board 1995–1996
- Received the Teacher of the Year Award, Otterbein College (2005)
- Recognized as the Middle School Educator of the Year by the Ohio Middle School Association (2008)

Selected Publications

Swaim, J. H. (1979). The transescent needs a break too. *Transescence: The Journal on Emerging Adolescent Education, 7*(1), 21–24.

Swaim, J. H. (1981). Middle school curriculum: An identity crisis. *Contemporary Education, 52(3),* 239–141.

Arth, A. A., Lounsbury, J. H., McEwin, C. K., & Swaim, J. H. (1995). *Middle level teachers: Portraits of excellence.* Columbus, OH: National Middle School Association and Reston, VA: National Association for Secondary School Principals.

Swaim, J. H., & Stefanich, G. P. (1996). *Meeting the standards: Improving middle level teacher education.* Columbus, OH: National Middle School Association.

Swaim, J. H., & McEwin, C. K. (1997). Middle level competitive sports programs. In J. L. Irvin (Ed.), *What current research says to the practitioner* (pp. 151–159). Westerville, OH: National Middle School Association.

Swaim, J. H., McEwin, C. K., & Irvin, J. L. (1998). Responsible middle level sports programs: What research says. *Middle School Journal, 30*(2), 72–74.

Swaim, J. H., & McEwin, C. K. (2005). Sports in middle schools. In V. A. Anfara, G. Andrews, & S. B. Mertens, *Encyclopedia of middle grades education* (pp. 347–350). Greenwich, CT: Information Age Publishing and Westerville, OH: National Middle School Association.

McEwin, C. K., & Swaim, J. H. (2007). *Clearing the hurdles: Issues and answers in middle school sports.* Westerville, OH: National Middle School Association.

Swaim, J. H. (2009). A visit to my junior high school 50 years later. *Middle School Journal, 40*(5), 46–51

McEwin, C. K., & Swaim, J. H. (2009). National Middle Association School research summary: Middle level interscholastic sports programs. Retrieved from http://www.nmsa.org/Research/ResearchSummaries/SportsPrograms/tabid/1886/Default.aspx

---

*John H. Swaim**

My parents were very influential in getting me involved in education. My mother was a career first grade teacher and my dad was a high school teacher. They were extremely influential in who I am as a teacher. The other person who has been equally influential is my wife, Sue Swaim. We attended junior high together, went to high school and college together, and both became teachers. Sue was an elementary teacher and I was a high school teacher. Then later we both fell into the middle school level. Sue has been very supportive and one of the most important influences on my life.

Outside of those individuals, considering people that are in the profession, John Lounsbury has been almost a father figure. I have done a lot of work with John. I admired him when I wrote my doctoral dissertation. To know him as a person is even more special. What he stands for is what I stand for in middle level education. I have a lot of contemporary people that mean a lot to me also. When I say contemporary I'd say that they're in the same generation. Two of my generation have influenced me considerably. One is Ken McEwin. Ken and I have done a lot together in teacher education. The other person is Ed Brazee. Ed went through a doctoral program with me and was one of my teachers when I was principal.

What kinds of middle school literature did you read?

As a doctoral student in the early to mid-1970s I was into a lot of the literature on what middle school was about, identifying what it was—mainly more philosophical literature. I got hooked on the developmental part. I read Herschel Thornburg on the social aspects of kids, Don Eichhorn on the physical development of kids, and Epstein with the cognitive development of kids. In the middle school, understanding this age is critical. You have to understand what developmentally responsive means. That made a lot of sense to me. I read Joan Lipsitz's book *Growing Up Forgotten*. Probably late 1970s early 1980s, I got into more the structural things of middle school: teaming and scheduling. At that time I was still a principal, so those things were of interest to a principal. Then probably in the late to mid 1980s I got more into curriculum. About that time Jim Beane's book came out on integrating curriculum and how that fits into the middle school structure. I have always been particularly interested in any literature on teacher education.

---

* John Swaim was interviewed for the Legacy Project in April 2004.

Are there particular theorists (or theories) or writings that have influenced your educational thought?

I think it would be the developmentalists. I have really looked into Piaget, and that focused me more on cognitive development and how that fits into early adolescence. Kohlberg was another developmentalist who looked at social/psychological development of kids. Understanding how all the developmental theories fit together is critical to understanding early adolescence. Sometimes we look at those as "Here is Piaget's work" and "There is Kohlberg's work." If you look at those developmental theories together, they really mesh very well with what we know about early adolescence. I think relative to curriculum, integrated curriculum or the interdisciplinary curriculum, I would adhere to Jim Beane's theories. Still, I struggle with my teacher education students as to how to put that into practice, particularly the democratic part of how you involve the young adolescents in developing an integrated unit. I am still searching for where I stand on the implementation of integrated curriculum. I very much believe in an integrated curriculum with a lot of student involvement, but I still struggle at times with how to do that. Obviously, if you look at teacher education as a topic, there are all kinds of theories out there about teacher education. The ones that match the way I teach reflect a democratic approach.

What was your primary motivation for becoming involved in the middle school movement?

I think the reason was probably pragmatic. I just switched from a high school to a middle school teacher. Then I got really intrigued and committed and dedicated to the idea that we have to make our educational system developmentally responsive. So I think that is what excited me the most and really drew me in as a movement that was grounded in: "Let's put the kids first." Who are we educating? We are educating young adolescents. As the cliché goes: "You build a system to fit the kids, not fit the kids to the system." Basically, that's my motto, my approach.

What is your primary motivation for your continuing involvement in middle school education?

I think it is to pursue the need to have specially prepared educators for the middle level. We need teachers that have the desire and the wherewithal to teach young adolescents. I am committed to that. If middle schools are to be successful we have to have middle level teacher education. I do not say that flippantly because I am not sure that middle school has really taken hold. It is there in numbers but it is not there in theory. We have too many middle schools that aren't middle schools. I believe the reason for that is we don't have teachers that have been really prepared to teach at that level. I believe that there are teachers in the field now that, given the opportunity to be involved in professional development, would provide leadership in middle school education. But also we need new people coming into the field. Our middle childhood teacher education program at Otterbein College has over a hundred students in the middle childhood education program. I get excited when they get excited about teaching young adolescents. I like to see that enthusiasm. That's what we have got to have to make the middle school work—teachers that are truly dedicated and committed to teaching at that level.

Teachers can't be saying, "Well I teach in middle school but you know when someone dies at the high school, I will move up." I think we are getting past that. There are good middle schools out there that our college students have been through so it is not a stretch for them to come back and to be a teacher in a middle school. I think we just are starting to get some of a generation who are coming from good middle schools into middle school teacher education programs. However, we have a lot of work to do. We don't have enough schools that are truly good middle schools, in practice and philosophy. I tell my teacher education students that the climate in a school is not set by the kids, it is set by the adults. So my motive is to continue to stay involved with the preparation and professional development of middle school teachers.

How would you describe the early years of the middle school movement (1960s and 1970s)?

I was fortunate in that I was at the beginning of my teaching career in the early part of the movement. Whereas some of the folks you have interviewed like John Lounsbury had been around in the 1960s and 1970s and involved in middle schools from the very beginning, I was just coming into education about the time the middle school was coming on the educational horizon. So, there was a second generation: Ken McEwin and myself, Howard Johnston, Tom Erb and some of the others including Tom Dickinson. There was kind of that generation that grew up, professionally, at the same time the middle school movement got started.

I think the early 1970s was a struggle for identity—the junior high versus middle school. In the 1960s and 1970s you still had lots of junior highs. So the thrust during the 1970s was trying to find an identity, trying to say what is unique about middle schools. We got into some real black and white stuff. You either had a defined component of a middle school or you didn't. So the 1970s were identifying who we are. In the late 1970s and 1980s we had a lot of middle schools go to middle schools for very pragmatic reasons, not philosophical reasons—dropping enrollments, busing, and a variety of different types of things. But that wasn't all bad, because in the 1970s, we had the philosophy developing, too. The middle schools that developed for pragmatic reasons changed the grade structure, and they often took advantage of making a philosophical change, too—provided the basis for the middle school movement. I am afraid there were a lot of middle schools that made the pragmatic changes, but never made the philosophical changes. We still have a lot of those out there.

I think in the 1980s we began to have more philosophical changes. School districts made decisions to build middle schools for philosophical reasons rather than for pragmatic reasons. The 1980s I would say were kind of glory years of middle school in public education: "Get on the bandwagon. Have a middle school. You may not know what it is, but you need a middle school." It was very open for schools to do what they thought was right to make it a good middle school. Of course there was *Turning Points* at the end of the 1980s, which gave some focus to what middle schools weren't doing. The 1990s provided more visibility, more growth. I think in the 1990s, we were beginning to look at the curriculum, rather than just looking at the middle school as a structure. We began to look at teaming in a different way. That was a giant leap for a lot of people to say, "We can change the structure; that's not too hard, but to change how we teach and the way we teach, that's pretty big." I think we are still making some of those changes in schools.

By 2000, we had arrived. People now know what a middle school is, or at least recognize it as a structure in the K–12 continuum. Any time you gain status and you are starting to do pretty well, then people start looking at negative things. I think we are in for a period of time that people are looking for what's wrong with middle level education. That is not all bad. I think we need to take a look at ourselves and be forced to justify why we're doing what we are doing. It may be too, that some of the things that we believed in need to be changed, if we truly believe that we've got to develop an educational system that can fit the needs of the ever-changing young adolescents. So, I think it's going to be healthy. We are going to come out in the end stronger than we were before.

How has the middle school concept changed since the early years of the middle school movement?

I don't think the concept has changed at all. That is what has made middle schools so strong. We have been able to maintain the middle school concept. Saying that, I am not sure we have gotten the word out what the concept is. Those of us who truly believe in and understand the middle school concept think that it is the basis of the whole middle school. I purposely didn't say movement, because I think it is beyond the movement. It is an established part of American educational society. I think the concept is solid. How people perceive the concept is what we need to work on and what we as middle level educators need to be advocating.

What have been some of the most significant events, incidents, or moments in the middle school movement?

I would have to say the creation or the development of the National Middle School Association has to be one of, if not the most significant event, that has contributed to the middle school movement. If we hadn't had the National Middle School Association, an association particularly for middle school, I don't think we would've had the impact on American education that we have had today. In fact, let me tell you a story which affirms that. It was in 1972, I believe, when I went with my doctoral advisor to an ASCD conference in Minneapolis. There was no national middle school association at that time. I was also starting my dissertation on middle school teacher education. There was a meeting at ASCD about starting a Special Interest Group (SIG) in ASCD that was geared toward middle school. Most of the big names in middle school at that time were there. I can remember there were about 15–20 people that came to the session. I can remember Connie Toepfer was there, John Lounsbury was there. I think Don Eichhorn was there also. Those are the three that I remember. The ASCD people were there too. The middle school people were trying to convince ASCD to start a special interest group for middle school. The tone of the conversation was that ASCD was not interested. At least that is what I picked up. From there, I think, the leadership of the middle school turned to the Midwest Middle School Association and that was the beginning of the National Middle School Association. So originally there was an effort to start through ASCD, to develop a closer tie with curriculum, and get into an organization that was already established. So, early on, ASCD did not seem to be interested in providing a home for middle school education.

Turning Points has had a big impact. Going back before that, in 1982, National Middle School Association through its publication of *This We Believe* had and has continued to have a big influence on a lot of schools and school districts. *Turning Points*, on the other hand, has had a big influence by taking a critical look at what we should be doing to educate young adolescents. When it first came out, some of the middle school advocates felt it was too critical. But I think it was critical in the sense that we were not doing what we should be doing at that particular point. I think over a 10-year period, we were able to make some significant changes. Those are the things that come to mind right now.

Who or what have been some of the greatest detractors or opponents (negative influences) of middle school education?

That is hard for me to respond to because I don't focus on that a whole heck of a lot. Somebody else is fighting those battles. I like a fight where we are proactive. I wouldn't say there have not been any individuals or groups that haven't opposed what middle school stands for. I would say overall that people who are looking for a more focused type of education, rather than a holistic type of education, would tend not to be supportive of the middle school concept. Maybe I could explain it this way: those who see the middle school's purpose as strictly a preparation for the high school may not be as supportive of the middle school concept because the whole middle school philosophy is built around the idea that the middle school is not just a preparation for the high school. Middle school must take young adolescents from where they are right now in their lives and build a system that is responsive to their needs. If we do a good job of that, they will be ready for high school. Some people have the old coaching philosophy that the best way to get ready for the game is to practice it. So to get ready for high school, you practice high school. I think the people that believe in that type of push-down theory of education, that elementary's sole purpose is to get them ready for middle school, middle school's sole purpose is to get them ready for high school, and high school's sole purpose is to get them ready for college, don't tend to have a developmental perspective on education.

What are some of the mistakes that have been made during the middle school movement that we might be able to learn from today?

Early on, we were perceived as just warm and fuzzy with little academic credibility. We didn't stress academics as much as we should have. Regarding young adolescent development—I am maybe coming from a little different point of view than some of my other middle school colleagues—I think intellectual development is equally as important, not necessarily more important. I know there are some people who believe that in schools intellectual development should be more important. But, I think the developmental stages are a hand and glove mixture of physical, social, psychological, and intellectual growth and development that you have to look at as equally important. I think we over-stressed the social, psychological part and maybe de-emphasized the intellectual part early on. And we got a reputation as not being as intellectually rigorous as we should. Obviously, the other thing would be teacher education. We did not jump on the bandwagon soon enough to start preparing teachers for middle school. Middle schools were established far ahead of teacher education and middle level certification, with the exception of a few states.

What are some of the most important factors that are influencing middle school education today?

The standards movement has had a strong influence on the middle school. I'm an advocate of standards. The old cliché is that you need standards in education but education shouldn't be standardized. I think we are moving toward the standardization of education. We are closing down some of our options that we have. We are becoming much too focused and narrowing our options in curriculum and instruction. Standards to me are something you set to meet. There should also be flexibility in how you meet standards. I think that we are becoming standardized in the sense that we are being prescriptive in how we measure standards, for example proficiency tests.

Who do you consider to be among the most influential leaders of the middle school movement? And as you think about that, why did you select these particular leaders?

Let me start with the founders that have been recognized by the National Middle School Association—John Lounsbury, Bill Alexander, Don Eichhorn, Connie Toepfer, and Gordon Vars. They have been recognized for their contribution not only early on but even today. Taking a stand for what middle school stood for, good middle level education early on was quite challenging. We have lost Bill and Don. But right up to the end they were very active. Those folks are in a league of their own as far as middle school is concerned. Contemporary leaders, I am going to mention a few, but there's a lot that have made lots of different contributions in a lot of different types of areas. We have Paul George and his writings. He is a prolific writer and advocate through his writings. Howard Johnston for his motivation. One that I would probably put with those top five that I mentioned before as the founders is Ken McEwin. Ken is a best friend and a colleague, and he has contributed in many ways. He is prolific in his writing. I have had the privilege of writing with him, working with him in teacher education. If he would have been born at the same time as the founders, he would have been considered as the sixth founder. Ed Brazee and Jim Beane, I think have made significant contributions in curriculum. And of course Jim's work speaks for itself. Ed's belief, as expressed in his book *Dissolving Boundaries*, helped turn middle school from a structure to more looking at a curriculum and where and what middle schools should be curriculum-wise.

Then I think as far as political influence and advocacy, I would say my wife, Sue, has been very instrumental in helping the National Middle School Association get to where it is. And because of that, the middle school movement has assumed a more political advocacy type of role.

Have there been major debates among middle school leaders focusing on particular issues or beliefs?

Yes, let me give you one example. When I formed the committee to prepare a position paper in 1980, which I thought would maybe take six months to write and in the end took about two and one half years before we got it done. I can almost guarantee you every word was fought over in that document. We just about lost a couple members off of that committee that were going to resign. I still have the letters from them, saying that we were defining middle school too much and that middle school was more of a philosophy and we were trying to make a check list out of it. God bless John Lounsbury, who worked with me and convinced those people to continue and stay with it. The document went through several revisions, but in actuality the first *This We Believe* ended up with ten components. However, eventually it got turned into more or less of a checklist in many respects. But it was a start. I think there is room in middle school for interpretation of how to implement the middle school concept but firm agreement on the concept itself. Even our founders, in those early years, had their differences. I think some of those debates still go on, but maybe in a little different arena.

What was at stake? And, which position won out, if there was one?

There were people at that time that wanted a stronger definition of middle school. If you notice the first version of *This We Believe*, teaming was noted, but not highlighted. There were those who said, "You can't be a middle school unless you have teaming." Ultimately it was written in such a way that you had to have collaboration rather than formal teaming. So, I think the first issue tried to keep the focus on the concepts of middle school not structure. But the ten components eventually ended up being more interpreted as structural components. One of the members of the committee wanted more interdisciplinary curriculum and integrated core curriculum. And we had to work that out. I think it was a series of compromises, not compromising the idea of what's good for young adolescents, but what was good for that time. And certainly some of those things that they were advocating in those early days are still things we believe in today.

**What have been the roles of women and minorities in the middle
school movement?**

Early on, we had a very strong emphasis on the Board to have minority
representation. In fact, Connie Toepfer was the champion of that. In his
presidency he made sure there was a committee dealing with representation of minorities. We have been very sensitive to that on the Board. Women
have been very much a central part of the National Middle School Association and rightfully so, because the last statistic I saw, 70 some percent of the
middle school teachers are women. I think actually as far as middle school
and who's teaching there, I think women are the backbone of the teaching
force in middle level education.

**What are some examples of ways the middle school movement
has affected American education?**

Let me say overall that it has been one of the most rapidly developing
movements that has changed the whole system of American education. I
believe that the middle school movement has the potential of focusing the
American education system on a more holistic approach to teaching kids.
But we have a lot of battles to fight because I think we are actually moving in
the opposite direction. We are focusing more on things that don't directly
address the total development of our students. I would hope that this more
comprehensive approach in dealing with our students would filter up to
the high school and filter down to the elementary level. We say elementary
is very humanistic, but I am not sure I can say that. I have been in enough
elementary schools where the instructional approach is pretty subject centered in those self-contained classrooms. Certainly not interdisciplinary in
the ones I have been in—you teach your reading at this time, you teach your
social studies at this time, you teach your language arts at this time, and never the twain shall meet. So, I think middle school has the potential to set the
direction for good educational practices for elementary and high school.

**Have particular legislative actions significantly influenced the
middle school movement (state and/or national levels)?**

Let me speak just about the teacher education. There obviously are
others, legislative actions that have made significant contributions. The
ones I am most familiar with in teacher education are: 1969, Pumerantz
did a study that found only two states had any kind of state licenses or endorsements for middle school or middle level teachers. Now according to
Peggy Gaskill's study, we have 46 states that have some kind of middle level
endorsement or licensing at that level. So I think there's been tremendous
movement with regard to the preparation of middle school teachers. Let

me just speak of Ohio. When I came here 13 years ago, they had a K–8 license for elementary and a 7–12 license for secondary level. We now have a middle childhood license, 4–9. It's got some problems that we are still working on, but I'll tell you, we are now preparing teachers to teach in middle schools. We aren't just taking anybody and everybody who can teach there. We now recognize that they have to have special preparation to be a middle school teacher. We now have 49 teacher education programs in Ohio that are fully accredited to offer middle childhood programs. I think that is one of the biggest areas in which we have made progress in middle school education.

The National Council for Accreditation of Teacher Education (NCATE) has had a big influence on middle school, and the growth of middle school teacher education. Through NMSA's involvement with NCATE and submitting our middle level teacher education standards for their approval, we now have states that have based their middle school standards on our standards as well as middle school preparation programs that have adopted our standards. I don't think we would have gotten that recognition unless we were a part of NCATE. If we would have tried to do it on our own, I am not sure that we would've had the clout to make the difference that we have.

As middle level educators, how do you think we should respond to the current emphasis on student achievement as measured by standardized tests?

I am a supporter of standards. But I am not a supporter of standardizing. I think that's the problem that we face. We have standardized the measurement of student performance, which leads to the standardization of our curriculum. I am an advocate of multiple assessments. I also realize that sometimes it's not economically feasible at a state level or a national level to administer anything else but paper–pencil tests. I think standardization has hurt the middle school movement but having standards has helped the middle school movement. We know what we stand for in middle schools. To standardize how we get to those standards, I think, could be detrimental to us.

Are there lessons we still need to learn from the history of the middle school movement?

The biggest lesson that we could learn is that middle school is always a process of becoming. Now let me give an example of that more specifically with regard to teacher education and teacher licensing. I've seen too many middle school educators after they have obtained middle school licensure for their state or developed a middle school teacher education program on their campus say, "Well, we've got it. So we don't have to do much more." You have to continually keep fighting. You have to continue to keep advocating for middle school teacher education. I have found in Ohio and in Colorado at two different types of higher education institutions and two different types of state departments that you constantly have to keep advocating (fighting) for middle school teacher preparation. My parents have taught me. "The stronger you believe in something, the stronger you will act on those beliefs." I believe that applies to middle school. We've got to hold on to our beliefs about middle school, but we've also got to act on those beliefs. We can't just believe in them. We have to continuously act on those beliefs. I really think that's true; I look at the things that I truly believe in, and that's what consumes my life, my family, my profession. That consumes my life because I strongly believe in them. There are things in life that I don't have a strong belief in, and I don't act on as much. I think as middle level educators, we've got to strongly believe in the middle school concept and, most importantly, we've got to act on those beliefs in many different types of ways. We as teacher educators will act on it in certain way. Acting together we will perpetuate what's good education for young adolescents.

How would you characterize the current status of the middle school movement?

I think we are in for some rough roads. I think we are in for some questioning. We've been accepted as a legitimate part of the K–12 system. I think we're going to have some serious challenges ahead of us from the outside, some of them legitimate and some not so legitimate.

Are there other comments you would like to make that you have not been asked about in this interview?

I would just commend the people involved with this project. I think it is a marvelous project, and I think we can learn from the past. We have a new generation of folks that'll have to step up to bat now and take the leadership in the middle school movement. I think this is really good motivation for them.

20

Sue Swaim

> *As middle level educators we must advocate for what we know is the right thing to do at the local, state, and national levels. We live it every day and have experience and expertise that is needed when these discussions are happening and decisions are being made.*

During her 14 years of service (1993–2007) as Executive Director of National Middle School Association (NMSA), Sue Swaim provided distinguished leadership that saw the Association gain new heights of national and international prominence and influence. Her tenure was highlighted by many notable events and achievements including the establishment of a satellite office in Washington, D.C., the initiation and continued celebration of October as the Month of the Young Adolescent, and the establishment of collaborative relationships and joint projects with other national organizations. She also provided leadership for the relocation and expansion in facilities and personnel of NMSA's headquarters, a doubling of membership, and the development of *Success in the Middle: A Policymaker's Guide to Achieving Quality Middle Level Education,* a major policy statement based on *This We Believe.* Swaim instituted the development of the second

The Legacy of Middle School Leaders, pages 327–342
Copyright © 2011 by Information Age Publishing
All rights of reproduction in any form reserved.

and third editions of *This We Believe* and was one of the writers in the development of the third and fourth editions. During her tenure as Executive Director of NMSA, the number of state and provincial affiliate organizations expanded to include nearly every state, all the Canadian provinces, and several other countries. Upon her retirement, the NMSA Board of Trustees recognized her contributions by granting her the status of Executive Director Emeritus.

Sue Swaim received her undergraduate degree in elementary education from Emporia State University, Emporia, Kansas, in 1967, and earned her master's degree in middle level curriculum and instruction from the University of Northern Colorado, Greeley, in 1980. For more than 20 years, she taught in elementary and middle schools and served as principal of the University of Northern Colorado's Laboratory School and faculty member before becoming Executive Director of NMSA. Ms. Swaim is a popular speaker who has made keynote addresses and presentations across the nation and in Canada, China, and New Zealand. She is the author or co-author of more than 70 professional publications and is a sought-after consultant who remains active in middle level education.

Selected Accomplishments and Contributions to Middle Level Education

- Executive Director of the Colorado Association of Middle Level Educators (1988–1992)
- National Middle School Association (NMSA) President (1991)
- Co-developed the Prentice-Hall National Teaching Teams Award (1995)
- Developed the international celebration and program, Month of the Young Adolescent (1997)
- Co-developer of the national television program and accompanying resource guide, *Opening the Door to Diversity: Voices from the Middle School* which received the Beacon Award, Cable Television Association's Highest Recognition (1999)
- Member of the writing team for *This We Believe: Successful Schools for Young Adolescents* (2003) and *This We Believe: Keys to Educating Young Adolescents* (2010)
- Received the John H. Lounsbury Distinguished Service Award from NMSA (2006)
- Received the Jim Garvin Distinguished Service Award from the New England League of Middle Schools (2007)

- Received the Donald Eichhorn Distinguished Service Award from the Pennsylvania Middle School Association (2007)
- Received Emporia State University's Distinguished Alumna Award (2010)

Selected Publications

Swaim, S. (1996). In defense of middle schools. *American School Board Journal, 183*(11), 60.

Swaim, S. (1996). The central office role in middle level school reform. *The School Administrator, 53*(6), 6–9.

Swaim, S. (2001). Developing and improving a shared vision. In T. O. Erb (Ed.), *This we believe... and now we must act* (pp. 20–27). Westerville, OH: National Middle School Association.

Swaim, S. (2003, Winter). What middle schools should and could be. *Middle Matters, 4*, 6.

Swaim, S. (2004–2007) Perspectives column, *Middle Ground,* 4 issues per year.

Swaim, S. (2005). A shared vision that guides decisions. In T. O. Erb (Ed.), *This we believe in action* (pp. 29–34). Westerville, OH: National Middle School Association.

Swaim, S. (2005) Lead Developer for NMSA's *Success in the middle: A policymaker's guide to achieving quality middle level education.* Westerville, OH: National Middle School Association.

Swaim, S., & Kinney, P. (2009). *Voices of experience: Perspectives from successful middle level leaders.* Westerville, OH: National Middle School Association and Reston, VA: National Association of Secondary School Principals.

*Sue Swaim**

Early in my career one of my main influences was John Lounsbury, and he continues to be a person I consider a mentor and friend. When I began working in the middle school, my husband was at the middle school as well. He was working on a doctorate in middle school curriculum and instruction. I began to periodically pick up some of the materials that he was reading. One of those was the *Middle School Journal* that John Lounsbury was editing. In it he wrote a column entitled *As I See It.* I read some of the initial columns and it was like, "This guy's been in my classroom. He is

---

* Sue Swaim was interviewed for the Legacy Project in April 2004.

talking about the things that are happening with my kids." At the time I thought, "Wow, wouldn't it be great if I could meet him and really get to visit with him?" Much to my surprise, within a year he was on the campus of the University of Northern Colorado as part of the faculty for a middle level institute, and I did get to meet him. I think he really was one of the key people who helped nurture my interest in middle school and initially mentored me as I began to work with this age group.

What kinds of middle school literature did you read?

The Middle School Journal was the first one and once I discovered it, I began reading it on a regular basis. Besides that, I began to read some of the other monographs that were being written at the time. I also read some of the middle school articles that were showing up in other associations' publications. When I began my graduate degree in Middle School and Junior High Curriculum and Instruction, I read a lot more of the in-depth curriculum and research material available at that time.

Are there particular theorists (or theories) or writings that have influenced your educational thought?

I typically read articles or books written by John Lounsbury, Gordon Vars, Connie Toepfer, Jim Beane, Ken McEwin, and Tom Dickinson. I also read quite a bit written by Art Combs. I quickly became interested in the early interdisciplinary curriculum writings because it made such sense to me as I worked on a daily basis with middle school students in language arts, social studies, and reading. I don't think I've ever sat down and thought about particular theorists, per se. I usually would pick a specific interest or topic, like reading in the content areas as an example, and then try to find as much written about that particular topic as I could find.

What was your primary motivation for becoming involved in the middle school movement?

I have had the opportunity to teach elementary, high school, and middle school. While I enjoyed teaching each level, the middle level became my primary love. I first heard of National Middle School Association through my husband's involvement in it. As I began to teach in a middle school, I felt NMSA was an organization that "spoke" to me. I began to build a network of like-minded, enthusiastic middle level educators not only at the national level but at the state and local levels as well. I got very involved in the Colorado Association of Middle Level Education early in my career. I loved getting to know people who were enthusiastic about what they were doing. It helped energize me and in a way I began to develop my own professional learning community through getting to know and working with these folks. I think we all realized that we were part of an emerging middle level movement and that was exciting.

What is your primary motivation for your continuing involvement in middle school education?

I believe very much in the importance of the work we are doing—more so today than ever before. I went into this because I wanted to make a difference in the lives of kids. The more I learned about middle level education, the more I learned about the needs of this particular age group and the things we needed to address if young adolescents were to be successful learners. I wanted to be involved in doing that kind of work, and I was lucky enough to find a group of people and an organization that based itself on doing what was best for young adolescents. Everyone I met through my middle school network was focused on putting kids at the center of their work. I felt our work was kid-focused and people-focused, and that was important to me. I've gotten the opportunity to watch the middle school movement grow over the years as well as be a part of NMSA's own growth and development by being a member, a board member, the association president, and today its executive director.

How would you describe the early years of the middle school movement? We define the early years as the 1960s and 1970s.

I think during the early years we were trying to find our own identity within the educational continuum. We knew that middle school needed to be a place that addressed the unique needs and characteristics of young adolescents. In the early years people talked about middle schools versus junior highs. I think during that time there was a lot of dialogue about the name over the school's entry way and the grade configuration (5–8 or 6–8 vs. 7–9) housed within the building. I know a lot energy was spent on trying to get people to understand why this was such a critical time in a child's development. We knew young adolescents needed and deserved an educational system that understood them, addressed their needs, and was staffed with educators who wanted to work with this age group and who were prepared to teach this age level. But, that was a hard sell to many people and in some ways that is still true today. I think we made some positive and strong strides in that direction in those early years. The reality was, however, that was just the beginning part of the conversation and change. The real work of impacting the curriculum, instruction, and assessment implemented during this time frame was not as vigorously pursued in the early years as it is today.

How has the middle school concept changed since the early years of the middle school movement?

Today, I think that most realize that middle level education is more than the name over the door or the grade configuration inside the building. It's about implementing successful middle level schools that focus on students' academic growth and achievement and their personal growth and development. Building a middle level identity was challenging work, but I believe we're now engaged in the hardest part of the work. Today's work focuses on middle level curriculum, instruction, and assessment based upon the needs of young adolescents. It focuses on developing safe and engaging learning communities not only for the students but also for the adults who work with them. We are wrestling with answering questions like, "What does it really mean to be a learning community? How do we really put the tenets outlined in *This We Believe* into action?" The depth and breadth of that kind of work can feel overwhelming at times, but it is critical work to pursue.

How have middle schools changed since the early years of the middle school movement?

Well, that varies a lot from school to school and community to community. One of the challenges we're facing today is that there are still too many middle schools that too narrowly define themselves. They may have changed the school's name and grade configuration from junior high to middle school; they may have even started to implement some of the middle level organizational structures such as teaming or block scheduling, but they only began the journey and have stalled out. They haven't implemented teaming or block scheduling to their fullest possibilities. They still talk about interdisciplinary units of study done periodically throughout the year rather than a more fully integrated curriculum on a daily basis. People will say to me, "Sue, we've been doing this middle level stuff for over ten years and it's just not working, we're not seeing any improved results." My answer is that in too many places the middle level concept has never been fully implemented with consistency over time. Too many states still do not prepare teachers or administrators specifically to teach this age group in the same way they require professional preparation for elementary and high school educators. However, we have schools and school districts throughout our country that have fully implemented the middle school concept and they prove this thing called *middle school* works. These schools have also made commitments to provide ongoing professional development and to hire new teachers specifically prepared in middle level education whenever possible. It's going to take this type of consistent commitment over time to reach the goal of successful middle schools for all young adolescents.

How were decisions about the directions taken by the middle school movement made?

I think we now benefit from years of continued successful practice and a growing body of quality research that work together to guide our decisions. In the early years of the movement our decisions were based upon trying to address the unique needs and characteristics of young adolescent learners. What were their characteristics? What were their unique needs? And then what were the instructional strategies we should use to address those successfully? We many times relied more on *gut* instinct or good common sense when implementing something more than anything else.

In 1982, NMSA released *This We Believe,* which was really the first time anyone had brought together a group of people to sit down and actually develop a document focused on what middle level education should include. That wasn't easy work, but it was a critical contribution to the field. Most importantly, *This We Believe* was thought of as a *living document,* meaning that it should grow and develop, as research and practice more fully informed us over time. It wasn't just something that you wrote one time, distributed, and then moved on.

What was the educational context at the time the middle school movement began?

Teacher preparation programs were divided into general K–8 preparation and specific content area preparation for high school. The new public three-tier system didn't match the teacher preparation or licensure system. Additionally, in many instances the junior high school had taken its name pretty literally and had become a miniature high school. When you look at the initial rationale for the junior high school, developed over 100 years ago, you'll find it was started to be a distinct educational entity for early adolescents. It was realized even then that something different from a high school setting best served this age group. History shows us that over time, however, educators moved away from the junior high's initial purpose. At the beginning of the middle school movement, the junior high schools were being closely examined. Many felt they were not meeting the needs of young adolescents.

What have been some of the most significant events, incidents, or moments in the middle school movement? Why did you select those particular ones?

One event would be William Alexander's 1963 speech because it was the first time someone had publically discussed a framework for educating young adolescents and called for the implementation of a *middle school.* I think that speech began the networking of people who were like-minded in this regard and helped facilitate their coming together to see how they could address these common issues.

I think the founding of the National Middle School Association in 1973 was really critical because it gave folks an opportunity to come together, to network, to learn from one another, to really begin to build a middle level voice on a national level. NMSA's long-standing commitment to middle level teacher preparation is important as well. When NMSA became a constituent member of NCATE and took over the responsibilities of writing the NMSA Standards for Teacher Preparation at the pre-service, master's level, specialist, and doctorate level, it was a big step forward. Through our NCATE partnership and work we have 30 states which now say that any college or university in their state preparing students to teach at the middle level must meet NMSA's standards to receive state program approval.

The releases of the all three editions of *This We Believe* have had a significant and far-reaching impact on middle level education. The release of *Turning Points* and the work that Carnegie funded for over ten years was very important. The release of *Turning Points 2000*, which focused on the lessons they learned and said, "Here is what we are getting good at, but here's the work we still have to do," is a critical contribution to the field.

Do you have any personal accounts related to those events that might be of interest to others?

People may or may not know that John Swaim and I are married and both ended up teaching in middle school together. One of the unusual things is that when he was president of NMSA in 1980, I was just beginning to be a middle school teacher. I had been an elementary teacher prior to that time. I got to watch a lot of the movement really through his engagement and his activities. John is the NMSA president who convened the group to write the first *This We Believe*. I got to experience what was happening from that vantage point, which is probably a lot different from anyone else. By the time that 1995 came around (the release of the 2nd edition of *This We Believe*), I, too, had been president of NMSA and in 1993 became its executive director. In 1995 I got to be part of the committee that revised the original *This We Believe*, as well as being a part of the committee that revised the 2003 edition. I would say that some of the most exciting professional development opportunities for me were to sit around the table with these folks, to talk about research, to look at current practice, to look at the input we received, and to get the chance to be personally engaged in the development of the second and third editions of *This We Believe*.

Likewise, the NMSA Middle Level Teacher Preparation Standards were written by a group of people on a retreat in Colorado. I got to be there and be part of that as an observer because I did the cooking for this group for several days. But if anyone ever doubted the passion or the commitment of this group, they just needed to be there to see it evolve. The Middle Level Teacher Preparation Standards as well as all of the *This We Believe* documents have had practically every word fully debated prior to being written in the final document. None of these documents came about easily or without great thought. I know, because I have been fortunate to be a part of all of them in one way or another.

Who or what have been some of the greatest detractors,
opponents, or negative influences on middle school education?

From the beginning, people challenged the idea that this was a unique age group and whether young adolescents really needed an equally valued and funded tier in the K–12 continuum. People questioned things like if having students in a middle school setting caused them to grow up too fast or if the academic rigor (or lack thereof) in middle schools held back gifted and talented students or didn't prepare them appropriately for high school. Also, people contended that specific teacher preparation for this level was not necessary. Depending on the grade level being taught, an elementary generalist licensure or content specific licensure in one area was all that was needed. There were also ongoing debates about the idea of teaching the *whole child* and including such things as advisor/advisee groups as part of the required school day.

Debates over academic rigor, grade configuration, and teacher and administrator preparation and licensure still exist today. In fact, I think the current interest by the press and larger school districts to return to a K–8 grade configuration is perhaps driven by an attempt to find a *quick and simple* fix to the problems of appropriately and successfully educating young adolescents instead of addressing the heart of the matter. The curriculum, instruction, assessment, and school organizational patterns that research and practice show best address the needs of young adolescent learners as well as having knowledgeable teachers and administrators in every classroom and school are the things we should be focused on.

I know there are concerns about No Child Left Behind and how it impacts middle level schools in particular. For example, how do we define a highly qualified middle level teacher? Middle level educators know we have to define it differently than the narrow definitions that are currently in the NCLB regulations. How do we deal with a single high-stakes test being the determinant of a successful school when we know that educating 10-

through 14-year-old students takes so much more than that? Middle level seems to have more than our fair share of issues to deal with today, and they all serve as detractors from the work we know we need to be doing.

What have been some of the most significant obstacles to the success of the middle school movement?

I think we really need to make a move towards implementing specific middle level teacher and principal licensure throughout the United States. We have too many states that don't make that a requirement. There are also many states that overlap the licensure areas so there is no distinct identity to middle level and no specific need to pursue middle level courses. The lack of specific professional preparation and licensure requirements is a major obstacle. It was an obstacle for the junior high movement as well and I think it contributed to its failure. There are a variety of reasons given by people for why specific middle level licensure is not needed. Sometimes people in the field feel it would narrow their hiring pools too much. I don't believe that's the case, and I don't think if they looked at states that have middle grades licensures they would find that happening. Nevertheless, we're dealing with these perceptions and a general public's lack of commitment to these issues. While the field of middle level teacher preparation and mandated middle level licensure is growing, we are not even close to having it universally in place as it is for the elementary and high schools.

We need to do more to engage the community in our middle schools so that they really understand their needs and issues. It's important that they see the successes as well as the challenges of middle schools so that when we need community support, we have informed parents, community members, and policymakers in place. Middle level advocacy at the local, state, and national levels is important, and every one of us has a role to play in accomplishing that. I think without more focused advocacy work, too many barriers will remain in place for middle level educators.

What are some of the mistakes that have been made during the middle school movement that we might be able to learn from today?

During our initial phase of raising middle level awareness, we got too excited about school name changes and grade configuration reorganizations. Perhaps we should have found a way to push harder at that time for the complete implementation of the concept because too many places started the journey with good intentions but stalled out along the way. You can't just tinker with the education of young adolescents. You've got to go the full mile with it. I think we have learned some lessons from this already. When we look at the recommendations or characteristics of what make a successful middle school today, we talk about how they're all interrelated. We recognize that providing a positive learning environment means addressing students' safety, wellness, and learning styles. We now talk about the importance of the adults in the learning process and how they should work together while ensuring the curriculum is challenging, motivating, and engaging. We talk about the need for active student and teacher engagement in the learning process rather than supporting a more passive, lecture approach to learning. Today we seek the connectedness of these things rather than thinking these issues are addressed in isolation of one another.

Were there regional differences in the way middle school education was developed or defined—say, comparing New England versus the South?

I don't think there were regional differences per se. I think you'll see differences for how middle level education evolved in rural settings, for example, versus large cities depending upon the region of the country they lived in and the community factors that impacted school decisions. I know there was a point in time where you probably saw the initial middle school movement further along in our country's Midwest and Southern regions before it began to really move west. I also know that suburban districts tended to move towards middle level schools sooner than urban or rural settings, but that is a pattern that occurred nationwide. I don't think that the concept, per se, or the kinds of things that we believed were important middle school components were different regionally.

Who do you consider to be among the most influential leaders of the middle school movement?

I think we'd start with those who are considered to be the founders of the middle school movement: Bill Alexander, Connie Toepfer, Gordon Vars, John Lounsbury, and Don Eichhorn. The leadership and commitment they brought to the movement was critical. Early in the middle school movement, these people would go just about anywhere and talk to anyone interested. They were very committed to the implementation of middle schools. After the founding fathers, I think you begin to look at those who had the opportunity to work directly with those folks, learn from them, who picked up their commitment and enthusiasm and carried it on. I've heard some of these folks referred to as the "second generation" of middle level leaders and includes such people as Ken McEwin, Paul George, Tom Dickinson, Tom Erb, John Swaim, Nancy Doda, Howard Johnston, Al Arth, and Sherrel Bergmann. These people and many others have made lasting impacts on the field. Then you think about current and emerging generations that include researchers as well as practitioners. Names that quickly come to mind are people such as Gayle Andrews, Steve Mertens, Vince Anfara, Kathy Hunt, and Rick Wormeli. It's hard to start making a list because you know you'll leave out important names but these are ones that come to mind today.

You specifically talked about Connie Toepfer and
John Lounsbury. Could you describe them?

I always have considered Connie Toepfer to be the conscience of the middle school movement. I served on the NMSA Board of Trustees when he was president of the Association, and I was continually impressed by his commitment to being student-focused in our schools. He also always pushed the status quo looking for what research was saying and how that research should inform our practice. I have the greatest respect and admiration for John Lounsbury's commitment to young adolescents, to the nature of human growth and development and its impact on curriculum and instruction. John Lounsbury is an example of a lifelong learner. He has stayed the course with the middle level movement and he continues to learn and grow, to address the current issues of today as strongly as he addressed the issues 35 years ago.

Have there been major debates among middle school leaders
focusing on particular issues? And as you think about that, what
were the debates about? What was at stake?

There have been debates and discussions among middle level educators from day one. I think a lot of them happened when you got middle level educators together. They tend to share their thoughts and debate back and forth about what is working best. If you look at some of the larger national debates, they have focused on such things as if this middle school movement isn't more about the warm and fuzzy, the *soft* side of education, and missed out on the academic rigor or the academic challenge. Based upon some of the challenges we still face today, I wonder if these particular debates changed anyone's viewpoint or not. We seem to have a consistency to the issues that are being raised.

I think those who listened and learned from the debates moved forward to a point that recognizes middle level education today should not be about academic rigor versus developmental responsiveness. It should instead encompass both and find the balance point of the two. Students who do not feel safe, nurtured, cared for, respected, in a positive learning environment are not going to achieve academically as far as they would otherwise. And so it's not either/or, but it's a balance of them coming together. It's a commitment to find that balance point for every child, not most of them, but every child.

What have been some of the roles of women and minorities in the middle school movement?

I think the roles of women and minorities are growing and expanding. But the reality of it is that when you look at the initial voices of the middle school movement and the initial people who were doing the writing and the research, it was very much male-dominated. I don't think that that is as true today. I think we are finding the woman's voice and we are finding more diversity among leaders in the field. But it's happening gradually. One of our challenges is the diversity found in the students in our classrooms is not found as equally in our middle level educators. Teachers and principals do not reflect the students that are in their classrooms, the diversity that's within the school community. And it's not just a middle level issue; it's an issue that cuts across education—elementary, middle, high, and higher education—that we have to be addressing.

Are there other groups that you particularly want to talk about?

The growth in AERA's Middle Level SIG is important to note. I think we would all agree we don't yet have enough quality middle level research, but we're finding a body of researchers who are committed to researching young adolescents in a variety of areas. I know that's having an impact on the field. Higher education middle level teacher preparation programs are having an impact on the field as well. Graduates of these programs get hired and enter teaching knowledgeable about this age group and their educational needs. They sometimes have the best currency in the field of anyone else in their building. I'm hoping someday their impact will be so strong that all states will seek middle level preparation and licensure.

Have particular legislative actions significantly influenced the middle school movement at the state and/or national level?

I think at both levels. In 2004, you can't answer this question without discussing No Child Left Behind and the impact it has had in a variety of ways. Certainly the testing component has an impact because NCLB has mandated grades 3–8 to be the testing grades. That means over 60% of the kids tested are middle school kids. So the success of that mandate rests squarely on the shoulders of middle school students and middle school educators. That, obviously, is creating all sorts of concerns about a single high-stakes test driving the curriculum of the school and narrowing the focus of what middle level education should include. Test results become so critical to funding, among other things, that many school districts are making unfortunate choices such as reducing the amount of physical education, social studies, art, or music from their school programs to make sure students have more focused test preparation time. What a loss to the education and well-being of young adolescents!

An interesting thing to note is that America's largest single education act is The Elementary & Secondary Education Act. That's where 80% of the federal education funding is found. Notice the word middle school or middle level aren't in that title nor are they mentioned anywhere in the law. It appears we only have a two-tier educational system, when we have a three-tier system in the vast majority of our country. People in Washington, D.C., will tell you "secondary" is the term that serves both middle school and high school, but the funding actually designated to middle level doesn't bear that out. Without this recognition you experience challenges in areas that elementary or high school people do not. Examples not only include difficulty in receiving specific funding for middle level needs in areas such as reading or science but the recent discovery that federal research data doesn't support a disaggregation of information for middle level researchers.

As middle level educators, how do you think we should respond to the current emphasis on student achievement as measured by standardized tests?

First of all, we need to develop an effective middle level advocacy outreach. Policymakers and others need to understand that middle level educators understand accountability and we want accountability but it must be appropriate for the level we teach. It must consist of more than a single high-stakes test. Standardized tests were always meant, in my opinion, to be snapshots of what is going on, to be used to give you a picture over time as to what your strengths are and the areas that you need to work on. I don't think they were meant to be used as they are being used today. Individually and collectively we have to find our voice and be willing to speak up regarding these issues and others.

We should be engaged in helping expand the thinking about assessment that goes beyond a single test and instead, values formative assessment practices. What about student self-assessment? Isn't that a critical skill for students to be learning if they're going to be lifelong learners? Where are we paying attention to that? There are other factors to consider besides assessment to determine if a school is successfully serving its students.

Are there lessons we still need to learn from the history of the middle school movement?

I think one of the lessons we've learned is that in too many places, schools and school districts started to implement the middle school philosophy but stalled out along the way. When people say we tried middle schools but they're just not working in our community or the student achievement is flat at this age group we have to ask, "Did you really implement middle school? Did you really implement the concept with consistency over time? Or did you stop along the way and it stalled out?"

When we look at the recommendations or components of what a middle school should be as seen in *This We Believe* or *Turning Points*, we have to realize they are not isolated components that can be picked in isolation of one another to be implemented. We can't choose our favorite six recommendations to implement and ignore the other four. We have come to more fully understand just how interrelated these are, and when you begin to work with one of the recommendations, the others are involved as well. We also have learned that naming a team of teachers or providing a block of time in the schedule for learning does not mean that teaming or block scheduling is being utilized correctly or to their fullest extent. Too many schools used the *terminology* but never fully implemented the practice. I hope we're also learning that you can't talk about curriculum that's relevant and challenging if you also don't address instructional strategies that actively engage every student in the learning process. That's true about the assessment strategies used every day so that students understand the growth they are making and become involved in setting their own learning goals and personal accountability. It has probably taken too much time for us to learn these lessons, but we know them now and we have to renew our commitment to ensuring every student in every middle school is experiencing these things.

How would you characterize the current status of the middle school movement?

I'm concerned. I think there is fragileness to it right now. Middle level education has a heightened visibility because of the political issues that are going on and tightened school budgets. Quite frankly, to fully support teaming and provide common planning time, it costs more than to departmentalize. As school districts are looking for financial cuts, they will consider those things. We have to be continually reaching out to our community members, central administration, and school board members to help them understand why cutting teaming, for example, is not a viable option at the middle level.

Many middle school educators feel these people don't understand their specific needs and challenges. I think in many communities they do not hence see the need for middle level educators to advocate for quality middle level education on a daily basis—not waiting until the crisis has already arrived. We are at risk and are taking some backwards steps at this time. I think it's so dangerous because this isn't the time to be moving away from implementing the middle level concept. This is the time to be moving towards it. This is the time to be rolling up our sleeves and saying we know what to do. Research tells us what to do. Practice has told us what to do. Join with us to ensure we make decisions and implement educational programs that are best for young adolescents.

This is the time to do more advocacy, more sharing the success stories, getting community and policy makers directly engaged in middle level classrooms and with middle level students and teachers. I am really beginning to think in teacher preparation and in professional development everyone needs to take an Advocacy 101 course. It's no longer something that can be left for someone else to do. When teachers visit with parents in the grocery store, at a football game, or they see a school board member, what they say and how they say it about middle level education can make a difference in the support they have in their community. I think it's a challenge to us right now, and I don't think enough people understand that yet.

PART **III**

*Voices of the Past
and Visions for the Future*

21

Participants' Perspectives on the Middle School Movement

At its beginning, the middle school movement was characterized by enthusiasm, excitement, and a pioneer spirit. Ideas were new and fresh, and participants seemed to feel they were on the path toward something immensely important. They were hopeful and optimistic. Now, as the early leaders have an opportunity to look back on the birth and development of the middle school movement, it seems appropriate to chronicle their experiences and learn from their wisdom. Though it was hard for the early leaders to know exactly how this effort would unfold and whether they would be successful in creating a significant social and educational movement, a retrospective view allows the public and academic communities to recognize that it was, in fact, a *middle school movement.*

Movements have been variously defined as groups of individuals in a certain time and place, characterized by (1) a common goal of changing social conditions through (2) advocacy and other individual actions (Laughlin, 2008); a group of people who consciously, and at their own cost,

The Legacy of Middle School Leaders, pages 345–385
Copyright © 2011 by Information Age Publishing
All rights of reproduction in any form reserved.

connect to change the status quo (Cochrum, 2007); and an ongoing, informal group action that is inspired by a passionately shared idea and directed toward positive change (Walton, 2008). Cochrum (2007) further explains that after a period of time, most movements dwindle or die. Sometimes this is because the stated objective has been achieved (e.g., the Women's Rights Movement declined when women were granted the right to vote). Sometimes the movement may fade due to poor leadership, a lack of ownership among the masses, or a perception that the cause is not compelling. With mixed emotions, several of our participants declared that the middle school movement may, in fact, be at an end. Some of them felt that the end signaled progress because middle schools are now established as a legitimate part of the K–12 continuum. George expanded on this position:

> I do sense as the reorganization of American middle level schools comes to an end...that the middle school movement may lose momentum as a consequence.... Somehow thirty years ago, it was a mission that everyone caught on to, but today it's very difficult. We've got to keep that history alive, but you know what, even if we don't, the middle school movement will stand out historically as the most comprehensive, complete, and successful liberalizing influence in the history of American education. It's already been a complete success.

In spite of George's declaration about the "complete success" and "end" of the middle school movement, he expressed concern that younger middle level educators are not taking up the mantle of the cause for which he and many others have invested their professional lives: "In our state, the people who were involved in the start up of the Florida League of Middle Schools thirty-two years ago are still the people who are running the Florida League of Middle Schools thirty-two years later. It is difficult to find young educators who are willing to get involved beyond their school." On this point—the position that leaders are needed to continue the work that has been started on behalf of young adolescents and the schools that serve them—our participants spoke with one voice. They do not believe that the objectives of the middle school movement have been fully implemented. They are concerned that the passion and intellectual energy that fueled those early years of conceptualization and implementation of middle schools is being extinguished by public and governmental forces that value quantitative data more than responsiveness to the needs of young adolescents. One factor that has to be recognized is the climate surrounding education in recent decades that has made it hard for the middle school message to receive a fair hearing and consideration.

In their interviews and conversations with us, these middle school leaders celebrated the successes and progress of the middle school movement, and they provided profound insights regarding its shortcomings and future challenges. This chapter provides a synthesis of their collective views on multiple aspects of the history of the movement, including the articulation and communication of the ideology and identity of middle school education; implementation of the various and collective components of the middle school philosophy; attention to the unique needs of young adolescents; the reorganization of middle schools; the influence of the middle school on American education; the implementation of appropriate curriculum for young adolescents; attention to appropriate teaching and learning practices; development of a substantial, scholarly knowledge base; commitment to specialized middle level professional preparation and development; and the influence of policy, politics, and accountability initiatives on middle school education. The chapter concludes with a synthesis of the participants' insights about the current status of deliberate efforts to appropriately educate young adolescents, their predictions about the future challenges of middle school education, as well as their recommendations for future action and advocacy on behalf of young adolescents and the schools that serve them.

The Ideology and Identity of Middle School Education

The earliest leaders in the middle school movement were determined to right the wrongs in the way that young adolescents were being educated. They wanted to address the shortcomings in the junior high school that had become too much like the senior high school. They had many clear ideas about how middle school education should look, and they possessed honorable motives for initiating change on behalf of young adolescents. In those early days, however, their individual ideas were as varied as their backgrounds. Many of the leaders were spread out geographically. In their fervor for the cause, they devoted their energy to making middle schools look and operate differently from their junior high school predecessors. It was some years before they began collectively examining and articulating their ideology about middle school education. In retrospect, some of the early leaders consider this a great weakness of the movement. With their common goal of improving education for young adolescents through action and advocacy and with their shared, passionate ideas directed toward positive change, the early participants met the prerequisite conditions for initiating a social and educational movement. However, Beane, some years later, lamented that "the movement failed to take on any kind of social sense of itself; failing to stand for something in a larger societal sense has been an obstacle in the movement." Instead, he believes that the movement tried to elevate puberty to the level of an ideology rather than to articulate clearly an ideology grounded in philosophy (his preference being democratic education) that is concerned with meeting the various, changing needs of young adolescents. Similarly, Arnold stated, "We've never had a clear enough vision of what we want for kids. I believe we need to embody the progressive education understanding that the aim of education is the development of good people. It's who people are that counts—their character, attitudes, values, integrity."

Some of our participants believed that early leaders did have a clear ideology, one grounded in progressive education. Among them were Arnold, Beane, Dickinson, Doda, George, and Lounsbury, who described the middle school movement as "progressive education in contemporary dress." Perhaps it was not a lack of ideology that impaired the movement but a failure to communicate that ideology clearly, widely, loudly, or consistently enough. Conceivably, those in the schools who heard and were supportive were necessarily so occupied with the organizational work and clarifying the purposes of the movement that limited time and opportunity were left to advocate for the philosophy. Doda reflected as follows:

> One of the things I am struck by as I look back on those early conversations in middle school is that we were so caught up in this passion to bring feeling and heart to the middle school, to the school, to the institution, to the lives of children. So desperate to create school in which whole human beings could be celebrated and valued, that children would be honored as human beings as well as students. And all that remains very critical in education, but because we were so passionate about that part of the story, we didn't articulate as clearly as we should have the connection between affect and academic achievement in learning.

Doda's comments corroborate the idea that passion and dedication among the leaders were almost tangible but that they did not communicate their message clearly to those outside middle school education. Therefore, the public was left to draw its own conclusions about middle school education. Doda believes that they, therefore, interpreted that middle schools were really just "soft, warm, fuzzy places that really weren't about deep intellectual learning."

Lipsitz expressed some of the same concerns about failure to communicate widely enough:

> Sometimes when you start something, you need for it to be protected and small and in a hothouse. But after that, if you really want to have an impact,

you have to ask not who the true believers are, but who the true believers need to be and how you can make that happen. In the end, I think, there could have been greater impact early on had a more strategic set of alliances been forged into the world of research, into the world of public policy setting, into the major political forces in urban education. It was a boutique movement for too long.

However, communicating the vision and ideology of the middle school movement to those outside of it is not the only issue. In addition, there has always been some level of disagreement about the collective middle school identity within members of the movement. This disagreement has not necessarily been a liability, however. Many of our participants suggested that a strength of the middle school movement has been that it has been open to debate. These debates among leaders have often resulted in important collective milestones. For example, in 1981, John Swaim was elected president of NMSA. He had been involved in NMSA since the mid-1970s, and he realized that the organization had a problem. For several years they had been meeting, and people across the country had been committing their professional lives to middle school education. However, the organization had no official position or set of principles to support and promote middle school education. Swaim appointed a committee to develop a position statement with a clear definition of the middle school. The committee was comprised of William Alexander, Al Arth (chair), Charles Cherry (Virginia school principal), Donald Eichhorn, John Lounsbury (editor), Conrad Toepfer, and Gordon Vars. John Swaim recalled thinking that it might take about six months for the group to write the document. In the end, it took about two and a half years. Swaim stated,

> I can almost guarantee you every word was fought over in that document. We just about lost a couple members off of that committee that were going to resign from the committee. I still have the letters from them, saying that we were defining middle school too much and that middle school was more of a philosophy and we were trying to make a checklist out of it. John Lounsbury worked with me and convinced those people to continue. The document went through several revisions, but the first *This We Believe* ended up identifying ten "Essential Elements of a 'True' Middle School." However, eventually it got turned into more or less of a checklist in many respects. But it was a start. I think there is room in middle school for interpretation of how to implement the middle school concept but firm agreement on the concept itself. Even our founders, in those early years, had their differences. I think some of those debates still go on, but maybe in a little different arena.

In 1982, the National Middle School Association published *This We Believe,* its landmark position statement about the organization's vision for schools for young adolescents. Many of our participants cite the publication of this document as one of the most significant events in the history of the middle school movement because it "gave schools a set of standards and a philosophy to implement" (Bergmann). Subsequent editions of *This We Believe* were published in 1995, 2003, and 2010, as participants in middle level education have continued to learn and grow and debate ideas. Paul George spoke to the power of evolving ideas: "You know, the middle school concept is a cauldron of ideas, and that's one of the things that has kept me interested all these years is that we keep unfolding what the middle school means."

Though these debates and struggles to come to agreement have often pushed the movement forward, they have also led to what some see as the movement having two distinct wings. Beane explained:

> Think about the middle school movement as having two wings, one much larger than the other. The largest one is what I would call the mainstream middle school movement. And that is people who are certainly caring about young adolescents. They speak well of young adolescents and they seem to enjoy young adolescents. But they're mostly interested in structural changes in the middle schools and in a sense, as we used to say with the curriculum work, what they are interested in is trying to find what bait to put on the hook to pull the kids in. So, there is that kind of mainstream group and it is the largest group and they have been incredibly important and they are extremely well intentioned and I have great respect for them. And then there is the other wing, to which I would belong, which is the progressive wing of the middle school movement. This wing is trying to be responsive to young adolescents, but also believes that the movement should be addressing larger social issues and obligations. In 1968, in a conversation with Connie Toepfer, he said to me: "You know, the thing about most educators, child-centered educators, is they don't understand that if you really love children you have to hate the things that crush their souls. You have to hate racism. You have to hate sexism. You have to hate poverty." I never forgot that. And I think probably if I were to explain my work in the middle school movement, it wouldn't be about trying to find a way to integrate subject areas, it would be about a search for democratic curriculum and a curriculum with a social conscience.

The middle school ideology, then, has been characterized somewhat differently for those who have spent much of their professional lives inside it. At its core is the intent to provide the best possible education for young adolescents. Individuals who have been involved have established their own positions about how that education might look and even why it is important. Among our participants, the attraction to educating young adolescents has often had a spiritual dimension. It has been called a moral imperative (Doda, Erb) and a mission (George, Johnston, Lounsbury). Bergmann explained that "there was such a commitment, such a deep, unselfish involvement in bettering the education and lives of children in that age group that you just couldn't help but be brought into it." Perhaps the middle school movement is still in search of its ideology and identity, and perhaps the efforts to continue the search, to keep moving forward toward the quest for an appropriate education for young adolescents, has been what has kept so many involved in the journey.

Implementation of the Various and Collective Components of the Middle School Philosophy

Most of our participants who discussed the implementation of middle school practices and programs characterized it as disappointing and too focused on structural changes. Sue Swaim described the current status of implementing the middle school ideal:

> One of the challenges we're facing today is that there are still too many middle schools that too narrowly define themselves. They may have changed the school's name and grade configuration from junior high to middle school; they may have even started to implement some of the middle level organizational structures such as teaming or block scheduling, but they only began the journey and have stalled out. They haven't implemented teaming or block scheduling to their fullest possibilities. They still talk about interdisciplinary units of study done periodically throughout the year rather than a more fully integrated curriculum on a daily basis. In too many places the middle level concept has never been fully implemented with consistency over time. Too many states still do not prepare teachers or administrators specifically to teach this age group in the same way they require professional preparation for elementary and high school educators. However, we have schools and school districts throughout our country that have fully implemented the middle school concept, and they prove this thing called *middle school* works. These schools have also made commitments to provide ongoing professional development and to hire new teachers specifically prepared in middle level education whenever possible. It's going to take this type of consistent commitment over time to reach the goal of successful middle schools for all young adolescents.

Some of the traditional components of middle school organization are easy to sell and fairly easy to implement. For example, many of our participants pointed out that teachers and schools were attracted to the idea of teaming. Teachers were drawn to the idea of collaboration and affiliation with their colleagues and students. Therefore, middle schools quickly organized teachers into teams. However, they often lost sight of the *purposes* of teaming and other middle school practices. Lounsbury lamented that one of his greatest disappointments in the development of the middle school movement has been the

> failure of teams to take advantage of common planning time and to take advantage of the opportunity to improve curriculum. I think in part we made great strides forward, and teaming has become well established, and well it should, but because we organized our teams by subject area, we still tended to teach by subject area, and if you go into most middle schools today, with teams, they are still largely departmentalized in their instruction. With limited exception, an occasional interdisciplinary unit, and an occasional correlation, but by and large most middle schools still teach subjects. So I think that's been a big disappointment that we haven't taken advantage of the concept of teaming with common planning time to really alter curriculum and instruction. We've done a great job of dealing with kids and their needs. We've done a good job of taking care of a lot of things in common planning time—meeting with parents, avoiding getting tests on the same day and those sorts of things—but we really haven't taken advantage of what teaming really is designed to do.

While teaming in an organizational sense has been a fairly easy practice to implement, advisory has not. Vars suggested that "the mechanics of making an advisory group work, especially if all teachers are required to take a group, are destroying the whole concept." He explained that the intent of advisory programs is to provide a "guidance" element to a young adolescent's middle school experience. Vars believes that teams should be given the freedom to decide how they will incorporate the advisory responsibility into their work. He believes that teachers who have an aptitude or willingness to do advisory should be given that opportunity. He also contends that advisory cannot be relegated to a particular time of the school day: "A kid doesn't wait until advisory period to have a spat with his girlfriend or to have a crisis come up. The team has to get on it right when it happens, and therefore, it needs to be embedded in the team."

Stevenson believes that one of the major mistakes made in implementing middle school practices and programs was that it was too incremental, that leaders tried to implement middle school practices a little at a time. Perhaps they organized teachers into teams one year and then implemented an advisory program the following year. Now, he's convinced that "overhauling a traditional school to move it in the direction of the middle level concept must be done in large strokes." He maintains that "kids seem to handle big changes easily" and to "welcome them." He says that early on "the logic of making changes incrementally seduced" him. This same logic has clearly influenced change in middle level education, often with a partial or half-hearted attempt at implementation. John Swaim concurred that "a lot of middle schools that made the pragmatic changes never made the philosophical changes." He contends that "we still have a lot of those out there." Sue Swaim also argued that "you can't just tinker with the education of young adolescents. You've got to go the full mile with it." She further explained that the recommendations and characteristics of what make a successful middle school are interrelated. For example, providing a positive learning environment means addressing students' safety, wellness, and learning styles. Adults work together in middle schools for the purpose of ensuring that the curriculum is challenging, motivating, relevant, and engaging.

Middle school leaders and innovators can no longer have a checklist or menu mentality about implementing best practices for middle level schooling. Such an approach is too simplistic to provide for the complex needs of young adolescents. Johnston warned about "procedural orthodoxy." He explained that local middle school leaders "must embrace deep commitments to produce high achievement, to be developmentally responsive, and to promote social equity" while also taking into consideration the unique needs of the students and community served by a particular middle school. In other words, the commitment to ideals must be steadfast, but the implementation of practices must be somewhat flexible. McEwin recounted a prophetic warning Alexander made very early in the middle school movement: "He [Bill] said we had to be really careful and not standardize the middle school. One of the problems with the junior high school was that it became the same everywhere; it became standardized." McEwin maintained that "there are certain essential elements that ought to be in every middle school, but how those are implemented depends on the students and teachers and the community."

Rather than providing a list of required characteristics or components, Arnold proposed that, in developing middle schools, four key questions need to be addressed *in order*:

(1) *Who?* Who are these students we are trying to educate? What are their needs, interests and abilities? This is the developmental question. (2) *What?* What do they need to know now, and are likely to need to know in the future, to meet their needs, interests and abilities? This is the curriculum question. (3) *How?* What strategies and techniques shall we use to teach the content and skills that meet the students' needs, interests, and abilities? This is the methodology question. (4) How can we structure the school experience so that it best facilitates the methods and curriculum to meet student's needs? This is the school organization question.

Arnold believes that many schools have failed to address the first three questions adequately, and in fact, they have reversed the order of the questions: "They've started with and been preoccupied by the organization question. Once the organization is set, that of course limits what kinds of methods and curriculum you can develop, and then you can only hope that kids' needs will be met."

The good news is that we now have a growing body of research to support empirically the implementation of middle school practices and structures. McEwin discussed in his interview and has found in his research that middle schools that more authentically follow the middle school concept (e.g., interdisciplinary team organization) have higher standardized test scores in reading and mathematics than do randomly selected middle schools (McEwin & Greene, 2010). Other studies have found that middle schools that have high levels of implementation of programs and practices associated with the middle school concept have higher achievement scores than schools that have only partially implemented the middle school plan (Backes, Ralston, & Ingwalson, 1999; Felner, Jackson, Kasak, Mulhall, Brand, & Flowers, 1997; Mertens & Flowers, 2006; Mertens, Flowers, & Mulhall, 1998). He stated that "the more middle school the middle school, the higher the standardized test scores."

Indeed, these findings are significant, for they provide much-needed evidence for leaders who advocate for middle school practices. To realize the ideal of appropriate education for young adolescents, we must have leaders committed to whole-hearted implementation. Vars stated, "People want the shape of a middle school but aren't willing to do the hard work of developing staff, students, and parents who support the kind of education that . . . is needed." It is time for middle school leaders to roll up their sleeves and get to (or back to) the labor of full-scale implementation of appropriate education for young adolescents.

Unique Needs of Young Adolescents

While our participants expressed mixed feelings individually and collectively about the success of the middle school movement to communicate effectively a clear ideology and then to implement best practices in schools based on those ideals, their opinions about the movement's efforts to respond to the needs of young adolescents were less varied. Clearly, they believe that young adolescents have benefitted from the efforts of middle school initiatives. Beane spoke emphatically about this element of the movement:

There's no question that young adolescents have benefited enormously from the middle school movement. That is so even in the most mainstream middle schools where people haven't really pushed the edges of the concept. I think more teachers than ever are more understanding and responsive to young adolescents. I think there is in schools a much greater understanding of kids than ever before. The greatest asset of the middle school movement has been a serious and more than rhetorical commitment to young adolescents. I really think that today that there are overwhelming numbers of people working in middle level schools who really do identify themselves as middle level educators, and one of the identifying features would be that they work with these young adolescents and they enjoy them.

Lipsitz's recollection helps us understand the magnitude of our progress in this area. She explained that when she wrote *Growing Up Forgotten* (1977), early adolescence was a "non-field." In her research, she discovered that a lack of attention to young adolescents was not an education anomaly. The age group was also not being studied or written about in the medical community or in social science areas such as psychology and sociology. She found that in the early 1970s, in all of the United States and Canada, there were only 15 residencies in adolescent medicine. She recalled her amazement at this lack of available research and information:

It was stunning to me that this age group was a non-field. It wasn't just about what was going on or not going on in schools; it was about what wasn't going on for a completely pivotal age group in the lifespan. It was amazing to me that you could have an age group that everybody knew was important and that nobody was willing to pay attention to.

Now, nearly 50 years after Alexander proposed the middle school in 1963 and nearly 40 years after the publication of *Growing Up Forgotten* (1977), millions of young adolescents have benefitted from an approach to education that was specifically conceived to attend to their needs. On the day of his interview, George (2003) heard Joycelyn Elders speak at a general session of the National Middle School Association annual conference. He commented on her remarks:

Joycelyn Elders today mentioned that there are 20 million young adolescents in middle school today. If you multiply 20 million by 30 years, I think you can say that by any means the last two generations of young adolescents have been the direct recipients of innovative education and benefited from it immeasurably far more than they would have had the middle school movement not been there for them.

Certainly, since Lipsitz brought national attention to young adolescence in the late 1970s, we have seen improvements in the lives of many young adolescents. However, our interview participants readily noted some areas where continued growth is needed to move the ideals of middle school education forward. Several of our participants indicated that, in the beginning, the middle school movement was strongest in suburban, white communities (see Beane, Doda, Johnston, for example). While the "larger assumption of the middle school movement was that every single child should have a first class seat" and "equal access and opportunity to the best curriculum, the best teachers, the best resources, and the richest learning opportunities we have" (Doda), this ideal has not yet been realized. The participants we interviewed believe reaching all young adolescents, regardless of their social, cultural, or academic status, is a challenge and opportunity for the next generation of middle level education leaders. Doda spoke earnestly about the need to broaden and intensify the scope of middle level education:

> Our most vulnerable students are the very students in middle school who need heightened affiliation, heightened intimacy, heightened connection with human beings, long-term accountability relationships with adults and other kids. They need environments that are extremely safe and trusting circles of friendship and security, and we've diminished the emphasis on that in the name of test accountability, and so ironically, in the short term, while things may shift and appear to be favorable for test scores, ultimately it will bottom out and those children who have needed those wonderful elements of middle school, the strong affiliation focus, will suffer and the gap will widen again.

> I keep hoping that people will get it, that they will get the connection between affiliation and academic accomplishment that it will become eminently clear that if you want to make a difference in the lives of children you have to let children be an incredible interruption in your life, which means that children have to be a part of the middle school experience, and we can't just *do* school to them, and I do think that there are people out there that do get that and maybe the contrast is becoming clearer as there is less and less of that good stuff, and problems start mounting in schools that people will become, like in the Columbine post window of time, a little bit more aware that you can't create good middle schools without that kind of affiliation.

Beane suggested that the lack of authentic middle schools in urban areas is a "two-way street." While he agrees that the middle school movement has not had a deliberate enough reach into urban areas, he also believes that "many of the administrators, central office, and others in large urban areas believe, like the general society, that poor kids of color need structure of the sort that is the drill and kill and rote memorization and that's antithetical to what we think of as the middle school concept." Beane further elaborated that the National Middle School Association has had some involvement from people of color but that, given the percentage of young adolescents in the United States who are in urban middle schools, it has not been nearly enough. Perhaps urban centers are the next frontier for middle school education.

Participants such as Doda, Gatewood, and Lounsbury spoke about the power of middle schools to provide places of affiliation for young adolescents and that such affiliation is connected to academic accomplishment and positive self-esteem. Lounsbury discussed the power of middle school education to affect the future: "Government can't do it, family can't even do it anymore, church can't do it anymore, and I regret that, but the middle school is the one place where we really have a chance to make a difference." Certainly the public who funds education wants to see young people who are connected to their schools and communities, who are achieving academically, and who feel good about themselves. In fact, to those inside the movement, advocacy for young adolescents likely seemed so morally justified that it might have seemed inconceivable that anyone could dispute it. However, Johnston warned that we have, at times, promised too much and therefore opened ourselves to criticism:

> When you promise much, and we do, if you fail to deliver on those promises you become the target of criticism. And in some respects we promise too much, I think. We're going to take care of the kids' self-esteem; we're going to make them literate, we're going to make them smart; we're going to make them well-adjusted, decent human beings; we're going to make them functional members of society; we're going to make them good neighbors; we're going to make them contributing members of their communities. Man, that's a tall order! You run the risk of having such a long shopping list of promises that if you don't do any of them well or even if you do 80% of them well, you're still not doing everything you promised you were going to do.

Finally, as with most aspects of education, we must communicate more effectively about young adolescents and their needs. We cannot let the portrayals of young adolescents in the media prevail as the public's perception of reality. Rather, we must emphasize the "wonderful, rich, beautiful, intellectual, philosophical, and spiritual side of [adolescent] development" (Doda).

The Reorganization of Middle Schools

Using the definition of middle schools as those containing grades 5–8, 6–8, and 7–8, there were 4,884 middle schools in the United States in 1970. By 2008, there were 13,227 middle schools with those organizational plans (McEwin & Greene, 2010). In addition, several of our participants believe that we have now reached a professional and public consensus about what middle schools look like. Beane described the consensus as follows:

> I think people have really come to expect middle schools and to expect them to be of a certain form. I think it is true that it has become more standardized. Despite protests about the litany of characteristics that would make up a middle school, there generally is such a litany. I think when most people talk about middle schools, they mean four-person teams, an exploratory program, an advisory program, a block time schedule, and so on.

Dickinson noted that one of the successes of the movement is that people understand that the middle school is focused on development. Erb claimed that "we now have a pretty strong research basis for interdisciplinary team organization in middle schools" and that team organization is a "better way to organize the delivery of core curriculum in schools for young adolescents than are separate, uncoordinated classes." George pointed out that we now have a common understanding that "teachers that share the same students make more sense than teachers that share the same subject when it comes to the education of young adolescents" and that "no one anywhere quarrels with the idea of interdisciplinary team organization."

Many of the organizational approaches in middle schools are related to matters of ideology, implementation, and responsiveness to young adolescents that have already been discussed. Lounsbury and Arnold discussed the importance of "smallness" in schooling for young adolescents: "Smallness has become a recognized factor in correlation with quality and that's why we've tried to develop looping, and multi-age teaming, and schools within a school. Things that create a sense of smallness and a continuity of relationship" (Lounsbury). Doda recalled that during her years teaching at Lincoln Middle School, teachers kept the same students for three years. At the end of the eighth grade year, students would line up to say good-bye with "tears and hugs and this magnificent display of affection." Meanwhile, she stated, "at the junior high just down the road the kids would be racing out the door." She remembered that people were always stunned by the contrast and often asked "What are you doing with those children?" Doda recounted with warmth, "We loved them, and we were committed to them, and we knew that we were more than facilitators of academic learning. We knew that we were committed to the whole child, and we took that very seriously." By creating small teams and communities within larger educational organizations, middle school professionals have been able to accomplish much on behalf of young adolescents.

Despite the progress and popularity of middle school organization and the proven success of middle school practices, organizational issues are not without controversy. Some middle school leaders remarked that the middle school movement became too preoccupied with organizational aspects of schools or "procedural orthodoxy" (Johnston). Lipsitz stated a concern that organization could become an excuse for not serving young adolescents adequately: "I don't want to give anybody an excuse, 'Oh, we didn't have the right grade organization, so I couldn't teach them.'" Rather, she explained that the focus in a middle school should be on how and what is taught: "To think you can change the grade organization of a school and thereby have an impact on outcomes without changing your approach to the culture of the school and the curriculum and the instruction, is just diversionary. The issue is what we do in those schools with those kids, whatever the grade organization."

Some of the research participants expressed a belief that, in recent years, the organizational focus has been changing to a more flexible understanding of middle schools:

> I think the concept has certainly adapted to changing conditions. And I think that the early years of the middle school were characterized by these sorts of lists of features that comprise the institution and if you had the right list of features, you were doing okay. I think the emphasis now has shifted, rightfully so, and in the last dozen years or so the emphasis has been on how all of these things come together and how they work. I also think there's also a fair amount of interest in alternative ways of organizing things for middle level kids. (Johnston)

The reorganization of middle-level schools in America has been profound and far-reaching: "Middle school is now a part of the education establishment" (Gatewood). With the restructuring work behind us, middle school leaders can hope that the best is yet to come, that we are now positioned to get to the work of developing and providing the best possible services and education within those structures to maximize the potential of young adolescents as the brightest human capital on earth.

The Influence of the Middle School on American Education

As part of this research project, we asked participants, "What effect has the middle school movement had on American education?" Their responses covered a wide range of influences. Perhaps the most obvious influence they reported was that the middle school has changed the structure and continuum of American schools and schooling from a two-tiered system of elementary and secondary (which included a junior and senior high school) to a three-tiered system of elementary, middle, and high school. Gatewood characterized this as middle school's greatest contribution to American education:

> I believe the greatest contribution that middle school has made to American education is legitimizing an organization in the middle grades that is truly unique. . . . I think it is clearly accepted. I think that the public has accepted middle school as a school, as an organization. I think there is a general feeling that it needs to be different from elementary, different from high school but it's a necessary, separate entity of its own.

Arth agreed that this was a very significant, positive development: "We use the term [middle school] now and it stands for something; it stands for a different program." He described this recognition of middle school as a unique institution as a "fantastic breakthrough." Lounsbury concurred that "we've remade the face of American education, no question about it. Middle school is now seen and heard everywhere." John Swaim stated that "people now know what a middle school is, or at least recognize it as the structure in the K–12 continuum." Arth and Swaim both commented on the relatively quick life of this transition. For example, Swaim emphasized, "It [the middle school movement] has been one of the most rapidly developing movements that has changed the whole system of American education."

Other contributions cited included the contribution of middle school education to the organizational structure of schools. Gatewood, for example, suggested that the concept of teaming communities in the middle school continues to be unique. Others commented on the more general approach of middle schools to develop smaller learning communities as mechanisms for providing affiliation for young adolescents and their teachers. Doda and Johnston, for example, noted that the middle school's approach to small learning communities is affecting school reform at the secondary level:

There has been a clear invitation from the middle school that there needed to be change at the secondary level, and now with the small schools movement and the Gates Foundation's monies devoted to reforming the American high school, it's no surprise to me that much of the high school reform could be traced back to the early developments in middle school and then the later invitation through *Breaking Ranks* and other documents to rethink the high school model. (Doda)

Interestingly enough, I work now extensively in high school reform initiatives and a lot of what is being considered to be innovative practice for high school reform has been going on in middle schools for thirty years. Smaller communities, student advocates, a focused, interdisciplinary hands-on curriculum, lots of real life experiences—it's all there. John Lounsbury and those guys were writing about that stuff forty years ago and I think it's had tremendous impact on what we expect of our schools. I think we expect them to be whole-child focused and compassionate, and we expect them to be developmentally responsive. And I think we have raised the bar for all school reform efforts in this country. (Johnston)

Arnold mentioned the importance of smallness and summarized a number of other contributions middle schools have made to American education:

Certainly it [the middle school movement] has caused education to focus more on young adolescents and to take their education more seriously. I think it's had a significant effect on interdisciplinary curriculum development, and also on scheduling practices. Its attempts to create smallness out of bigness have influenced the high school house system. It has given a big boost to advisories. The camaraderie and the spirit the middle school movement has engendered I think have spill-over effects to American education in general. It has surely affected clearly the lives of the kids, teachers, and professors involved.

Another contribution to American education and perhaps to American society in general is that the middle school movement has raised awareness of young adolescence as an important and distinct developmental stage. Beane stated that "we have brought a lot of attention outside of the middle level movement to young adolescents. Let's face it: people know who we are. They know what we stand for. So I think we've definitely impacted American education."

In spite of these great contributions to American education, not all news is good. Johnston suggested that "middle schools have been unfairly targeted as the weak link in the system.... The institution has never caught the imagination, or the commitment, of the American people to the extent that it deserves." Perhaps lack of recognition in public policy and federal legislation is partly to blame for the inconsistency between a public *acknowl-*

edgement in the legitimacy of middle schools and public *action* to support them. Sue Swaim, for example, expressed disappointment that, after all these years and after so much progress toward legitimizing American middle schools,

> America's largest single education act is The Elementary and Secondary Education Act.... The word 'middle school' or 'middle level' isn't in that title nor is it mentioned anywhere in the law. It appears we only have a two-tier educational system when we have a three-tier system in the vast majority of our country. People in Washington, DC will tell you "secondary" is the term that serves both middle school and high school, but the funding actually designated to middle level doesn't bear that out. Without this recognition, you experience challenges in areas that elementary or high school people do not. Examples not only include difficulty in receiving specific funding for middle level needs in areas such as reading or science, but the recent discovery that federal research data doesn't support a disaggregation of information for middle level researchers.

Without governmental support of middle schools as a critical, unique tier in the American education system, we will continue to struggle for public support and commitment.

John Swaim suggested, "Any time you gain status and you are starting to do pretty well, then people start looking at negative things. I think we are in for a period of time that people are looking for what's wrong with middle level education. That is not all bad. I think we need to take a look at ourselves and be forced to justify why we're doing what we are doing." The optimists among us may find hope in Swaim's statement: "We are doing well." However, optimism without action at this critical time in our history is meaningless. As Swaim suggested, middle level leaders must rise to the challenges of retrospection and introspection. We must examine our motives, our advocacy, our practices, and our role in American education. We must work collaboratively to rededicate ourselves to present and future generations of young adolescents.

The Implementation of Appropriate Curriculum for Young Adolescents

As we began to code the transcript data from this project for topics and themes, the topic with the most "coverage" across our participants was *curriculum*. This should not be surprising since Alexander, Lounsbury, Vars, and Toepfer—four of the five founders of the middle school movement—had advanced graduate education in curriculum. Dickinson asserted that "we happen to be blessed with one of the best curriculum minds in this century—as the father of our movement [William Alexander]. Now that goes a long way to give us legitimacy from the early 1960s." John Swaim recalled some of the first efforts to organize a national effort to support middle grades education. In 1972, there was a meeting at the annual conference of the Association for Supervision and Curriculum Development (ASCD) about starting a special interest group in ASCD that focused on middle school education. Swaim remembered that Toepfer, Lounsbury, and Eichhorn were there, trying to convince ASCD to start a special interest group or subgroup for middle school. "The tone of the conversation," Swaim recounted, "was that ASCD was not interested." So, originally there was an effort to start a middle school initiative through ASCD, to develop a closer tie with curriculum, and get into an organization that was already established. Since this effort was not successful, middle school leaders looked to the Midwest Middle School Association to broaden its reach to become a national association.

Vars's emphatic response to our question about the "influence of the middle school movement on curriculum and instruction" demonstrates his deep roots in curriculum:

> I jotted down a question mark on that because I'm not sure I understand that question. How has the middle school movement influenced middle level curriculum and instruction? The movement *is* curriculum and instruction! If it is viewed as just organizational, then it isn't middle level education.... They are two sides of the same coin. Organizational structure and all of that should serve the curriculum, and the curriculum should serve the student.

In spite of the rich curriculum heritage of the middle school movement, and perhaps because of it, almost all of our research participants expressed disappointment about the implementation of appropriate curriculum for young adolescents. Arnold stated, for example, "I think curriculum, outside of the interdisciplinary emphasis, has been one of the most neglected things in the middle school movement." Similarly, Dickinson lamented, "If there's one indictment of the movement—that is one ... that we did not pay attention to the curriculum probably from day one as we should have because we had an inheritance from the junior high school with the separate subject curriculum which we should have looked at as part of our organizational changes and we didn't." George concurred that "our influence on what the curriculum is has been far less than what our influences have been on school organization like team organization, flexible schedules and that sort of thing. I don't think the curriculum is very different than it was when the Committee of Ten laid it out" in the 1890s. Doda called the publication of James Beane's book, *A Middle School Curriculum: From Rhetoric to Reality* (1990), a huge landmark in the history of the middle school movement because it "jarred folks into recognition that we hadn't paid attention to the curriculum. We had been working on structure and scheduling and advisory programs and we really didn't have this deeper curriculum investigation going on so that was huge for the middle school movement." An examination of various models of curriculum development for young adolescents is outside the scope of this book; however, a synthesis of the participants' comments obligates us to emphasize their position that we have not adequately and collectively examined, discussed, articulated, organized, or implemented an appropriate curriculum for young adolescents.

Though our participants could not report widespread progress in implementing appropriate curriculum for young adolescents, they did mention several smaller successes. For example, Arth pointed out the extensive availability of materials and resources for the age group: "Walk through any National Middle School Association convention in the past four to six years. There are materials for middle school kids. There were none when we first started. There are materials, there are programs, there are people recognizing that teachers need separate involvement with materials; it's been a heavy influence on the curriculum." Beane and Stevenson expressed their deep respect and admiration for middle school teachers who have designed and implemented curriculum specifically intended to meet the needs of young adolescents. Beane explained that curriculum theories were enacted in teachers' classrooms and that the teachers' work "shaped the sense of what a progressive and democratic middle school curriculum looks like." He emphasized that "in terms of influence, the teachers who were doing the work with democratic and integrative curriculum in the 1990s were influential in enormous ways if you think about what was happening in the 1990s at NMSA conferences. These teachers would go into a room to present about the units they were doing or to talk about how they involved kids in planning and assessment and so on. There would be 500 people in those rooms to listen to these teachers talk about what they were doing. And I think they generated a new wave of excitement in the 1990s." Stevenson also mentioned glimpses of promise in curriculum development and implementation:

> Through innovation and integrated curricular programs, we've been able to demonstrate that organic learning is a real thing, and it can be seen and understood and it is in evidence when conditions are changed to truly integrate curriculum.... There are many brilliant examples of such fabulous curriculum work. Judy Carr and I put together a project with Vermont teachers that resulted in a book, *Integrated Studies in the Middle Grades: Danc-*

ing Through Walls. That's the kind of work that has taught me beyond any shadow of a doubt that we can create learning experiences at school that children will thrive in, that they will mature rapidly through, and through which they will grow into better citizens and better human beings for themselves and others. When we get the conditions right in our schools, amazing things come to pass.

Beane and Stevenson remembered fondly specific moments and times when curriculum innovation on behalf of young adolescents was alive, but like many other participants, they spoke with regret about missed opportunities. Beane elaborated an historical view of curriculum opportunities that the movement missed:

> I believe that the door has been opened on two occasions for the middle school movement to take seriously the question, "What should be the middle school curriculum?" One was in the late 1970s when Vars and Lounsbury published *Curriculum for the Middle School Years* and tried to bring back to life the concept of the core program. I remember the publication of that book. I remember how excited I was about it. People I was working with at the time started into curriculum conversations and started debating, "Is that how it should look?" and so on and so forth. So that was one moment for a door opening for the curriculum question. The other moment was in the 1990s when the work around the integrated and democratic curriculum got started through NMSA. I think we opened that door, and I think it was a mistake for the Association not to see that as the next move for the whole movement. I don't mean to say, by the way, that the Association should necessarily have opened their arms and coffers to those of us who were doing the really progressive work. But they could have used the work that we were doing as a moment to really do a hard look at the curriculum.

Beane's recollection that the "door has been opened" for curriculum innovation two times makes us hope that there will be another time when the door of opportunity will swing open and that there will be middle level education leaders waiting to go through the door to begin the complex, rewarding work of developing and implementing appropriate curriculum for young adolescents. Better yet, perhaps we have middle level leaders reading this book who are not willing to wait, who will storm the door of curriculum innovation on behalf of young adolescents who deserve a curriculum that honors their questions, their interests, and their intellect.

Participants mentioned several hindrances or barriers that have prevented maximum success in the development of a curriculum appropriate for young adolescents. Interestingly, while most candidates agreed that the middle school movement had been open to debate, Beane, who has valued and participated in these debates, suggested that some of the curriculum debates have been detrimental to progress in that area. He and George debated issues related to integrative middle school curriculum in several public venues, several hosted by the National Middle School Association. He argued that one problem with having these open debates hosted by NMSA was that people walked away thinking that NMSA did not have a clear position about curriculum issues and that it apparently recognized multiple positions. Subsequently, Beane maintained that this situation was unfortunate because people walked away believing nearly any position about curriculum was acceptable. Beane also said that the nature of the protests against integrative curriculum is not usually about its appropriateness for young adolescents; rather, "most of the opposition that was raised had to do with the skill of teachers or problems with schedules and things like that. It never really got to be a debate about the organization of the curriculum."

Doda suggested that many middle school leaders in the 1970s and 1980s were focused on restructuring rather than re-culturing schools. They spent most of their energy on the question of "How do we organize schools in the middle?" versus "What do we teach kids in the middle?" Because making the transition from junior high to middle schools seemed such a large task, Doda maintained that middle level leaders took a sequential rather than integral approach. They began by re-organizing the schools with an intention to get back to issues of curriculum; however, the re-organization took so much effort and time that they never got back to the curriculum, in many cases.

More recently, curriculum innovation has clearly been hindered by federal, state, and local mandates. Doda lamented that teachers have been telling her that they have pacing guides and that the pacing guides are such that they are departmentalized and lock teachers into curriculum organization that follows a certain linear sequence. Such a limited view of the purpose and implementation of pacing guides limits the time that teachers will sit down with their interdisciplinary team and map their curriculum and look for connections across the curriculum. Doda stated that this development "scares me more than anything." Doda had a teacher recently tell her that in her building, teachers have to all be on the same page the same month, the same day on the same topic and that as a new teacher that she is hardly willing to worry about the needs of kids because *she has got to get through this curriculum* (italics added for emphasis). This teacher's interpretation of the local priorities of her district demonstrates her belief that the district values curriculum coverage over responsiveness to students' needs.

Perhaps the greatest contemporary impediment to curriculum innovation for young adolescents has been a proliferation of public policies and practices that compel schools and teachers to segment knowledge for the purpose of making teaching and the assessing of it more "efficient." Erb explained that "high-stakes tests tend to limit the curriculum to easily testable skills in separate disciplines." Similarly, this segmenting mindset is "forcing the development of a new definition of a highly qualified teacher for the middle level. It's having a negative impact on our movement towards integrated curriculum and teachers who are knowledgeable in two subject areas" (S. Swaim). As a result, when teachers are forced to hyper-focus on one content area, they are less able to spend intellectual time and energy developing more integrated curriculum. In addition, a subject-focused approach to curriculum tends to make schools organize themselves into departments by subject area, which provides limited opportunities for interaction with teachers in other disciplines. In addition, curriculum dialogue becomes constrained by budget decisions that have led to discontinuing interdisciplinary teaming and funding for professional and curriculum development not directly connected to raising test scores. The fate of integrated curriculum, therefore, is often determined more by outside factors than by any debate about its educational merits. It seems important here to distinguish between our participants' perspectives on standards and standardization. Most of our participants valued academic standards. Erb, for example, discussed that

> when scholarly associations and state departments of education develop standards about what students should know about history, geography, mathematics, science, economics, life skills, the arts, physical health and well-being, or English, they often tend to go beyond information to be memorized and isolated skills to learn. Standards tend to include problem-solving skills, inquiry-based learning, interdisciplinary connections, and applications to real-world activities. Juxtaposed to high-stakes tests, standards tend to expand the curriculum to make it richer and deeper.

Erb, Jphnston, Lipsitz, McEwin, and other participants expressed that they value standards and their potential to influence curriculum innovation for young adolescents. Without exception, it was the standardization of curriculum and the overemphasis on *standardized* tests that our participants opposed.

The tradition of a separate-subject approach to curriculum has also been a barrier to curriculum innovation for middle schools. Dickinson argued that "the separate-subject curriculum organization is inappropriate for young adolescent thinkers. It's antithetical to where they are in their larger thinking and their developmental orientation. I think that is something that a lot of people don't argue with any more, but I think we're also in a period of time where we have high-stakes testing, and we have a climate and culture that wants to know how Johnny or Susie scored on their history test, rather than what is their thinking about humanities topics." While Erb praised academic standards for their attention to valuing sophisticated knowledge in the disciplines, he expressed concern that "virtually all the standards are written from a separate disciplines perspective. Standards are written by discipline, and universities educate their teachers by disciplines. How are teachers to become aware of and skilled in interdisciplinary or integrated approaches to curriculum and instruction?" Erb discussed the tension between separate subject and interdisciplinary approaches: "At the same time the supports for disciplinary curriculum are being strengthened, the supports for interdisciplinary curriculum are being weakened."

Our participants had many observations about the nature of appropriate curriculum for young adolescents. Dickinson provided an historical and philosophical context for an appropriate middle school curriculum and credited Beane with continually raising our collective conscience about curriculum issues:

> The whole thrust of what middle school education is about is very much a Deweyan Progressive democratic school. And the secondary subject matter, separate orientation, does not match up with that well at all. I mean, everything is sliced and diced and organized and laid out and it's almost "swallow it now, and chew it later" in certain manifestations. So, one of the things that Jim [Beane] did was reminded us of our philosophical roots with integrated curriculum as a school that is supposed to be about the democratic ideal of helping these children develop and develop who they are, which means we need to be responsive and flexible and that an interdisciplinary, and integrated curriculum can do that.

Erb further supported the ideal of an integrated curriculum that involves young adolescents in making decisions about their learning:

> We have argued for a number of years, with increasing evidence to support our position, that the more a curriculum can be integrated the better it is, because you involve students in learning activities that are more natural and more meaningful. Consequently, students tend to learn various skills and knowledge based in different disciplines that enable them to perform better academically by solving integrated learning problems.

Stevenson offered a balanced and common-sense perspective on curriculum for young adolescents and warned against creating falsely dichotomous comparisons:

I think it has been falsely posited that it's integrated curriculum versus separate-subject curriculum because it's often easier to debate things when you can create two straw men and pit them against each other. However, through the process of integrating children's questions, ideas, concerns, priorities and personal goals into curriculum decisions, we are personalizing the learning experience and I know in the long run contributing much more to its durability than if we did not involve children in planning curriculum.... Integrated curriculum at the middle level entails building curriculum around the questions and curiosities and interests that children have. That is how to arouse the cognitive processes that are instrumental to learning and growing in healthy, productive ways.

Beane stated simply that "the road to rigor with young adolescents has to run through relevance." In the midst of the standards and accountability movement, and in spite of it, middle level leaders persist in their belief that young adolescents must be involved in making decisions about their learning. It is most centrally what defines an appropriate curriculum for the age group.

Given the history and origins of the middle school movement, it seems no surprise that thoughtful conversations about curriculum persist in the middle school ranks. Beane, often cited by our participants as one of the greatest and certainly most radical curriculum thinkers in our movement, explained his interest in curriculum work, especially at the middle school level:

I see the middle level as the ground for the most contentious of curriculum debates. It's the place where elementary and high school come together and becomes contested terrain. It's where the historic curriculum debates take on the most vivid forms: What should all kids learn? How should content be organized? And so on. People have an expectation in elementary schools that there can be some variety and it's not unusual to have units and things like that. At the high school, people clearly expect to have a straight, separate-subject program. They are not so sure at the middle level, and so it turns out to be tremendous debate. I think my interest in it, aside from the fact that I just really like young adolescents, has to do with the fact that my major field, which is curriculum development, really applies better at this level than at any other level.

In spite of a fairly widespread agreement about the appropriate nature of curriculum for young adolescents, our participants continually raised concerns about the current status of our efforts in this arena. With the benefit of an historical perspective, they were able to look back at the history of the movement and point to opportunities that had been missed to make substantial progress. For example, Beane, Bergmann, and Erb argued that the middle school movement has not worked hard enough to ensure exploratory opportunities for young adolescents. Bergmann pointed to the current "battle that we are fighting right now to keep the arts and exploratory programs in the middle school. There is a lot of research in the music and art fields that says that kids that have music and art do better in school. But that doesn't get publicized as that's why we have exploratory courses in the middle school." In addition to this research that Bergmann mentions, Erb linked opportunities for exploratory courses to the development of young adolescents who he believes ought to have choices and a chance to explore their talents and interests and not be shortchanged by being foreclosed prematurely. He contended, for example, that "educators should not be just picking the ten best students to be the cheerleading squad to the exclusion of all others. Instead, many middle schools provide opportunities for as many girls and boys who want to be involved. That is part of the middle school concept. If it is a good activity for young adolescents, then everybody who wants to ought to be able to do it." Not only have young adolescents been shortchanged by a lack of exploratory opportunities, but also Beane maintained that the exploratory teachers have been overlooked as a critical force in the implementation of appropriate curriculum:

> I would say exploratory teachers have not benefited from the middle school movement. If there is a single sort of mainstream idea in the middle school concept that has not been even remotely addressed, it's how to bring the exploratory teachers in from the edges of the curriculum. They really are overwhelmingly simply the place where the kids go while the "real" teachers plan. In a lot of schools that I have worked with, the exploratory teachers have been early leaders in pushing the middle school concept, but at the end of the day they certainly don't benefit from it and so a lot of them become pretty cynical about it.

As the emphasis on standardized tests and curriculum has increased, exploratory teachers and their curriculum have been further alienated because time for their courses and students' opportunities to attend their classes are often taken away because time and resources are directed to teaching and remediating in the "real" subjects.

Perhaps the limited progress in the curriculum area is evidence of a decline in the curriculum field more on a larger scale. Whereas American universities used to have dedicated programs and departments in curriculum, that focus seems to be changing. Toepfer provided a story to illustrate this trend:

> When Bill Alexander retired from the University of Florida, his line [position] was taken and replaced by three instructor lines of business edu-

cation. Within a decade, the nationally recognized University of Florida Curriculum Department was gone. That wave spread into graduate educational schools across the nation. Now, the discipline of Curriculum Planning and Development no longer exists. From my perspective, today's emphasis on school organizational issues focuses almost entirely on form. There is virtually no concern with planning curricula that respond to developmental and learning needs. Back in the early 1960s, many school districts had assistant superintendents for curriculum and instruction and curriculum coordinators in schools. There was high priority for funding them in school district budgets.

Again, Toepfer points to a trend toward specialization. Curriculum is a field that often brings people from various disciplines together to discuss larger issues of what is valued and should be taught. Increasingly, individuals and groups set themselves apart to focus on single subjects without considering their relationship to other disciplines. The apparent demise of the curriculum field may be viewed as a setback not just at the middle level, but in every level of education.

Attention to Appropriate Teaching and Learning Practices

While advances in curriculum have been somewhat disappointing, most of our participants expressed a positive view about innovations in instruction for young adolescents. Beane noted that "the middle school movement has been tremendously influential with regard to instruction. That is to say that middle school classrooms today more so than thirty or forty years ago involve much more hands-on, engaging type activities, to some degree projects, and to some degree inter-disciplinary or multi-subject units and activities." Similarly, Doda believes that "teachers today are more likely to engage in collaborative teaching methods than they did in the 1960s." She stated that generally speaking, middle school classrooms today are "livelier and more engaging in methods and pedagogy than they were in the 1960s." Several participants commented that middle school teachers are more likely now to engage in hands-on activities, cooperative learning, flexible grouping, and experiential learning, and that teachers are less dependent on textbooks than they have been in years past.

One area that participants seemed to cite as needing attention in contemporary middle schools was related to raising the level of social conscience with our programs, practices, and instructional approaches. Looking back, Doda recalled that teachers and leaders in the early years of the middle school movement failed to discuss some very important issues and to incorporate them into their practice:

> We didn't talk about race, we didn't talk about class, we didn't talk about gender very much. And you know, the middle school movement was a white movement, and ethnicity was not reflected in our early work. . . . I think that was a huge mistake and there are now with the standards movement, we're talking about closing the achievement gap, you know using the "learn or I will hurt you" model of educational accountability to sort of reduce the gap between rich and poor and black and white and so on. And what I'm observing today is that the shift away from the original middle school concepts which focused on affiliation and inclusion and are leaning more towards test score achievement and accountability are really pushing the urban schools to dismantle middle schools even though they are dying for affiliation; those children are desperate for inclusion.

Doda's comments offer a challenge to present-day middle level leaders—a challenge to return to some of the early principles and approaches of the middle school movement that offered affiliation to all students and their teachers. Rather than abandon the middle school concept, she maintained that the middle school concept offers hope for urban schools to make school relevant for their students. Further, she insinuated that the collective middle school movement must correct the mistakes of the past by raising our conversations to new levels of inclusiveness.

Development of a Substantial, Scholarly Knowledge Base

Participants in our study discussed the importance of a substantial, scholarly research base for middle school education. They cited both progress and limitations in the current research base. Middle school education is a relatively new field, and as Joan Lipsitz reminded us, young adolescence was a non-field less than four decades ago. On the side of progress, Erb, McEwin, Sue Swaim, and others observed that there is a growing body of research related to middle school education and young adolescence. Bergmann discussed this development:

> There is more research right now, available to us as to what works and what doesn't. It may not necessarily be called middle school research, but we know so much about adolescents and young adolescents now that we didn't know even ten years ago. So what we have done by identifying this age group as different, has been able to start new research projects that have to do with these kids.

Erb and McEwin asserted that the research has shown that implementing middle school practices makes a positive difference for young adolescents. Arnold discussed that middle school teachers have benefitted from a growing body of descriptive data about what good middle school teaching looks like. Another area of progress related to research in middle level education has been its "water cooler effect." Now that middle school education and young adolescence have become legitimate areas of research, more individuals and groups are talking about them. People involved in medicine, psychology, sociology, education, and other fields focus their studies on the issues of education of young adolescents. Then, these individuals and groups can read each other's work, meet at conferences, collaborate on research, and continue building the research base. Bergmann and Dickinson discussed the importance of this development. Bergmann, for example, discussed how the medical community began researching issues of young adolescent health and development:

> A big moment for me was when people began to question what athletics ought to be for middle school kids. Pediatricians, like Lee Salk, began doing research on young adolescents and their development, and the American Academy of Pediatrics made some statements about what was and wasn't good for kids athletically in the middle school. So we saw a big difference then in competitive sports. We saw a removal of some of the more dangerous sports for middle schools and an attitude towards physical fitness for all students. I think for me, personally, another big moment was when we drew in the medical profession to do research on this age group. We saw, particularly at Johns Hopkins, an amazing increase in middle school research on child development. And people saying "What do we know about this age group and what do we need to know?" They began to do early puberty research, and they began looking at anorexia and all of the social issues. Alan Dresh's research at University of Pittsburg Medical Center on nutrition and how often early adolescents need to eat, led to changes in school schedules as snack breaks were allowed. So that was a focus that was a turning point.

Dickinson discussed the involvement and influence of researchers in fields like psychology and in organizations and foundations:

> There is a whole thread of psychological research. Jeanne Brooks-Gunn is one that comes to mind. Jacquelynne Eccles comes to mind, who have never been part of the "middle school movement," but who have done tremendous amounts of research outside of the mainstream educators. Yet their work is really what we base all of our work on. The psychologists and the researchers have been primary in giving us a knowledge base to stand on. And then there'll be others, and you have to look to places like the Center for Early Adolescence with Lipsitz. You have to look at the different foundations: Carnegie, early-on Ford, Pew Charitable Trust, and others which were really repositories of a lot of very thoughtful creative people who supported a lot in what went on in middle grades. And there are some parallel tracks

out there and only every now and then when you have a group like now the National Forum to Accelerate Middle Grades Reform do you see the cross-over and broad participation. Early on there were a lot of parallel tracks, but they didn't mix and that was to our detriment.

Dickinson's comments provide both a celebration of the progress that has been made in reaching across disciplinary lines to consider, influence, share, and act on the research of others as well as a challenge to do more to collaborate with individuals and groups whose research and professional advocacy can benefit young adolescents and the professionals who serve them.

While participants acknowledged progress in research, they also expressed a unanimous belief that more research is needed. Bergmann recalled work with schools and districts who wanted more research. She indicated that an early lack of definitive research that middle school concepts make a difference was a barrier to success. She stated that district leaders would say things such as, "Prove to me that it works," "Prove to me that this concept makes any more difference than doing it any other way," "Don't give us theory; give us numbers," and "We don't want to talk about theory; we want to talk about how it is going to raise our reading and math scores."

Conversely, Toepfer and Erb expressed a belief that research is not necessarily a guarantee of good practice. Erb supplied an example about research related to teaming:

> Since the enactment of No Child Left Behind and various budgetary cut backs, we see teaming beginning to disappear. This phenomenon has not occurred because of a change in the middle school concept. On the contrary, we now have a pretty strong research base to support a theoretical basis for interdisciplinary team organization in middle schools. This is a better way to organize the delivery of core curriculum in schools for young adolescents than are separate, uncoordinated classes. Yet we know that many schools are steering away from it.

Though the research about teaming suggests that it is positive for young adolescents, budget and accountability concerns thwart efforts to implement interdisciplinary teaming. Toepfer raised similar points about the effect of research on American education:

> The greatest problem with American education is that it has never been largely research based. Substantially belief and politically based, it remains prone to all manner of outside pressures. An example is that the campaign against middle schools persists, despite the evidence showing that they are more effective for the age group they serve. I have yet to find data that

confirms young people do, or will do better after being put back into elementary schools and secondary-oriented programs. It has *not* been shown that a two-level school system achieves the success of a three-level one with developmentally responsive middle schools. Again, a large body of research, a lot of it done by Paul George, validates the success of middle schools.

Toepfer's comments raise an even larger concern about research: Perhaps it does not matter. The challenge is for researchers to develop well-designed and implemented studies about young adolescents, their schools, their teachers, their communities, and other aspects of their healthy development and to communicate that research far and wide. Like the middle school philosophy, we cannot limit our advocacy to those within our "camp"; rather, we must reach into the public. We must provide accurate research-based information to the media. We must counteract the stereotypes of young adolescents as raging bundles of hormones and middle schools as merely soft centers of socialization by providing research that demonstrates their value, intellect, and potential.

Commitment to Specialized Middle Level Professional Preparation and Development

Without exception, participants in this study are advocates of specialized middle level teacher preparation. They see it as critical to the success of young adolescent students. In addition, they see it as critical for middle level teachers whose confidence, effectiveness, and efficacy are increased when they feel knowledgeable about what and whom they are teaching. In addition, when middle level teachers are knowledgeable about young adolescents and the programs needed to serve them, they are better positioned to lead innovative efforts on behalf of their students. If they come to the profession knowledgeable about their content, the developmental age group they will be teaching, and effective teaching approaches, they can begin; they do not have to "make up ground" trying to learn these aspects of teaching before they can move forward as leaders.

Many of our study participants have been involved in teacher education in universities. From that vantage point, they have been able to observe progress in middle level teacher education over time; however, they are also in a position to see that the potential for providing the very best preparation and continuing education has not yet been realized. Dickinson described the complexity of the issue:

> I don't think you can underestimate the problems and difficulties that have been visited upon this movement by the lack of across-the-board, across the

50 states, separate and distinct teacher preparation and teacher licensure standards. You cannot create and sustain any educational endeavor without appropriate preparation. And throughout the history of this movement, teachers that teach in it have been prepared for other developmental ages, or prepared differently for subject-matter orientations rather than a combination between children and knowledge. And it's been one of those handicaps that continues to revisit itself. You'll have certain states like North Carolina, Ohio, or Georgia that will be in the vanguard, and then you'll have other states.

I don't think anymore that it's really a problem with the universities and deans and provosts. At one time it was, but it's not now. Now it's with a cadre of people at the state levels who are on licensure boards, who are in political power positions, that don't want to have anything but the flexibility to put a warm body in front of a classroom, regardless of whether they are qualified or not. And I think that's where we are, and I find it shameful.

There are other terms that Ken McEwin and I have used, including "malpractice." And it really is, if you prepared to teach young children, you should teach young children. If you prepared to teach older adolescents and separate subjects, you should do that. We shouldn't be all in the middle in the dumping ground. And I think that's one of the big problems that continues to haunt us even to today, despite a large number of people's best efforts.

Gatewood, George, Lipsitz, Lounsbury, McEwin, and Vars suggested that the failure of the middle school movement to advocate for and establish specialized middle school teacher education programs early became a barrier to maximizing its progress. George provided that a part of the mistake was that he (and others) thought they needed to work on establishing quality middle schools first so that pre-service teachers could be placed in those schools during their field experiences. Now, in retrospect, he believes those efforts should have been parallel rather than sequential. McEwin stated that after all these years, he has "tried to be patient." Further, he stated,

We know what to do. We just need to do it. And we know how to do it, and we're doing it better than we used to do, but every time a young adolescent walks into a classroom of a teacher with no special knowledge of that age group or how he or she should be teaching them, then I think it's almost a crime. It's a shame, to say the least. So many people just don't understand that; they think any teacher will do. If we really want to change American education, including middle-level education, then the best way to do that is to help teachers be well prepared and knowledgeable. They already care about young people. They already have degrees. They're already smart persons. But just loving a kid isn't enough. They need that special knowledge, including content knowledge, of course. You can't teach what you don't know, but just knowing the content alone is not enough.

In spite of these observations that we have not come far enough, many participants did comment on progress in middle level teacher education. Erb, Sue Swaim, and others discussed that during the transition to middle school education, we had a history in teacher education of having elementary teacher education programs that provided a general K–8 preparation and secondary programs that focused on content area specialization. John Swaim cited a study by Pumerantz (1969) that found only two states that had any kind of state license or endorsement for middle level education. During their interviews, McEwin and Swaim cited Gaskill's research (2007) that shows we now have 46 states with some type of middle level teacher licensure. Certainly, this trend demonstrates progress. Sue Swaim also discussed the advocacy of NMSA in specialized middle level teacher preparation:

> NMSA's long-standing commitment to middle level teacher preparation is important as well. When NMSA became a constituent member of NCATE and took over the responsibilities of writing the NMSA Standards for teacher preparation at the pre-service, master's level, specialist, and doctorate level, it was a big step forward. Through our NCATE partnership and work, we have 30 states which now say that any college or university in their state preparing students to teach at the middle level must meet NMSA's standards to receive state program approval.

John Swaim also noted that we are now beginning to have college majors who matriculated through quality middle schools themselves. They are intentionally entering middle level teacher education programs informed and influenced by their own experiences and determined to provide a good experience for their own young adolescent students.

It is important to recognize that recently specialized middle level teacher preparation has suffered in the context of a compromised view of teacher education at all levels. George cautioned:

> We've got to find a way to save middle school teacher education. You of course know that teacher education is under attack nationally and wholly. There are people in the national government and surrounding the national government who have found the favor of the national government who would very much like to do away with traditional teacher education as a whole, and they are making tremendous progress. They may win. So one of the battles we've got to fight right now is to hang onto as much of quality teacher education as we can. We've got to change a lot of the things we have done poorly because a lot of people don't support traditional teacher edu-

cation. So fighting for middle school teacher education is a very important part of it.

In the spirit of middle school collaboration and teaming, perhaps an appropriate course of action in this context is to advocate for specialized middle level teacher preparation in a system of quality specialized teacher preparation—a system that values the developmental stage for which teachers are prepared to work as well as the content for which they are prepared to teach. In addition, it would likely be wise to support a research agenda that provides data about our suspicions regarding the efficacy of specialized middle level teacher programs. The success of our schools depends on the success of teachers:

> We have to focus on teacher preparation; and I know I'm pounding on that that, but I believe if you really want to change schools then you support and empower teachers. Who's making those daily decisions, minute-by-minute, even second-by-second on some days, all year long? If you think about some principals who are problems, where do those principals come from? What kind of preparation do they have? Well, if you have a middle school principal who's been a middle school teacher and taught on a team and really understands the school, it's more likely they're going to be supportive of an "authentic middle school plan," when they become principals. If you continue to hire people without middle-level knowledge and without middle-level experience, they may be very well-intended, good persons who do care about kids and want to do a good job, but they may not know what to do. Also, it's good to have a really strong teaching force who understands what needs to happen for the middle school plan to be authentically and systematically applied, so that when a new principal does come in he or she can be trained quickly, as far as what really needs to happen in the school, if that person's not already knowledgeable.

The overall course of action, it seems, is to do whatever we can to support the training and preparation of all professionals (e.g., teachers, principals, counselors) who work with young adolescents in middle-level schools so that they will feel prepared, confident, and determined to have an impact. McEwin and Dickinson have often stated that any other approach is the equivalent of "malpractice."

The Influence of Policy, Politics, and Accountability Initiatives on Middle Level Education

State and national politics and policies affect education at every level, and middle level education has been especially vulnerable to the changing tides of politics. At the state level, perhaps the two most influential elements of policy are related to teacher licensure and the curriculum. In many states, the middle school movement has made progress in both areas. For example, many states now have specialized middle level teacher licensure or endorsement. Also, many states have a curriculum that is divided into elementary, middle, and high school levels. McEwin stated that such policies and organizations "carry the message that there are three distinct levels in American public education." He also mentioned that many district and state departments now have support for individuals to work specifically with middle level teachers and curriculum.

On the other hand, policies at the national level have not been so friendly to middle level education. Lipsitz recognized that "major national bills like Title I and No Child Left Behind reorient our schools. They deflect us for better and for worse onto a different trajectory." More specifically, Sue Swaim discussed that America's largest single education act, the Elementary and Secondary Education Act, completely ignores schooling that happens at the middle level. Toepfer stated that "a persisting national problem is that the United States Department of Education has never recognized middle schools...and lists all of the nation's schools as either elementary or secondary." He called this an "anachronistic, misinformed stance" stating that the evidence is clear that "a middle school unit can better address the educational needs of young adolescents." The implications of this act, and its most recent iteration, the No Child Left Behind (NCLB) Act are deep and far-reaching in middle schools. Sue Swaim explained that NCLB has mandated that grades 3–8 be the testing grades, and "that means over 60% of the kids tested are middle school kids." In other words, she maintained, "the success of the mandate rests squarely on the shoulders of middle school students and middle school educators," even though they are not formally recognized in the law. Furthermore, since "middle level" or "middle school" is not mentioned in NCLB, Swaim further lamented that it is difficult to obtain specific funds for middle level needs in areas such as reading or science. George echoed Swaim's observation: "Virtually every state in the country provides less money to funding young adolescents than it does for young children or young adults, so middle schools have been crippled all along by being literally less money per child than other levels of education." Swaim also explained that federal research data does not support a disaggregation for researchers who might be interested in studying the effectiveness of middle schools.

Of course, NCLB also has disturbing implications for defining quality teaching. George argued that the NCLB "mystical interpretation of highly qualified teachers is making it very difficult for states to produce teachers who can teach more than one subject." He called this a "giant step back-ward." Similarly, McEwin expressed concern that NCLB communicates that "all the emphasis should be on content knowledge, and nothing else is important." In his words, NCLB defines "highly qualified teacher...as a teacher who has a degree in something, does not have a criminal back-ground, and can pass a state-approved content test." He protested, "It re-ally irks me to hear 'highly qualified' being defined as those very minimal criteria." The concerns raised by these participants and others are related to their commitment to high quality specialized middle level teacher prepa-ration which seems to be completely discounted by NCLB.

In addition to narrowly defining highly qualified teacher, NCLB also narrowly defines student success. Lipsitz characterized the "testing issue" broadly: "It's not a small technical issue. It's an enormous question about public accountability." Lipsitz, Gatewood, and others discussed the difficul-ty of schools, teachers, and students to "balance" their values with public accountability. Lipsitz warned that "this country is in danger of losing its commitment to public education." However, many of our participants have observed that this balancing act is not going particularly well. For example, Stevenson recounted being in a school

> where teachers were so afraid and anxious about their kids' performance on tests that all they were doing was drilling and grilling them to come up with correct answers. Privileges and punishments were meted out based on the numbers of questions answered correctly. I found it so consummately de-generate in comparison to what is possible and infinitely more appropriate with young adolescents that I excused myself and left as quickly as I could. My friend John Arnold refers to this syndrome as a preoccupation with get-ting kids to memorize answers to questions they haven't asked.

Lipsitz seemed to suggest that we cannot merely reject the entire notion of public accountability. Rather, we must offer alternatives, ways to demon-strate that the time young adolescents spend in our schools adds value to their individual lives and adds to the cohesion of our democratic society. She worried that failure to do so might lead to a rejection of the "Jefferso-nian ideal of taking children from all quarters, and using the public coffers to educate them." Her appeal seems to be related to the point made about middle level teacher education. Perhaps all teacher education and all pub-lic education are in jeopardy. We must work within the ranks of middle level education to ensure our continued survival, but we must also lift our heads to work with others within our larger ranks. We must secure alliances and allegiances to protect the larger educational agenda as well. In other words, if teacher education and public education fail, middle level education will likely collapse with them. If teacher education and public education endure, then middle level education has a good fighting chance.

George discussed the larger context of the political environment that has fostered policies such as NCLB:

> I believe that ultraconservatives in America are opposed to the concepts and the values that lie at the heart of middle school education and that those people are doing basically everything that they can to drive out the kinds of things that middle school education stands for, and we are in a tremendous struggle certainly for the rest of this decade, maybe forever, to try and keep the middle school concept alive and to keep the light of middle school education on during a period that I perceive to be growing darker and darker with people whose views about human nature are dark—people whose views about human potential are dark, people who believe in accountability, people who don't trust, people who want to monitor and supervise and test. Those are the people who threaten the middle school concept in 2003 and beyond. Those are the people who don't believe in integrating the academic disciplines. Those are the people who don't believe that curriculum can actually spring from the needs of young adolescents themselves. Those are the people who believe that curriculum needs to come from on high somewhere. That people who have already learned and taken power should decree what young people need to know for the future. Those are the threats to middle school today.

George and Sue Swaim challenged their middle level counterparts and descendents. Swaim urged: "Middle level advocacy at the local, state, and national levels is important, and every one of us has a role to play in accomplishing that." George stated, "I think we should reject it [the accountability movement], reject it, and reject it, and I think we should do it loudly and angrily and publicly." He also said that "we've got to get political. We've got to support candidates who understand and support quality and enlightened education rather than narrow, punitive, negative, and hostile approaches to education." In George style, he credited Sam Houston, a Texas pioneer, with providing great advice for middle level educators: "We've got to do right and damn the consequences!"

Accomplishments and Possibilities:
Legacy Participants Evaluate the Current Landscape
of Middle Level Education

In the Middle Level Education Legacy Project interviews, we asked our participants directly about the current status of middle school education. Similar to other topics, they reported both good news and bad news. As examples, Beane, Doda, and Erb commented on various positive aspects of the progress of middle school education:

> I think more teachers than ever are more understanding and responsive to young adolescents. I think there is in schools a much greater understanding of kids than ever before.... The greatest asset of the middle school movement has been a serious and more than rhetorical commitment to young adolescents.... I think the middle school concept has brought more teachers into better relationships with young adolescents. And I think it has made their lives better. I think they are happier about being a teacher than they would have been had the concept not opened the door for them. (Beane)

> On the positive side, we know more about best practices than we've ever known before; we know what good pedagogy looks like; we know what good middle schools can look like; we know that the research supports these practices that we can articulate. There is a convergence of understanding about great teaching; the advances of looking at quality of student work have improved conversations around teaching and learning. I think we know that schools have to become professional learning communities so the knowledge we have is the wind beneath our feet. (Doda)

> I think it is an exciting time to be alive. Middle school advocates have much to offer to the national dialogue about the role of public education in a liberal democracy. We have an increasing body of sound research documenting the impact of applying middle school principles to the education of young adolescents. We have evidence-based talking points to support what we are trying to do for the education of 10- to 14-year-olds. (Erb)

Gatewood, McEwin, and John Swaim noted that the middle school is established as a legitimate part of the continuum in K–12 American public education system. Most school districts have three tiers. It seems that, unless we start moving backward, as some of our participants have suggested could happen, the reorganization of American schools is nearly complete.

However, while schools and school districts have gone through widespread organizational changes, the middle school philosophy of education has not been so widely implemented. McEwin observed that "the part of the movement that is not over is trying to make schools be authentic and serve young adolescents and their teachers well." Sue Swaim elaborated on the less than optimal implementation of middle school education:

> I think one of the lessons we've learned is that in too many places, schools and school districts started to implement the middle school philosophy but stalled out along the way. When people say "We tried middle schools, but they're just not working in our community," or "The student achievement is flat at this age group," we have to ask, "Did you really implement middle

school? Did you really implement the concept with consistency over time?" or "Did you stop along the way and it stalled out?"

When we look at the recommendations of what a middle school should be as seen in *This We Believe* or *Turning Points*, we have to realize they are not isolated components that can be picked in isolation of one another to be implemented. We can't choose our favorite six recommendations to implement and ignore the other four. We have come to more fully understand just how interrelated these are and when you begin to work with one of the recommendations, the others are involved as well. We also have learned that naming a team of teachers or providing a block of time in the schedule for learning does not mean that teaming or block scheduling are being utilized correctly or to their fullest extent. Too many schools used the terminology but never fully implemented the practice.

I think we know what we need to do; now we must re-commit to doing it.

Doda spoke with frustration about the untimely emergence of the public and policy priorities that created a hostile environment for middle school education:

We're still struggling to have that conversation about the deeper substantive issues of change, and I think one of the sad stories about the middle school movement and disappointing stories is that just about the time we were ready, poised really for the next question, the question of the deeper changes in the middle school and the classroom experience changes and the curriculum changes and the student voice changes, you know the public was bent on accountability and test score monitoring, and suddenly we had this competing agenda that pushed aside our concerns for really good human affiliation in the middle school, safe havens for learning to look at how do we prepare for these state tests.

Many of the participants in our study described the suspension of full implementation of the middle school. They described it variously as in limbo (Arnold), in a pause, in neutral (Arth), stagnant, at a standstill, not growing, no new ideas (Beane), in a state of arrested development (Dickinson), a plateau, losing ground (Doda), at a peak, but could be starting downhill (Gatewood), in a defensive mode (George), under assault, unfairly targeted as the emblem of school failure in the United States (Johnston), shaky (Lipsitz), struggling (Lounsbury), a process of becoming, in for some rough roads (J. Swaim), fragile (S. Swaim), being eroded, in trouble, the whipping boy for public education (Vars). These words and phrases suggest that participants characterize the movement as being in a passive, neutral stance. They described their own dispositions as reluctantly cynical (Beane), wanting to be hopeful (Doda), and cautiously optimistic (McEwin).

In horology, a *movement* is the internal mechanism of a clock or watch, as opposed to the *case*, which encloses and protects the movement, and the *face*, which displays the time. In the middle school movement, it seems we worked to create a model of a school, a *case* to enclose and protect young adolescents and our beliefs about their sacredness; we also worked to communicate that model to others, to expose the right *face* for middle schools. Some schools literally changed their faces by changing the signs on their door from "junior high school" to "middle school." However, the essence of those schools, their inner workings, were not fully developed.

Fortunately, the middle school leaders who participated in our study did not concede defeat with a passive characterization of middle school education. Rather, they offered many insights for reigniting middle school education as a vibrant, dynamic, "green and growing edge of educational reform" (Lounsbury).

References

Alexander, W. (1963). The junior high school: A changing view. *Middle School Journal, 26*(3), 21–24.

Backes, J., Ralston, A., & Ingwalson, G. (1999). Middle level reform: The impact on student achievement. *Research in Middle Level Education Quarterly, 22*(3), 43–57.

Beane, J. A. (1990). *A middle school curriculum: From rhetoric to reality* (2nd ed.). Westerville, OH: National Middle School Association.

Cochrum, K. (2007, August 15). On leading well: What is a movement? [Web log post]. Retrieved from http://onleadingwell.blogspot.com/2007/08/what-is-movement.html

Felner, R. D., Jackson, A. W., Kasak, D., Mulhall, P., Brand, S., & Flowers, N. (1997). The impact of school reform for the middle years: Longitudinal study of a network engaged in Turning Points-based comprehensive school transformations. *Phi Delta Kappan. 78*(7), 528–532, 541–550.

Gaskill, P. E. (2007). *The current status of middle grades teaching credentials: Executive summary.* Retrieved from http://www.peggygaskill.com/images/Executive%20Summary-March%202007.pdf

Laughlin, B. (2008, July 5). *What is a movement?* [Web log post]. Retrieved from http://aristotleadventure.blogspot.com/2008/07/what-is-movement.html

Lipsitz, J. (1977). *Growing up forgotten: A review of research and programs concerning early adolescence.* Lexington, MA: D. C. Heath and Company.

Mertens, S. B., & Flowers, N. (2006). Middle Start's impact on comprehensive middle school reform. *Middle Grades Research Journal, 1*(1), 1–26.

Mertens, S. G., Flowers, N., & Mulhall, P. (1998). *The Middle Start initiative, phase I: A longitudinal analysis of Michigan middle-level schools.* Center for Prevention Research and Development, University of Illinois.

McEwin, C. K., & Greene, M. (2010). Results and recommendations from the 2009 national surveys of randomly selected and highly successful middle level schools. *Middle School Journal, 42*(1), 48–62.

Pumerantz, P. (1969). Few states certify teachers for growing middle schools. *Phi Delta Kappan, 5*(2), 102.

Walton, S. (2008, September 9). Movement builders: Movement defined. [Web log post]. Retrieved from http://movementbuilders.com/2008/09/movement-defined/

22

Navigating the Middle School Expedition

For nearly five decades, middle school educators and leaders across America have been involved in a bold educational expedition focused on improving educational opportunities and experiences for young adolescents. Like any other expedition, this journey has been subject to the ebbs and flows of progress. For the first three decades, the activities associated with the creation of middle schools were widespread and characterized by a high degree of enthusiasm. In the last decade or so, however, the middle school movement has been characterized by many of its most committed participants as dormant or flat. Perhaps a more positive and optimistic way to view the current situation is to consider that middle school education, as John Swaim suggested, is "a process of becoming." If we visualize the task of improving middle school education as analogous to climbing a towering mountain and a challenge worthy of pursuing, we can garner hope that emerging middle school educators will stand confidently on the shoulders of the giants that used their knowledge, experience, and skills to establish safe routes and passages in earlier stages of this ascent. The expedition leaders, the climbers and sherpas of the middle school movement, have guided

The Legacy of Middle School Leaders, pages 387–405
Copyright © 2011 by Information Age Publishing
All rights of reproduction in any form reserved.

us safely to an elevated plateau. Here, they have secured an advanced base camp, a place for trekkers to rest, recover, rejuvenate, acclimatize to the altitude, and plan their next push towards the summit. From the perspective of this altitude, one can look back at the ascent that has thus far been made on Mount Middle School and see the successful reorganization of American schools that resulted in a middle level institution becoming all but the universal central unit in a three-tiered school organization pattern. In addition, important progress was made in increasing attention to the education and development of young adolescents, in establishing distinctive preparation programs for teaching the age group, and in creating a good many schools that put into practice—successfully—the tenets of the middle school philosophy.

While the view from this elevation may be impressive, emerging and prospective middle school mountaineers cannot remain content to travel on the routes established in the past or simply transform a temporary base camp into a permanent residence. Rather, they must look up and ahead toward the summit of middle level education reform and organize new climbs. Legacy participants have suggested that the Middle School Expedition has, indeed, stalled on the slopes. They expressed concern that too much rest and acclimatization to the current altitude may have led to a diminished vision of the true educational excellence that drove the pioneer climbers on their ascent.

In their interviews, these pioneer leaders offered their wisdom and experience to help us chart the course for the next portion of our ascent up Mount Middle School. From the security of the present base camp, the next generation of leaders can and must stage collective attempts toward the summit of excellence in education for every young adolescent. Careful analysis of the interviews illuminated several important and specific beliefs or conclusions that can serve as guideposts or goals in directing efforts as we challenge the treacherous topography of reform. Note that each goal begins with a verb because action is the critical factor in our continued success.

For the sake of clarity, we have provided headings for each goal. However, we hope readers will not view these guideposts or goals as singular, independent concepts, or as an a la carte menu from which one can select preferences. These goals are intimately interrelated. For example, promoting advocacy is related to preparing teachers to be advocates for their students and schools and promoting the worth and significance of young adolescents suggests that we should provide specialized preparation for their teachers. One of the mistakes of the past and current iterations of middle level education has been half-hearted implementation, a menu mentality of implementation, in which schools, districts, principals, and teachers have said, "I'll take a serving of developmental responsiveness, but I wouldn't care for any advocacy," or "We'd like specialized teacher preparation, but please hold the integrated curriculum." In the new era of the Middle School Expedition, we must work courageously, collaboratively, and boldly to implement what we know is best for the education of young adolescents. We must heed the wisdom found in *Turning Points* (Carnegie Council of Adolescent Development, 1989), *Turning Points 2000: Educating Adolescents in the 21st Century* (Jackson & Davis, 2000), *This We Believe* (National Middle School Association, 2010b), and the growing middle level research base (NMSA, 2010a), the Legacy Project participants' reflections, and in the school-based experiences of countless incredible middle level teacher-servants who have shared daily their compassion, insight, and experience with 10–15 year olds.

Goal: Promote the Worth and Significance of Young Adolescents in America and the World

If we are to continue successfully on this critical mission, we must counteract the pervasive caricatures and stereotypes about young adolescents that remain pervasive in the media and promote positive, authentic, research-based portraits of them. Though real progress has been made, Arnold characterized much of the nice talk about children in America of every age as mere "rhetoric," and maintained that we must foster deeper understandings about young adolescents. He further explained that the goal is not for teachers to be able to recite Piaget's stages or Kohlberg's levels; rather, it is about "being deeply interested and observant" of kids' intellectual, moral, and social development and to develop strategies to help them grow in those areas. Beane argued that "we ought to be speaking for young people and their interests and their rights, and we're not doing that." Doda and Stevenson emphasized the importance of inviting young adolescents into our conversations about their education: "We can't forget to include student voice. We can't just talk about it so much that we forget that we're not doing it. We really need to do it; we need to take kids seriously and invite them into the conversation" (Doda) and "Pay careful attention to the children and get them to tell about themselves and listen to them and believe them and trust them and build your program to a large extent around your best knowledge of those children" (Stevenson).

Vars recommended making young adolescents their own ambassadors:

> Some marvelous public projects have been initiated by kids at the middle level. There are books and pamphlets about how to carry out social action

projects with elementary and/or middle level school students. A woman out in Denver, I think, demonstrated how kids can literally transform a community or a neighborhood if they are turned on to it as a problem or challenge that affects them. We sell the kids short on what they can do. We must take them into our confidence and involve them wisely in doing things that are really important, instead of memorizing stuff to pass a test.

Vars implied the importance of showing the world the "best" side of our young adolescents. He further discussed that we must be better at publicity. Caricatures of young adolescents draw people to the movies, the news, magazines, and concerts. These portrayals are not usually the very best of our young people. So, where are the best young adolescents? Sitting in classrooms every day in middle schools across America. How do we invite the public in to see their faces, to hear their fears and intellectual promise, to understand their complexity, and to support their individual and collective prospects as the bright future of global citizenship?"

Erb stated, "We need to expand the arena for our teaching to become educators of not only young adolescents, but members of other constituencies beyond the membership of our own associations to respond to critics and to educate the public on behalf of the welfare of young adolescents." Bergmann and Toepfer reminded us that our attention and advocacy on behalf of young adolescents must honor *all* of them:

> I think there are still kids out there who fall through the cracks for a variety of reasons. And I think those cracks are going to be larger and larger because of issues of which they have very little control in the middle school. I think we have to take a special look at the at-risk group in the middle school because it's really a lot easier to deal with them and help them there than it is when they get to the high school. So I would just say that in the future that we need to spend some time looking at that group of kids who come into the classroom and say, "Teach me, I dare you." (Bergmann)

> My belief has been that education should allow youngsters to learn as fast as they can, or as slow as some must. Not all students have the ability to master the same amount of material by the end of specific grades as required in the educational standards rubric. . . . However, the educational standards system expects virtually all to achieve specific progress at common "check points." Punitive and discriminatory, that assumes those not blessed with the abilities of others can pass common tests at the same intervals. Would it not make sense to develop a paradigm allowing all to learn the essential skills and information life will require of them as fast as they can or as slow as they must? That would allow most students to learn what they need to "complete the course." Possible back in the 1970s and 1980s, now such learning and internalizing of facts, skills, concepts, and information have been replaced with teaching for tests. (Toepfer)

Our collective, united message of the beauty, promise, and sacredness of young adolescents must become so loud and so compelling that it rings, reverberates, and resonates throughout the world.

Goal: Implement Educational Practices That Are Responsive to the Needs of Young Adolescents, and Implement Them Comprehensively

The consensus among Legacy participants as reported earlier was that the middle school concept in most places has only been partially or half-heartedly implemented. Middle school educators must be vigilant and aggressive in research, development, and implementation of the middle school concept. Beane explained the significance of our past and current efforts:

> We need to be absolutely certain about what kind of footprints we're leaving. That is to say, at a time in the future when people come back to the concept in its fullest version, they need to have access to information and ideas about the things we did well and the things we didn't do well so that they can hit the ground running and move ahead. I think we need to be thinking about what kinds of things we are doing right now as a record that people can use in the future.

This book provides a record from many prominent leaders about the successes and shortcomings of middle school education to this point. However, if our current middle level leaders do not read it and other scholarly works and discuss them and learn from them, we continue unnecessary cycles of disappointment. Erb reminded us that "we have a lot of work to do to maintain our integrity and the integrity of effective middle school programs" without repeating mistakes of the past. From here, we should focus on moving forward with the benefit of past research and experience. For example, Erb, George, Gatewood, and Lounsbury warned that middle school education should not become so fixed (George), institutionalized (Gatewood, citing Alexander), and rigid (Erb) that we fail to bring about real change. Lounsbury said that we need to "quit trying to make schools better as they are and make them different instead." These warnings point to the fact that a good many American middle level schools have changed their organization and their names but they have not changed their practices very much. Acknowledging that implementation must be flexible to the needs of the young adolescents, families, and communities being served, we must move forward to get to the heart of reform. For example, we must tackle the question of an appropriate curriculum for young adolescents rather than succumbing to the separate-subject approach simply because it has been the traditional approach since American education was fashioned from an industrial model many decades ago. George elaborated the need to keep learning and growing in our knowledge of best programs and practices when he recounted a warning from Bill Alexander that "the day the middle school concept was fixed would be the day that it started to die." Further, George suggested that "we need to do our best to keep tinkering, keep tweaking, keep challenging, keep debating, and keep it alive as a consequence." Our dogma is not sufficient; we must be willing to learn and grow and innovate as we move into a new era of middle school education.

We now have a sound research base that supports our basic tenets (NMSA, 2010a). We know, for example, that team organization is correlated with higher levels of student achievement (Flowers, Mertens, & Mulhall, 1999; Mertens & Flowers, 2006). We need descriptive data, case studies, anecdotes, and examples of practices that happen within team organizations that make students more successful. We need to know, in addition to achievement gains, what benefits students, and families derive from being affiliated with interdisciplinary teams of teachers. We need to understand *why* we have teams and exploit their potential. Teams provide a way to help make large schools seem smaller and to promote community, responsibility, and affiliation for their members. In common planning time, teams can plan integrated instruction that is responsive to the needs of their particular students. Teaming is not an end; it is a means to the end of meeting the needs of the teachers, students, and families involved in the middle level education enterprise. In all our practices, we must keep our eyes on the prize of purpose. Otherwise, it is as if we are all sitting in the middle school car together, but we are not traveling toward any significant destination.

McEwin warned that, in our discussions about implementation, we must always "watch out for the 'it.'" He explained:

> We tried to do "it," but "it" did not work; we tried "it," but somebody would not let us keep doing "it." People are always talking about the "it" instead of "*we* failed." We have to be willing to say, "*We* tried to implement this and *we* failed at it, so we need to try again," instead of backing away and saying "it" did not work. It is easier to blame our shortcomings on the "it," that's not a good explanation. "It" is a real enemy.

Finally, one of the middle school founders, Toepfer, offered these sage recommendations about the continued implementation of middle school practices:

- Look at middle level schools and identify those things that are working now.
- Identify those things that merit being preserved, enhanced, and nourished.
- Identify programs that need to be re-thought, reconsidered, and/or changed. The entire effort must be data-based.
- Never take anything for granted. Don't believe that what is in vogue today will persist on its own. If you think present practice is effective, identify what must be done to insure its continuation.
- Provide continuing opportunity to research and develop successful practices and/or refine the effectiveness of what is in practice.

Goal: Cultivate Middle Level Education Leaders

Mountaineering is challenging, invigorating work. It involves hiking, camping in the open, and strenuous climbing, often in inclement weather and in high altitudes. Danger and changing conditions can lurk with each step and around every corner. Proper training is of paramount importance to the success of any expedition. As is evidenced in the transcripts in this book, the middle school movement has had a rich heritage of bold leadership. But the Middle School Expedition is not yet complete; many of our guides have retired, and the Expedition is in need of new leaders to continue the journey. Specialized middle level teacher preparation and continued professional development is one powerful way to cultivate future leaders. Citing a context of political suspicion about the importance and relevance of teacher education in general, George, asserted that "we've got to find a way to save middle school teacher education." McEwin argued, "If you want to change schools, then you support and empower teachers." Specialized middle level teacher preparation should allow prospective teachers to learn about the heritage of the movement, including its history and purposes. It should provide a strong foundation related to the healthy development of young adolescents. It should provide middle level field experiences that enable teacher candidates to interact with young adolescents and examine, apply, and analyze the knowledge they have gained in their courses. We must not only advocate the importance of specialized middle level teacher preparation within colleges of education, but also we must argue for it with our policymakers and licensure boards. We must demonstrate that middle school teachers with specialized preparation are the preferred professionals to provide quality teaching and leadership in our schools. We must partner with schools and districts to place middle level teachers and to support them into and throughout their profession as leaders and innovators of change. Otherwise, McEwin argues, "If we continue to hire people without middle level knowledge and experience, they may be very well-intended, good people who care about kids and want to do a good job, but they may not know what to do." Energy and resources that could be spent working on curriculum and instruction innovations will instead be spent remediating teachers about the students they are teaching. Lounsbury optimistically highlighted that in the relatively short life of specialized middle level teacher preparation, we have been "building a new group of pre-service teachers in many institutions, including some in Georgia where the graduates are just excellent, just excellent, who are committed middle school educators. They're going to make the difference."

McEwin pointed out the far-reaching benefits of specialized training for middle school teachers. These teachers can become more effective middle school principals, or they can train the principals who are assigned to their schools about the appropriate education for young adolescents. Sue Swaim agreed that "we have to keep our focus on improved middle level teacher and administrator preparation and licensure as well as quality professional development for those already in the field."

In addition to concentrating on teacher preparation as a means to cultivate future leaders, Beane discussed the importance of extending invitations to prospective leaders and of sustained mentoring of prospective leaders. He expressed concern that the leadership in organizations such as National Middle School Association (NMSA), state affiliates of NMSA, and the National Forum to Accelerate Middle Grades Reform have had the same "faces" for "twenty or thirty years." He elaborated that the consistency is not all bad; it demonstrates long-term commitment and dedication to a great ideal. He recounted,

> I was lucky Connie Toepfer brought be into the movement, Paul George was lucky that he happened to study under Bill Alexander, Judy Brough was lucky that she studied under Connie Toepfer, and Sherrell Bergmann that she studied under Gordon Vars. There's this group of us who all studied under the people who started the movement. We were brought into it. We had a way in.

Yet, he worried that middle level education now almost seems like a closed group. For new leaders, he contended, "I don't know what the entry points would be. I don't know how people would get into it now. It doesn't feel, to me, as open as it should be, and that's tremendously important because the movement definitely needs new blood, it needs new life, it needs new energy.

The message here seems to be that current middle level education leaders and organizations must be about the business of cultivating new leaders.

Our efforts to invite new leaders to join us on the Middle School Expedition must be deliberate. We must work to collaborate, inform, mentor, motivate, and inspire those in our ranks who are eager, willing, and capable to re-ignite the fires of middle level education reform. We must educate them, prepare them, and equip them for the journey; millions of present and future young adolescents are depending on their success.

Goal: Communicate, Collaborate, and Advocate

If middle level education is to continue moving forward, those involved must be active, engaged, alert, and vigilant in their efforts. Though the daily work of teaching young adolescents and preparing their teachers is critically important, it is not sufficient to sustain and advance the Middle School Expedition. The cause of responsive schooling for young adolescents must be understood by not only those within the work but also those outside who influence local, state, and national policies, resources, and strategic planning. Middle level educators must work to communicate, collaborate, and advocate the cause of appropriate education for young adolescents. Every friend of middle level education must work continuously to stir the still waters. We must position ourselves around the Lake of Middle Level Education Reform and hurl our stones in, creating thousands of individual ever-expanding ripples that spread and join until the entire lake is moving. Within our various circles of influence, we can affect voters, policymakers, parents, influential community members, state officials, business executives, and even national leaders who need to understand the critical nature of young adolescent development.

Communicating a complex message in what Erb characterizes as a "sound-bite culture" of "cable TV shouting matches, 140-character tweets, and information overload in general" is certainly a challenge. We must consider how, when, where, and to whom we communicate our message. Beane, Erb, and Johnston stressed the importance of listening attentively in addition to talking and writing about our own agenda. Beane, for example, remarked that "middle school people" sometimes spend "too much time talking to each other and not enough time looking at the world outside and anticipating some of the issues" that are causing concern beyond middle school education. Similarly, Erb explained, "In the continuing discussion on how best to educate young adolescents, we need to listen as well as talk. . . . Foundational as it is, education exists as part of a larger society. We must always interface with that larger society if we are going to be effective in what we do. One of the last things we want to be doing is to morph into a kind of little cult that exists apart from the larger society." Arnold, Arth,

Doda, Johnston, Lounsbury, and Sue Swaim emphasized the importance of listening to and communicating with parents, citizens, and communities. Johnston suggested that we should "invite communities into deeper, more sustained conversation about what they expect and want from their middle school," thus making them partners in the cause for young adolescent education and development. He also cautioned that we should be open to hearing their first request: we "want high test scores." Then, we should stay tuned for their next set of comments. He maintained that parents and community members are "pretty much like you and me—regular people concerned about their kids and their community." He said parents and communities are "going to tell you they want a place where their kid wants to go to school, they want a place where their kid feels safe, where their kid feels involved, and can develop as a person. They want a place where their kid can learn to make good ethical decisions." "Once we invite parents into the conversation, and then work collaboratively with them to create the kinds of schools that produce those results," Johnston assured, "I think our future is golden."

Legacy participants stressed the importance of open, honest communication. Erb and Arth contended that open discussions and forums, debates, and public disagreements are just as important as efforts to find common ground. The goal with effective communication is for participants to understand each other's positions. As a result, all parties can speak knowledgeably about the issues.

Understanding the issues and what is at stake is also critical in the timing of our communication. Legacy participants indicated variously that our communication about the cause of middle level education should happen immediately, continually, daily, and regularly. Sue Swaim explained that the time to communicate is now, not when a crisis arises. If we take every opportunity to pave the path of communication and to prepare the way for enlarging our collective and concentric circles of influence, when a crisis arises (e.g., budget cuts), we will likely have more informed friends who are willing to stand with us on behalf of young adolescents.

In addition to considering how and when we should communicate, Arnold asserted that we must think about who is hearing, receiving, and transmitting the middle school message. In addition to parents and community members, he advocated communicating with other agencies and organizations who are interested in the welfare of young adolescents. For example, he suggested that we must be communicating with health care providers. Vars stated the importance of taking the case for middle level education to "all teachers, not just those in the middle grades." "The backbiting between elementary and middle and middle and high school and high school and college," Vars lamented, "is a shame in this education profession." Lipsitz further articulated the importance of communicating broadly and inclusively:

> I think that the tent has to be big and wide and open. Sometimes when you start something, you need for it to be protected and small and in a hot house. But after that, if you really want to have impact, you have to ask not who the true believers are, but who the true believers need to be and how you can make that happen. Otherwise you don't have enough impact. In the end, I think, there could have been greater impact early on had a more strategic set of alliances been forged into the world of research, into the world of public policy setting, into the major political forces in urban education. It was a boutique movement for too long.

Lipsitz's reference to a "strategic set of alliances" with the worlds of research, public policy setting, and political forces in urban education provide insight into the importance of collaboration with individuals and groups beyond the inner circle of middle level education. McEwin stressed that many people and agencies have roles to play in the healthy development and education of young adolescents and that we must play those roles in concert with each other. Public education in the 21st century is a demanding enterprise. With so much emphasis placed on accountability as measured by standardized test scores, educators hardly have time to collaborate with their own students and colleagues. Even more energy will be needed to collaborate with those beyond the schoolhouse door. However, the investment is worth the dividends that could be realized for young adolescents and the schools and professionals who serve them. With so much pressure on teachers, it is increasingly important that they support each other—that elementary, middle, and high school teachers work together. In addition, Doda asserted that middle level educators "need to collaborate, and we need to model what we believe and become a professional learning community ourselves, those of us who are involved in this work need to learn from each other and learn together and to constantly continue that learning process so that we're growing as a movement of educators as well as a model of education." Arth suggested that the "National Middle School Association should bring together all the organizations that care about young adolescents and get them to work more closely together." NMSA's efforts to establish and promote October as Month of the Young Adolescent have raised awareness of the age group. In fact, 55 agencies and organizations have joined as partners in this effort (see http://www.nmsa.org/moya/Partners/tabid/1173/Default.aspx). Concentrated, deliberate collaboration among the groups is a logical next step.

Parents of middle school students are often struggling to establish or maintain a career and provide the basic needs for their families. Middle level education professionals and parents must recognize each other as partners and allies. Collaboration is more than talking and listening; it is working side by side to develop creative solutions to complex problems. Collaboration can lead to activism, advocacy, and collective bargaining power on behalf of the promise of young adolescents.

Sue Swaim made middle level advocacy the bailiwick of her term as Executive Director of the National Middle School Association. She argued that how we advocate individually and collectively on a daily basis has a significant impact. Specifically, she suggested that we need to do more advocacy, more sharing of the success stories, getting community and policy makers directly engaged in middle level classrooms and with middle level students and teachers:

> I am really beginning to think in teacher preparation and in professional development everyone needs to take an Advocacy 101 course. It's no longer something that can be left for someone else to do. When teachers visit with parents in the grocery store, at a football game or they see a school board member, what they say and how they say it about middle level education can make a difference in the support they have in their community.

Lipsitz made a related claim that we must be opportunistic in our approach to middle level education. Whenever an opportunity, formal or informal, arises to advance the cause of appropriate middle level education, we should reach out naturally and speak out zealously and boldly.

Vars offered that young adolescents should be their own advocates as well: "Kids should be involved in some of the political battles we fight, such as school funding, censorship, and so forth. By the time they are in the middle school, they should be able to tackle some of these issues."

The fervor and advocacy of the Legacy participants is evident in their passionate belief, commitment, and commentary about the importance of activism in middle level education:

> I hope that when the movement really begins to hit the end that people stand up and go down in a blaze of glory. Go down screaming, go down yelling in moral outrage, and go down speaking for children. It just makes no sense to me that we would limp along trying somehow to comply with rules that are eventually going to do us in. (Beane)

> I think we're in a defensive mode and we've got to shift to an attack mode. We've got to take the offensive. We've got to stand up and shout out the

principles that underlie the middle school movement. Otherwise, the darkness is going to overtake us, so we really need to be active. We need to be militant. We need to be out there. We can't apologize. What we are doing in the middle school movement, I believe, is saving the best of American education during a difficult time. (George)

We all need to continue to be active. Simply thinking about things or quietly speaking to others about how things are not the way they ought to be doesn't serve anyone well. So I think we all have to be activists. We need to continually be out there, even if people get tired of listening to us. Simply liking young adolescents and thinking the middle school plan is a good idea just will not cut it. We have to stay the course. We know what we are doing is right. We have to stay the course because young adolescents are too young to take care of themselves, too young to lobby. We know what we need to do and have to do it. We have to help educate policymakers and our colleagues in some cases, and make sure that they understand that when you 'stay with' the middle school concept, positive things happen. One of my fears is, out of ignorance, some decision makers will go backward. They will say, "Well, we really think the middle school plan is a good idea. We really think you ought to integrate curriculum. We do think that young adolescents are different, but we cannot do it." (McEwin)

My parents have taught me, "the stronger you believe in something, the stronger you will act on those beliefs." I believe that applies to middle school. We've got to hold on to our beliefs about middle school, but we've also got to act on those beliefs. We can't just believe in them. We have to continuously act on those beliefs. I really think that's true; I look at the things that I truly believe in, and that's what consumes my life, my family, and my profession. (John Swaim)

We are at risk and are taking some backwards steps at this time. I think it's so dangerous because this isn't the time to be moving away from implementing the middle level concept. This is the time to be moving towards it. This is the time to be rolling up our sleeves and saying we know what to do. Research tells us what to do. Practice has told us what to do. Join with us to ensure we make decisions and implement educational programs that are best for young adolescents. (Sue Swaim)

These words are powerful reminders that middle level educators cannot sit passively at the base camp halfway up Mount Middle School. We cannot be mere observers of the ascent; we must be the doers, the climbers, the risk-takers, and the trail-blazers of reform.

Goal: Get Political

Political activism is a specific type of advocacy. Public education is a civic enterprise, with battles fought and wars waged within and among district school boards, state legislatures, and the federal government. Middle level educators must extend their classrooms to include tax payers, voters, and policy makers. Sue Swaim maintained that "we must advocate for what we know is the right thing to do at the local, state, and national levels. We live it every day and have experience and expertise that is needed when these discussions are happening and decisions are being made."

Erb offered, "If we look at the bigger picture of what we would like to have happen with young adolescents as they grow and develop, there are many commonalities across the political spectrum." At the local level, school board members should be provided information about the purposes and value of middle level practices so that when capital, budget, personnel, and other decisions are made, they are informed. By way of example, Sue Swaim explained that middle level education currently has a heightened visibility because of the political issues that are going on and tightened school budgets. "Quite frankly," she added, "to fully support teaming, it costs more than to departmentalize. As school districts are looking for financial cuts, they will consider those things." She contended that "we have to be continually reaching out to our community members, central administration, and school board members to help them understand why cutting teaming, for example, is not a viable option at the middle level."

Toepfer discussed the significance of state policies:

> We need to define effective middle school program elements and establish them in state educational regulations. Not providing the latter allowed middle school programs to erode. We cannot allow political judgments and similarly vested interests to determine whether or not school practice is good. Greater respect for middle level educational theory and practice and the professional knowledge authority for middle grades educators is still lacking. If people have cancer, most wouldn't go to their doctor and suggest a procedure. However, most people wouldn't hesitate to tell a middle school teacher what to do with their child or what classroom practice the school should use or disregard. Educators require the same prerogatives given other professions. Had that been accorded educators working with young adolescents, the middle level movement would have fared much better than it unfortunately did. Lack of such professional regard helped dismantle effective middle school programs and practice. As well, public understanding of the difference of young adolescents both from younger children and from high school adolescents would have helped continue the three-level school system initiated during the middle school movement.

Part of Toepfer's message is that middle level educators must make themselves known—individually and collectively. We must communicate our goals and purposes to those with decision-making authority so that they become powerful partners in the Middle School Expedition.

George suggested that the greatest challenge to middle level education today is the standards-based reform movement. His opinions about this initiative and his political leanings are pretty clear:

> State standards-based reform programs and the No Child Left Behind Act to me are the embodiment of all of the negative thinking that we could possibly summon about the capacity of human beings and how they should be educated. Middle school educators need to join the ranks of the rising angry left. We need to join Al Franken and Michael Moore and Jon Stewart and Bill Maher and throw up the window and say we are mad as hell and we are not going to take it anymore. We need to be as loud and as angry as the conservative critics have been. It's worked for them. They need to get some of their own medicine back.

Regardless of one's individual level of agreement with George, what is critical to note is his intense rage about the injustice he perceives. Though he does not demand this level of fervor for every middle level educator, he does recommend that we remain informed and at least "support candidates who understand and support quality and enlightened education rather than narrow, punitive, negative, and hostile approaches to education." While some middle level educators have an interest and ability to become political lobbyists, others may be more effective working to communicate the middle level education message closer to home. What George and many other Legacy participants implied is that taking no political action is irresponsible and unacceptable.

Goal: Contribute to and Disseminate Research

In an increasingly data-driven world, many Legacy participants emphasized the importance of scholarly research that informs our decisions and practices. Many asserted that, based on research, "we know what works." Unfortunately, it appears that the research is not so widely known by others within and outside middle school education. Therefore, we must not only continue contributing to the growing body of research about best practices in middle level education, but also we must work to disseminate these findings to the larger education community, to policymakers, to the general public, and to the students, families, and communities we serve. Toepfer implied that we must model, promote, and require research-based decisions so that we do not become victims of public whims and impulses:

I believe we must learn how to find ways of encoding things into regulation so that if something is established as valid, and effective that, lacking data to the contrary, it cannot be suddenly changed by a 4-to-3 vote. Major evidence has to prove the need to change or discontinue existing practice. Data must be provided as to the advantages of what is being proposed to replace something. As Paul George identified in *Evidence for the Middle School*, no such data were provided in removing and replacing the elements in effective middle school programs with the "clap-trap" of the present national standards and standardized testing movement. Tragically, effective middle schools were jettisoned despite the lack of evidence proving specific shortcomings. Their demise lacked any research base for dismantling them. What replaced them was not data-based. Abandonment of middle schools was largely based on whimsy, political moves, and the like.

Goal: Be Proactive About Accountability

Legacy participants expressed multiple opinions about questions related to how middle level educators should respond to the current emphasis on student achievement as measured by standardized tests. What was similar about their responses, however, was that, to varying degrees, they all criticized current accountability systems, and they all called for strong action to bring about change. Lounsbury said we should respond "with alarm, with distress, and with advocacy of alternatives." Beane expressed with disappointment that middle level educators have talked about how they can maneuver around No Child Left Behind, for example, but that we have not "talked about standing up and saying it is absolutely wrong for young adolescents; it's wrong for our society; it's wrong for our schools." Johnston, Lipsitz, Lounsbury, McEwin, and Sue Swaim all expressed some level of acceptance of accountability. However, their criticisms were mostly about the narrow measures and the limited scope of what is being measured. Lounsbury's complaint was that the over-emphasis on test measures compromises attention to authentic, enduring learning.

In his interview, Erb mentioned the danger and allure of false dichotomies that attempt to simplify complex issues. Toepfer discussed one of those false dichotomies: "People seem to think that if you come out against the standards and the national testing programs you are anti-achievement. That is neither true nor correct." Lounsbury and Toepfer argued that middle school education at its best very much values *learning* in an academic sense. However, they and other Legacy participants argued that middle level education also values other outcomes, such as character and citizenship, that are not reflected in current educational standards or standardized testing achievement targets.

Perhaps the most controversial responses about how middle level educators should respond to the current emphasis on student achievement as measured by standardized tests came from Lipsitz, who asserted, "I think we need to embrace it." Though her view seems exactly opposite from most other Legacy participants, her further elaboration reveals that her views are not so polarizing. Her evaluation of the current system is equally disapproving, yet her approach to counter the system is very different. She acknowledges that "embrace it" is a "very controversial thing to say, but sometimes you alter something or transform it or even kill something by embracing it. I don't think in this political environment you can go head up against it." Furthermore, she contended that we should not only embrace accountability but also up the ante: "We need to come up with accountability measures that are much more challenging and that educate the public about what we do." Like Toepfer, she proposed that we should develop assessment models that demonstrate what we value—and that we must value the good in people. With the current system, instead of holding ourselves accountable on our own terms and communicating to the public our own terms for accountability, Lipsitz stated that "we waited until it happened *to* us." Calling herself an opportunist, Lipsitz stated, "I truthfully feel that if people now spent more time and effort on *what* we hold ourselves accountable for and *how* we should hold ourselves accountable, we could use the current mania about testing to our advantage. Through that opportunity, with everybody being focused on testing, we could strengthen middle schools by articulating a clear set of priorities for accountability and by creating the measures." Lipsitz reasoned that if we "embrace accountability as part of what it means to have children in public trust," we have a better chance to reform it. She further explained that we have to make the case for middle schools "based not on ideology, but based on outcomes, based on the value added of the middle school experience." Instead of rejecting accountability, we should be defining the measures based on our values and documenting the impact that an appropriate middle level education can make. Similarly, Sue Swaim argued for expanded measures of school effectiveness:

> We should be engaged in helping expand the thinking about assessment that goes beyond a single test and instead, values formative assessment practices. What about student self-assessment? Isn't that a critical skill for students to be learning if they're going to be lifelong learners? Where are we paying attention to that? There are other factors to consider besides assessment to determine if a school is successfully serving its students. We should be looking at attendance and discipline referral records; student equity issues; professional development opportunities; and parent engagement, to name a few.

Again, citing her opportunistic approach, Lipsitz maintained, "If you have to plow with the mules you've got, and you do, then you have to show not only that you're excellent on that very narrow measure, but also show how much else you do excellently."

Conclusion

As a social and educational movement, perhaps the middle school movement is nearing a conclusion. This does not mean that the quest to develop developmentally responsive programs and schools for young adolescents should or will end. Indeed, as pointed out throughout this book by middle level leaders, much remains to be accomplished (e.g., a stronger commitment to an appropriate middle school curriculum). However, middle school principles and ideals have been articulated and in many places across America; schools have been established or re-organized; teachers are being specifically prepared to work as members of interdisciplinary teams to provide an appropriate education for young adolescents. Research is demonstrating that the tenets of middle school education are benefitting the young adolescents who are fortunate enough to attend schools that have implemented developmentally responsive programs and practices. Though it has faced challenges, "The middle school concept has survived and surmounted those challenges. I think because the middle school concept is a wonderfully grand idea based on all of the good things about human beings and education. It's an idea that has light and that light isn't going to be put out by those challenges. It has persistence. It has strength and it will continue" (George). *In Their Own Words*, the giants of the middle school movement have offered their experiences, their wisdom, and their perspectives for the consideration of emerging middle level mountaineers, and they encourage others to join the Middle School Expedition in the push toward the summit. Being content with current achievements or slipping back to previously achieved heights is unconscionable. The education and welfare of millions of young adolescents are at stake.

References

Carnegie Council on Adolescent Development. (1989). *Turning points: Preparing American youth for the 21st century*. New York: Carnegie Corporation of New York.

Flowers, N., Mertens, S. B., & Mulhall, P. (1999). The impact of teaming: Five research-based outcomes of teaming. *Middle School Journal, 31*(2), 57–60.

Jackson, A. W., & Davis, G. A. (2000). *Turning points 2000: Educating adolescents in the 21st century*. New York: Teachers College Press.

Mertens, S. B., & Flowers, N. (2006). Middle Start's impact on comprehensive middle school reform. *Middle Grades Research Journal, 1*(1), 1–26.

National Middle School Association. (2010a). *Research and resources: In support of This We Believe.* Westerville, OH: Author.

National Middle School Association. (2010b). *This we believe: Keys to educating young adolescents.* Westerville, OH: Author.

About the Authors

Dr. Tracy W. Smith is Professor and Coordinator for the Undergraduate Middle Grades Teacher Preparation Program at Appalachian State University, in Boone, North Carolina. Prior to taking a faculty position at Appalachian State, she was a middle school language arts and social studies teacher and later a school district coordinator for middle grades and gifted education. In 2005, she was the recipient of both the Reich College of Education Outstanding Teaching Award and the Appalachian State University Student Government Association Outstanding Teacher Award. She has been involved in middle level education on the national, state, and local levels. Her service has included work as Executive Director of the South Region for National Professors of Middle Level Education (NAPOMLE), secretary of the North Carolina Professors of Middle Level Education, member of the North Carolina Middle School Journal publications committee and editorial board, lead reviewer and auditor for the National Middle School Association/National Council for Accreditation of Teacher Education Program Review Board, and advisor for the Appalachian State University Collegiate Middle Level Association. In 2001, she received the Outstanding Dissertation Award from the American Association of Colleges for Teacher Education (AACTE). Her research interests include performance-based middle level teacher preparation, the history of the middle school movement, the relationship between teaching expertise and student learning, and evaluating the depth of student understanding. She has had articles published in journals such as the *Middle School Journal, Journal of Teacher Education, Clearing House,* and *Teacher Education and Practice.*

The Legacy of Middle School Leaders, pages 407–408
Copyright © 2011 by Information Age Publishing
All rights of reproduction in any form reserved.

Dr. C. Kenneth McEwin is Professor of Curriculum and Instruction and Co-ordinator of Graduate Middle Grades Teacher Preparation at Appalachian State University, Boone, North Carolina. He is a former sixth grade teacher and principal and has extensive experience as a consultant to school districts, state departments of education, universities, and policy-making groups. McEwin is a past-president of National Middle School Association and author of more than 150 professional publications that focus on middle school education, middle school sports, and the professional preparation of middle level teachers. He has served as a member of many national committees and task forces for the National Middle School Association, the National Association of Secondary School Principals, and the National Forum to Accelerate Middle Grades Reform. He is the Program Review Coordinator for National Middle School Association/National Council for Accreditation of Teacher Education reviews of middle level teacher preparation programs. McEwin is recipient of the National Middle School Association John H. Lounsbury Distinguished Service Award and the North Carolina Middle School Association Distinguished Service Award, which is named in his honor.

The Middle Level Education Legacy Project

Interview Protocol

Name of Person Interviewed _____

Position _____

Location _____

Date of Interview _____

Length of interview _____

Start time _____ Stop time _____

Interviewer _____

Taped? ☐ Video ☐ Audio

Original copy of the videotape (mini DV) _____

mini DV copy _____

VHS copy of videotape (ASU) _____

VHS copy of videotape (WU) _____

Audio tape of interview _____

Copy of transcription _____

The Legacy of Middle School Leaders, pages 409–412
Copyright © 2011 by Information Age Publishing

The Middle Level Education Legacy Project
Interview Protocol

Videotape **Off**:

> Thank you very much for completing the questionnaire and allowing me to interview you.
>
> The survey/questionnaire was introductory; we may be asking some of the same questions the same way, but now we are interested in getting your responses and reactions to these questions.
>
> With your permission, I would like to videotape and tape record the interview so that I can concentrate on what you are saying rather than on note-taking. Is that okay?
>
> Please take a few minutes to read over our consent form and sign it. If you have any questions please feel free to ask.

Videotape **On**:

This is _____ interviewing _____
           (interviewer)   (interviewee)

in _____ on _____
           (location)   (date)

Introductory Question(s):

- ☐ How did you get involved in the middle school movement?
- ☐ What/who were your main influences?
- ☐ What kinds of middle school literature did you read?
- ☐ Are there particular theorists (or theories) or writings that have influenced your educational thought?
- ☐ What was your primary motivation for becoming involved in the middle school movement?
- ☐ What is your primary motivation for your continuing involvement in middle school education?

History of the Middle School Movement:

- ☐ How would you describe the early years of the middle school movement (1960s & 1970s)?

☐ How has the middle school concept changed since the early years of the middle school movement [plan]?

☐ How have middle schools changed since the early years of the middle school movement [implementation]?

☐ What were some of the motivations that fueled the growth of the middle school movement?

☐ How were decisions about the directions taken by the middle school movement made?

☐ How were other individuals and groups outside middle level education involved in the early years of the middle school movement?

☐ What was the educational context at the time the middle school movement began?

The Middle School Movement:

☐ What have been some of the most significant events, incidents, or moments in the middle school movement?

☐ Why did you select these particular events?

☐ Do you have any personal accounts related to these events that might be of interest to others?

☐ Who or what have been some of the greatest detractors or opponents (negative influences) of middle school education?

☐ What have been some of the most significant obstacles to the success of the middle school movement?

☐ What are some of the mistakes that have been made during the middle school movement that we might be able to learn from today?

☐ What are some of the most important factors that are influencing middle school education today?

☐ Who has benefited the most from the middle school movement?

☐ Who has benefited the least from the middle school movement?

☐ Were there regional differences in the way middle school education was developed or defined —New England, South?

Middle School Leaders:

☐ Who do you consider to be among the most influential leaders of the middle school movement?

　　☐ Why did you select these particular leaders?

☐ Have there been major debates among middle school leaders focusing on particular issues or beliefs?

    ☐ If so, what were these debates about? What was at stake? Which position won out? Why?

☐ What have been the roles of women and minorities in the middle school movement?

Influence of the Middle School:

☐ What are some examples of ways the middle school movement has affected American education?

☐ What educational groups, organizations, and institutions have influenced the middle school movement?

☐ What are some examples of ways these groups influence middle school education?

☐ Have particular legislative actions significantly influenced the middle school movement? (state and/or national levels)

☐ What are some ways the middle school movement has influenced middle level curriculum and instruction?

☐ As middle level educators, how do you think we should respond to the current emphasis on student achievement as measured by standardized tests?

Concluding Questions:

☐ Are there lessons we still need to learn from the history of the middle school movement?

☐ How would you characterize the current status of the middle school movement?

☐ Are there particular efforts that need to be made to help ensure the future success of the middle school movement?

☐ Are there other comments you would like to make that you have not been asked about in this interview?

THANK YOU